INTERNATIONAL CRIMINAL LAW

Intersections and Contradictions

BETH VAN SCHAACK
Leah Kaplan Visiting Professor of Human Rights
Stanford Law School

RONALD C. SLYE
Professor of Law
Seattle University School of Law

CONCEPTS AND INSIGHTS SERIES®

FOUNDATION PRESS

444 Cedar Street, Suite 700
St. Paul, MN 55101
1-877-888-1330

Printed in the United States of America

ISBN: 978-1-68467-001-7

To Harold Hongju Koh
B.V.S. & R.C.S.

PREFACE

International criminal law (ICL) can be, and is, taught in a number of different ways depending on the text utilized and the interests and expertise of the particular professor. For example, ICL can be taught as a subset of public international law, with an emphasis on relevant treaties and customary international law, international law-making, and the creation and operation of institutions and organizations that adjudicate ICL. By contrast, ICL can be taught as a specialized or upper division criminal law course, with an emphasis on the elements of crimes, the burdens on the prosecution and defense, and the parties' strategic moves in the adversarial or inquisitorial context. Given that many professors come to the field with a domestic law background, the course can also be taught as the transnational extension of domestic criminal law. This perspective includes attention to issues of interstate cooperation in law enforcement matters and extraterritorial and international assertions of jurisdiction. It is hoped that this book will complement all of these approaches.

To this end, in Part I of the book we provide chapters that address the major institutions and international crimes with reference to important features and open questions. We do not dwell on doctrinal minutiae on the assumption that the cases highlighted in the primary text will adopt this approach. Instead, we identify broad themes undergirding the entire field, summarize the origins and elements of the major international crimes, and identify doctrinal areas that remain the subject of debate, litigation, advocacy, and negotiation. We also present some of the jurisdictional issues surrounding the major fora in which ICL norms are contested and adjudicated: international tribunals, hybrid tribunals, and domestic courts. In addition to these more standard topics, we have endeavored to expound upon themes that may only be treated briefly in a two- or three-unit course on ICL. For example, we have included chapters on the history of the field and the sources of ICL that are more detailed than many primary texts provide. The latter chapter will, we hope, be helpful to students who have not yet taken a general course on international law. In addition, we have included a chapter on a defense that is almost ubiquitous in ICL—*nullum crimen sine lege*—that provides insights into ICL reasoning and rhetoric. In so doing, we hope to convey some of the deep structural underpinnings of the field, with all its uncertainties, inconsistencies, *lacunae*, and idealism. Throughout the book, we move between macro and micro perspectives to convey the full panoply of issues presented by this increasingly established area of law. As a result, this book is meant to operate only partially as a comprehensive "nutshell" text for the field of ICL. Taken as a whole, we hope this book will provide a useful framework for understanding the fascinating and ever-evolving field of ICL.

Although we touch on some central questions of procedure concerned with enforcement and adjudicative jurisdiction, we primarily approach the field as one of substantive international law adjudicated before international, or quasi-international, institutions. We are thus concerned with the origins, elements, and evolution of international crimes. In Part II, we discuss the definition of, and jurisprudence devoted to, specific international crimes, as well as novel issues concerning forms of responsibility and defenses found in the field of ICL. In this regard, we focus on what we consider to be the core ICL crimes: genocide, crimes against humanity, and war crimes. These are also termed *atrocity crimes* in the literature to distinguish them from other crimes that may also be defined or prohibited by international law, such as drug trafficking or money laundering. All of the *ad hoc* tribunals included some combination of these atrocity crimes within their jurisdiction. They are now being actively adjudicated before the International Criminal Court (ICC). These are also the crimes over which many states can by treaty or statute exercise universal jurisdiction. As such, although most of the case law mentioned in the text forms part of the jurisprudence of the international (and hybrid) criminal tribunals, we occasionally address proceedings in national courts on the understanding that ICL is subject to a high degree of concurrent jurisdiction, with domestic and international authorities having a role to play in ensuring comprehensive and complementary enforcement.

From this core, we also venture into the periphery by providing materials on the crimes of aggression and the so-called treaty crimes (such as torture and terrorism). The ICC's jurisdiction over the crime of aggression was recently activated, yet the definition of the crime, and the wisdom of prosecuting it, remain hotly contested even within circles that generally support international criminal prosecutions. Unlike the prosecution of the other core crimes, prosecution of the crime of aggression has the potential to complicate determinations of threats to the peace that are textually committed in the United Nations Charter to the "political" branches of the United Nations—the Security Council and, to a lesser extent, the General Assembly. A determination in a penal proceeding that the crime of aggression has occurred has the potential to contradict political determinations involving the same situation or state and thus to invite institutional conflicts. There is also concern that the activation of the crime of aggression will overburden an already stretched ICC, consuming valuable resources that could be devoted to the other atrocity crimes. In a series of negotiations that culminated at the 2010 ICC Assembly of State Parties' Review Conference in Kampala, Uganda, agreement was reached on the definition of the crime of aggression. In order to encourage further engagement and discussion on this newly activated crime, we provide a summary of those negotiations and the compromises that were reached to bring aggression fully within the jurisdiction of the Court.

We refer to the crimes of torture and terrorism as "treaty crimes," as they are subject to their own specialized treaty (in the case of torture) and treaties (in the case of terrorism). They are not found as freestanding crimes within the jurisdiction of the international criminal tribunals, yet acts of torture and some acts of terrorism enter the jurisprudence as constitutive acts of the core international crimes. Notwithstanding the fact that 170 states have ratified the Torture Convention, which includes a detailed definition of the crime, the interpretation of the definition of torture remains contested, particularly in light of efforts by elements within the United States following the attacks of 9/11 to limit the force and effect of the prohibition against torture in the so-called "war on terror." The crime of international terrorism, to the extent that there is such a concept in general international law, also gives rise to unique conceptual difficulties in part because it is often implicated in circumstances in which the prohibitions against war crimes, crimes against humanity, and even genocide may be equally applicable. Nonetheless, a strong sentiment has emerged that terrorism *stricto sensu* is something altogether different and deserves separate treatment in the canon of ICL. By exploring these crimes and the conceptual difficulties they raise, we hope to shine light both on how they fit within the pantheon of core international crimes and how they continue to exist and evolve outside of the core international criminal law institutions.

Our focus is primarily on *international* criminal law. We do, however, make reference to some crimes that more accurately may be considered *transnational* crimes. Transnational criminal law encompasses crimes with a transnational dimension that are prohibited and prosecuted primarily at the domestic level (although they may also be the subject of multilateral treaties). The emphasis on transnational implies that the borders of at least two states are crossed in some fashion during the inception, commission, or prosecution of the offense or where the offense creates direct or indirect effects on more than one country. For some crimes, this transnational dimension is inherent to the offense itself (as in export crimes or various forms of trafficking or smuggling). Other crimes may be committed domestically or transnationally, depending on the circumstances (such as mail fraud or money laundering).

In light of our focus on substantive law, this book gives only cursory treatment to procedural issues relevant to the domestic prosecution of crimes with international dimensions, such as questions of extradition, transnational mutual assistance, choice of law, and the recognition of foreign penal judgments. On the whole, we think these topics are best taught as specialized courses in transnational criminal law and procedure. Although the international community is increasingly generating international law norms to address these dimensions of transnational crime, prevailing norms still vary and are largely the product of the unique constitutional, statutory, and jurisprudential frameworks of individual nations and adjudicative institutions. We also spend little time on the growing international body of criminal procedural and evidentiary law being developed by the various *ad hoc* criminal tribunals. Although the international law governing criminal procedure and evidence presents a fascinating and *sui generis* blend of elements from the common law and civil law traditions, this material is also best covered in a specialized procedural or comparative law course. The field of international criminal procedural law is destined to continue to evolve in the next few years as the *ad hoc* tribunals wind down their work and the ICC becomes the primary international tribunal adjudicating international crimes.

Although ICL is ultimately a course of substantive law, it is impossible to consider the relevant law without reference to background issues of state sovereignty, foreign policy, national security, and the exercise of power in international relations. The international community and individual states do not resort to ICL in a vacuum. Rather, choosing to implement a regime of international criminal justice is a political choice, among other available and competing policy choices. The decision to pursue criminal trials is influenced by a number of variables often at odds with the legalistic principles underlying criminal justice in its platonic state and the ideals of human rights advocates. As you read the materials assigned for your course, consider what role ICL is playing in the particular historical moment in which it has been invoked and what other options—including resort to military force—may have been available to elites with decision-making power. When it comes time to address the crimes of the past, there are a range of other transitional justice options available to states—such as amnesties, reparations, efforts at reconciliation and rehabilitation, symbolic memorials, exile, and so on—that are the subject of our chapter on alternatives to ICL. As you progress in this course, you will see that ICL is often an exercise in idealism reflecting the belief in a world governed by law and altruism rather than power or apathy. At the same time, it is a course on the limits of such idealism in the face of *realpolitik*.

In closing, we would recommend that you keep abreast of developments in the law. Although ICL is at its height of codification, the field is still very much in a state of evolution, and courts around the world continue to issue important judgments that resolve outstanding doctrinal issues or introduce new ones. In addition, new institutions—for the Central African Republic, South Sudan, and Colombia—are being considered or still evolving. This text, by providing the basic framework for understanding the field of ICL, will lay the foundation for assimilating new developments when they inevitably occur. Although the contexts and institutions of ICL may vary, the substantive law is converging to a certain extent, making this one of the most dynamic topics of public international law and a fascinating addition to your course of legal study.

Seattle, Washington
Palo Alto, California
July 2020

ACKNOWLEDGMENTS

The authors express their sincere thanks to the many people who contributed to this volume. We would also like to acknowledge several students from Stanford University—Bailey Ulbricht and Dillon Leet—and Seattle University School of Law—Justin Loveland and Thea Jennings—for their expert research assistance. We are grateful to Michele Tedeschini and Eric Stover for their excellent suggestions on the draft. We would also like to thank Deans Annette Clark and Jenny Martinez for providing us with the time and resources to make this project possible. Finally, our gratitude goes out to the staff at Foundation Press for their support, assistance, and patience as we completed this manuscript.

TABLE OF CONTENTS

INTERNATIONAL CRIMINAL LAW

Intersections and Contradictions

Part I

THE DISCIPLINE OF INTERNATIONAL CRIMINAL LAW

A. Introduction

This part addresses fundamental questions concerning international criminal law as a distinct discipline of public international law. It begins by tackling the question of what areas of law the field of international criminal law encompasses. This preliminary definitional discussion is followed in Chapter 1 by a concise history of this body of law, with reference to key precedents, treaties and other legal instruments, institutions, and historical moments. Chapter 2 introduces the primary institutions that adjudicate international criminal law and the way in which these bodies mediate, accommodate, and even threaten state sovereignty—a foundational principle of international relations. Chapter 3 focuses on the way in which international criminal law is made, with reference to the traditional sources of public international law. Chapter 4 discusses the justifications for treating certain violent conduct as an international crime—in other words, why a particular assault should allow for cases to be brought at both the international and domestic levels. Finally, Chapter 5 considers the way in which modern tribunals have addressed situations in which the extant international criminal law is incomplete, vague, or indeterminate while remaining faithful to the principle of legality. These chapters should enable you to better evaluate the relative authoritativeness of the various sources of law being cited by parties and tribunals as they resolve contested doctrinal issues before them in the cases you read.

B. What Is International Criminal Law?

Academics and practitioners often do not agree on the full contours of the field of international criminal law (ICL) as a distinct discipline. Part of this definitional disagreement stems from the fact that ICL is a relatively new discipline. Although ICL has a few long taproots (as discussed in the chapter on the history of ICL), the field really came to fruition in the post-World War II period when two major bodies of law converged. Modern ICL sits at the intersection of public international law—which historically regulated the behavior of states when they acted on the world scene—and domestic criminal law—which metes out individualized criminal penalties for breaches of the peace. Although the individual arrived late on the scene as a full subject of public international law, she now sits front and center in ICL as a potential victim, witness, and perpetrator.

This definitional disagreement also reflects the fact that contemporary devotees (both practitioners and scholars) have entered the field from different places, including from the disciplines of domestic criminal law, international human rights (IHR) law (which generally governs the treatment states may and must accord individuals within their jurisdictions), and international humanitarian law (IHL, also known as the law of armed conflict). One's understanding of a field is heavily influenced by one's point of entry. Criminalists therefore tend to build the field outward from a domestic foundation to cover the transnational dimensions of domestic criminal law and the various ways that states endeavor to extend their penal law abroad. This approach encompasses what would be more accurately described as transnational criminal law, rather than ICL *stricto sensu,* although the two bodies of law often draw from and influence each other. Transnational criminal law focuses in part on issues of substantive law—such as the ways in which states incorporate international crimes into their domestic penal codes or otherwise criminalize conduct with extraterritorial dimensions—but also on procedural issues, such as the provision of mutual legal assistance among states, processes of extradition and prisoner transfer, and the recognition of foreign judgments. Individuals who approach the field from the human rights tradition tend to focus on the prosecution of so-called atrocity crimes—genocide, war crimes against civilians, and crimes against humanity. When human rights advocates take up ICL, their focus tends to be on the prerogatives of the prosecutor or ending entrenched impunity, rather than on executive overreach or the rights of the accused that tend to dominate the focus of criminalists. Finally, individuals who approach ICL from the perspective of military justice are primarily interested in crimes committed in the context of armed conflicts involving prohibited means and methods of war and harm to specifically-defined protected persons (civilians, prisoners of war, and the wounded). This dimension of the field at times requires a high degree of technical knowledge about military tactics and technology.

In this text, and in our work, we approach the field from a fourth perspective: public international law. We thus define ICL as the body of law that assigns individual criminal responsibility for breaches of public international law. Given this emphasis on the field's international law pedigree, we take international law sources—treaties, international custom, general principles of law, jurisprudence generated by international institutions, jurisprudence generated by domestic institutions applying substantive international law, and the writings of publicists—as our point of departure. To facilitate this approach, this text provides an overview chapter on the sources of ICL for those students who have not yet taken a basic course in public international law or who would value a refresher of basic principles from an ICL perspective. At the same time, we recognize that ICL is not purely a field of international law. States have incorporated many substantive norms of ICL—with varying degrees of fealty to their international origins—into their domestic penal codes, particularly as they have ratified the Rome Treaty establishing the International Criminal Court. On the basis of these statutes, domestic courts are increasingly prosecuting international crimes under various forms of extraterritorial jurisdiction, including universal jurisdiction. The contemporary field is thus characterized by a fascinating cross-fertilization between domestic and international legislative, judicial, and executive actions.

Modern ICL has gathered together once unconnected strands of public international law under one rubric. Some elements of ICL have their origins in the IHR edifice. Many multilateral IHR treaties, conventions, and covenants (such as the International Covenant for Civil & Political Rights) and the human rights machinery they created (such as the Human Rights Committee) concern themselves with the allocation of state responsibility. Other treaties (such as the Convention Against Torture and Other Cruel, Inhuman or Degrading Treatment or Punishment) combine a focus on state responsibility with obligations to impose criminal penalties on individuals who violate treaty provisions. Thus, acts of genocide, torture, slavery, and other crimes against humanity may give rise to both state civil responsibility as IHR violations and individual criminal responsibility as ICL violations. Other elements of ICL have their origins in IHL, or the law of armed conflict. Although much of IHL concerns state responsibility, certain violations of this body of law also carry criminal penalties when committed in the context of armed conflict. Such "war crimes" include abuses of civilians or prisoners of war (POWs), using weapons calculated to cause unnecessary suffering, or employing methods of war that cause harm that is disproportional to the military advantage to be gained.

ICL materialized into a discrete field of law in the modern period as a reaction to a global war of catastrophic proportions. Since then, it has been a feature of civil war armistices, postwar occupations, and multilateral responses to global crises. During the democratic transitions in Latin America and elsewhere, ICL became part of the repertoire of any transitional government moving from a period of repression and state terror to one emphasizing the rule of law. ICL is also employed outside of conflict zones by states asserting jurisdiction over individuals with transient presence within their territory but with little other connection to the crimes in question. Even more controversially, states sometimes attempt to assert jurisdiction over individuals who are not in their custody and who have never stepped foot on their territories. ICL thus supports expansive assertions of international and extraterritorial jurisdiction, including through the concept of universal jurisdiction, although the outer limits of these authorities are still in flux. The cases and materials you will no doubt read in your ICL course will be drawn from these disparate contexts. The next chapter on the history of ICL outlines how the field reached this point.

Chapter 1

A CONCISE HISTORY OF INTERNATIONAL CRIMINAL LAW

A. Introduction: The Genesis Story

The international criminal proceedings following World War II (1939–1945) are credited with launching the modern regime of international criminal law (ICL). Antecedents, however, trace back for centuries and across the globe.[1] In particular, ICL draws on four main strands of international law history: the once theological and later secular theory of just war, nineteenth-century prohibitions against piracy, the subsequent regulations of the slave trade and then slavery, and what we now call international humanitarian law (IHL) or the "law of war." On this foundation, the international community gradually built the norms, rules, instruments, and institutions that now make up the modern ICL ecosystem. This chapter interweaves the history of substantive norms with that of evolving principles of domestic and international jurisdiction, as these narratives are virtually inseparable in ICL.

Several features of this evolution are worth emphasizing. First, with the exception of the post-World War II period, when the international community simultaneously created the law to be applied and the tribunals to apply it, many ICL norms developed well before there were judicial institutions available to enforce them. In the terminology of Professor Dan-Cohn, ICL had conduct rules without corresponding enforcement rules (rules enabling officials to enforce the conduct rules).[2] As is the case with much public international law, it took some time before the international community was willing to put principle into practice. Second, until recently, the design of much of the system was *ad hoc* and reactive to world events rather than the result of any sort of coherent forward-looking process. A notable exception is the permanent International Criminal Court (ICC), which has only prospective jurisdiction (i.e., it cannot adjudicate crimes committed prior to its establishment). Third, the history of ICL is marked by greater and greater incursions into arenas that were historically the exclusive province of sovereign states. Thus, not only do ICL norms increasingly regulate a state's treatment of its citizens and others under its jurisdiction (as well as

[1] *See* THE HIDDEN HISTORIES OF WAR CRIMES TRIALS (Kevin Jon Heller & Gerry Simpson eds. 2013).

[2] Meir Dan-Cohn, *Decision Rules and Conduct Rules: On Acoustic Separation in Criminal Law*, 97 HARV. L. REV. 625 (1984).

the behavior of non-state actors), but conduct that violates these norms is increasingly the subject of international scrutiny, condemnation, and criminal prosecutions.

B. Substantive Law Antecedents to Modern ICL

This short section will highlight elements of the antecedents to ICL that were available to the architects of the Nuremberg and Tokyo tribunals as they embarked upon their grand experiment with international criminal justice. In some respects—for example when it came to the war crimes provisions within the tribunals' respective Charters—the victorious Allies were able to build on a relatively firm legal foundation. In other respects, however, they had to innovate, particularly when it came to defining crimes against the peace and against humanity and building judicial institutions, for which there was little historical precedent.

1. Just War: The *Jus Ad Bellum*

Although early Christian theology manifested an "extreme pacifism" that prohibited participation in war, by the time of St. Augustine (C.E. 354–430) a theory of *just war* had developed, which stated that resort to war was permitted only if the ends were just. Other religious and national traditions also preserved the right to engage in war against "infidels" or to avenge a wrong as just ends. Efforts to identify the necessary conditions for war constitute the *jus* (or *ius*) *ad bellum*—the set of rules regulating the decision to use military or armed force in international relations. In his *Summa Theologica,* for example, St. Thomas Aquinas (C.E. 1225–1274) set forth the following requirements for a war to be considered just: (1) it must be authorized by a legitimate sovereign; (2) it must be necessary for the achievement of a just cause; and (3) it must be inspired by a "right intention," that is the restoration of a good and just order and not in furtherance of injustice.[3] Self-defense against an unjust act of aggression, punishment for an unjust act of aggression, or recovery of something wrongly taken all qualified as just causes for Aquinas.

By the sixteenth century, however, it became accepted that there may be a claim of just war on both sides, and the laws of war gradually shifted attention away from identifying the acceptable reasons for going to war to regulating the effects of war—the *jus* (or *ius*) *in bello*. Eventually, the notion of just war dissipated almost entirely. By the time of World War I, war was viewed as the prerogative of the sovereign and a valid instrument of foreign policy. Efforts to "outlaw" war in the form of the Kellogg-Briand Pact in the

[3] St. Thomas Aquinas, *Question 40 of War,* in SUMMA THEOLOGICA 1359–1360 (Fathers of the English Dominican Province trans., Benzinger Brothers, Inc. 1947).

interwar period did little to constrain the rise of militarism or German and Japanese aggression in World War II.[4] International law had thus dramatically shifted focus. It went from evaluating the morality and justice of going to war, but only weakly regulating the means and methods of warfare, to a resignation that the justness of war was too difficult to universalize combined with renewed efforts to humanize the means and methods of warfare. This shift in emphasis from *jus ad bellum* to *jus in bello* still largely describes the state of the law of armed conflict today, although the development of the crimes of terrorism and aggression harkens back to the *jus ad bellum* tradition.

2. Penal Antecedents: Piracy, the Slave Trade, and Slavery

Piracy and the slave trade were two of the earliest international crimes outside of war that states coordinated among themselves to criminalize and prosecute. Up until this point, what we now call ICL had primarily focused on acts committed by one state against the nationals of another state in the context of an armed conflict—the traditional paradigm for war crimes. With the recognition of piracy, the slave trade, and eventually slavery as international crimes, ICL turned its attention to private, non-state actors that operated within the interstitial space separating nation states. With these prohibitions, we thus see a shift from a focus solely on activity that is international, or activity *between* distinct nation states, to an acceptance of international jurisdiction over activity that affects the efficient operation of the international system (piracy) or that implicates universal moral values (slavery and the slave trade).

Piracy was a widespread phenomenon in the eighteenth and nineteenth centuries. Because piracy was committed on the high seas (and thus not within the territorial jurisdiction of any state), and because there were no international tribunals before which the offender could be prosecuted, any state that obtained custody of a pirate was permitted to prosecute. The prohibition against piracy thus gave rise to the notion of universal jurisdiction, now a central feature of modern ICL. Universal jurisdiction permits a state to prosecute the perpetrator of certain crimes that are considered of universal concern to the community of nations, regardless of the nationality of the perpetrator or victim or the place of commission.

Piracy was one of the earliest crimes defined internationally and incorporated by reference into domestic criminal law. In *United States v. Smith*, for example, the United States sought to prosecute an American citizen, one Thomas Smith, and others for the capital crime of piracy after they seized and captured several foreign ships.

[4] General Treaty for the Renunciation of War as an Instrument of National Policy, Aug. 27, 1928, 46 Stat. 2343, 94 L.N.T.S. 57.

The defendant argued that there was no definition of piracy in U.S. law, so the prosecution was invalid. In support of its charges, the government pointed to the Congressional Act of 1819, in which Congress declared that anyone convicted of piracy, as defined by the law of nations, could be put to death.[5] The Court noted that it was universally agreed that piracy is "robbery, or forcible depredation, upon the sea" and an "offense against the universal law of society . . ., a pirate being *hostis humani generis* [enemy of all humankind]."[6] Accordingly, the Supreme Court ruled that Congress could incorporate the law of nations by reference into the federal penal code. Justice Livingston dissented, arguing that the law of nations' definition of piracy was too vague to use in a capital case. He reasoned that the Constitution, at Article I § 8 (empowering Congress to "define and punish piracies and felonies committed on the high seas, and offenses against the law of nations"), specifically directed Congress to promulgate its own definition of the offense, not to borrow one from elsewhere. In 1820, the United States extended the domestic definition of piracy to include participation in the international slave trade in an effort to compel other states to criminalize slavery. The Third Circuit later ruled, however, that slavery could not be conceptualized as an act of piracy under international law, meaning that—at that time—the United States could not assert universal jurisdiction over individuals involved in the slave trade.[7] Congress, incidentally, has since legislatively overturned this ruling.[8]

Collective international efforts to combat piracy in many respects began with the 1856 Paris Declaration Respecting Maritime Law promulgated at the end of the Crimean War, which abolished forms of piracy (deemed "privateering") in armed conflict and was signed by nearly all the imperial powers.[9] As the international community convened the League of Nations after World War I, there was talk of regulating piracy more generally through an international agreement; however, this effort was abandoned as delegates thought it insufficiently pressing to merit international attention and got bogged down in distinctions between definitions of piracy under international and domestic law. It was not until a

---

5 The federal piracy statute (18 U.S.C. § 1651) still reads: "whoever, on the high seas, commits the crime of piracy as defined by the law of nations, and is afterwards brought into or found in the United States, shall be imprisoned for life."

6 *United States v. Smith*, 18 U.S. 153, 163 n.8 (1820) (citing Blackstone).

7 *United States v. Darnaud*, 3 Wallace 143 (3rd Cir. 1855).

8 18 U.S.C. § 1596 (allowing for the assertion of universal jurisdiction over a range of slavery and human trafficking crimes if the perpetrator is present in the United States).

9 Declaration Respecting Maritime Law, signed by the plenipotentiaries of Great Britain, Austria, France, Prussia, Russia, Sardinia, and Turkey, assembled in Congress at Paris, April 16, 1856, 115 CTS 1.

century later when four of the first Law of the Sea Conventions were drafted in Geneva that an omnibus treaty-based definition of the offense emerged. Article 15 of the 1958 Convention on the High Seas defines piracy as

> (1) Any illegal acts of violence, detention or any act of depredation, committed for private ends by the crew or the passengers of a private ship or a private aircraft, and directed:
>
> > (a) On the high seas, against another ship or aircraft, or against persons or property on board such ship or aircraft;
> >
> > (b) Against a ship, aircraft, persons or property in a place outside the jurisdiction of any State;
>
> (2) Any act of voluntary participation in the operation of a ship or of an aircraft with knowledge of facts making it a pirate ship or aircraft;
>
> (3) Any act of inciting or of intentionally facilitating an act described in sub-paragraph 1 or sub-paragraph 2 of this article.[10]

This definition appears, with stylistic changes, in Article 101 of the 1982 United Nations Law of the Sea Convention.[11] The once customary practice of states asserting universal jurisdiction over piracy now finds expression in the 1982 Convention at Article 105: "On the high seas, or in any other place outside the jurisdiction of any State, every State may seize a pirate ship . . . and arrest the persons and seize the property on board . . . [and] may decide upon the penalties to be imposed." The example of piracy illustrates the evolution of state responses to an international crime from an *ad hoc* regime of self-help, to the first appearance of universal jurisdiction as a rule of customary international law, to the codification of the crime in a formal treaty. As we will see, the evolution of international criminal law from state practice to customary international law to treaty has accelerated, and often forgoes the earlier stages for more immediate codification in either a treaty or a tribunal statute.

The abolition of the slave trade and then slavery marks another important chapter in the story of ICL and international human rights.[12] Abolitionists working across the globe were responsible for gaining the passage of domestic laws outlawing these abhorrent

---

[10] Convention on the High Seas, Apr. 29, 1958, 13 U.S.T. 2312, 450 U.N.T.S. 82 (entered into force, Sept. 30, 1962).

[11] U.N. Convention on the Law of the Sea, Dec. 10, 1982, 1833 U.N.T.S. 3.

[12] *See generally* Jenny S. Martinez, *Antislavery Courts and the Dawn of International Human Rights Law*, 117 YALE L. J. 550 (2008) (recounting this history).

practices and convincing nation states to enter into multilateral treaties doing the same. Great Britain led the charge, entering into a network of bilateral and multilateral treaties that both permitted the searching of ships suspected of transporting individuals to be sold into slavery and established mixed tribunals in ports of call around the world to condemn slave ships. As early as the 1815 Congress of Vienna, which followed decades of turmoil in Europe, signatories called for the voluntary abolition of the slave trade, which they described as "repugnant to the principles of humanity and universal morality."[13]

The 1890 General Act for the Repression of the African Slave Trade ("the Brussels Act") finally called on all signatories to criminalize slave trading and to prosecute offenders—an early example of the concept of treaty-based universal jurisdiction.[14] States also established an international monitoring commission, the Temporary Slavery Commission (1924–1925), which expanded its own mandate to consider analogous practices of forced labor, debt slavery, and sexual slavery. This was followed a year later by the relatively anodyne Slavery Convention of 1926, which called for the "progressive" suppression of slavery. Although it contained no concrete enforcement regime, the 1926 Convention contains one of the first provisions calling upon states to criminalize slavery itself, stating at Article 6 that state parties are required to "undertake to adopt the necessary measures in order that severe penalties may be imposed in respect of [the slave trade and slavery]."[15] The subsequent Supplementary Convention on the Abolition of Slavery, the Slave Trade, and Institutions and Practices Similar to Slavery (1956) returned to the regime of the Brussels Act and required domestic criminalization and prosecution. In particular, Article 6(1) provided that:

> The act of enslaving another person or of inducing another person to give himself or a person dependent upon him into slavery, or of attempting these acts, or being accessory thereto, or being a party to a conspiracy to accomplish any such acts, shall be a criminal offence under the laws of the

---

13 Randall Lesaffer, *Vienna and the Abolition of the Slave Trade*, OXFORD PUBLIC INTERNATIONAL LAW, https://opil.ouplaw.com/page/498.

14 The Act's effects were not all beneficial or beneficent; part of its enforcement regime involved establishing colonial administrations in the African interior, putting "an anti-slavery guise on the colonial occupation and exploitation of Africa." Suzanne Miers, *Slavery and the Slave Trade as International Issues 1890–1939*, 19(2) SLAVERY AND ABOLITION 16, 19 (1998).

15 Convention to Suppress the Slave Trade and Slavery, March 7, 1927, 60 L.N.T.S. 253.

> States Parties to this Convention and persons convicted thereof shall be liable to punishment.[16]

This legal response to slavery and related acts also finds expression in international treaties prohibiting forced labor—such as the 1932 Convention Concerning Forced or Compulsory Labour[17]—and the trafficking of persons—such as the 2000 Protocol to Prevent, Suppress and Punish Trafficking in Persons Especially Women and Children (the so-called Palermo Protocol), which supplements the United Nations Convention against Transnational Organized Crime.[18]

While this progression is generally a good news story, it is worth noting that the international community was willing to abolish the slave trade before slavery itself. The former effort occurred at a time when the slave-holding states subjugated a critical mass of slaves who essentially reproduced themselves—including through the mass rape of enslaved women. Indeed, at a certain point, the southern U.S. states were producing enough slaves that the slave trade was actually reducing the price of slaves in the domestic market.[19] Nonetheless, the abolition of the slave trade—which benefited from a convergence of arguments premised on morality as well as economics—laid the groundwork for the steps to be taken to abolish slavery itself. In 1981, Mauritania finally abolished slavery (it was the last state to do so), although the practice continues there in various form.

The legacy of these two earlier international criminal law developments remains salient today. Piracy is still the touchstone that is cited to justify the application of universal jurisdiction to a broad range of international crimes. While piracy developed as an international crime because it did not fit within the traditional basis of criminal jurisdiction (i.e. territory), the prohibition against slavery opened the door to criminalizing activity over which many states in fact did have jurisdiction but, for a variety of self-interested reasons, were reluctant to assert or even criminalize. In addition, the mass mobilization of what we would today call civil society to pressure governments to criminalize and abolish slavery is an early model of the role that civil society, and in particular international and local

---

[16] The Supplementary Convention on the Abolition of Slavery, the Slave Trade, and Institutions and Practices Similar to Slavery, 1956 Commentary: The Supplementary Convention, April 30, 1957, 226 U.N.T.S. 3.

[17] Convention Concerning Forced or Compulsory Labour (ILO No. 29), May 1, 1932, 39 U.N.T.S. 55.

[18] Protocol to Prevent, Suppress and Punish Trafficking in Persons, Especially Women and Children, supplementing the United Nations Convention against Transnational Organized Crime, Nov. 15, 2000, 2237 U.N.T.S. 319.

[19] *See* William Spivey, *America's Breeding Farms: What History Books Never Told You*, MEDIUM (Mar. 20, 2019).

human rights organizations, play in pushing states to continue to innovate in efforts to prevent international crimes and to hold those responsible for their commission accountable.

3. International Humanitarian Law

Modern international criminal law also borrows heavily from international humanitarian law. IHL, also called "the law of war" or the "law of armed conflict," describes those international rules governing armed conflict. As long as groups of people, and later states, have waged war, rules have been in place governing acceptable behavior in armed conflict, giving lie to Cicero's claim that *silent enim lēgēs inter arma*—in war, the law falls silent. Although the history of the law of war is often told from the perspective of international conferences held in The Hague and Geneva, as described in more detail later, all human cultures manifest efforts to regulate this seemingly inherent aspect of our shared humanity.[20] Recorded history confirms that the ancient Israelites, Greeks, and Romans, for example, distinguished between combatants and civilians and made only the former the lawful object of attack. Certain African and Islamic traditions dictated that captured combatants and civilians should be humanely treated. Likewise, in ancient combat, certain weapons or tactics were prohibited if they caused excessive damage. The codes of chivalry developed in Medieval Europe set forth rules of combat that applied within the knighthood. In 1139, for example, the Second Lateran Council condemned the use of the crossbow, foreshadowing subsequent efforts to ban the use of weapons viewed as unnecessarily cruel or inhumane.

The first modern codification of the laws of armed conflict is found in the Lieber Code, drafted during the American Civil War by Professor Francis Lieber of Columbia College and promulgated by President Abraham Lincoln to govern the Union forces.[21] While the Code only applied to the U.S. internal conflict, it provided inspiration for other states to issue similar regulations, and for the first multilateral conventions on the laws of war in the late 1800s, including the Hague Conventions on land warfare of 1899 and 1907. Many of the provisions in the Lieber Code, along with antecedent codifications going back to the earliest era of recorded history, are now contained in a web of bilateral and multilateral treaties, making IHL the most codified area of ICL. A rich body of customary international law—painstakingly documented by the International

---

[20] *See generally* ANDREW GILLESPIE, ALEXANDER, A HISTORY OF THE LAWS OF WAR (2011).

[21] Instructions for the Government of Armies of the United States in the Field, General Orders No. 100 (1863), https://www.loc.gov/rr/frd/Military_Law/Lieber_Collection/pdf/Instructions-gov-armies.pdf.

Committee of the Red Cross (ICRC)[22] in an online database—supplements this extensive treaty regime to this day.

The codification of IHL historically evolved along two parallel tracks. The first track, originating from a series of international conferences in The Hague and elsewhere, concerns the means and methods of warfare and seeks to limit the tactics of war and prohibit the use of certain weapons designed to cause excessive suffering ("Hague Law"). The second track, originating from a series of treaties sponsored by the ICRC in Geneva, establishes protections for individuals uniquely impacted by war, especially those who do not—or who no longer—participate directly in hostilities, such as the shipwrecked, prisoners of war (POWs), and civilians and non-combatants ("Geneva Law"). With the notable exception of the 1863 Lieber Code governing the U.S. Civil War, the laws of war originally and almost exclusively addressed *international* armed conflicts. That is no longer the case. IHL now regulates *non-international* armed conflicts (i.e. those armed conflicts that are primarily contained within the territory of one state or that do not involve formal government armed forces). Over time, the legal distinctions between international and non-international armed conflicts have diminished and the two tracks of IHL have converged to create a more complete corpus of law that applies to all armed conflicts. Article 8 of the Statute of the International Criminal Court reflects this gradual merging of Hague and Geneva Law and of the law applicable in international and non-international armed conflicts.

The first multilateral IHL treaty was the 1856 Paris Declaration Respecting Maritime Law, referenced earlier in connection with the history of piracy, which addressed privateering and the neutrality of commercial ships in times of war, among other topics. It was followed by the First Geneva Convention of 1864, widely considered the founding IHL text.[23] This treaty was the brainchild of Henry Dunant, an inadvertent witness to the Battle of Solferino between Austria and the kingdom of Sardinia prior to the Italian unification. After seeing thousands of wounded and dying soldiers on the battlefield, Dunant organized Italian citizens to provide care. He later wrote a highly influential book, *Un Souvenir de Solferino* ("A Memory of Solferino"), in which he advocated the creation of a neutral organization to care

---

[22] The ICRC is a non-governmental organization based in Geneva, Switzerland that operates as a neutral, impartial, and independent organization to protect victims of armed conflict. Although non-governmental, it has been empowered by states to carry out various functions under IHL. In this capacity, the ICRC monitors compliance with the Geneva Conventions by warring parties, organizes care for those wounded on the battlefield, supervises the treatment of prisoners of war, traces those missing in armed conflict, and mediates between warring parties.

[23] Convention for the Amelioration of the Condition of the Wounded in Armies in the Field, Aug. 22, 1864, 22 Stat. 940.

for the wounded in war. He also convinced the Swiss government to convene a diplomatic conference of states to draft rules to prevent the suffering he had witnessed. The conference led to the signing of the first Geneva Convention by several European and American states. Aside from creating the ICRC, the treaty established rules governing the duty to provide relief to the wounded without distinction of nationality, confirmed the neutrality of medical units, and designated the red cross symbol as a protected insignia.

By the turn of the century, the international community increasingly turned its attention to codifying the laws of war. Peace conferences were held in The Hague in 1899 and 1907 that led to the conclusion of multiple conventions addressing land and maritime war. (Ironically, preparations for a third conference were interrupted by World War I). The 1899 Hague Conventions, signed but never ratified, addressed themselves to the Pacific Settlement of International Disputes (Hague I), the Laws and Customs of War on Land (Hague II), Maritime Warfare (Hague III), the Launching of Projectiles and Explosives from Balloons (Hague IV, 1), Asphyxiating Gases (Hague IV, 2), and Expanding Bullets (Hague IV, 3). Delegates reconvened in The Hague in 1906 to draft additional treaties, which superseded their predecessors and expanded consideration to the Opening of Hostilities (Hague III), the Rights and Duties of Neutral Powers and Persons in Case of War on Land (Hague V), the Status of Enemy Merchant Ships at the Outbreak of Hostilities (Hague VI), the Laying of Submarine Automatic Contact Mines (Hague VIII), Bombardment by Naval Forces in Time of War (Hague IX), and the Discharge of Projectiles and Explosives from Balloons (Hague XIV).

The most important treaty to emerge from this latter Conference was undoubtedly the fourth, Respecting the Laws and Customs of War on Land,[24] which contained a detailed set of regulations in its annex. The fundamental principle of *jus in bello* is found in Article 22, which states that "[t]he right of belligerents to adopt means of injuring the enemy is not unlimited." The regulations go on to forbid poisoned weapons; the killing or wounding of those belligerents who are *hors de combat* (i.e., those who have laid down their weapons and no longer present a threat); means of warfare "calculated to cause unnecessary suffering"; the destruction or seizure of enemy property unless "imperatively demanded by the necessities of war"; and the attack of undefended towns, villages, dwellings, or buildings.

The Hague Conventions also introduced the so-called Martens Clause, named after the Russian delegate to the first Hague Conferences, Professor Fyodor Fyodorovich Martens. The Clause

---

[24] Convention Respecting the Laws and Customs of War on Land, Oct. 18, 1907, 36 Stat. 2277.

appears in the preamble of the Hague Conventions of 1899 and 1907, in a modified form in the 1949 Geneva Conventions and the 1977 Protocol II of the Geneva Conventions, and in the main text of Protocol I. In its inaugural formulation, it provided that:

> Until a more complete code of the laws of war is issued, the High Contracting Parties think it right to declare that in cases not included in the Regulations adopted by them, populations and belligerents remain under the protection and empire of the principles of international law, as they result from the usages established between civilized nations, from the laws of humanity and the requirements of the public conscience.

Martens introduced the declaration after delegates at the Peace Conference failed to agree on the status of civilians who took up arms against an occupying force. Large military powers argued that they should be treated as *francs-tireurs*—a term first used to describe irregular military formations that had taken up arms against the Germans during the Franco-Prussian War (1870–1871) and from then on used to refer more generally to guerrilla fighters. Conversely, smaller states contended that these irregular fighters should be treated as privileged combatants. Although the clause was originally formulated to resolve this particular dispute, it has subsequently reappeared in various but similar forms in later treaties regulating armed conflicts and has been cited as authority to fill gaps in IHL.

The clause, although somewhat abstruse, contains several important ideas. First, it highlights the legal and moral bases of humanitarian obligations by making reference to natural law ideas, such as the sentiments of humanity. Second, by invoking the practice of states,[25] the Clause directly incorporates customary law principles as a source of rules to fill *lacunae* in codified law. Third, although framed from the perspective of potential victims of violations ("populations and belligerents"), it also suggests that courts should refer to principles of international law and morality in assigning responsibility for abuses.

Although the Fourth Hague Convention retains modern currency, today's rules of IHL are largely founded on the four Geneva Conventions of 1949, drafted on the heels of World War II and supplemented by their two 1977 Protocols.[26] The 1949 Conventions were developed to provide specific protections to four classes of

---

[25] The offensive reference to "civilized states" was eventually dropped in subsequent formulations.

[26] In 2005, a third Protocol recognized the red crystal as a fourth protected symbol alongside the red cross, the red crescent, and the lion and sun, and put to rest a longstanding dispute between the ICRC and the State of Israel, which had long advocated a nonsectarian symbol.

individuals not actively involved in combat: the wounded and the sick in the field (Geneva Convention I), the wounded and sick at sea (Geneva Convention II), prisoners of war (Geneva Convention III), and civilians and other non-combatants (Geneva Convention IV).[27] The four Geneva Conventions primarily apply to international armed conflicts, although common Article 3 as a "convention in miniature" applies to conflicts "not of an international character." The four Conventions criminalize so-called "grave breaches," which in Geneva Convention III include willful killing, torture or inhuman treatment, including biological experiments, willfully causing great suffering or serious injury to body or health, depriving a POW of the rights of fair and regular trial, and the taking of hostages and extensive destruction and appropriation of property not justified by military necessity and carried out unlawfully and wantonly. It is notable that these provisions protect core due process rights alongside the physical and mental integrity of persons affected by armed conflict.

The international community adopted two Protocols to the Geneva Conventions in 1977 in response to the changing nature of armed conflict. Protocol I provides a detailed set of rules concerning the obligation to discriminate between military and civilian targets, defines international conflicts as including "armed conflicts in which people are fighting against colonial domination and alien occupation and against racist regimes in the exercise of their right of self-determination," expands the category of privileged combatants to include some members of guerrilla movements in such conflicts, and further defines and clarifies the rules with respect to mercenaries. Protocol II elaborates on the minimum rules in common Article 3 governing non-international armed conflicts. It thus clarifies what constitutes a non-international armed conflict and sets out detailed rules of conduct in terms of the means and methods of warfare that mirror, though are not as extensive as, those that regulate international armed conflicts.

When it comes to treaty provisions, many more rules govern international armed conflicts as compared to non-international armed conflicts. However, over the years, a customary international law of non-international armed conflicts has developed that mirrors, in most respects, the rules governing international armed conflicts. Many developments contributed to this advancement, including the jurisprudential innovations of the modern war crimes tribunals, the war crimes provisions included in the Rome Statute establishing the ICC, and domestic courts adjudicating war crimes cases.

---

27 All the IHL treaties are available in a treaty database on the website of the International Committee of the Red Cross.

C. Efforts to Enforce International Criminal Law

The IHL treaties all contain substantive rules that apply across the conflict-classification spectrum from non-international to international armed conflicts. Other ICL prohibitions that do not depend on the existence of an armed conflict emerged later. We summarize below the range of institutions and doctrinal innovations the international community developed in an attempt to enforce these rules, including international and domestic judicial institutions and expansive principles of jurisdiction.

1. Pre-World War I: Antecedents

The original customary and conventional law of armed conflict implicated only state responsibility. In the event of a breach, responsible states were liable to pay reparations or provide other civil remedies to aggrieved nations. Only later did states begin to impose individual criminal liability on breaches of the law of armed conflict. Although many point to the war crimes trial of Peter von Hagenbach in 1474 in Austria as the first prosecution of an individual by an international tribunal (convened by the Holy Roman Empire), the earliest recorded trial of an individual for war crimes appears to be the prosecution by an English court in 1305 of Scottish national hero and warrior Sir William Wallace. Sir Wallace was charged with, convicted of, and executed gruesomely for waging the First War of Scottish Independence against the English "sparing neither age nor sex, monk nor nun." The first treaty mention of individual criminal liability for breaches of IHL is found in the work of the Brussels Conference of 1874, which produced a final protocol that 15 European states signed but never ratified. Paragraph III stated:

> The laws and customs of war not only forbid unnecessary cruelty and acts of barbarism committed against the enemy; they demand also, on the part of the appropriate authorities, the immediate punishment of these persons who are guilty of these acts, if they are not caused by an absolute necessity.[28]

Jurisdictionally, most early prosecutions for violations of the laws and customs of war were based on the territorial or nationality principles of jurisdiction—i.e., based upon the crime being committed on their territory or by or against their nationals, respectively. This was the case with the trials of Sir Wallace and von Hagenbach. A prominent example of such a prosecution by the United States is the 1865 military commission trial of Henry Wirz, a Confederate Captain accused of mistreating and murdering Union soldiers detained in

---

[28] *See* THE LAW OF ARMED CONFLICTS 21 (Dietrich Schindler & Jiri Toman eds., 2004).

Andersonville prison in violation of the laws and customs of war. This prosecution also presents one of the earliest examples of a defendant unsuccessfully arguing that he should not be held responsible for implementing the orders of his superiors. Wirz argued that he was unable to ensure proper conditions in the prison and was otherwise just following orders. In pleading his case, he wrote:

> I do not think that I ought to be held responsible for the shortness of rations, for the overcrowded state of the prison (which was in itself a prolific cause of the fearful mortality), for the inadequate supplies of clothing, and of shelters &c. Still I now bear the odium, and men who were prisoners here seemed disposed to wreak their vengeance upon me for what they have suffered, who was only the medium, or I may better say, the tool in the hands of my superiors.[29]

The Union military commission rejected Wirz's defense and sentenced him to death by hanging. Notwithstanding that many wrote to President Andrew Johnson pleading Wirz's pardon, or at least the commutation of the death sentence, Wirz was hanged on November 10, 1865. On the gallows, he reputedly declared: "I know what orders are. And I am being hanged for obeying them."

At the turn of the twentieth century, during an insurrection in the Philippines launched in opposition to the U.S. annexation of the territory following the Spanish-American War (1898), the United States convened a number of military commissions to prosecute Filipino insurgents and courts martial to prosecute U.S. service members. These institutions adjudicated both war crimes and common crimes, the latter as a function of the United States' obligations as an occupier to maintain public order. Most of the 800 military commission cases involved abuses against Filipino victims (so-called *Americanistas*) who had been accused of collaborating with the American occupiers or opposing the guerillas. These institutions confronted a number of key issues that continue to vex the modern tribunals, such as the definition of crimes triable under the laws of war; forms of liability for lesser participants, accomplices, superiors, and co-conspirators; and legal defenses. The Filipino insurrection marks one of the few times that the U.S. Congress suspended the writ of *habeas corpus*.[30]

---

29 May 7, 1865 letter from Capt. Hy Wirz to Maj. Gen. J. H. Wilson. This letter, the indictment, and judgment against Wirz are available in U.S. Army publication THE WAR OF THE REBELLION: A COMPILATION OF THE OFFICIAL RECORDS OF THE UNION AND CONFEDERATE ARMIES.

30 Additional suspensions occurred in the South to combat the Ku Klux Klan and in Hawaii during World War II.

2. World War I: A False Start

The first world war of the modern era launched the first global effort to address international crimes through the exercise of international and domestic criminal jurisdiction. World War I (1914–1918)—which pitted the Central Powers (composed of the German, Austro-Hungarian, Bulgarian, and Ottoman Empires) against the Allied and Associated Powers (Great Britain, France, Imperial Russia, later the United States, and others)—witnessed the commission of abuses against combatants, POWs, and civilians on an unprecedented scale. German atrocities included unrestricted submarine warfare, brutal occupations, the targeting of civilians and undefended towns, breaches of neutrality, and—from the perspective of the rest of Europe—the initiation of the war in the first place. The Ottoman Empire, with the Young Turks at the helm, stands accused of staging one of the first genocides of the twentieth century in its effort to eradicate the Christian Armenian population from what is now Turkey—an accusation that Turkey continues to contest. Under the pretext of averting an Armenian revolutionary uprising or a "treasonous" alliance with Russia during the war, the Ottoman Empire launched wholesale deportations and massacres that amounted to a virtual extermination of the Armenian population. In all, more than a million people were reportedly killed.

In the face of these offenses, the Allies convened a Commission on the Responsibility of the Authors of the War and on Enforcement of Penalties to inquire into culpable conduct by the Central Powers during the "Great War." The Commission was also to consider the propriety and feasibility of asserting penal jurisdiction over particular individuals "however highly placed" accused of committing such breaches. During the ensuing debates over the notion of ascribing individual criminal responsibility for crimes of war, a confluence of ideological and pragmatic objections emerged. On the merits, naysayers—led primarily by the Americans—took issue with the very premise that the principle of state sovereignty could be pierced so dramatically as to hold heads of state and other state actors liable for the collective actions of their sovereigns. Objectors also noted the lack of precedent for such a project and pointed to gaping *lacunae* in available substantive law. Others argued that trials could lengthen the war if the threat of prosecution was hanging over the parties. As the war ended, realists argued that trials would exacerbate instability in the fledgling Weimar Republic and in Turkey, where new governments were struggling to consolidate their authority in the wake of the war. Others warned that trials could create a dangerous precedent that might come back to bite the Allies in subsequent conflicts. Even where there was support for holding trials in theory, there was little agreement on secondary issues of venue, rules of procedure and evidence, standards of proof, and so on.

In 1919, the Commission presented its final report to the Paris Peace Conference that was at the time negotiating peace agreements with the Central Powers. This report documented "outrages of every description committed on land, at sea, and in the air, against the laws and customs of war and of the laws of humanity."[31] These included

> murders and massacres, tortures, shields formed of living human beings, collective penalties, the arrest and execution of hostages, the requisitioning of services for military purposes, the arbitrary destruction of public and private property, the aerial bombardment of open towns without there being any regular siege, the destruction of merchant ships without previous visit and without any precautions for the safety of passengers and crew, the massacre of prisoners, attacks on hospital ships, the poisoning of springs and wells, outrages and profanations without regard for religion or the honor of individuals.[32]

The report concluded that such crimes should be prosecuted before an international "high tribunal" composed of representatives of the Allied and Associated Powers or before national tribunals. Foreshadowing the notion of crimes against the peace later developed at Nuremberg and Tokyo, the Commission also considered "not strictly war crimes, but acts which provoked the war," such as deliberate violations of the neutrality of Belgium and Luxembourg. Notwithstanding early support for prosecuting German officials for initiating the war, the Commission concluded that acts of aggression should not be the subject of prosecution in light of the lack of legal authority for such a charge and the complexity of undertaking an investigation into the politically-charged question of the causes of the war. It reasoned:

> The premeditation of a war of aggression, dissimulated under a peaceful pretence, then suddenly declared under false pretexts, is conduct which the public conscience reproves and which history will condemn but by reason of the purely optional character of the institutions at The

---

[31] This latter reference to the "laws of humanity" planted one of the first seeds of the idea that there were crimes against humanity that were punishable separate and apart from conventional war crimes. The first use of the term "crimes against humanity" that we can find occurred in 1890 in a letter from the African American journalist, George Washington Williams, to the U.S. Secretary of State, James Blaine, describing the atrocities committed in the Belgian Congo (present-day Democratic Republic of Congo).

[32] Commission on the Responsibility of the Authors of the War and on Enforcement of Penalties, *reprinted at* 14 AM. J. INT'L L. 95, 113 (1920).

> Hague for the maintenance of peace . . . a war of aggression may not be considered as an act directly contrary to positive law, or one which can be successfully brought before a tribunal.

The Commission, however, recommended that in the future "penal sanctions should be provided for such grave outrages against the elementary principles of international law."[33]

The United States at Annex II advanced four fundamental reservations to the report's recommendations. First, it objected to the proposal of creating an international criminal tribunal—for which, it argued, there was "no precedent, precept, practice, or procedure"—instead of coordinating existing national military tribunals. Second, it invoked the limitations of jurisdiction when it argued that nations could not legally take part in the prosecution of crimes committed against the subjects of other nations. Third, it rejected the notion that any court of law could prosecute violations of the "laws or principles of humanity," on the ground that such violations were moral rather than legal breaches and were, as such, non-justiciable. Fourth, it argued that to prosecute a head of state outside of his national jurisdiction would violate basic precepts and privileges of sovereignty. The Americans indicated their intention not to participate in any international trial and instead focused their energies on President Woodrow Wilson's project for the League of Nations.

From this point, the potential liability of German and Ottoman defendants proceeded along separate tracks. The 1919 Treaty of Versailles ending the war with Germany required Germany to accept full responsibility for causing the war (the so called "war guilt" clause), make substantial territorial concessions, and pay reparations. Most important for our purposes, Article 227 envisioned the establishment of an international tribunal composed of representatives of the United States, Great Britain, France, Italy, and Japan to try the former German Emperor, Kaiser Wilhelm II, who was thus singled out for his central role in orchestrating German crimes during the war. In agreeing to this provision, the United States capitulated on its prior position in favor of domestic trials. The envisioned tribunal was to prosecute the Kaiser for "a supreme offense against international morality and the sanctity of treaties" and was to be "guided by the highest motives of international policy, with a view to vindicating the solemn obligations of international undertakings and the validity of international morality."[34] According

---

[33] *Id.* at 118–120.

[34] Treaty of Versailles, June 28, 1919, *reprinted in* 13 AM. J. INT'L L. 151 (Supp. 1920).

to Article 228 of the Treaty of Versailles, lesser German defendants were to be tried before the domestic military tribunals of the Allied and Associated Powers. This same provision obligated Germany to hand over "all persons accused of having committed an act in violation of the laws and customs of war, who are specified either by name or by the rank, office or employment which they held under the German authorities." Mixed military tribunals were to prosecute individuals "guilty of criminal acts against the nationals of more than one of the Allied and Associated Powers" pursuant to Article 229. By these terms, the Treaty of Versailles thus became the first peace treaty to contemplate war crimes trials.

By the time the Versailles Treaty entered into force, six months after the signing of the 1918 general armistice, the Kaiser had fled to the Netherlands, which had remained neutral during the war. The Netherlands refused to extradite him for trial, invoking a long history of providing asylum to political refugees and the double criminality rule, which prevented the Kaiser's extradition to face justice for acts that were not crimes under Dutch law. An unauthorized attempt by American soldiers, led by the former U.S. Senator from Tennessee Luke Lea, to kidnap the Kaiser was thwarted, and he died in 1941 a free man.[35] Although it is easy to blame the Dutch for this outcome, the truth is that the allies had lost interest in the trial. Article 227 thus remained a dead letter.

The Allies never enforced the other penal provisions of the Treaty either. In the face of continued Allied equivocation over war crimes trials and fierce objections among the German public to the possible extradition of German nationals, Germany artfully proposed hosting domestic trials before the German Supreme Court in Leipzig. The Allies, desperate to salvage some vestige of the project, agreed. To the extent that cases were brought (out of more than 800 individuals accused of war crimes, including high-level German officials, only 12 proceedings were held), trials proceeded sluggishly against low-level defendants and resulted in acquittals or disproportionately low sentences. Although the Allies protested and then quit the proceedings, they never made good on their threats to further sanction Germany, and no additional cases were pursued.

With respect to the Ottoman Empire, the new Turkish regime—under pressure from the British and perhaps in an effort to head off international trials of its own former leaders—court-martialed in Constantinople an impressive array of once prominent officials for "crimes against humanity and civilization" and other wartime offenses. Some defendants were tried *in absentia* because Germany refused to extradite them. The trials provoked a surge of Nationalist

---

[35] *See* WILLIAM A. SCHABAS, THE TRIAL OF THE KAISER (2018).

backlash, prompting the Turkish government to release a number of important defendants, ostensibly on the ground that there was no case against them. The British took many of these individuals into custody in Malta and elsewhere to prevent their release. As the Turkish civil war heated up, however, the British eventually swapped or released its prisoners, who had been languishing in pretrial detention.

The first treaty of peace with Turkey, the 1920 Treaty of Sèvres, contained accountability provisions mirroring those in the Treaty of Versailles with respect to the right of the Allies to convene military tribunals to prosecute persons guilty of having committed acts in violation of the laws and customs of war. Article 230 also contemplated a tribunal created by the League of Nations to address "the massacres committed during the continuance of the state of war on territory which formed part of the Turkish Empire on August 1, 1914." After the Turkish War of Independence, Mustafa Kemal (a.k.a. Atatürk), who led the Nationalists to victory in the civil war, denounced and refused to ratify the Treaty of Sèvres. Renegotiations produced a successor treaty, the 1923 Treaty of Lausanne, which was silent on the question of international justice or legal accountability for abuses. To this day, Turkey has never acknowledged responsibility for the campaign against the Armenians and vehemently protests whenever it is mentioned.

The World War I experiment with international criminal justice thus proved short-lived, a "fiasco" even, according to Henry Morgenthau, Sr., ambassador to the Ottoman Empire from 1913 to 1916. The fragile unity and resolve among the Allies dissipated in the immediate postwar period. Evolving events overtook idealism. In the end, only a handful of individuals were tried, and those who were prosecuted were essentially exonerated. This failed history was ever present a mere two decades later as a world war once again ravaged the globe.

3. The Interwar Period: Efforts to Avert Another World War

"The end of a great war frequently brings a revision of the laws of war in its wake."[36] World War I was no different. In the tenuous peace during the short interwar period, the international community came together to build institutions to minimize and settle international disputes and to fill some of the legal *lacunae* that had become so apparent in the post-World War I period. Institutionally, the League of Nations—which included as its "judicial branch" the Permanent Court of International Justice (PCIJ), the precursor to the International Court of Justice—announced its goal of providing

---

[36] Allison Marston Danner, *When Courts Make Law: How the International Criminal Tribunals Recast the Laws of War*, 59 VAND. L. REV. 1, 2 (2006).

a global forum for "safeguard[ing] the peace of nations" by resolving international disputes without recourse to war. In 1920, an advisory commission convened in connection with the League of Nations recommended the creation of a permanent international criminal court to have jurisdiction over "crimes constituting a breach of international public order or against the universal law of nations." The proposal, however, was rejected as "premature," and only the PCIJ was created with civil jurisdiction over states.

In response to the new weapons systems deployed during World War I, treaties were drafted regulating or prohibiting the use of various means and methods of war, such as bacteriological agents, poison gas, and submarines, and protecting vulnerable classes of persons, such as POWs and the wounded and sick. The catastrophic war also revived aspects of the just war theory as reflected in the optimistic, if not naïve, Kellogg-Briand Pact (or Pact of Paris). The Pact, originally a bilateral treaty between the United States and France that was later opened to global ratification, pledged its members to

> condemn recourse to war for the solution of international controversies, and renounce it as an instrument of national policy in their relations with one another . . . [and] agree that the settlement or solution of all disputes or conflicts of whatever nature or of whatever origin they may be, which may arise among them, shall never be sought except by pacific means.

The Pact reflected the organizing principle of the international order in the inter-war period: the prohibition of inter-state wars. Almost immediately after it entered into force, however, the Pact became a nullity, as Japan invaded Manchuria (1931), Italy invaded Ethiopia (1935), and Germany invaded Poland (1939), effectively launching World War II. Equally troubling were the three Moscow show trials (1936–1938) against old guard Bolsheviks in the Soviet Union. All of the defendants were convicted of treason based upon fabricated evidence and forced confessions. The trials successfully eliminated (through imprisonment and execution) real and potential rivals to Stalin, and thus is often referred to as the Great Purge. Notwithstanding their use of torture and fabricated evidence, these trials were once described as the "missing link between Versailles and Nuremberg."[37] Many of the architects of these trials later joined the Soviet delegation in Nuremberg.

---

[37] Gerry Simpson, *Human Rights with a Vengeance: One Hundred Years of Retributive Humanitarianism*, The Annual Kirby Lecture on International Law, ANU College of Law (2015), https://www.youtube.com/watch?v=bxzJK0nlNrY.

4. World War II: A Return to First Principles

The post-World War II period is nothing less than a watershed moment in the development of ICL. This period heralded the establishment of two international tribunals for adjudicating international crimes—the International Military Tribunal for the Trial of German Major War Criminals (the IMT or Nuremberg Tribunal) and the International Military Tribunal for the Far East (the IMTFE or Tokyo Tribunal). The Allies established these Tribunals to prosecute, respectively, high-level German and Japanese military and civilian authorities whose crimes "had no particular geographic localisation."[38] The Nuremberg Tribunal was established by agreement (the London Agreement of August 8, 1945) among the four victorious allied powers: France, the Soviet Union, the United Kingdom, and the United States. By contrast, the Tokyo Tribunal was technically established by a special proclamation issued by the Supreme Allied Commander of the Far East, U.S. General Douglas MacArthur, although with the acquiescence of the other Allied powers. International judicial proceedings before these institutions were followed by hundreds of trials before military and civilian tribunals in the various zones of occupation throughout Europe and the Pacific theatre. As these enforcement efforts were underway, the codification of ICL also began in earnest, with the promulgation of treaties addressing genocide (the 1948 Convention on the Prevention and Punishment of the Crime of Genocide) and war crimes (the four Geneva Conventions of 1949, discussed above).

That the Allies would adopt a strategy of international criminal justice in the post-World War II period was not a foregone conclusion. For one, the memory of the abject failure of the last effort at international justice following World War I remained fresh. The British and Soviets were more inclined to purge, punish, and in some cases simply execute defeated principals without elaborate legal processes. (The devastated French played little role in the initial decision making). Even Prime Minister Churchill argued in favor of executions for Nazi leaders and summary legal proceedings for the rank and file. In the end, it was pressure from the United States—and in particular from the Secretary of War, Henry Stimson—that resulted in the adoption of strictly legal processes to adjudge German and Japanese officials accused of violations of international law.

Although Stalin would have executed upwards of 50,000 German officers, he too was keen on holding a didactic trial of the

---

[38] Declaration of the Four Nations on General Security ("Moscow Declaration"), signed at Moscow, October 30, 1943, 9 U.S. Dep't of State Bulletin 308 (1943) (entered into force 30 October 1943). The Moscow Conference, October 19–30, 1943 (Declaration of German Atrocities), 1 November 1943, 1943 For. Rel. (I) 749 at 768, *reprinted in* 38 AM. J. INT'L L. 3, 7 (1944) (Supp).

Nazi masterminds. He recognized the value of such a proceeding to expose the enormity of the Nazi enterprise, foster Soviet unity, highlight the immense sacrifices made by the Soviets to defeat the Nazis, vindicate the national suffering, establish a legal claim to "reparations in kind" from Germany (a troubling euphemism for forced labor), and position the Soviet Union as a postwar international power (even as it was still reeling from wartime devastation at home). However, as it turned out, Stalin's vision of a propagandistic show trial with pre-determined outcomes was fundamentally at odds with the legalistic traditions of the other allies, who were operating under the deeply ingrained assumption that, if the captured Nazis were to be put on trial, the defendants were entitled to present a defense and enjoy strict due process.[39]

This dramatic change in the U.S. position toward international justice provides one of the most fascinating chapters of the history of ICL. As you will recall, after World War I, the United States was the staunchest opponent of the creation of an international tribunal, considering such an institution to be unprecedented and potentially dangerous. The United States also rejected both the justiciability of crimes against humanity as separate and apart from more traditional war crimes and the notion of a crime of initiating and waging an aggressive war. By the end of World War II, however, the United States had become the champion of trials, domestic and international (even single-handedly establishing the Tokyo Tribunal by executive fiat). The United States also directed the prosecution of crimes against the peace and conspiracy charges.

How can we explain this *volte-face*? Much may have turned on a key protagonist in this story—Stimson, a lawyer by training. Stimson never wavered in his advocacy that the Nazi defendants should face trials rather than firing squads, a counter-majoritarian position when U.S. public opinion at the time strongly favored summary execution or immediate imprisonment. Stimson remained staunchly opposed to alternative proposals that hundreds if not thousands of Nazis be summarily shot, insisting that even the Nazi defendants deserved due process of law in keeping with the best of the American legalistic tradition. Stimson was able to pass the baton to Justice Robert H. Jackson, a Supreme Court Justice (the last one without a law degree incidentally) who represented the United States at the Paris Peace Conference and eventually became chief U.S. prosecutor at Nuremberg. Once the Allies arrived at the Paris Peace Conference, the American delegation imposed its postwar strategy on the rest of the Allies, and the Nuremberg Tribunal was established. The

---

39 *See* FRANCINE HIRSCH, SOVIET JUDGMENT AT NUREMBERG: A NEW HISTORY OF THE INTERNATIONAL MILITARY TRIBUNAL AFTER WORLD WAR II (Oxford University Press, 2020).

Tribunal convened November 20, 1945 to October 1, 1946. The Tokyo Tribunal (sitting from May 3, 1946 to November 12, 1948) followed closely on its heels.

The subject matter jurisdiction of the two tribunals (i.e., the crimes they could prosecute) reflects the ideas being cast about in the post-World War I period. Notwithstanding the original Allies' reticence about criminalizing the resort to war, the Nuremberg and Tokyo Charters at Articles 6(a) and 5(a), respectively, enabled the prosecution for "crimes against the peace," defined as the "planning, preparation, initiation or waging of a war of aggression, or a war in violation of international treaties, agreements or assurances." Prosecutable war crimes, uncontroversially defined in sub-section (b), included "murder, ill-treatment or deportation to slave labor or for any other purpose of civilian population of or in occupied territory, murder or ill-treatment of prisoners of war or persons on the seas, killing of hostages, plunder of public or private property, wanton destruction of cities, towns or villages, or devastation not justified by military necessity." The Charter heralded the revival of the concept of crimes against humanity, although little reference was made in the judgment to the crime's World War I ancestry. The crime was defined as "murder, extermination, enslavement, deportation, and other inhumane acts committed against any civilian population, before or during the war, or persecutions on political, racial or religious grounds in execution of or in connection with any crime within the jurisdiction of the Tribunal, whether or not in violation of the domestic law of the country where perpetrated."

Twenty-four Nazi leaders were indicted before the IMT, which was composed of judges from the four Allies. One defendant was too ill to go to trial (Krupp);[40] one committed suicide (Ley); and one was tried and convicted to death *in absentia* (Bormann). The Tribunal tried the other 21 defendants.[41] Three of those were acquitted (Schacht, von Papen, and Fritzsche); seven were sentenced to prison terms ranging from ten years to life (Hess, Funk, Doenitz, Raeder, von Schirach, Speer, and von Neurath). The other 11 were sentenced to death (Goering, von Rivventrop, Keitel, Kaltenbrunner, Rosenberg, Frank, Frick, Streicher, Saukel, Jodl, and Seyss-Inquart). These defendants were all hanged except Goering, who committed suicide hours before he was scheduled to be executed. It

---

[40] IMT prosecutors attempted to substitute his son Alfried (who ran his family's armaments company during the war) as a defendant, but the judges ruled the substitution came too close to trial. Alfried was later tried in subsequent proceedings for his use of slave labor. As a result of U.S. intervention during the Cold War, Krupp was eventually released from prison with his property restored.

[41] The full IMT judgment is available at: *Judicial Decisions Involving Questions of International Law—International Military Tribunal (Nuremburg), Judgment and Sentences*, 41 AM. J. INT'L L. 172 (1947).

has been suggested that he accomplished this with the help of a young American guard who, perhaps unwittingly, smuggled a cyanide pill into Goering's cell.

At the time of Japan's surrender, the Japanese Cabinet launched war crimes trials of Japanese defendants, perhaps thinking that the principle of double jeopardy would prevent subsequent trials by the Allies. Eight accused were tried according to this plan, but all were subsequently retried by the Tokyo Tribunal. The defendants at Tokyo were four former premiers (Hiranuma, Hirota, Koiso, and Tojo), three former foreign ministers (Matsuoka, Shigemitsu, and Togo), four former war ministers (Araki, Hata, Itagaki, and Minami), two former navy ministers (Nagano and Shimada), six former generals (Doihara, Kimura, Matsui, Muto, Sato, and Umezu), two former ambassadors (Oshima and Shiratori), three former economic and financial leaders (Hoshino, Kaya, and Suzuki), one imperial adviser (Kido), one theorist (Okawa), one admiral (Oka), and one colonel (Hashimoto).

The United States, through General MacArthur, exercised far more control and influence over the Tokyo trials than at Nuremberg. Whereas the prosecutions at Nuremberg were led by a multinational team that shared relatively equal power and responsibility, the Tokyo prosecution was led by a single Chief of Counsel from the United States chosen by MacArthur with Associate Counsel from the Allies. The Tribunal itself was composed of judges from newly independent states in addition to representatives of the Allies. All of the decisions of the Tokyo Tribunal were subject to review by MacArthur, although he never exercised this power; there was no provision for review of any of the Nuremberg decisions. In addition, each of the accused at Tokyo had an American defense counsel in addition to one or more Japanese defense counsel. The majority opinion, authored by Judge Webb of Australia, resulted in the sentencing of seven defendants to death by hanging, 16 to life imprisonment, one to 20 years' imprisonment, and one to seven years' imprisonment.[42] Interestingly, Emperor Hirohito was not indicted or called as a witness by the Tokyo Tribunal, notwithstanding that he was viewed by many as the architect of Japanese imperialism. There is speculation that members of the U.S. government thought the occupation would proceed more smoothly with the emperor in place, albeit with a renunciation of any claims to divinity. By the 1950s, most of the Tokyo defendants sentenced to terms of imprisonment had been paroled. Two defendants returned to high government positions in Japan.

---

42 *United States v. Araki*, 101 THE TOKYO MAJOR WAR CRIMES TRIAL (R. John Pritchard ed., 1998).

Notwithstanding the importance of the work of the Nuremberg and Tokyo Tribunals, the vast majority of post-World War II prosecutions did not occur before these two international tribunals, but were conducted by the victorious powers in their respective zones of occupation. For example, Allied Control Council Law No. 10, which largely mirrored the terms of the Nuremberg Charter, authorized trials in Germany. The United States hosted 12 key trials, each with a theme and appropriate nickname. The Hostages Trial, for example, involved allegations against German generals leading troops during the Balkans Campaign who were charged with civilian hostage-taking and murder. The RuSHA Trial targeted 14 officials of various SS organizations responsible for the implementation of the Nazi "pure race" program through racial cleansing and resettlement. Defendants included principals from the Rasse-und Siedlungshauptamt (RuSHA) bureau, the office of the Reich Commissioner for the Strengthening of Germanism, the Repatriation Office for Ethnic Germans, and the Lebensborn society. The Einsatzgruppen Trial involved mobile death squads operating primarily behind the frontline in Eastern Europe that indiscriminately targeted Jews, partisans, Roma, disabled persons, lesbians and gay men, and otherwise uncooperative civilians. The Doctors Trial involved medical doctors accused of engaging in human experimentation, and the Justice Case involved German jurists and lawyers held responsible for implementing the Nazi "racial purity" program envisioned by the odious eugenic laws. The Ministries Trial involved officials of various Reich ministries, who faced charges for atrocities committed both in Germany and in occupied countries during the war. The High Command Trial focused on high-ranking generals and former members of the High Command of Nazi Germany's military forces charged with having participated in, planned, or facilitated the execution of the war.

Trials proceeded against civilian industrialists as well. For example, the Flick Trial centered on Friedrich Flick and five other high-ranking directors of Flick's group of companies and involved the use of slave labor and plundering. (Flick himself was sentenced to seven years' imprisonment. After serving three years, he was released and went on to rebuild his industrial empire. His son later became one of the richest men in Austria). The IG Farben Trial concerned the manufacture of Zyklon B, the poison gas used in extermination camps (the other supplier of the gas was the firm Tesch/Stabenow). IG Farben was also charged with participating in crimes against the peace, because it had developed processes for synthesizing gasoline and rubber from coal and thereby contributed to Germany's ability to wage war without access to petroleum resources. Twelve former directors of the Krupp Group were accused of having enabled the armament of the German military forces and for having used slave laborers. In total, more than 5,000 trials were held of German and Japanese POWs accused of committing war crimes and crimes against humanity.

It is difficult to overstate the significance of the post-World War II period to the field of ICL. Together, these legal proceedings established many core principles of the field, and modern tribunals continue to cite these proceedings as persuasive authority. We touch here on the most salient of the tribunals' contributions. First, the Nuremberg and Tokyo proceedings established that many violations of IHL that had theretofore given rise only to state responsibility also gave rise to individual criminal responsibility, even if the relevant treaty was silent as to criminal penalties. Therefore, when the Nuremberg defendants argued that they could not legally be prosecuted for certain acts because they were not technically crimes under international law at the time the acts were committed, the Tribunal responded that "[c]rimes against international law are committed by men, not by abstract entities, and only by punishing individuals who commit such crimes can the provisions of international law be enforced."[43] All of the post-World War II ICL treaties are premised on this notion of individual criminal responsibility for breaches. In particular, it is the cornerstone of the enforcement regime contained in the four Geneva Conventions of 1949, which with 196 parties are the first treaties to enjoy universal ratification (the most recent being Palestine, which is significant because there have been lingering questions about whether Palestine constitutes a state). Each state in the world has now agreed to apprehend and prosecute, or extradite for prosecution, any individual found to have committed a "grave breach" of one of the four Conventions in an international armed conflict.

Second, the two tribunals established the primacy of international law over domestic law. In many cases, the conduct for which the accused had been charged was authorized by domestic law. Indeed, the tribunals' statutes made clear that crimes against humanity in particular were punishable "whether or not in violation of the domestic law of the country where perpetrated." That international law placed limits on the content of domestic law governing purely domestic affairs was groundbreaking under the prevailing view that international law primarily governed relations between states and not relations within states. The Nuremberg and Tokyo proceedings mark the first time that the international community pierced the veil of sovereignty to hold governmental actors responsible for the mistreatment of their compatriots.

---

[43] *Nuremberg Judgment*, 41 AM. J. INT'L L. at 221.

Third, two new crimes officially came into existence with the promulgation of the Nuremberg and Tokyo Charters: crimes against the peace and crimes against humanity. The Allies' prosecutorial strategy focused primarily on the crimes against the peace charge, which the Allies considered the primary justification for punishing individual representatives of the Axis Powers. Jackson, in his opening statement, spoke of aggressive war—not genocide—as the "greatest menace of our times."[44] Indeed, the crimes against humanity allegations appear in parts of the Nuremberg Judgment as mere afterthoughts. Nonetheless, this latter charge was revolutionary in establishing once and for all that international law applied to crimes committed within the borders of a single state. The inclusion of both crimes in the Charter was controversial in light of the principle of legality, defined in international law through the maxim *nullum crimen sine lege, nulla poena sine lege*, which dictates that an individual cannot be prosecuted for conduct that was not criminalized at the time the individual acted. As mentioned, this was a primary defense of all the defendants, yet it had no effect on the tribunals. The Nuremberg Tribunal in particular ruled that the defense was inapplicable in light of the obvious wrongfulness of the acts in question. Where the treaties were silent as to the criminality of the prohibited acts therein, the Tribunal found precedent for their prosecution under national law. Accordingly, it argued that the customary international law prohibition of the acts went beyond what the treaties provided. As discussed in a fuller chapter on the *nullum crimen* defense, these arguments are repeated in modern ICL jurisprudence when judges are faced with new atrocities that do not fit nicely into the framework of existing crimes.

Fourth, although their legacy remains plagued by charges of "victors' justice," the tribunals established clear precedent for the exercise of international penal jurisdiction as distinct from domestic jurisdiction. Indeed, in many respects, this precedent gave rise to a distinct preference for international and multilateral, as opposed to national and unilateral, efforts at international criminal justice. This option remains compelling today in light of concerns about the potential for abuse and politicization inherent in the practice of universal jurisdiction, although the high cost associated with international tribunals has diminished the enthusiasm for international judicial institutions, a phenomenon called "tribunal fatigue." Depending on the political will of the international community, international courts can assert a more robust jurisdiction, freed from the limitations that international law and the

---

[44] *Second Day, Wednesday, 11/21/1945, in* II TRIAL OF THE MAJOR WAR CRIMINALS BEFORE THE INTERNATIONAL MILITARY TRIBUNAL (11/14/1945–11/30/1945), 98–102 (1947).

principle of international comity might place on their domestic counterparts.[45] International tribunals are also able to tap into the existing U.N. enforcement machinery, such as the Security Council. Notwithstanding this firm foundation for the exercise of international jurisdiction, the international community did not significantly build on this precedent until the post-Cold War period. The mending of entrenched Cold War rivalries created space for the United Nations to revive the promises of the post-World War II era in the face of civil wars in the former Yugoslavia and Sierra Leone, crimes against humanity and genocide in Rwanda and Cambodia, the destruction of East Timor by forces loyal to its former occupier Indonesia, and acts of terrorism in Lebanon. In particular, the Security Council, once paralyzed by East-West obstructionism, could suddenly act unanimously without the threat of an automatic veto of one of the permanent five members. These modern international and hybrid tribunals have the blessing of the entire United Nations, either as organs of the Security Council (the Yugoslav and Rwandan tribunals), as the products of treaty negotiations between the state in question and the U.N. Secretary General (the Special Court for Sierra Leone, the Extraordinary Chambers in the Courts of Cambodia, and the Lebanon tribunal), or as a feature of a U.N. transitional authority (the East Timor Special Panels).

Fifth, the postwar tribunals confirmed that even high-ranking state officials could be held individually criminally liable for international crimes committed in war. In particular, the IMT proclaimed that "the very essence of the [Nuremberg] Charter is that individuals have international duties which transcend the national obligations of obedience imposed by the individual State."[46] High-ranking state agents thus cannot hide behind state sovereignty when international jurisdiction is at issue. In so holding, the tribunals rejected common law doctrines of head of state and sovereign immunity that might have shielded particular defendants from liability, a result that has been followed by the modern international tribunals in cases involving Yugoslav President Slobodan Milošević, Liberian President Charles Taylor, Khmer Rouge Foreign Minister Ieng Sary, and Sudan ex-President Omar Al Bashir. Complementing this rejection of official immunity, the post-World War II tribunals also rejected the claim that individuals implementing superior orders should be exonerated: "That a soldier is ordered to kill or torture in violation of the international law of war has never been recognized

---

[45] Comity refers to the respect and mutual recognition of legislative, executive or judicial acts that is deemed to be owed to co-equal sovereigns.

[46] *Nuremberg Judgment*, 41 AM. J. INT'L L. at 221.

as a defense to such acts of brutality, though . . . the order may be urged in mitigation of the punishment."[47]

Sixth, the tribunals convicted civilians and military men as well as private actors—financiers and industrialists—for war crimes and crimes against humanity. State action is not an element of these crimes, although in many situations of mass violence and repression the state is the source of, or inspiration for, the abuses. Together, this collection of rulings—since ratified by the U.N. General Assembly—became known as the "Nuremberg principles" and they have shaped the field of ICL ever since.[48]

5. Post-World War II: The Cold War Freeze

The post-World War II period heralded a wave of optimism about the power of law and judicial institutions to restrain state violence and protect the vulnerable. However, just as the ink was drying on the U.N. Charter and the tribunals' judgments against the major World War II defendants, the Cold War set in, paralyzing efforts to put permanent ICL institutions in place. As a result, for many years, the development of ICL was largely relegated to obscure U.N. drafting committees, a smattering of domestic proceedings in transitional societies, and the writings of a few dogged academics.

This stagnation did not set in immediately, however. Continuing the typical reactivity of international law, the close of World War II brought about a flurry of drafting endeavors. The international community constructed the United Nations from the ashes of the League of Nations. The lynchpin of its Charter is Article 2(4), which codified a default rule against the use of force subject to two express exceptions—actions undertaken with Security Council approval (Article 42) and measures taken in self defense (Article 51). The Charter forbids the use of force undertaken "against the territorial integrity or political independence of any state." The legality of the use of force to stop atrocities or to otherwise assist people in need (also known as humanitarian intervention) is thus an open question, especially in light of the proliferation of human rights treaties.

The immediate postwar era also witnessed the promulgation of the 1948 Genocide Convention[49] and the four Geneva Conventions in 1949 protecting various classes of people in times of war. These treaties confirmed the new expectation of individual criminal responsibility for international law breaches. The Geneva Conventions, in particular, codified the war crimes recognized at

---

[47] *Id.*

[48] G.A. Res. 95(I), 188 U.N. Doc. A/64/Add.1 (1946).

[49] Convention on the Prevention and Punishment of the Crime of Genocide, Dec. 9, 1948, 78 U.N.T.S. 277.

Nuremberg and Tokyo and others—officially deeming them "grave breaches." The treaties also made such breaches subject to universal criminal jurisdiction, distinguishing them from those other treaty breaches that give rise only to state (civil) responsibility. These instruments were followed by other multilateral treaties prohibiting or criminalizing acts of torture, the policy of apartheid, various manifestations of terrorism, war crimes in non-international armed conflicts, human trafficking, and the international sale and distribution of narcotics. Many of these subsequent treaties contain boilerplate language obliging signatories to either prosecute offenders or extradite them elsewhere for prosecution, regardless of the place of the act's commission or the nationality of the perpetrator or victim (the *aut dedere aut judicare* compulsion). This drafting process remains seemingly without end, as international law struggles to keep pace with increasingly destructive and cruel methods of warfare and repression. One of the more recent additions to this pantheon is the 2006 Convention against Enforced Disappearances,[50] and work continues on drafting a convention on crimes against humanity.

In addition to this norm proliferation, members of the international community also tried to build a permanent judicial institution, untainted by the stain of victors' justice, to prosecute international crimes. It was assumed that this work would proceed in parallel with the drafting of substantive law. Indeed, the drafters of the Genocide Convention contemplated the establishment of a permanent international criminal court at Article VI, which provides that individuals charged with committing genocide shall be tried "by a competent tribunal of the State in the territory of which the act was committed, or by such international penal tribunal as may have jurisdiction." Thus, in 1947, the General Assembly requested the International Law Commission (ILC)[51] to study "the desirability and possibility of establishing an international judicial organ for the trial of persons charged with genocide or other crimes." The ILC was also asked to codify the Nuremberg and Tokyo principles in a Draft Code of Offenses Against the Peace and Security of Mankind that would provide the subject matter jurisdiction of the proposed tribunal.

On other fronts, the international community began the process of building a regime of international human rights that in many respects is the progeny of the crimes against humanity charge at

[50] International Convention for the Protection of All Persons From Enforced Disappearance, Dec. 20, 2006, 2716 U.N.T.S. 3.

[51] The General Assembly established the ILC that year to promote the progressive development and codification of (primarily) public international law. The ILC is composed of independent legal experts and played a key role in creating a draft code of international crimes and a draft statute for a permanent international criminal court that served as the starting point for creating the modern ICC.

Nuremberg. The groundbreaking Universal Declaration of Human Rights in 1948 established a holistic view of human rights. When states decided to convert the Declaration into a binding instrument, they moved away from this admirable approach. Reflecting the ideological schisms of the day, twin Covenants finalized in 1966 separately protect civil and political rights on the one side[52] and economic, social, and cultural rights on the other.[53] Subsequent specialized treaties sought to guarantee equal and fair treatment for racial and ethnic groups, women, children, indigenous people, the disabled, and migrant workers. Over time, states increasingly built more robust enforcement regimes in these treaties, granting expert committees the power to receive reports, monitor human rights practices, accept individual complaints and petitions, mediate inter-state complaints, recommend reforms and reparations, conduct site visits, and so on—all subject to state consent, of course. This proliferation of partially overlapping institutions—domestic, regional, and international bodies with varying degrees of adjudicative power—has generated a productive cross-fertilization of norms that is approaching a veritable common law of ICL and international human rights law.

With the advent of the Cold War, however, work on many of these fronts slowed or stalled. In particular, the project to create a permanent international criminal court hit an impasse, in part because delegates could not agree on a definition of the crime of aggression against the backdrop of United States and Soviet "proxy wars" throughout the developing world. As a result, prior to the establishment in the mid-1990s of the *ad hoc* criminal tribunals, ICL was characterized by a panoply of articulated rights without judicial institutions in which to launch prosecutions—a rights-remedy gap that characterizes much of public international law.

Notwithstanding the lack of international prosecutions, there were some important domestic prosecutions that are worth noting. The most high profile of these is probably the trial of Adolf Eichmann, whose job under the Third Reich was to manage mass deportations from Eastern Europe to brutal ghettos and extermination camps. Following Germany's surrender after World War II, U.S. troops detained Eichmann briefly in an internment camp, although he escaped unrecognized. On a false Red Cross passport obtained through the Nazi underground, Eichmann traveled through "ratlines" to Argentina where he lived under an assumed name until 1960. That year, Israeli Mossad agents abducted him, causing a

---

[52] International Covenant on Civil and Political Rights, Dec. 16, 1966, 999 U.N.T.S. 171.

[53] International Covenant on Economic, Social and Cultural Rights, Dec. 16, 1966, 993 U.N.T.S. 3.

major diplomatic rift between Israel and Argentina that went before the U.N. Security Council. The Council condemned the kidnapping and ordered Israel to make "appropriate restitution."[54] In Israel, Eichmann was charged with crimes against humanity, war crimes, and "crimes against the Jewish people" under the 1950 Nazi and Nazi Collaborators (Punishment) Law. His primary defense was jurisdictional, arguing that the Israeli courts could not prosecute him under *ex post facto* legislation for acts that he allegedly committed before the State of Israel existed. The Israeli court ruled that it had both universal and passive personality jurisdiction—jurisdiction premised on the nationality of the victim—over him.[55] Eichmann did not contest the factual charges against him, but claimed he was just following orders. He was convicted and hanged in 1962.

In 1987, France prosecuted Klaus Barbie—the former head of the Gestapo in Lyon, dubbed the "Butcher of Lyon"—for crimes against humanity committed in connection with his involvement in the deportation of French Jews and partisans during World War II.[56] He had already been prosecuted *in absentia* for war crimes, but these verdicts lapsed while he was in exile in Bolivia. The crimes against humanity case went forward on the basis of a ruling that the crime carried no statute of limitation. During this trial, he was represented by Jacques Vergès, who subsequently made a name for himself ("the Devil's Advocate") representing high-profile accused war criminals and Holocaust deniers. Vergès—an avid anticolonialist—invoked a modified *tu quoque* ("you also") defense by analogizing Barbie's actions to those of France in Algeria during that country's quest for independence. Barbie ultimately died in prison after serving four years of a life sentence.

In the United States, civil suits involving ICL and human rights norms—in other words, lawsuits initiated by the survivors themselves and seeking compensation—have proceeded under the Alien Tort Statute (ATS)[57] and related statutes since the seminal case of *Filártiga v. Peña-Irala* in 1980,[58] although the U.S. Supreme Court has significantly truncated the reach of this statute in recent rulings.[59] For example, civil plaintiffs have obtained personal

---

[54] S.C. Res. 138, ¶ 2, U.N. Doc. S/4349 (June 23, 1960).

[55] *Attorney General of Israel v. Eichmann*, reprinted in 36 I.L.R. 5 (Jm. 1961), *aff'd*, 36 I.L.R. 277 (S.Ct. 1962).

[56] *Fédération Nationale des Deportés et Internés Résistants et Patriotes v. Barbie, reprinted in* 78 I.L.R. 125 (1985), *aff'd* 100 I.L.R. 331 (Court of Cassation 1988).

[57] 28 U.S.C. § 1350; *see also* Torture Victim Protection Act, 28 U.S.C. § 1350 note; Anti-Terrorism Act, 18 U.S.C. § 2333(a).

[58] *Filártiga v. Peña-Irala*, 630 F. 2d 876 (2nd Cir. 1980).

[59] *See Kiobel v. Royal Dutch Petroleum Co.*, 569 U.S. 108 (2013) (recognizing a presumption against extraterritoriality and thus requiring a showing that the claim has a U.S. nexus).

jurisdiction over defendants hailing from the former Yugoslavia, Rwanda, East Timor, the states of the Southern Cone and Central America, the Philippines, and elsewhere. For several years, corporations could be sued for violating these norms in places where they do business; the Supreme Court ruled recently that the ATS does not support suits against foreign corporations.[60] Under certain circumstances, victims can also assert claims against sovereign states directly, for example if the state in question has been designated a state sponsor of terrorism or if the state commits, or is complicit in, acts of domestic terrorism.[61] Although serving important purposes, these tort cases—which are akin to personal injury lawsuits and occasionally proceed in default—often are a poor substitute for more robust criminal processes and penalties that better reflect the severity of the offenses involved.

6. Post-Cold War: A Renaissance

In the late 1980s, a consortium of Latin American and Caribbean states reinvigorated the project of international criminal justice, primarily because they sought an international mechanism to combat the transnational illicit drug trade. With prompting from the General Assembly, the ILC again turned its attention to drafting a statute for a permanent international criminal court. The ILC completed a draft statute in 1994 that formed the basis for intensified consideration by an Ad Hoc Committee and then a Preparatory Committee on the Establishment of an International Criminal Court.

In the meantime, genocide appeared to return to Europe in the form of deportations, concentration camps, "ethnic cleansing," and mass killings of Bosnian Muslim civilians during the war on the territory of the former Yugoslavia. (Violations were in fact committed by all three of the immediate parties to the conflict—Bosnian Muslims, Croats, and Serbs—as well as by agents of the former Yugoslavia and recently independent Croatia, which had territorial designs in Bosnia). In the midst of the war, the U.N. Security Council addressed the conflict in seriatim resolutions. In Resolution 780 adopted on October 6, 1992, the Security Council directed the Secretary General, at the time the Egyptian diplomat Boutros Boutros-Ghali, to establish a Commission of Experts to document violations of international law. As this investigation was ongoing, governments (prominently the United States) and intergovernmental and nongovernmental organizations called for the creation of an *ad hoc* international tribunal in the Nuremberg tradition to assign individual responsibility for the documented abuses. The interim report of the Commission of Experts echoed

---

[60] *Jesner v. Arab Bank, PLC*, 138 S.Ct. 1386 (2018).

[61] Foreign Sovereign Immunities Act, 28 U.S.C. §§ 1605A & B.

these recommendations. In Resolution 808 adopted February 22, 1993, the Security Council unanimously decided "that an international tribunal shall be established for the prosecution of persons responsible for serious violations of international humanitarian law committed in the territory of the former Yugoslavia since 1991." It directed the Secretary General to prepare specific proposals for such a tribunal. In his subsequent report, Boutros-Ghali presented a tribunal blueprint and appended a draft statute setting forth existing international humanitarian and criminal law. Invoking its Chapter VII powers, the Security Council unanimously adopted the draft statute in Resolution 827 on May 25, 1993. The International Criminal Tribunal for Yugoslavia (ICTY) was thus established.

The next year, genocide was committed in Rwanda. All told, upward of 800,000 Tutsi and moderate Hutu individuals perished within the span of a mere four months—a rate of killing that far exceeded the Nazi Holocaust. Having convened a tribunal for the former Yugoslavia, the Security Council could not readily ignore almost a million dead in Rwanda, especially given that the international community had largely stood immobile as the death toll mounted. The Security Council through Resolution 955 thus established the International Criminal Tribunal for Rwanda (ICTR), finding that widespread violations of international law largely within the confines of a single state, although with regional ramifications, constituted a threat to international peace and security within the meaning of Chapter VII of the U.N. Charter.

As first constructed by the Security Council, the *ad hoc* tribunals shared an Appeals Chamber and a Chief Prosecutor. South African jurist Richard Goldstone originally held the latter post. Canadian jurist Louise Arbour, who was later chosen to be the U.N. High Commissioner for Human Rights, next occupied the position. The Security Council then appointed Swiss Prosecutor Carla Del Ponte. From the Tribunals' beginning, observers expressed concern that the Rwandan prosecutions were not getting the Chief Prosecutor's full attention. As the Security Council began to contemplate the completion of the Tribunals' missions, it split the Office of the Prosecutor into two positions over the objections of Del Ponte. Hassan Bubacar Jallow—a former Solicitor General, Attorney General, Minister of Justice, and Supreme Court Justice of Gambia—was then appointed Chief Prosecutor of the ICTR. In 2007, Del Ponte retired and was replaced by Belgian jurist Serge Brammertz, who was also the chief U.N. investigator into the terrorist assassination of former Lebanese Prime Minister Rafik Hariri. Later, additional *ad hoc* tribunals were established by efforts from outside the Security Council to respond to massive crimes committed in Sierra Leone,

Cambodia, Lebanon, Kosovo, East Timor, Chad, and the Central African Republic. New models are under contemplation elsewhere, including South Sudan and the Democratic Republic of Congo. In the meantime, the two *ad hoc* tribunals have transitioned their legacy work—including tracking the few remaining ICTR fugitives, hearing lingering appeals, supervising sentences, ensuring witness protection, maintaining archives, and providing assistance to national judiciaries—to a U.N. International Residual Mechanism for Criminal Tribunals.

The two *ad hoc* tribunals were successful at implementing their mandate but had high startup costs. This served as further inspiration for the formation of a standing international criminal court. After convening six separate sessions, the Preparatory Committee produced a consolidated draft statute that served as the basis for comprehensive negotiations at a Diplomatic Conference of Plenipotentiaries on the Establishment of an International Criminal Court held from June 15 to July 17, 1998 in Rome, Italy. A final treaty—called the Rome Statute of the International Criminal Court (ICC Statute or Rome Statute)—was completed and adopted at the Diplomatic Conference, which was attended by delegations from 120 states, multiple observers and intergovernmental organizations, and hundreds of nongovernmental organizations. Only seven states voted against the final text: the United States, China, Israel, Qatar, Libya, Iraq, and Yemen. The ICC entered into force in 2002 with the deposit of the 60th instrument of ratification.

The ICC originally exercised jurisdiction over war crimes, crimes against humanity, and genocide as defined by its Statute. Although the crimes against the peace charge was the lynchpin of the Nuremberg and Tokyo proceedings, the crime of aggression (as the crime is now known) has eluded modern definition. Drafters of the ICC Statute were unable to come up with a consensus definition of aggression in time for the treaty to be opened for signature, so they punted. Article 5(2) promised that "[t]he Court shall exercise jurisdiction over the crime of aggression once a provision is adopted defining the crime and setting out the conditions under which the Court shall exercise jurisdiction with respect to this crime. Such a provision shall be consistent with the relevant provisions of the Charter of the United Nations." A subsequent Working Group was mandated to determine a number of open issues, such as (1) the proper role of the Security Council, the General Assembly, and the International Court of Justice in adjudications of the crime of aggression; and (2) whether the definition should make reference to specific acts that constitute aggression, or be left open for future interpretation by the Court. A full penal definition and jurisdictional regime were finally achieved at a Review Conference held in

Kampala, Uganda in 2010, and the crime became prosecutable—albeit under exceedingly narrow circumstances—on July 19, 2018, the 20th anniversary of the promulgation of the Rome Statute.

Events from 1994 onward attest that the Nuremberg and Tokyo Tribunals are not mere historical footnotes. Although it took decades and remains a work in progress, the international community has built on the promises of that era in significant ways. Key moments include the 1998 arrest of General Augusto Pinochet of Chile in the United Kingdom in response to an arrest warrant from Spain for him to stand trial for torture, genocide, and other international crimes over which Spain asserted universal jurisdiction; the 1999 indictment of President Slobodan Milošević, the first ever against a sitting head of state; the 2012 conviction of former Liberian President Charles Taylor for abetting crimes against humanity in Sierra Leone, even though it does not appear he ever set foot in the country; the first order for payment of reparations by the ICC in 2015; and the ICC Appeals Chamber's 2020 authorization of an investigation into crimes committed in Afghanistan, which may include custodial abuses committed by U.S. personnel, and thus an assertion of ICC jurisdiction over nationals of a powerful non-party state. Dozens of states have domesticated the Rome Statute crimes in their own penal codes as part of the process of ratifying the treaty and are increasingly invoking those provisions in atrocity trials at home.

Progress toward a more comprehensive system of international justice has not been linear or continuous. Rather, it has featured a number of oversteps and backslides that include the failure of international troops and domestic officials to arrest key indicted war criminals from the Yugoslav war; the *in absentia* indictment in Belgium of high-level political figures from powerful states, which resulted in an international backlash and a contrite amendment of Belgium's universal jurisdiction law; the failure of the East Timor Special Panels to gain jurisdiction over any defendants of real consequence as a result of Indonesian obstructionism and international neglect; the summary execution of Saddam Hussein after a controversial trial and while important charges remained pending against him; the dismissal of a number of high profile cases by the ICC for failure by the Office of the Prosecutor to carry its burden;[62] and the systemic impunity for the myriad crimes being

---

[62] *See, e.g.*, *Prosecutor v. Bemba*, Case No. ICC-01/01-01/08-3636-Red, Judgment on the Appeal of Mr. Jean-Pierre Bemba Gombo against Trial Chamber III's "Judgment pursuant to Article 74 of the Statute" (June 8, 2018); *Prosecutor v. Gbagbo & Blé Goudé*, Case No. ICC-02/11-01/15, Dissenting Opinion of Judge Herrera Carbuccia to the Chamber's Oral Decision of 15 January 2019 on the 'Requete de la Defense de Laurent Gbagbo afin qu'un jugement d'acquittement portant sur toutes les charges soit prononce enfaveur de Laurent Gbagbo et que sa mise en liberte immediate

committed in Syria, Iraq, and Yemen. A concern that the ICC was disproportionately "targeting" Africa and African heads of state led certain members of the African Union to advocate for a collective ICC Withdrawal Strategy. South Africa, The Gambia, and Burundi took steps in this regard, although only Burundi ultimately withdrew from the treaty. (South Africa's effort was declared unconstitutional and a newly-elected government in The Gambia reversed course). Add to this all the delays, wasted resources, and corrupt functionaries that seem to plague international bureaucracies, no matter how noble their mandate. On the domestic front, the tragic events of September 11, 2001, led to the creation of "legal black holes" at Guantánamo and elsewhere where pure power has all but eclipsed law. Yet, the field's movement is inexorably forward, and the system of international criminal justice—however imperfect—is undoubtedly here to stay.

---

soit ordonnee' and on the 'Ble Goude Defence No Case to Answer Motion' (Jan. 15, 2019) (dissenting to majority's granting of the defense's no case to answer motion).

Chapter 2

SOVEREIGNTY, JURISDICTION, AND POWER

International criminal law (ICL), like all of public international law, implicates the principle of state sovereignty. States have historically considered scrutiny by international and foreign tribunals of events within their territory or involving their nationals to be an infringement on such sovereignty, especially when this scrutiny takes the form of criminal investigations and prosecutions of individuals accused of committing international crimes. State authorities often assert the prerogative to decide whether and how to prosecute their own citizens for crimes they may have committed as well as criminal acts committed in their territories. As a result, governments frequently resist exercises of international or extraterritorial jurisdiction over their nationals or over events that have occurred within their borders. Yet with the reemergence of international criminal tribunals on the global stage in the 1990s, and the increased use of universal jurisdiction occasioned by the overlapping wars in Syria and Iraq, such exercises of scrutiny are increasingly common. As a result, the enforcement of ICL has occasioned a reinterpretation of the principle of state sovereignty—a development that not all states have accepted quietly.

ICL is now applied, interpreted, and developed through three different types of judicial institutions: domestic, international, and hybrid. Historically, prosecutions for what we would today call international crimes primarily occurred in domestic courts, if they took place at all. Today, international and mixed national-international ("hybrid") tribunals have joined domestic courts as adjudicators of ICL. These multilateral institutions have been created by two primary means. First, they have been created through an exercise of state consent, usually with the promulgation of a bilateral or multilateral treaty, by which a state agrees to subject individuals within their jurisdictions to prosecution before an international or quasi-international tribunal. The International Criminal Court (ICC) and Special Court for Sierra Leone (SCSL) are examples of this approach. Second, institutions have been created through the coercive power of the international community acting collectively through the auspices of the U.N. Security Council. The two *ad hoc* criminal tribunals for Yugoslavia and Rwanda exemplify this approach. Notwithstanding the recent focus on international institutions, domestic courts remain important fora for ICL development, especially given the increasing acceptance and prevalence of various forms of extraterritorial jurisdiction.

This chapter provides an overview of the origins of the institutions in which ICL is adjudicated and various procedural mechanisms (such as extradition) that effectuate such proceedings. It also discusses the jurisdictional frameworks at work with reference to the three types of jurisdiction—prescriptive, adjudicative, and enforcement—and the classic bases for exercising jurisdiction—territoriality, nationality, protectivity, and universality. Finally, it discusses some of the structural limitations that states impose on these tribunals to cabin their juridical power. The subject matter jurisdiction of the various international and hybrid tribunals is often quite similar in terms of the crimes that can be prosecuted. Their jurisdictional power over the individuals and events of concern varies as a result of the different circumstances and power dynamics at play during their formation. This chapter serves as a reminder that although the principle of state sovereignty has been under attack, it remains a potent force in international relations and the field of international criminal law.

A. Creatures of Consent

This section discusses the most prominent example of the creation of an international criminal tribunal by consent—the multilateral Rome Treaty that gave rise to the ICC. It also discusses the hybrid tribunals and mixed panels that were created by virtue of international agreements, although the treaties in question were bilateral rather than multilateral. Treaty-based institutions have the advantage of high (or higher) "buy in" by participating states. At the same time, this requirement that states express affirmative support for the future institution comes with its own, not insignificant, weaknesses. For one, important states may choose not to participate, thus weakening the strength and legitimacy of the tribunal. In addition, states that negotiate the terms of these tribunals' constitutive treaties may insist on the inclusion of significant structural limitations to control the amount of discretion, independence, and judicial power these institutions can exercise and to ensure some measure of state control over the judicial process. This can result in both a significantly weaker institution and one vulnerable to political manipulation.

1. The International Criminal Court

The ICC illustrates the strengths and weaknesses of the consensual treaty-based approach. The ICC was created by a treaty that was finalized in Rome, Italy in 1998 (often referred to as the Rome Treaty). The treaty came into force on July 1, 2002, after ratification by 60 states. As of April 1, 2020—and following the withdrawals of Burundi, the Philippines, and Malaysia—there are 123 state parties to the Court's constitutive treaty. The refusal of three of the five permanent members of the U.N. Security Council (China, Russia, and the United States) to join the Court, and the aggressive opposition mounted by Republican administrations in the United States against the Court (under Presidents George W. Bush and Donald J. Trump), illustrate one of the weaknesses in the consensual approach. At the time of this writing, the ICC Prosecutor is investigating multiple situations that have resulted in indictments. A number of these situations—including Uganda, the Democratic Republic of the Congo, the Central African Republic, Mali, and the Comoros—were brought to the Court by virtue of a referral by the affected state itself or by other states, such as a 2018 referral of Venezuela by a consortium of the Southern Cone joined by Canada. The idea that states would submit themselves to the Court was not anticipated and reveals a strength of a consent-based approach. Although each of these referrals has its own peculiarities, together they illustrate a high level of reliance by those states on the ICC to address the crimes committed in their midst.

Drafting the ICC Statute involved juggling a number of moving parts. With respect to each jurisdictional and substantive law element, states engaged in protracted and multipolar negotiations, with self-described Like-Minded States and most nongovernmental organizations advocating provisions that would ensure a strong, impartial, and independent institution, while other participants pushed in the opposite direction by trying to incorporate significant limitations and checks on the future Court's power at every turn. Two of the most contentious issues to arise during the Rome Treaty negotiations concerned the persons over whom, and situations over which, the Court would have jurisdiction (the so-called preconditions for the exercise of jurisdiction) and how the Court's jurisdiction could be initiated, triggered, or otherwise controlled. Drafters also had to work out a system of resolving jurisdictional conflicts between the future Court and the domestic courts of states that may also be empowered to assert jurisdiction over the events and individuals in question (the question of admissibility).

a. Preconditions for the Exercise of Jurisdiction

The Court has jurisdiction over an individual suspected of committing genocide, a crime against humanity, or a war crime if: (1) the act was committed within the territory of a state that is a party to the treaty; or (2) the individual is a national of a state that is a party to the treaty. In other words, the preconditions for the Court's assertion of jurisdiction are based on the territorial and active nationality principles of jurisdiction. (The one significant exception to this involves referrals by the Security Council which, as we discuss below, automatically imposes jurisdiction over responsible individuals irrespective of their nationality or the place of the alleged crime). As of July 17, 2018, the Court also has jurisdiction over the crime of aggression, though there are significant restrictions on the exercise of jurisdiction over this crime. In particular, the Court does not have jurisdiction over the crime of aggression if committed by a national of a non-party state, or if committed on the territory of a non party state. This limitation marks a significant victory for the U.S. negotiating team at the 2010 Assembly of State Parties meeting in Kampala where the definition of the crime of aggression was adopted.

The two alternative bases for the assertion of ICC jurisdiction over crimes other than aggression derive from general principles of international law regulating when a state can assert jurisdiction over an individual. Territoriality is the most common, and least controversial, justification for the assertion of criminal jurisdiction and provides that a state may assert jurisdiction over any individual who commits a criminal act within its sovereign territory. The Genocide Convention, for example, states that persons charged with genocide shall be tried by a competent tribunal of the state in which the genocide occurred, thus incorporating the territoriality principle. (Interestingly for our purposes, the Genocide Convention also states in the alternative that such a person may be tried before an international tribunal, although no such tribunal existed at the time the Convention was opened for signature or for several decades afterwards).

There are two versions of the territorial principle. First, under the *subjective territorial principle,* a state may assert jurisdiction over acts commenced within its territory but consummated abroad. This principle is tangentially at play in the ICC's consideration of harm to the Rohingya Muslim minority in Myanmar (a non-party state), who find themselves seeking refuge in the territory of Bangladesh, an ICC state party.[1] There, a Pre-Trial Chamber of the ICC ruled that the Office of the Prosecutor can proceed with a preliminary examination of crimes only partially committed within Bangladesh, such as deportation, persecution, and other inhumane acts. Second, under the *objective territorial principle,* a state may assert jurisdiction over acts committed abroad that are consummated within the territory of the prosecuting state. A variation of this latter principle—applied most often in the antitrust, trafficking, and

[1] Pre-Trial Chamber I, Case No. ICC-RoC46(3)-01/18, Decision on the "Prosecution's Request for a Ruling on Jurisdiction under Article 19(3) of the Statute" (Sept. 6, 2018).

securities law contexts—allows a state to regulate acts that cause effects within the state, even if the criminal act itself is committed outside the state.

The nationality justification for the ICC's assertion of jurisdiction is also well established under international law. There are also two types of nationality jurisdiction. The ICC's nationality jurisdiction derives from the *active nationality principle,* wherein the state of which the alleged perpetrator is a national may assert jurisdiction over that individual's acts wherever they may occur. Under this rationale, a state asserts the right to regulate the activities of its citizens outside of its territory. All the major ICL treaties permit, and in some cases oblige, member states to prosecute nationals who commit international crimes.

The second type of nationality jurisdiction is based on the *passive personality principle* of jurisdiction. This principle allows a state to assert jurisdiction over a crime committed against one of its own nationals. In other words, a state may assert jurisdiction based on the nationality of the victim, regardless of the nationality of the offender or where the offense took place. Whereas active nationality is an uncontroversial basis for the assertion of jurisdiction, passive personality jurisdiction has historically received less support from states. Today, however, passive personality jurisdiction has experienced a revival as states aggressively legislate against acts of terrorism. As a result, many states can prosecute acts of terrorism and other international crimes committed against their own citizens anywhere in the world. Notably, the ICC does not have jurisdiction based on the principle of passive personality; that is to say it does not have jurisdiction over a suspect if the only link to a state party to the Rome Statute is the nationality of the victim.

The Court does not have jurisdiction based on the principle of universal jurisdiction, although many states supported such a basis for ICC jurisdiction during the negotiations at Rome. The principle of universal jurisdiction allows any state to assert jurisdiction over an individual suspected of committing the worst crimes under international law (such as genocide, crimes against humanity, and certain war crimes), even if there is no formal link to the state asserting jurisdiction. (We discuss the principle of universal jurisdiction later in the context of the prosecution of international crimes by national courts). States supporting an ICC with "universal" jurisdiction argued, for example, that the Court should have the power to assert jurisdiction over any individual in the world suspected of committing genocide or any other international crime giving rise to universal jurisdiction before domestic courts.

Other states also argued that the Court should be able to assert jurisdiction over any individual who was in the custody of a state party to the treaty, even if neither the territorial nor nationality state were treaty parties. This would have allowed the Court to proceed whenever the perpetrator was in the custody of a state party, even—potentially—temporarily or forcibly. In addition to expanding the grounds on which the Court could prosecute, custodial jurisdiction would have had the useful side effect of limiting the ability of perpetrators of international crimes who otherwise would not be within the jurisdiction of the Court to travel to the territories of any ICC state party. Drafters of the ICC Statute also rejected this notion of custodial jurisdiction, however.

The final jurisdictional regime governing the ICC—territoriality and active nationality—formed part of a "take it or leave it" proposal advanced toward the waning days of the Rome Conference. As it stands, it is only in cases in which the perpetrator hails from a state party or commits crimes on the territory of a state party that the ICC can go forward absent a Security Council referral. In practice, this often amounts to the same state, which constitutes a significant limitation on the Court's ability to prosecute international crimes committed worldwide. Although the ICC's jurisdiction is relatively limited as compared to the failed proposals for universal and custodial jurisdiction, the United States and other nations continue to raise concern about whether non-party states are adequately protected from politically-motivated prosecutions. The territorial basis of jurisdiction is particularly troubling to a state like the United States with thousands of troops stationed abroad, many in states that are members of the ICC, such as Afghanistan, which is currently a situation under investigation.

One significant exception to these jurisdictional preconditions applies to referrals to the Court initiated by the U.N. Security Council. The Security Council may refer any matter to the Court for investigation, regardless of whether there is a link between the individual or act and a state party. Thus, the Security Council has referred the situations in Darfur (2005) and Libya (2011) to the Court, even though neither the Sudan nor Libya is a party to the Rome Treaty and none of the suspects is a national of a state party. Although states and civil society actors have encouraged the Council to refer other pressing situations to the Court—most notably Syria and North Korea—so far, Russia and China have blocked these efforts. The inclusion of a Chapter VII Security Council referral as a trigger mechanism injects an element of coercion into what is otherwise a highly consensual arrangement. This arrangement also shrouds the Court in geopolitics, since any referral requires the concurrence of nine Council members, including either a yes vote or an abstention by the five permanent members of the Council (China, France, the Russian Federation, the United Kingdom, and the United States)—the so-called P-5.

In addition to Security Council referrals, states themselves may make *ad hoc* referrals to the Court pursuant to Article 12(3) for particular crimes that fall within the Court's subject matter jurisdiction. So far, Côte d'Ivoire, Palestine, and Ukraine have availed themselves of this option. Article 12(3) has the benefit of allowing a state to dip its toes into the ICC's waters without ratifying the treaty and accepting the full reach of the Court's jurisdiction. It also enables states to vest the Court with retroactive jurisdiction as far back as 2002, when the Rome Statute entered into force. While this option may encourage more states to engage with the ICC, it also allows a non-party state to pick and choose when the ICC may have jurisdiction, and thus introduces another element of selective jurisdiction to the ICC regime.

b. Trigger Mechanisms

The Court's jurisdiction may be triggered in one of three ways: (1) by a state party (Article 14); (2) by the Security Council (Article 13(b)); and (3) by the prosecutor acting *propio motu* ("on his or her own motion") (Article 15). Granting the power of referral to a state party was widely accepted. In designing this regime, it was assumed that state parties would refer matters concerning another state party to the Court.[2] In practice so far, Article 14 has been used primarily for "self-referrals"; that is, situations referred to the Court by the impacted state itself. For example, Uganda invoked Article 14 when it self-referred the "situation concerning the Lord's Resistance Army" to the Court in December 2003. Such self-referrals were not contemplated by the drafters of the Statute. As a result, it is unclear to what extent these self-referrals may be revoked by the state in question. Allowing a state to turn the Court's jurisdiction on and off at will in the case of a self-referral could open the Court up to political manipulation by the referring state. Such a mechanism, for example, might permit a state to withdraw its referral if it did not support a particular charge or person being investigated by the Prosecutor. For example, it has been argued that the ICC referral eventually complicated peace negotiations in Uganda. This experience may cause states to rethink the propriety of externalizing justice for international crimes. While states that have self-referred have at

[2] The state referral trigger mechanism was modeled after enforcement regimes contained within the various human rights treaties, which allow state parties to allege that another state party is not upholding its obligations under the treaty. In practice, very few states have ever referred another state to one of these human rights treaty-enforcement bodies. Most matters come before these institutions through individual petitions.

times raised concerns about the ICC, none has attempted to annul its referral to date.

Much more contentious during the negotiations was the role of the Security Council in referring matters to the Court and potentially interfering in ongoing proceedings. The United States and other permanent members of the Security Council argued that no situation should be considered by the Court unless the Security Council affirmatively approved. This would mean that any one of the five permanent members of the Security Council, including the United States, could have blocked any investigation or prosecution from going forward by utilizing its veto power. This attempt to circumvent the state-consent model was rejected in Rome. Instead, the Security Council may use its Chapter VII powers to refer a matter to the Court (Article 13(b)) or to defer any investigation or prosecution for renewable 12-month terms if the work of the Court would interfere with the Council's exercise of its U.N. Charter mandate (Article 16). This means that once the Court is involved in a situation, none of the five permanent members can unilaterally block an investigation or prosecution from going forward. Rather, the P-5 can only block a Council referral to the Court or block an attempt to defer an investigation or prosecution. As noted earlier, there are no jurisdictional preconditions for the Court to investigate or prosecute a case referred by the Security Council except with respect to the Court's temporal jurisdiction. It is thus unlikely that the Security Council could refer a matter to the Court involving crimes committed prior to July 1, 2002 (although even this is not entirely clear from the statute itself).

The power of the prosecutor to initiate an investigation or prosecution *proprio motu* was also a source of acute disagreement during the negotiations in Rome. As the treaty stands, the prosecutor may initiate an investigation into crimes committed on the territory, or by the nationals, of ICC state parties subject to certain procedural safeguards. The prosecutor may initiate an investigation only if she can convince a three-judge panel that "there is a reasonable basis to proceed with an investigation, and . . . the case appears to fall within the jurisdiction of the Court" (Article 15(4)). In addition, under the Court's admissibility provisions, the prosecutor must defer to an investigation or prosecution by a national authority unless a three-judge panel concludes that such national authorities are unwilling or unable to genuinely investigate the alleged criminal conduct (Article 18). These safeguards were introduced at the behest of a number of states, including the United States, that were uncomfortable with vesting unrestricted power to initiate an investigation with the prosecutor.

c. *Admissibility*

In addition to requirements of jurisdiction, the ICC is also limited by requirements of admissibility, most clearly set forth in Article 17 of the Rome Treaty. Although the *ad hoc* tribunals for the former Yugoslavia and Rwanda exercised primacy over national courts—i.e., their assertions of jurisdiction took precedence over any attempt by a national court to prosecute a particular individual—the ICC is subject to the reverse regime of complementarity, which gives initial primacy to proceedings before domestic courts. According to this principle of complementarity, a cornerstone of the ICC, the Court should not assert jurisdiction over a situation if:

> (a) The case is being investigated or prosecuted by a State that has jurisdiction over it, unless the State is unwilling or unable genuinely to carry out the investigation or prosecution;
>
> (b) The case has been investigated by a State that has jurisdiction over it and the State has decided not to prosecute the person concerned, unless the decision resulted from the unwillingness or inability of the State genuinely to prosecute;
>
> (c) The person concerned has already been tried for conduct that is the subject of the complaint, and a trial by the Court is not permitted under article 20, paragraph 3 [referring to the prohibition against being tried for the same offense twice, also known as double jeopardy or *ne bis in idem*];
>
> (d) The case is not of sufficient gravity to justify further action by the Court (Article 17).

Essentially, the ICC may only proceed if there is no national court that has initiated a good-faith effort to investigate or prosecute the case.

The Court has adopted a two-prong test concerning admissibility. The first prong looks at whether the domestic investigation or prosecution is directed against the same person for substantially the same conduct as the challenged prosecution before the ICC. If the domestic prosecution does not meet this test, then the ICC prosecution is admissible, and the inquiry ends. If there is an investigation or prosecution concerning the same individual for substantially the same conduct, then the second prong of the inquiry is triggered, *viz.* is the state *unwilling* or *unable* to conduct a genuine investigation or prosecution. This same person-same conduct test is not without its detractors because it appears to set quite a high bar for the state to meet to divest the Court of jurisdiction. Furthermore, it risks duplicative proceedings where a particular perpetrator has been the subject of prosecution for a different set of crimes in the domestic courts than those within the ICC Prosecutor's sights.

The Court has provided little guidance on how to interpret *unwilling* and *unable* in the context of an admissibility determination. In the Libya matters, the Court reached divergent conclusions with respect to two defendants—Saif Gaddafi and Abdullah Al Senussi—both indicted by the Prosecutor but also subject to prosecution in Libyan courts as part of a mega-trial of top figures of the *ancien régime*. Pre-Trial Chamber I dismissed the complementarity challenge concerning Gaddafi *fils*—on the grounds that he was in the custody of the renegade Zintan militia at the time of the Libyan proceedings and was being prosecuted *in absentia* in Tripoli without access to counsel—but held the case against Al Senussi inadmissible before the Court, even though he did not have individual representation either. The complementarity principle assumes that domestic courts may be used to shield a powerful defendant from prosecution; the formulation of the principle in the Rome Statute does not account for an over-zealous domestic prosecution that might result in deficits in due process.

The Libya admissibility decisions arose out of a procedural posture that was not anticipated by those who negotiated these treaty provisions in Rome. It was generally assumed that the issue of admissibility would arise in circumstances in which the state was aligned with an ICC suspect and thus trying to protect them from accountability. Yet in the Libya cases, the suspects and the state were on opposite sides of the admissibility argument. For due process and fairness reasons, both Gaddafi and Al Senussi wanted their cases to be transferred to the ICC, while the state of Libya wanted the cases to remain in domestic courts. The admissibility challenge in the case against Jean-Pierre Bemba presents another variation of a conflict between the suspect and the state. Bemba challenged the admissibility of his prosecution before the Court, arguing that he had already been investigated by the Central African Republic's prosecutorial authorities and they had decided not to prosecute him. While a state's decision not to prosecute could be made to protect a suspect like Bemba from accountability, the CAR authorities decided not to prosecute because they wanted the ICC to take up the prosecution. The Court concluded that the case was admissible. While it appears that in this case the domestic courts were "unwilling" to prosecute Mr. Bemba, the Court confined its decision to the first prong of the admissibility test, finding that there was no ongoing investigation or prosecution and, contrary to Bemba's argument, that there had been not been a decision not to prosecute.

How the Court will develop its jurisprudence on admissibility is at the core of the relationship between the ICC and state parties. On the one hand, a restrictive interpretation of admissibility may narrow the reach of the Court, undercutting one of the fundamental purposes to ensure accountability for the worst international crimes. On the other hand, a liberal interpretation of admissibility might overburden the Prosecutor and the Court, risks provoking claims of overreach by states, and may discourage the development of domestic mechanisms to address atrocity crimes. As the few cases that have addressed admissibility demonstrate, we are still at an early stage of the development of this jurisprudence.

2. Consensual Hybrid Tribunals

Following the Security Council's establishment of the International Criminal Tribunal for Yugoslavia (ICTY) and International Criminal Tribunal for Rwanda (ICTR), other elements within the United Nations subsequently created a number of additional tribunals. These newer *ad hoc* tribunals have been called *hybrid* or *mixed tribunals,* because they are situated within the host state as opposed to being established abroad; are staffed by international and domestic personnel (judges, prosecutors, investigators, defense counsel, and support staff) working in tandem; and apply a mixture of international and domestic law, including local criminal law and procedure.

Hybrid tribunals have a number of advantages over purely international and national courts. First, the mix of national and international attributes makes it more likely that the tribunal will be perceived as legitimate by both the domestic and international communities. Second, because they take advantage of a functioning domestic legal system, hybrid tribunals are less likely to have the same startup costs as a fully international tribunal. Third, the use of international law within the domestic legal system may increase the acceptance of international penal law standards. This can lead to the incorporation of ICL and fair trial rights within national law, further strengthening the effectiveness of these prohibitions and, derivatively, the domestic rule of law. Fourth, because they are generally located within the host country, hybrid institutions are closer to evidence and witnesses, and are more accessible to survivors and the population at large. Fifth, hybrid tribunals may enable the transfer of legal skills and experience, as local professionals work alongside their international counterparts. These advantages are dependent on the strength and resources of the relevant domestic legal system, of course, and thus may not be borne out in all cases.

Hybrid tribunals also manifest unique challenges when compared with national or international tribunals. As hybrid institutions are being established, the host government may exact key compromises that weaken the institution. Tensions may arise between staff members from the host country and members of the international staff. Both such contingencies occurred with respect to the Extraordinary Chambers in the Courts of Cambodia (ECCC), convened to prosecute surviving members of the Khmer Rouge, who terrorized Cambodia from 1975–1979. At the insistence of the Cambodian government, the ECCC are characterized by a dual staffing model: each key position is occupied by a Cambodian and an international professional, who have often disagreed on whether indictments or convictions should be issued. The government of the host country may also attempt to use its influence over the tribunal to affect who is investigated or prosecuted, and may withhold financial and other support for domestic political reasons. Lacking the authority of a Chapter VII Security Council resolution (which can bind all U.N. member states), these tribunals may have difficulty gaining the cooperation of third-party states that may have custody of defendants or access to important evidence. These problems have led many human rights organizations to argue against the continued use of hybrid tribunals, and to instead advocate for the return to purely international tribunals that are free from domestic political pressure and are more likely to apply a consistent interpretation of applicable law to similar conduct.

In addition, hybrid tribunals that incorporate elements of a civil law system may face additional challenges in furthering some of the goals of international justice. For example, mass atrocity crimes often involve an enormous amount of evidence arising out of an often complex political and military environment. The quantity and complexity of evidence places an enormous burden on civil law judges as they are the primary investigators and fact finders. This produced institutional challenges at the ECCC, for example, where the sheer magnitude of the task facing the investigating judges led to delays and inefficiencies. In addition, civil law proceedings tend to be less public (as evidence is collected by the judge rather than presented in an open courtroom), and often less dramatic, presenting challenges for engaging and educating the public about the atrocities.

It was thought that the creation of the ICC would preclude the establishment of additional *ad hoc* international or hybrid tribunals. Four situations remain, however, in which such tribunals may be necessary and appropriate. First, a hybrid or international tribunal is necessary to prosecute crimes committed prior to the coming into force of the Rome Treaty, as the ICC only has jurisdiction over crimes committed after July 1, 2002—an issue that becomes less important with the passing of time. The hybrid tribunal created in Cambodia (the ECCC) to prosecute crimes that occurred in the late 1970s is an example of a hybrid institution engaged in historical justice. Second, an *ad hoc* tribunal may still be necessary to prosecute crimes committed within the territory of, and by nationals of, states that are not parties to the ICC (unless the U.N. Security Council refers the matter to the Court). There have been a number of hybrid tribunals established with the consent of the territorial state without the involvement of the Council. In addition, there have been proposals for *ad hoc* courts without the consent of the territorial state, but these have yet to come to fruition.

Third, *ad hoc* tribunals can be empowered to prosecute criminal acts that are not included within the subject matter jurisdiction of the ICC, such as terrorism. The assassination of the former prime minister of Lebanon, Rafik Hariri, does not clearly fit within the subject matter jurisdiction of the ICC. The Security Council thus passed a resolution in 2007 leading to the creation of the Special Tribunal for Lebanon to investigate and prosecute those responsible for the Hariri assassination and related acts of terrorism. Fourth, and finally, an *ad hoc* tribunal may be paramount where there has been systemic criminality that would overwhelm the ICC and there is no domestic system available to work in tandem with the Court. Syria offers a prime example of this situation, although with Russia protecting the regime of Bashar Al Assad, there is no easy route to the creation of a dedicated international or hybrid tribunal for this tragic situation.

The first hybrid tribunals were established for Sierra Leone and Cambodia by virtue of an agreement between the U.N. General Assembly and the country itself. Hybrid tribunals created by this consensual model can be either embedded within (Cambodia) or independent from (Sierra Leone) the domestic court system. The ECCC was the product of over a decade of negotiations between the United Nations and the Cambodian government. Throughout these negotiations, the Cambodian government pushed for a tribunal controlled by Cambodians. The United Nations, along with most of the international human rights community, pushed for a tribunal controlled by "internationals"—that is, individuals appointed by the United Nations. The result is a body with a complex dual structure that embodies and, some might argue, exacerbates the tensions between the two sets of personnel. The majority of the judges are appointed by the Cambodian government, but decisions of the Court require a supermajority, effectively requiring the vote of at least one "international" judge for the will of the majority of Cambodian judges to become a decision of the court. In addition, the Office of the Prosecutor is a dual one; there are two co-prosecutors, one appointed by the United Nations and the other by the Cambodian government. Disagreements between the co-prosecutors are resolved by a panel of

ECCC judges. These divisions between U.N. and Cambodian government personnel exist throughout the structure of the ECCC, including among the defense counsel, who appear to have collectively adopted the one "international" and one "national" counsel model even though this is not required by the agreement establishing the ECCC. This awkward and unwieldy structure has resulted in gridlock, as questions have arisen as to how many defendants the ECCC will ultimately prosecute, with the international co-investigating judges and co-prosecutors pushing for new indictments against the wishes of their Cambodian counterparts. Attitudes among Cambodian political elites toward the ECCC ranged from outright hostility (with the ECCC seen as a threat to their domestic political power) to greedy support (with the ECCC seen as a source of badly needed hard currency in the form of ex-patriot investments and staff salaries).

Although also created by an agreement between the United Nations and the country at issue, the Special Court for Sierra Leone was markedly different in its structure. Unlike the ECCC, the SCSL was not a part of the domestic court system. Rather, the SCSL operated wholly separate from the Sierra Leonean legal framework. The majority of the judges were "internationals," and the government of Sierra Leone used some of its appointments to select non-Sierra Leoneans for key posts. Having just emerged from a brutal civil war, the Sierra Leoneans were more willing negotiating partners than their Cambodian counterparts, whose views about the ECCC vacillated over time. This resulted in better cooperation and fewer allegations of political interference.

A new regional model of hybridity was born in the Extraordinary African Chambers (EAC) established by the African Union and Senegal to prosecute former Chadian President Hissène Habré. The EAC marked the culmination of years of advocacy and litigation following determinations that Senegal (where Habré had sought refuge) lacked the domestic ability to prosecute him. At one point, Belgium opened proceedings against Senegal before the International Court of Justice, arguing that Senegal must either prosecute Habré itself or extradite him to Belgium in keeping with obligations under the Torture Convention. Even the Community Court of Justice of the Economic Community of West African States (ECOWAS) weighed in, reasoning that Senegal could not amend its domestic penal code to enable Habré's prosecution without running afoul of the principle of legality and the prohibition against *ex post facto* legislation.

The African Union and Senegal ultimately entered into an agreement to create an *ad hoc* chamber within the Senegalese court structure applying Senegalese criminal procedure and substantive international criminal law, and staffed by judges from Senegal and elsewhere on the continent exercising what amounts to a form of internationalized universal jurisdiction. Habré was convicted of crimes against humanity and war crimes in 2016 and is serving a life sentence, marking the first time an African head of state faced justice in the courts of another African state. The trial represented a form of "victims' justice;" for decades, victims' groups had pushed for Habré's prosecution and over 4,000 victims registered as civil parties. Efforts to convince the League of Arab States to follow suit with respect to Syria have not borne fruit.

One of the newest hybrid tribunals is the Special Criminal Court (SCC) in the Central African Republic. This marked one of the few times that a sovereign government created through national law a temporary hybrid court where national and international judges and prosecutors are working to adjudicate international crimes committed during serial armed conflicts involving government forces and a range of armed groups. The creation of the SCC reflects the recognition that the local courts were too weak and ravaged by war to administer justice effectively. Interestingly, the CAR also twice referred itself to the ICC. As such, the situation presents the opportunity for the ICC to work together with a hybrid institution rather than the ordinary criminal courts. The U.N. peacekeeping mission is tasked with supporting these judicial efforts.

The emergence of these hybrid tribunals has given rise to the question of under what circumstances should a hybrid tribunal be viewed as national or international tribunal. The determination of whether a judicial body is a domestic or an international court has some practical ramifications with respect to a number of legal doctrines. For example, a domestic court may be bound by a statute of limitation or an amnesty law enacted by the local legislature whereas an international court would not be.[3] In addition, it may be expected that domestic courts respect certain immunity doctrines—such as sovereign immunity or head of state immunity—that reflect the sovereign equality of states and the imperatives of international comity; such immunities do not apply before international courts.[4]

In two key decisions emerging from the SCSL, one concerning the constitutionality of the Court[5] and the other addressing the argument that former Liberian President Charles Taylor should

---

[3] *Prosecutor v. Kallon*, Case No. SCSL-2004-15-AR72(E), Decision on Challenge to Jurisdiction: Lomé Accord Amnesty (Mar. 13, 2004).

[4] *Prosecutor v. Omar Hassan Ahmad Al Bashir*, Case No. ICC-02/05-01/09 OA2, Judgment in the Jordan Referral re: Al Bashir Appeal (May 6, 2019).

[5] *Prosecutor v. Kallon*, Case No. SCSL-2004-15-AR72(E), Decision on Constitutionality and Lack of Jurisdiction (Mar. 13, 2004).

enjoy head of state immunity,[6] the Special Court embraced its international identity. It based its ruling on the following factors: (1) its provenance (a treaty negotiated by the U.N. Secretary-General between Sierra Leone and the U.N. General Assembly prompted and approved by the U.N. Security Council), (2) domestic ratification legislation asserting that the Court is not part of the Sierra Leonean judiciary, (3) its independent legal personality and ability to enter into agreements with sovereign states, (4) its enjoyment of the privileges and immunities of an international institution, and (5) its subject matter jurisdiction (mostly, although not exclusively, international crimes). Although the ECCC are more firmly embedded in the domestic judicial system and, as noted earlier, are governed by a supermajority of Cambodian jurists (who need the vote of an international judge to prevail), the Chambers reached similar conclusions when defendants being prosecuted for crimes committed during the Khmer Rouge era attempted to assert domestic amnesties and pardons as bars to prosecution.[7]

It remains to be seen to what extent the international community is willing to add further hybrid institutions to the modern pantheon. On the horizon is a hybrid tribunal for South Sudan, which has its roots in the Agreement for the Resolution of the Conflict in South Sudan (ARCSS). Chapter V of the Agreement is devoted to transitional justice and envisions the creation of the Hybrid Court for South Sudan (HCSS) by the African Union Commission (with other transitional justice mechanisms to be established by the government). The judges are to be prominent African principals, from outside of South Sudan, lending a regional flavor to the Court and minimizing perceptions that the hybrid court is an imperialist enterprise. Indeed, the African Union Executive Council described the HCSS as an "African-led and African-owned legal mechanism."[8] Per the terms of the agreement, the African Union could theoretically create the proposed tribunal without the involvement or support of the current government of South Sudan, although it would be difficult for the HCSS to operate without some cooperation from the government. So far, however, the Union has refrained from doing so, and the HCSS exists only on paper, although memoranda of understanding have been exchanged with the government in 2017.

Also under consideration on the African continent is the first regional criminal court. The African Union has adopted a protocol to

---

6 *Prosecutor v. Taylor*, Case No. SCSL-2003-1-I, Decision on Immunity from Jurisdiction (May 31, 2004).

7 Decision on Ieng Sary's Rule 89 Preliminary Objections (*Ne Bis In Idem* and Amnesty and Pardon), Case File 002/19-09-2007/ECCC/TC (Nov. 3, 2011).

8 AU Executive Council, Decision on the Supplementary Budget for the 2017 Financial Year, AU Doc. EX.CL/Dec.940 (XXX), at 1 (Jan. 27, 2017).

the instrument establishing the main regional human rights body, the African Court of Human & People's Rights (ACHPR). The so-called Malabo Protocol would create a criminal chamber within the ACHPR with jurisdiction over the four ICC crimes as well as a long list of other international crimes with particular resonance on the continent: the crime of unconstitutional change of government, piracy, terrorism, mercenarism, corruption, money laundering, trafficking in persons, trafficking in drugs, trafficking in hazardous wastes, and illicit exploitation of natural resources. It envisions jurisdiction over natural and legal persons.[9]

This initiative reflects, in part, a laudable effort to devise African solutions to African problems; at the same time, some African leaders were responding to universal jurisdiction cases in Europe involving African defendants and the ICC charges brought against Sudanese President Omar Al Bashir and President Uhuru Kenyatta and Deputy President William Ruto of Kenya. Controversially, Article 46A*bis* of the Protocol reads:

> No charges shall be commenced or continued before the Court against any serving African Union Head of State or Government, or anybody acting or entitled to act in such capacity, or other senior state officials based on their functions, during their tenure of office.

There are concerns that this provision would effectively immunize government actors from jurisdiction, leaving the new chamber to prosecute non-state actors only. Once created, the chamber would be the first regional criminal court and, given the above amendment, would be the first international criminal tribunal to expressly provide immunity to senior government officials. Every other international criminal tribunal to date has been governed by express language making clear that the official status of an accused, including that of Head of State or Head of Government, does not affect the criminal responsibility of any individual. Though it was finalized in 2014, the Malabo Protocol has yet to garner the necessary signatures to enter into force.

B. Creatures of Coercion

This brings us to the second way in which international or hybrid tribunals are created: through the exercise of a sovereign power—either international (usually the U.N. Security Council) or domestic (the nation-state itself). The latter is not controversial, as it is consistent with the idea that states retain the power to determine

---

[9] *See* Protocol on Amendments to the Protocol on the Statute of the African Court of Justice & Human Rights, Assembly/AU/Dec.529(XXIII) (2014) (the "Malabo Protocol").

how, if at all, to engage with international law. The former is more controversial, as it involves the use of coercive power that may result in institutions that do not reflect the priorities or preferences of interested and implicated states.

1. Nuremberg and Tokyo

The first international criminal tribunals ever formed—the Nuremberg and Tokyo Tribunals—were created by the exercise of collective sovereign power. The four victorious powers—France, the then-Soviet Union, the United Kingdom, and the United States—established the Nuremberg Tribunal pursuant to the London Agreement of August 8, 1945. By contrast, the United States established the Tokyo Tribunal through a special proclamation issued by the Supreme Allied Commander of the Far East, U.S. General Douglas MacArthur, with the acquiescence of the other Allied states. Thus, although the Nuremberg Tribunal was created by a treaty, the four states involved in its creation essentially dictated the terms of the new institution and imposed them on Germany and the rest of the international community. In addition to being established by a small number of states, these two tribunals are unique among their peers in being created by victorious powers after a military defeat.

2. The *Ad Hoc* International Tribunals

Almost 50 years would pass before the appearance of another set of international criminal tribunals—the ICTY and ICTR. These *ad hoc* tribunals were also created by a different global collective: the Security Council under the authority of the U.N. Charter. Unlike their predecessors, however, they were not created following a military victory. The Security Council created the ICTY—its official name is the International Tribunal for the Prosecution of Persons Responsible for Serious Violations of International Humanitarian Law Committed in the Territory of the Former Yugoslavia Since 1991—in response to the violent breakup of Yugoslavia while the war was ongoing. Between the end of World War II and 1991, the Republic of Yugoslavia was a federation of six republics (Slovenia, Croatia, Bosnia-Herzegovina, Serbia, Montenegro, and Macedonia) and two autonomous units (Vojvodina and Kosovo). The federation broke apart in 1991 and 1992 when Slovenia, Croatia, Macedonia, and then Bosnia-Herzegovina declared their independence, resulting in a brutal conflict that generated images evocative of the Nazi concentration camps, horrific accounts of mass rape, and the newly coined concept of "ethnic cleansing," which many equated with genocide.

The Security Council created the ICTY under the authority vested in it by Chapter VII of the U.N. Charter, which empowers the Council to pass resolutions that are binding on all states in response to breaches of the peace, threats to the peace, or acts of aggression. Why would the Security Council create the tribunal using its Chapter VII powers rather than initiating a treaty-based consensual method of formation? At least three explanations suggest themselves. First, it was clear at the time that the Federal Republic of Yugoslavia and its break-away republics would not agree to subject their citizens to the jurisdiction of an international criminal tribunal. Thus, one of the advantages of Security Council action under Chapter VII is that it can trump the unwillingness of the affected state(s) to hold individuals accountable for crimes committed within their territories or jurisdictions, including by their nationals.

The second reason the ICTY was created by the Security Council and not by treaty is time. Drafting, negotiating, and convincing states to ratify a treaty takes far more time than Security Council action. The Rome Treaty took a number of years to negotiate, and four years passed between the conclusion of the drafting of that treaty and the ratification by enough states (60) to bring it into force. Because the ICTY was created to address an ongoing conflict in the hope of exerting a deterrent effect, any significant delay in its creation would have undermined one of its central purposes. Third, there was a need on the part of the members of the Security Council, particularly the major powers, to appear to be doing *something* in the face of the first mass atrocities in Europe since the Nazi Holocaust. However, the United States and Europe were unwilling to commit significant troops to end the ethnic cleansing and other international crimes underway. Creating the ICTY gave the Security Council and its members a concrete response to these atrocities. This third explanation raises the question of whether the creation of the ICTY was sufficient. In other words, should the United Nations, Security Council, or regional states acting through the North Atlantic Treaty Organization (NATO) have done more at the time to address the atrocities in the former Yugoslavia?

As the first such tribunal to be established since the post-World War II tribunals, the ICTY was faced with a number of unprecedented legal questions. The first defendant prosecuted before the Tribunal, Duško Tadić, challenged the legality of the Security Council's creation of the Tribunal. The Trial Chamber dismissed this challenge, reasoning that it did not have the power to ascertain its own legitimacy. The Appeals Chamber also dismissed Tadić's appeal but held that it did have the power to evaluate its own legitimacy pursuant to the doctrine of *compétence de la compétence*. In this, its inaugural decision, the Appeals Chamber held that the Security

Council had the authority to create an international criminal tribunal under its Chapter VII powers even though the U.N. Charter does not list judicial institutions as among the available Chapter VII responses.[10]

The ICTY had subject matter jurisdiction over the following crimes: war crimes (in both international and non-international conflicts), crimes against humanity, and genocide. The temporal jurisdiction began on January 1, 1991 and was open-ended. Thus, NATO forces became subject to the jurisdiction of the ICTY when they intervened militarily in 1999 to repel the Yugoslav onslaught against the Kosovar minority population. In response to requests that she investigate allegations of violations committed by the NATO forces, the ICTY Prosecutor established a committee to advise her on whether there was enough evidence to initiate such an investigation. The committee looked at a number of specific incidents and concluded that the applicable law was under-developed and that there was insufficient evidence of wrongdoing to warrant a more formal investigation. Needless to say, this conclusion generated significant criticism.

The U.N. Security Council created a second tribunal under its Chapter VII powers in response to the 1994 genocide in Rwanda, formally known by the rambling and inconsistently capitalized moniker of "the International Criminal Tribunal for the Prosecution of Persons Responsible for Genocide and Other Serious Violations of International Humanitarian Law Committed in the Territory of Rwanda and Rwandan citizens responsible for genocide and other such violations committed in the territory of neighbouring States, between 1 January 1994 and 31 December 1994."[11] The ICTR differs from the ICTY in that the former was created in response to an internal conflict and genocide that was largely over at the time the Tribunal was established. Although questions were raised by some commentators about the use of the Security Council's Chapter VII powers to address what was mostly an internal conflict, such a challenge was not brought before the Tribunal itself. The ICTR had jurisdiction over the same crimes as the ICTY (war crimes, crimes against humanity, and genocide), although the definitions and scope of some of these crimes differed between the two resolutions. Unlike the ICTY, the ICTR's temporal jurisdiction was not open-ended, but instead only covered acts committed during the calendar year of 1994.

---

10 *Prosecutor v. Tadić*, Case No. IT-94-1-A, Judgment (July 15, 1999).

11 Note that the inconsistent capitalization is from the Security Council Resolution creating the Tribunal. S.C. Res. 955 (1994), U.N. Doc. S/RES/955 (Nov. 8, 1994).

Both the ICTY and ICTR were *ad hoc* tribunals, limited to a specific country, a specific set of crimes, and a specific time period. Both were subsidiary organs of the United Nations that benefited from funding from U.N. assessed contributions (at one point, consuming 10% of the United Nations' budget). Because they were intended to be temporary, both eventually wound down their affairs pursuant to a "completion strategy" announced in Security Council Resolution 1503.[12] To facilitate their closing, the tribunals were each directed to transfer some of their cases to appropriate and competent national jurisdictions for prosecution. Both tribunals transferred a number of mid- to low-level defendants to national courts, although the ICTR delayed sending defendants to Rwanda given concerns about judicial capacity and the availability of the death penalty. These two impediments were eventually removed (with Rwanda suspending the death penalty), so a number of cases were transferred.

The ICTR formally closed its doors on December 31, 2015, and the ICTY on December 31, 2017. While most of the cases pending before both tribunals had been completed by the time of their respective closure, each still had a number of outstanding appeals and, in the case of the ICTR, a number of accused are still at large. The U.N. Security Council created the International Residual Mechanism for Criminal Tribunals (IRMCT) to hear any appeals or new trials, including those of the ICTR fugitives and trials for contempt or false testimony; it is also supervising the enforcement of sentences handed down by the ICTY and ICTR, assisting national jurisdictions in prosecuting cases related to both conflicts, ensuring protection for victims and witnesses, and preserving and maintaining the archives of both *ad hoc* tribunals. In 2020, one of the ICTR fugitives was finally brought into custody—Félicien Kabuga who stands accused of bank-rolling the genocide in Rwanda, among other allegations against him. It is anticipated that he will be tried by the IRMCT.

3. Imposed Hybrid Tribunals

As noted earlier, hybrid tribunals have been created by both methods we highlight here: through an exercise of consent and by the imposition of sovereign power. As compared with the ECCC and the SCSL, which were created by treaty, the hybrid judicial systems established in Kosovo and East Timor were created by U.N. transitional authorities essentially holding these territories' sovereignty in trust in an immediate post-conflict situation. In both cases, there was concern that the domestic court system was either unable or unwilling to adequately and impartially address the

---

[12] S.C. Res. 1503, U.N. Doc. S/RES/1503 (Aug. 28, 2003).

violations of criminal law (both domestic and international) committed in their respective territories. In Kosovo, the U.N. Mission in Kosovo (UNMIK) appointed (without consultation with the local authorities) international judges and prosecutors to work with their local counterparts within the Kosovo judicial system. This move was in reaction to complaints that the domestic legal system was not impartial. Initially, international judges did not constitute a majority of the judges hearing a particular case, but UNMIK eventually established special tribunals consisting of three judges, the majority of whom were international. Cases could be referred to these special tribunals by the United Nations, the prosecutor, the accused, or the defense counsel. This was considered insufficient to address security concerns and the risk of political interference. As a result, in 2015 a Specialist Chamber and prosecutor's office were established in the Hague with the agreement of the government of Kosovo.[13] While staffed with international judges and prosecutors, the Kosovo Specialist Chamber is not an international tribunal, but part of the Kosovo judiciary. In June 2020, the first name was made public, that of Kosovo President Hashim Thaçi, a former guerilla fighter who is being charged with crimes against humanity and war crimes during the Kosovo war between 1998 and 2000.

In Timor-Leste, the Security Council created the United Nations Transitional Administration in East Timor (UNTAET) to administer the executive, legislative, and judicial functions of the country and bring to justice those responsible for international human rights violations committed during that country's independence referendum. Pursuant to this mandate, UNTAET created "Special Panels with Exclusive Jurisdiction over Serious Criminal Offenses" within the district courts and courts of appeals in the capital of Dili. Prosecutions were conducted by a Serious Crimes Unit (SCU), composed almost entirely of international staff. The existing court management serviced the Special Panels, presided over by a majority of international judges. The Special Panels had jurisdiction over crimes—including war crimes, crimes against humanity, and genocide—committed in East Timor since 1975. They were to operate until May 2005, but the Security Council, by Resolution 1543, extended their operation for a year to organize evidence for continued East Timorese prosecutions, if pursued. As with Kosovo, the United Nations created these panels unilaterally without significant negotiations with the local government.

As it turned out, the vast majority of perpetrators resided in Indonesia and were thus effectively out of reach of the Special Panels. Although technically outside the Special Court's mandate, the

---

[13] More information about the Specialist Chambers and the Specialist Prosecutor's Office can be found here: https://www.scp-ks.org/en.

Special Panels nonetheless issued indictments for individuals abroad, including General Wiranto, who once headed the Indonesian armed forces. After 55 trials, 84 defendants were convicted and four were acquitted. Few of these defendants can be described as leaders or individuals with significant command authority. All told, the Special Panels system is widely considered a failure of international justice. Besides the crippling inability to assert jurisdiction over the key architects of the violence, the Timorese legal system lacked indigenous capacity and could not hold up its side of the hybridity equation. The difficulty in recruiting for both the international and domestic sides led to delays, inefficiencies, and inconsistent jurisprudence. The proceedings also suffered from political interference on the part of a local government eager to improve relations with Indonesia and from a lack of dedicated resources from the international community.

C. Domestic Legal Systems

Historically domestic courts (both civilian and military) have been the venue where most international crimes have been prosecuted—if they have been prosecuted at all. Indeed, most ICL treaties assumed this indirect enforcement by signatories' domestic authorities under their ordinary procedural codes. Even with the proliferation of international and hybrid tribunals, and particularly with the creation of the ICC, domestic courts will continue to develop, and implement, ICL. In fact, the ICC's complementarity principle envisions a central role for domestic courts in the enforcement of ICL. In the process of ratifying the ICC Statute, states have codified ICL to harmonize their domestic penal codes with the Rome Statute and, presumably, to enable them to preempt any assertion of jurisdiction by the ICC. Thus, many states have passed legislation that for the first time criminalizes the major international crimes within their jurisdiction; states that already had such statutes (often dating from the World War II period) have modernized their codes to reflect the current state of the law. In many situations, these statutes allow for the assertion of extraterritorial criminal jurisdiction. Some academics and human rights advocates have argued that there is a "duty to prosecute" grave international crimes, citing a growing jurisprudence of the world's human rights courts which have articulated a right to truth, to a remedy, and to judicial protection.[14]

1. Civilian Courts

As discussed previously, international law recognizes four overarching bases by which a state may assert jurisdiction:

---

[14] *See* Alexandra Huneeus, *International Criminal Law by Other Means: The Quasi-Criminal Jurisdiction of the Human Rights Courts*, 107 AM. J. INT'L L. 1 (2013).

territoriality, nationality, protectivity, and universality. Domestic prosecutions for international crimes have often proceeded on the basis of territoriality and nationality jurisdiction—classical bases of jurisdiction discussed earlier in connection with the ICC's jurisdictional preconditions. The protective principle of jurisdiction permits a state to assert jurisdiction over acts that threaten the integrity and interests of the state. Although the protective principle could be interpreted quite broadly to encompass anything that a state deems in its vital interest, it has traditionally been limited to a narrow range of activities such as counterfeiting, espionage, falsification of government documents, perjury before a consular official, or violations of immigration or customs laws. The protective principle thus justifies the criminalization of activities that violate the integrity of core governmental functions. All of these bases of jurisdiction allow for the prosecution of crimes that have a clear nexus to the forum state.

The last basis of jurisdiction, universality, is the one most relevant to ICL, and thus one to which we devote a bit more discussion. Under the universality principle, a state may assert jurisdiction over an offender regardless of the nationality of the offender or victim, the place of commission of the wrongful act, or any other link to the state asserting jurisdiction.[15] The universality principle, often referred to as universal jurisdiction, asserts that certain acts are so heinous—and so violate the integrity, and so undermine the interests, of the international community—that any state may prosecute or otherwise assert jurisdiction over an individual suspected of committing them. The principle has been justified on grounds of the "exceptional moral gravity" of the offenses subject to it—a descriptor that fits most modern universal jurisdiction crimes but not necessarily robbery-at-sea, the original universal jurisdiction crime—but also as a tool to fill systemic enforcement gaps when it comes to these crimes.[16]

Universal jurisdiction arose in connection with efforts to repress the crime of piracy in eighteenth- and nineteenth-century Europe and North America. Pirates—deemed *hostis humani generis* ("enemies of all humankind")—were often effectively stateless and committed their crimes on the high seas (although attacks on flagships often triggered territorial jurisdiction since such vessels were considered an extension of their state of registration). Consequently, it was at times difficult for states to assert jurisdiction over pirates under any of the traditional principles of jurisdiction.

---

15 *See* Princeton Principles on Universal Jurisdiction, Princeton Project on Universal Jurisdiction (Princeton University Press, 2001).

16 Jiewuh Song, *Pirates and Torturers: Universal Jurisdiction as Enforcement Gap-Filling*, 23(4) J. POL. PHIL. 471 (2015).

Under the then-novel theory of universal jurisdiction, any state could prosecute a pirate even if that state or its citizens had not been directly harmed. The crime of piracy became universalized precisely at a time when the international community was consolidating sovereign authority into territorially-bound states as first envisioned by the Treaty of Westphalia that ended the Thirty Years' War in 1648.

Today, those responsible for violations of the most serious prohibitions of ICL join pirates as "enemies of all humankind." Although there is some debate about which specific violations trigger universal jurisdiction, it is generally accepted that the following offenses do: slavery, genocide, war crimes, crimes against humanity, human trafficking, transnational terrorism, and torture. Universal jurisdiction over these offenses exists as a function of treaty or customary international law. Treaty obligations may render the exercise of universal jurisdiction mandatory, at least where an offender is found on national territory and is not extradited. Under these circumstances, the nexus states have essentially waived any jurisdictional defenses that might be lodged in the forum state. Absent a treaty obligation, universal jurisdiction is generally considered permissive (rather than mandatory) under customary international law.

There is general agreement that a state may invoke the universality principle to prosecute or otherwise hold accountable an individual accused when the suspect is found on the prosecuting state's territory (in effect, a form of custodial jurisdiction). Treaties that embody the *aut dedere aut judicare* principle (extradite or prosecute) presume that the forum state has custody of the accused and accordingly mandate the exercise of universal jurisdiction only where that condition precedent is satisfied. In addition, several states have presumed that the universality principle allows a state to apprehend or otherwise seek the extradition of a suspect who is physically present outside of its own territory (a concept called "pure" universal jurisdiction by some in contrast to jurisdiction conditional on the presence of the accused). Many states, particularly from the civil law legal tradition, allow the criminal prosecution of individuals *in absentia*, which has enabled cases to proceed under universal jurisdiction even in the absence of the accused. States that disallow *in absentia* prosecutions generally discontinue the criminal proceedings at a certain point, as directed by the relevant domestic rules, in the event they are not able to obtain the custody of the accused through extradition, negotiation, abduction, or other means. Depending on when this point is reached, however, significant progress may be made toward investigating and publicizing the commission of international crimes.

The distinction between pure and conditional universal jurisdiction was raised when Belgium issued an arrest warrant in 2000 against Abdulaye Yerodia Ndombasi, the Minister of Foreign Affairs of the Democratic Republic of the Congo (DRC), pursuant to an indictment alleging serious violations of international humanitarian law committed against the Tutsi population prior to his becoming Foreign Minister. The DRC brought suit against Belgium before the ICJ claiming that the issuance of the arrest warrant against an incumbent foreign minister was unlawful under international law. As the pleadings evolved, the case eventually centered on the question of immunity, with the majority of the ICJ finding that incumbent foreign ministers were immune from the criminal jurisdiction of other states (but not from the jurisdiction of an international criminal tribunal). The majority limited its analysis to the question of immunity without addressing the question of whether international law would otherwise allow Belgium to assert universal jurisdiction absent such immunity.[17]

Three judges—hailing from the Netherlands, the United Kingdom, and the United States—felt that the question of jurisdiction was antecedent to the question of immunity and thus had to be answered first.[18] They concluded that international law does allow assertions of universal jurisdiction, including over individuals not physically present within that state's territory. They laid down the following conditions for a state to assert universal jurisdiction *in absentia*: (1) the national state of the accused must be given an opportunity to act on the allegations; (2) the prosecution must be initiated by a prosecutor or *juge d'instruction,* who is independent from control by the government; (3) special circumstances must exist to justify the assertion of jurisdiction, such as a request by the victims for the initiation of such a case; and (4) such jurisdiction must only be asserted over the most heinous crimes.

By contrast, Judge Raymond Ranjeva of Madagascar stated in a declaration that customary international law only recognized universal jurisdiction for maritime piracy, and that conventional law only provides for universal jurisdiction by national courts in a limited number of circumstances.[19] Judge Rezek of Brazil took an even more skeptical view of universal jurisdiction, in effect arguing that a state could only exert such jurisdiction if there was some connection to the forum state.[20] In contrast, Judge Van den Wyngaert of Belgium asserted in her dissent that universal jurisdiction is permitted under

---

17 Arrest Warrant of 11 April 2000 (Democratic Republic of the Congo v. Belgium), 2002 I.C.J. Rep. 3 (Feb. 14).

18 *Id.* at 63 (Joint Sep. Op. Higgins, Kooijmans & Buergenthal).

19 *Id.* at 54 (Decl. Ranjeva).

20 *Id.* at 91 (Sep. Op. Rezek).

international law by both national and international tribunals without any link to the forum state, thus going further than any of the other dissenters.[21] As this brief summary of the opinions makes clear, the status of universal jurisdiction under international law remains somewhat in flux. In 2009, Tanzania, on behalf of the Group of African States, asked the General Assembly to take up the question of the "scope and application of the principle of universal jurisdiction," a multilateral debate that remains ongoing over a decade later.[22]

Despite this uncertainty, a number of states in the last few decades have asserted universal jurisdiction over major international crimes. The Spanish attempt to prosecute former Chilean dictator Augusto Pinochet in 1998, and the Senegalese/African Union prosecution of the former Chadian dictator Hissène Habré in 2005, were both justified at least in part by the universality principle. The *Habré* case raises a question of competing assertions of universal jurisdiction, as prosecutions were initiated in both Belgium and Senegal. Habré was overthrown in 1990 and fled to Senegal. A Chadian truth commission concluded that Habré was responsible for systematic torture and the murder of more than 40,000 people during his dictatorship. Victims of his atrocities initiated a criminal prosecution in Senegal, but the Senegalese court dismissed the case, reasoning that Senegal had not incorporated ICL, including the Torture Convention, into its domestic law, so the Senegalese courts did not have jurisdiction. The victims then pushed for the initiation of proceedings against Habré in Belgium under that country's universal jurisdiction law. Pursuant to an extradition request by Belgium, the Senegalese authorities arrested Habré in 2005. The Senegalese court ordered the release of Habré, arguing that pursuant to the *Yerodia* case Habré was entitled to immunity from Belgian jurisdiction. Under pressure from the international community, including many African states, Senegal rearrested Habré and submitted the question of his immunity to the African Union. The African Union convened a panel of eminent African jurists who concluded that Senegal should amend its laws and assert jurisdiction over Habré for the alleged crimes he committed "on behalf of Africa." As a result, the African Union and Senegal created the Extraordinary African Chambers, discussed above.

---

[21] *Id.* at 137 (Diss. Op. Van Den Wyngaert).

[22] *See* Request for the Inclusion of an Additional Item in the Agenda of the Sixty-third Session: The Scope and Application of the Principle of Universal Jurisdiction, U.N. Doc. A/63/237/Rev.1 (July 23, 2009); G.A. Res. 73/208, The Scope and Application of the Principle of Universal Jurisdiction, U.N. Doc. A/RES/73/208 (Jan. 14, 2019). Some of these debates can be found here: https://www.un.org/en/ga/sixth/71/universal_jurisdiction.shtml.

As a policy matter, universal jurisdiction is not without its concerns and detractors. Many of the more successful assertions of universal jurisdiction have been by former colonial powers in the Global North against alleged perpetrators from developing countries in the Global South. Indeed, in many cases, the accused hails from a state that was a colony of the state asserting jurisdiction, provoking criticism that the assertion of jurisdiction is another manifestation of neo-colonialism. There are exceptions to this colonial valence, most notably in the form of dozens of proceedings against state and non-state actors arising out of the wars in Syria and Iraq that are being pursued in Belgium, Germany, Sweden, Spain (who, while colonial powers, did not colonize either Syria or Iraq), and elsewhere around Europe (although most cases against the personnel of powerful countries have been dismissed). In addition, Argentina and South Africa have initiated cases according to universal jurisdiction as well.

More generally, some express unease that universal jurisdiction places the decision of whom to prosecute with individual national authorities, arguing that only officials from politically unpopular or weak states will be targeted while officials from powerful states will enjoy *de facto* immunity. Moreover, many argue that universal jurisdiction encourages forum shopping, undermines double jeopardy protections, and creates judicial chaos, as foreign officials become incapable of travelling to states with universal jurisdiction laws on the books. In addition, critics often argue that universal jurisdiction provokes unrest in international relations and undermines state sovereignty. Henry Kissinger, the former U.S. Secretary of State and National Security Adviser, for example argued that it is inappropriate to subject foreign policy decisions to "the tyranny of judges"—a position that may reflect self-interest as much as ideology given that he was subject to investigation abroad for his involvement in human rights abuses in South America, S.E. Asia, and Timor-Leste.[23]

2. Domestic Military Courts

In addition to trials before regularly constituted civilian courts, courts martial and military commissions can exercise jurisdiction over violations of IHL. Courts martial are military courts that prosecute members of the armed forces subject to military law, including the laws of war. Courts martial may also be employed to prosecute enemy prisoners of war (POWs) for war crimes, individuals subject to martial law, or belligerents within occupied territory. In the United States, for example, trials by courts martial are governed

---

[23] Henry Kissinger, *The Pitfalls of Universal Jurisdiction*, FOREIGN AFFAIRS (July/Aug. 2001). *See also* CHRISTOPHER HITCHENS, THE TRIAL OF HENRY KISSINGER (2012).

by the Manual for Courts-Martial (MCM), prescribed by executive order, which contains the procedural and evidentiary rules for courts martial as well as the Uniform Code of Military Justice (UCMJ). Some of the military offenses within the UCMJ have domestic law analogs, whereas others are specific to the military (e.g., the crimes of dereliction of duty or conduct unbecoming an officer).

Although military commissions have become associated with the modern "war on terror," they are not a new phenomenon. Indeed, throughout history, the United States and other nations have utilized military commissions to prosecute individuals for violations of the laws of war. Military commissions were born of military necessity and have been constituted when the civilian courts are either unavailable or impractical, or in the context of martial law or belligerent occupation. For example, the United States prosecuted saboteurs and war criminals before military commissions during and following World War II. At that time, the U.S. Supreme Court issued several rulings confirming that military commissions can lawfully prosecute enemy belligerents for violations of the laws of war.[24] Historically, although military commissions have not been governed by statute, they were conducted largely according to the procedural rules then governing courts martial. In such proceedings, the international law of war has been held to be applicable, in effect as "military common law," within the commissions.

The 1949 Geneva Conventions require that POWs on trial for war crimes be prosecuted under the same procedures that would apply to the prosecuting army's own members ("the parity principle"). In *Hamdan v. Rumsfeld*, the U.S. Supreme Court cited the safeguards embodied in the Geneva Conventions (as well as the UCMJ) to invalidate the military commissions originally established to prosecute individuals detained at Guantánamo Bay.[25] A plurality opinion also reasoned that the charged offense, conspiracy to violate the laws of war, was not a cognizable violation of international law and therefore could not be tried by military commission. The U.S. Supreme Court later held that those individuals detained at Guantánamo Bay were entitled to challenge their detention in U.S. federal courts under the ancient writ of *habeas corpus*.[26]

D. New ICL Models

The international community has not established any of the above models for the most contemporary conflict situations in Syria, Iraq, Myanmar, China, or Yemen, in part due to political paralysis

---

[24] *See, e.g., Ex Parte Quirin*, 317 U.S. 1 (1942); *In Re Yamashita*, 327 U.S. 1 (1946); and *Johnson v. Eisentrager*, 339 U.S. 763 (1950).

[25] *Hamdan v. Rumsfeld*, 548 U.S. 557 (2006).

[26] *Boumediene v. Bush*, 553 U.S. 723 (2008).

and the availability of the veto in the U.N. Security Council. However, international actors have used other available mechanisms and fora to advance the accountability norm, primarily through the documentation of abuses in preparation for subsequent accountability exercises, whether international, regional, or domestic. For example, Syria has been the subject of multiple fact-gathering exercises by internationally-mandated organizations. Besides a U.N. Commission of Inquiry devoted to Syria deployed by the U.N. Human Rights Council and fact-finding around the use of chemical weapons by the Organisation for the Prohibition of Chemical Weapons (OPCW), an innovative new mechanism created by the U.N. General Assembly—the International, Impartial and Independent Mechanism to Assist in the Investigation and Prosecution of Those Responsible for the Most Serious Crimes under International Law Committed in the Syrian Arab Republic since March 2011 (IIIM)—has been tasked with consolidating existing documentation with an eye towards supporting future criminal trials.[27] The IIIM is meant to operate not only as a clearinghouse of information produced over the years by other entities—including the U.N. Commission of Inquiry, civil society actors, and governments—but also as a proto-investigative team gathering its own information to fill gaps in the evidentiary record and prepare files for future prosecutions before whichever court may eventually assert jurisdiction. Although an international tribunal has proven to be a bridge too far when it comes to Syria, national prosecutorial authorities—and particularly their dedicated war crimes units—are already proving to be avid consumers of the IIIM's work.

The Security Council created a similar body focused on Iraq—the United Nations Investigative Team to Promote Accountability for Da'esh/ISIL Crimes (UNITAD)—with the goal of supporting "domestic efforts to hold ISIL (Da'esh) accountable by collecting, preserving, and storing evidence in Iraq of acts that may amount to war crimes, crimes against humanity and genocide committed by the terrorist group ISIL (Da'esh) in Iraq, to the highest possible standards."[28] In some respects, UNITAD's mandate is more limited than the IIIM's; in other respects, the new entity is more empowered and has fewer constraints on its ability to make its holdings useful. The resolution has a singular focus on crimes committed by ISIL, with no instructions to look into crimes associated with other actors, including governmental forces, at the federal or regional level (e.g., Kurdistan Regional forces); militia such as the Popular Mobilization Forces; or international forces for that matter. Like the IIIM, UNITAD is ultimately only an investigative body; it has no

---

27 G.A. Res. 71/248, U.N. Doc. A/Res/71/248 (Dec. 21, 2016).

28 S.C. Res. 2379, U.N. Doc. S/Res/2379 (Sept. 21, 2017).

prosecutorial powers or formal ability to influence the imposition of charges or the criminal justice process writ large. If the authorities in Iraq are unable to host genuine trials, and European states are unwilling to take back their nationals who have flocked to the region to join the fight, there is a risk that UNITAD will find no ready outlet for its investigations. UNITAD has the benefit of a Chapter VII provenance and funding from U.N. assessed contributions; by contrast, the IIIM has only the support of the General Assembly and, at first, was reliant upon voluntary contributions (since upgraded).

In many respects, this proliferation of investigative innovations is a good news story. States are finding ways around the Security Council to support international justice efforts. However, a less sanguine trend is also apparent: it cannot be gainsaid that these new justice mechanisms are decidedly weaker than those developed in response to historical atrocities, such as the ICTY and ICTR. Indeed, in the genealogy of international criminal law since its renaissance, each generation of justice institutions has emerged weaker than the last.

E. Extradition, Transfer, Rendition, and Abduction

Although a number of domestic systems allow *in absentia* criminal trials, many do not; nor do the existing international and hybrid tribunals, except the Special Tribunal for Lebanon. As a result, the exercise of international and domestic jurisdiction over international crimes is often dependent on the ability of the prosecuting authority to obtain custody of the accused. Domestic legal systems are thus crucially important in transferring suspects from their custody to another jurisdiction, such as another state's legal system or an international tribunal. This is also an area in which one sees the use of highly coercive powers (sometimes rising to the level of international abduction) as states alternatively resist and acquiesce in requests for such transfers.

In most transnational cases, the accused is transferred between nation states through an exercise of *extradition*—the process by which one state (the requested state) transfers to the custody of another state (the requesting state) an individual wanted for trial in the latter. Extraditions are usually governed by a web of bilateral treaties between states, although the European Union features a multilateral treaty that renders intra-European transfers relatively seamless. Extradition provides an example of cooperation among states in the enforcement of international criminal law, but states continue to assert their sovereign prerogative not to extradite someone if (1) the act for which the requesting state wants to prosecute the individual is not a crime in the requested state (the so-called double criminality rule); (2) the act for which the requesting state wants to prosecute the individual is a political act (the political offense exception); (3) the individual is a national of the requested state; and (4) humanitarian reasons or concern about the lack of due process in the requesting state counsel against extraditing the individual. Each of these exceptions to extradition is premised on powers reserved to the requested state.

These exceptions are also designed to benefit and protect the individual accused. For example, in allowing Augusto Pinochet to return to Chile rather than be extradited to Spain where he was wanted for violations of ICL committed in Chile, the United Kingdom cited humanitarian concerns arising from Pinochet's age and health. At the same time, the Chilean government made it quite clear to the United Kingdom that it did not want Pinochet sent to Spain. The inevitable diplomatic friction that would have been created by extraditing Pinochet to stand trial was undoubtedly a factor in the decision of the U.K. government to return him to Chile. There was some concern that, in opposing extradition, the Chilean government was acting to protect Pinochet from any form of accountability. While this was certainly the motivation for some within the Chilean government, the litigation arising from Spain's request to the U.K. contributed to the mobilization of victims and civil society in Chile to demand that Pinochet be prosecuted at home. Eventually, he was indicted for corruption as well as numerous atrocity crimes, including disappearances and assassinations. He died a few days after being placed under house arrest at the age of 91.

When an international tribunal requests that a state hand over a suspect for prosecution, we speak of "transfer" or "surrender" and not extradition, which generally governs the horizontal rendering of a suspect to a sister sovereign. Although these are different processes, many of the doctrines and procedures that are applicable to extradition proceedings have been adapted to the context of surrender proceedings involving international tribunals. With respect to the two original *ad hoc* tribunals, states were obligated to transfer a suspect if the tribunal so requested by virtue of the tribunals' statutes and their Chapter VII provenance. For example, Article 28 of the ICTR Statute indicated that all states must cooperate in the investigation and prosecution of accused persons and "shall comply without undue delay with any request for assistance" issued by a Trial Chamber, including for "the arrest or detention of persons [or] the surrender or the transfer of the accused." Further, Rule 58 of the ICTR's Rules of Procedure and Evidence stated that these obligations "shall prevail over any legal impediment to the surrender or transfer of the accused to the Tribunal which may exist under the national law or extradition treaties of the State concerned." This coercive obligation established the primacy of the *ad hoc* tribunals' jurisdiction over domestic courts. Theoretically, any state that refused to cooperate could be subject to sanction by the U.N. Security Council.

Security Council backing did not necessarily guarantee state compliance, even from a permanent member of the Security Council. Early in the life of the ICTR, the tribunal requested that the United States transfer a suspect found in Texas, Elizaphan Ntakirutimana, to it for prosecution. The United States had entered into an executive agreement with the ICTR—the "Agreement on Surrender of Persons Between the Government of the United States and the International Tribunal for the Prosecution of Persons Responsible for Genocide and Other Serious Violations of International Humanitarian Law Committed in the Territory of Rwanda and Rwandan Citizens Responsible for Genocide and Other Such Violations Committed in the Territory of Neighboring States"—which was subsequently codified within the annual National Defense Authorization Act.[29] The legislation applied the federal extradition statutes (18 U.S.C. §§ 3181 *et seq.*) to the surrender of persons to the ICTR. According to that procedure, a hearing may be held to consider a request for surrender. If a judicial officer finds the evidence sufficient to sustain the charges, then the officer certifies to the Secretary of State that the individual may be legally surrendered. The Secretary of State then has final authority to order the surrender.

Ntakirutimana sued the U.S. government in a U.S. federal court to halt his transfer to the ICTR, arguing that this arrangement was unconstitutional in the absence of a proper extradition treaty. After a protracted legal battle, the 5th Circuit Court of Appeals ultimately ruled that the surrender legislation was constitutional, that there was probable cause, and that the transfer could go forward.[30] This degree of resistance by a national court is remarkable given that the ICTR enjoyed a Chapter VII pedigree. Ntakirutimana and his son were ultimately convicted by the ICTR for their involvement in the genocide in Rwanda. The ICTY experienced similar obstacles to obtaining custody over its accused, most notably from Serbia and—to a lesser degree—Croatia. These examples illustrate the tensions that can arise between efforts to further international justice, respect state sovereignty, and ensure the rights of criminal suspects.

A similar obligation exists under the Rome Treaty, whereby state parties are required to cooperate with the ICC to make suspects available to the Court. Unlike the *ad hoc* tribunals, which had

---

[29] *See* National Defense Authorization Act, Pub. L. 104–106, § 1342, 110 Stat. 486 (1996).

[30] *Ntakirutimana v. Reno*, 184 F.3d 419 (5th Cir. 1999).

recourse to the Security Council, the Court lacks any in-house ability to coerce states; rather, the obligation to cooperate is one accepted by states on ratification of the Rome Statute. It is only with respect to Security Council referrals that the Court enjoys analogous powers of coercion, assuming the Council is willing to oblige. Yet, even under these circumstances, cooperation has been spotty and the Council has received criticism for failing to follow up on its referrals. For example, ex-President Omar Al Bashir of Sudan traveled the world for many years while subject to an ICC arrest warrant, including to ICC member states and to Russia, a member of the P-5 ultimately responsible for referring Darfur to the Court. In their defense, states argued that while Al Bashir enjoyed no immunity before the ICC by virtue of Article 27 of the Rome Statute, he did still benefit from head of state immunity vis-à-vis the exercise of their "horizontal" enforcement jurisdiction (i.e., efforts by co-equal sovereigns to arrest or transfer him to The Hague). The ICC Appeals Chamber ultimately dismissed this argument, ruling that such immunities did not apply to states' cooperation duties towards an international tribunal.[31]

On the other hand, state cooperation was quite robust in a case involving offenses against the administration of justice under Article 70 of the ICC Statute filed in conjunction with the crimes against humanity cases against Jean-Pierre Bemba for crimes committed in the Central African Republic. Following an unprecedented joint arrest operation involving Belgium, the Democratic Republic of Congo, France, and the Netherlands, a number of suspects—including members of Bemba's legal team—were arrested and ultimately convicted of witness tampering. Evidence in the case included Western Union records and telephone intercepts provided by European countries pursuant to requests for assistance from the ICC. Bemba was acquitted of the underlying international criminal charges in a controversial ruling by the Appeals Chamber. Some commentators expressed disapproval of the Prosecution for pursuing the Article 70 charges, which consume prosecutorial resources and do not involve the Court's core crimes. The final outcome of the *Bemba* proceedings—which proved the existence of witness tampering and resulted in the only judgment against Bemba himself—suggest that such criticism is misplaced.

Even though not a party to the ICC Statute, the United States has twice effectuated the transfer of a suspect to The Hague. The first was Bosco Ntaganda who appeared at the U.S. embassy in Kigali, Rwanda, in April 2013 and asked to be transferred to The Hague. The second was Dominic Ongwen, who reportedly surrendered himself in early 2015 to U.S. special forces deployed to Central Africa

---

31 *See supra* note 4.

to assist in the hunt for Lord's Resistance Army leader Joseph Kony. Ongwen was the subject of one of the ICC's first arrest warrants and an INTERPOL red notice. Both indictees were designated under the United States' War Crimes Reward Program.[32] Originally designed to pay rewards leading to the arrest or capture of individuals indicted by the Yugoslav, Rwandan, or Sierra Leonean war crimes tribunals, Congress—with strong bipartisan support—amended the Program twice to extend to individuals indicted by any international or hybrid criminal tribunal, including the International Criminal Court, as well as to individuals accused of crimes in the war in Syria.

More controversially, individuals may be abducted to bring them within international or domestic custody. For example, as mentioned in the history chapter, the Israeli government kidnapped Adolf Eichmann in Argentina and brought him to Israel, where he was prosecuted, convicted, and executed for his involvement in the Nazi Holocaust. The United States has also resorted to such extrajudicial abductions to bring suspects into the United States to be tried criminally. The U.S. Supreme Court in a series of opinions has found that U.S. courts retains personal jurisdiction over such individuals even if they are forcibly brought into U.S. territory in violation of local law or an extradition treaty with the territorial state,[33] and that such abductions (at least where the individual was transferred to lawful custody within 12 hours) do not violate a clear and universal rule of international human rights law that would give rise to a civil claim for relief on the part of the person abducted.[34]

The ICTY essentially adopted this so-called *male captus, bene detentus* doctrine (which states that an improper capture can nonetheless result in valid detention) in a case in which private parties abducted the accused and brought him into the custody of the multinational force in Bosnia-Herzegovina.[35] The Trial Chamber did contemplate, however, that there may be a legal impediment to jurisdiction if the accused had been seriously mistreated before being handed over to the Tribunal or if Tribunal staff played a part in the abduction. The ICC has generally followed suit, rejecting a defendant's argument that his case should be found inadmissible under the doctrine of "abuse of process" because he was "unlawfully detained and ill-treated" by the national authorities that arrested him. The Appeals Chamber held that "abuse of process" is not a ground for finding a case inadmissible under Article 17 of the Rome Statute or dictated by any inherent or indispensable judicial

---

32 22 U.S.C. § 2708.

33 *United States v. Alvarez-Machain*, 504 U.S. 655, 670 (1992).

34 *Sosa v. Alvarez-Machain*, 542 U.S. 692 (2004).

35 *Prosecutor v. Dragan Nikolić*, Case No. IT-94-2-Pt, Decision on Defence Motion Challenging the Exercise of Jurisdiction by the Tribunal (Oct. 9, 2002).

function.[36] However, the Chamber nonetheless asserted that Article 21(3) of the Statute—which commands that the Court's interpretation of the law must be consistent with internationally recognized human rights—requires the dismissal of any case in which a fair trial has become impossible due to breaches of the rights of the accused.[37] Similarly, the Appeals Chamber held in the case involving Abdullah Al Senussi that although the Statute "was not designed to make principles of human rights per se determinative of admissibility," egregious violations of the rights of the suspect render a case inadmissible.[38]

Even more controversial is the U.S. practice of *rendering* individuals to offshore prisons or the custody of willing allies, all for the purpose of taking advantage of the ability to engage in aggressive interrogation techniques that in some cases rise to the level of torture. Some European states have initiated suits *in absentia* against Central Intelligence Agency operatives involved in such "extraordinary renditions." Numerous international human rights bodies—including the Committee Against Torture,[39] the Human Rights Committee,[40] and the European Court of Human Rights[41] have concluded that such renditions violate the Convention Against Torture, the International Covenant on Civil and Political Rights, and the European Convention for the Protection of Human Rights and Fundamental Freedoms, respectively. The international community continues to grapple with how to evaluate the legal implications of these assertions of state power. In particular, whereas abductions for the purpose of prosecuting an individual for an international crime (the Eichmann example) may be more palatable, those committed for the purposes of effectuating an

---

36 *Prosecutor v. Lubanga,* Case No. ICC-01/04-01/06-772, Judgment on the Appeal of Mr. Thomas Lubanga Dyilo against the Decision on the Defence Challenge to the Jurisdiction of the Court Pursuant to Article 19(2)(a) of the Statute of 3 October 2006, ¶¶ 34–35 (Dec. 14, 2006).

37 *Id.*, ¶¶ 37, 39.

38 *Prosecutor v. Gaddafi & Al Senussi,* Case No. ICC-01/11-01/11 OA 6, Judgement on the Appeal of Mr. Abdulla Al Senussi Against the Decision of PTC I of 11 October 2013 Entitled "Decision on the Admissibility of the Case Against Abdullah Al Senussi," ¶¶ 229–30 (July 24, 2014).

39 Committee Against Torture, Consideration of Reports Submitted by States Parties Under Article 19 of the Convention, Conclusions and Recommendations of the Committee Against Torture (United States), U.N. Doc. No. CAT/C/USA/CO/2, 36th Sess. (July 25, 2006).

40 *See Case of Lilian Celiberti de Casariego,* U.N. GAOR, 36th Sess., Supp. No. 40, U.N. Doc. A/36/40 (1981), at 185; *Case of Sergio Ruben Lopez Burgos,* U.N. GAOR, 36th Sess., Supp. No. 40, U.N. Doc. A/36/40 (1981), at 76; *Case of Almeida de Quinteros,* Comm. No. 107 (1981), July 21, 1983; and *Garcia v. Ecuador,* Comm. No. 319/1988, U.N. Doc. A/47/40 (1994), at 290.

41 *See* European Court of Human Rights, Secret Detention Cases, https://www.echr.coe.int/Documents/FS_Secret_detention_ENG.PDF.

indefinite or *incommunicado* detention without trial for the purposes of interrogation raise more acute concerns.

F. Conclusion

As should be apparent, a high degree of jurisdictional redundancy is apparent in the ICL system, as ICL norms are codified and adjudicated in both the international and domestic contexts. In addition, these jurisdictional regimes are created by very different types of processes—some cooperative, some more coercive. In some circumstances, international tribunals exercise primacy over domestic tribunals that may have parallel jurisdiction over the crimes in question (such as the state in whose territory the crimes were committed). In the case of the ICC, by contrast, international jurisdiction is complementary to domestic jurisdiction such that if a domestic court is prosecuting a particular crime, the ICC should stay its hand. Furthermore, there are no firm rules governing how competing exercises of jurisdiction are to be resolved between these institutions or whether and how future such jurisdictional regimes should be created at the international level. As you review your primary ICL materials, consider whether the forum in question is likely to be the most impartial, fair, and robust or whether the case would have been better pursued elsewhere.

Chapter 3

THE MAKING OF INTERNATIONAL CRIMINAL LAW

Fundamental to any legal system are processes, doctrines, and conventions concerning the development and identification of the applicable substantive rules—these rules of recognition are known as "secondary rules."[1] How law is created, and where one looks to determine the applicable rules, is particularly important in a system of law that imposes criminal penalties on individuals. The criminal law may result in the deprivation of an individual's fundamental right to liberty through incarceration, and—in some domestic jurisdictions—the ultimate penalty of capital punishment. *Nullum crimen sine lege* (NCSL), a fundamental principle of justice that applies to all criminal law systems, requires that the penal law be clear and easily ascertained, and thus provide adequate notice to individuals that certain conduct may result in criminal liability. This enables all of us to conform our behavior to the law, if we are so inclined. Given its centrality to the field, we discuss the uneasy relationship between international criminal law (ICL) and NCSL in its own chapter.

There is a core set of rules concerning sources of public international law over which there is little controversy. These rules derive from the definitive articulation of the primary sources of public international law found in Article 38 of the Statute of the International Court of Justice (ICJ).[2] Article 38 lists treaties, customary international law (CIL), and general principles of law as co-equal primary sources of international law, and judicial decisions and the writings of publicists as subsidiary sources. This article operates very much like a "choice of law" provision for the ICJ. To this canon of binding rules must be added resolutions from the U.N. Security Council under Chapter VII of the U.N. Charter, which are binding on all member states.[3] Indeed, the statutes of the International Criminal Tribunals for the former Yugoslavia and Rwanda were both contained in Security Council resolutions.[4] In

---

1 H.L.A. HART, THE CONCEPT OF LAW (3d. ed. 2012).

2 Statute of the International Court of Justice, April 18, 1946, 33 U.N.T.S. 993, 59 Stat 1055.

3 U.N. Charter art. 103, Oct. 24, 1945, 1 U.N.T.S. XVI ("In the event of a conflict between the obligations of the Members of the United Nations under the present Charter and their obligations under any other international agreement, their obligations under the present Charter shall prevail.").

4 *See e.g.*, S.C. Res. 827, U.N. Doc. S/RES/827 (May 25, 1993).

addition, following the attacks of September 11, 2001, the Council has required all states to ratify the suite of terrorism treaties and amend their domestic legal frameworks to enable domestic terrorism prosecutions.[5]

Although many ICL tribunals have relied upon Article 38 for the standard recitation of international law sources, in other contexts, separate rules with respect to sources of law have been established for particular ICL tribunals. For example, Article 21 of the Rome Treaty creating the International Criminal Court (ICC) sets forth a hierarchical set of sources of law applicable to the ICC that deviates from Article 38 by, among other things, de-emphasizing general principles of law and leaving the application of CIL somewhat ambiguous. This may reflect the fact that these traditional, uncodified sources of public international law sit uncomfortably in a system of penal law. Given the grave consequences of criminal liability, concerns over the rights of criminal defendants are raised when there is significant uncertainty about the applicable law or when the applicable law is not easily ascertainable. Source-of-law doctrines that are relatively uncontroversial in the context of most fields of public international law may thus evince more controversy in the criminal context. Codified rules, such as those found in treaties, are the least troubling; rules that derive from CIL, and thus arise out of a history of state practice undertaken out of a sense of legal obligation, or from general principles of law are more susceptible to uncertainty and raise special concerns with respect to ICL. As is true in all areas of international law, treaties and custom may address the same subject matter, leading to questions about which rule should prevail in the event of discrepancies.[6]

At the same time, a recurring tension arises in ICL between the requirement that the law be certain and explicit, as embodied in the NCSL imperative, and the concern that the more specificity and detail we include in the definition of a crime, the more likely we are to provide those responsible for some of the worst atrocities known to humankind with a technical defense to avoid criminal liability. This dilemma was evident at the birth of the modern ICL regime in the post-World War II period, when individuals were prosecuted for the novel offenses of crimes against humanity and against the peace at Nuremberg and Tokyo. A strict application of the principle of NCSL to these offenses at Nuremberg would have limited the ability of the Allies to hold the Nazi high command accountable for aggressive war and most of the crimes of the Holocaust.

[5] S.C. Res. 1373, U.N. Doc. S/RES/1373 (Sept. 28, 2001).

[6] Military and Paramilitary Activities in and against Nicaragua (Nicar. v. USA) (Merits), 1986 I.C.J. Rep. 14, ¶¶ 175–79 (June 27).

As we will see, this tension between wanting to keep the law flexible enough to adapt to the seemingly endless innovations of criminal activity without violating the fundamental rights of those accused of such atrocities is still present today. The dilemma is summed up by Professor Alain Pellet, who, in criticizing the decision to include in the Rome Treaty detailed definitions of the crimes within the jurisdiction of the ICC, noted:

> by freezing [international law] in a sometimes daring but often inadequate and regressive text, the authors of the Statute have limited the chances of making the Court an efficient instrument in the struggle against the crimes it is supposed to repress. . . . Unfortunately men's criminal imagination appears unlimited and, by enclosing the definition of the crimes in narrow, punctilious formulations, they have forbidden the judges in advance to suppress future malevolent inventions of the human spirit.[7]

Despite Pellet's characterization of the Rome Statute, the applicable sources laid out in Article 21 contemplate moving outside the specific terms of the treaty if necessary. Thus, as it adjudicates the cases before it, the Court is to first apply the Statute, the Elements of Crimes, and the Rules of Procedure and Evidence. States—including states that had not yet ratified the Rome treaty—drafted the Elements of Crimes to define the substantive offenses in the Statute with even greater detail. Second, the Court is to look, "where appropriate, [to] applicable treaties and the principles and rules of international law, including the established principles of the international law of armed conflict." According to this provision, if "applicable" treaties external to the ICC—which would likely include at a minimum the Geneva Conventions, the Genocide Convention, the Torture Convention, and the Enforced Disappearances Convention, but perhaps also the panoply of human right treaties—more clearly criminalize activity than the Rome Statute, then the Court may rely on those texts for interpretive guidance. In addition, where neither the Statute nor applicable treaties provide a clear rule of decision, the Court may look to general principles of law derived from the national legal systems of the world—and particularly from the legal systems of the relevant states—so long as such principles are not in conflict with either the Statute or international law. It is assumed that general principles of law will be most relevant to procedural questions given the relatively high degree of substantive law codification. This expansive grant of authority is tempered by the requirement that the Court apply and interpret the enumerated

---

[7] Alain Pellet, *Applicable Law*, *in* THE ROME STATUTE OF THE INTERNATIONAL CRIMINAL COURT: A COMMENTARY 1058–1059 (Cassese, Gaeta, and Jones eds., 2002).

sources of law consistently with "internationally recognized human rights."

In addition to these sources identified in Article 21, the ICC Appeals Chamber has noted that the Code of Professional Conduct for Counsel, which is mandated in the Rules, is "part of the Court's applicable law under article 21(1)(a) of the Statute," even though that article makes no mention of the Code.[8] The Court's Regulations (mandated by Article 52 of the Statute) are also influential. Regulation 55 is particularly controversial, as it empowers the judges to recharacterize the charges against the accused if the facts adduced at trial suggest that a different crime was committed or a different form of responsibility was involved.[9] The Appeals Chamber has cautioned that this practice could undermine the rights of the accused if the new characterization exceeds the facts and circumstances of the original charging document.[10] The judges have also produced a Chambers Practice Manual, in part in response to the difficulty of amending the Rules of Procedure and Evidence (which requires a 2/3 majority of the Assembly of State Parties).[11] In an opinion addressing the Court's first guilty plea, Judge Péter Kovács wrote separately to criticize the majority for relying too heavily on the Manual in justifying its approach to weighing the probative value of, and resolving inconsistencies in, the evidence adduced in connection with the Court's first guilty plea.[12] Besides these types of subsidiary sources, ICL tribunals also resort to inherent judicial functions to define applicable powers and law. A Trial Chamber of the ICC, for example, has held that the Court has the implied power to subpoena witness testimony, even though the Statute only refers to the voluntary appearance of witnesses.[13]

---

8 *Prosecutor v. Muthaura & Kenyatta*, Case No. ICC-01/09-02/11-365 OA3, Judgment on the Appeal of the Prosecutor against the Decision of Pre-Trial Chamber II dated 20 July 2011 entitled 'Decision with Respect to the Question of Invalidating the Appointment of Counsel to the Defence', ¶ 48 (Nov. 10, 2011).

9 *Prosecutor v. Katanga*, Case No. ICC-01/04-01/07-3319, Decision on the Implementation of Regulation 55 of the Regulations of the Court and Severing the Charges Against the Accused Persons, ¶¶ 26–34 (Nov. 21, 2012).

10 *Prosecutor v. Katanga*, Case No. ICC-01/04-01/07-3363, Judgment on the Appeal or Mr. Germain Katanga Against the Decision of the TC II of 21 November 2012 Entitled "Decision on the Implementation of Regulation 55 of the Regulations of the Court and Severing the Charges Against the Accused Persons", ¶¶ 90–91 (Mar. 27, 2013).

11 CHAMBERS PRACTICE MANUAL (May 2017), https://www.icc-cpi.int/iccdocs/other/170512-icc-chambers-practice-manual_May_2017_ENG.pdf.

12 *Prosecutor v. Al Mahdi*, Case No. ICC-0-1/12-01/15-84-Anx, Separate Opinion of Judge Péter Kovács, ¶¶ 13–16 (May 9, 2016) (arguing that the Manual has "no legal authority" and thus does not empower the judges to depart from or disregard the formal evidentiary rules).

13 *Prosecutor v. Ruto & Arap Sang*, Case No. ICC-01/09-01/11-1274-Corr2, Decision on Prosecutor's Application for Witness Summonses and resulting Request for State Party Cooperation (Apr. 17, 2014).

Given this background, this chapter surveys the relevant sources of ICL with an emphasis on the ways in which they have been invoked by the various ICL tribunals in their proceedings. As we shall see, the original *ad hoc* tribunals relied much more heavily on customary international law, in part because their constitutive statutes were less detailed. The Rome Statute and the suite of ICC instruments are much more intricate; nonetheless, the ICC judges continue to explore the full meaning and scope of Article 21 as they carry out their mandate.

A. Treaties

Treaties are the least controversial source of international law, and the one that domestically trained lawyers find the easiest to grasp. The law of treaties—the body of rules that governs the formation, interpretation, implementation, and exit of treaties—is itself codified in a series of treaties on treaties, most importantly the 1969 Vienna Convention on the Law of Treaties.[14] Almost 120 states have ratified the Vienna Convention, and there is general consensus that the provisions of the Convention have risen to the level of customary international law, which is to say that the treaty sets forth a default legal regime that is binding on all states, not just those that have joined the Convention. Indeed, the ICC has relied upon the Vienna Convention to interpret the Rome Treaty.[15]

ICL is a field replete with treaty law. In fact, the field of international humanitarian law (IHL) is one of the earliest subjects of international treaty law, and is today one of the most codified areas of international law. The Geneva Conventions of 1949, which require states to exercise universal jurisdiction over enumerated war crimes committed in international armed conflicts, enjoy the unique distinction of being the only treaties—as of this writing—that have been ratified by every state in the world. Besides war crimes, there are today treaties dedicated to defining, prohibiting, and obliging state parties to criminalize the crimes of torture, genocide, slavery and the slave trade, apartheid, terrorism, enforced disappearances, and human trafficking, in addition to the whole panoply of international human rights. Crimes against humanity are conspicuously absent from this list. No dedicated treaty on crimes against humanity emerged in the post-World War II period. It was only recently, in 2019. that the International Law Commission produced Draft Articles on crimes against humanity that are being

---

[14] Vienna Convention on the Law of Treaties, May 23, 1969, 1155 U.N.T.S. 331 (entered into force Jan. 27, 1980).

[15] Situation in the Democratic Republic of Congo, Case No. ICC-01/04-168, Judgment on the Prosecutor's Application for Extraordinary Review of Pre-Trial Chamber I's 31 March 2006 Decision Denying Leave to Appeal, Appeals Chamber, ¶ 33 (July 13, 2006).

considered by the General Assembly.[16] Treaties establishing international crimes arguably provide adequate fair notice to nationals of treaty members (and others for that matter), and thus pose fewer problems with respect to the NCSL principle than other sources of ICL, such as custom and general principles. In addition to these ICL treaties, the U.N. Charter, binding on all U.N. member states, remains relevant, particularly in connection with the crime of aggression and in so far as it establishes duties vis-à-vis Security Council referrals to the ICC.[17] And finally, the International Criminal Tribunal for Yugoslavia (ICTY) incorporated as part of its law international agreements that were already binding on the states of the former Yugoslavia (even if those treaties did not reflect customary international law), such as an agreement ratified by the breakaway republics on May 22, 1992, making various IHL treaties applicable to the conflict (regardless of how the conflict was classified under IHL).[18]

Treaties come in two basic types. Bilateral treaties are entered into between two states, or between a state and another entity, usually an international organization. Multilateral treaties are open for ratification to a large number of states and often to all states in the world. Regional treaties are multilateral treaties but are geographically restricted with respect to the states that may ratify them. For example, the American Convention on Human Rights is open to all members of the Organization of American States (OAS).[19] Multilateral treaties are a primary building block of ICL. That said, bilateral treaties do play an important role in some aspects of ICL; for example, extradition treaties that govern the procedures by which a suspect may be transferred from one jurisdiction to another are usually bilateral.

Some analogize bilateral treaties to contracts and multilateral treaties to legislation. As with many such analogies, these comparisons often confuse more than they assist. Some contract law doctrines, including interpretive principles aimed at gleaning the intent of the parties, apply to bilateral treaties, but they apply equally to multilateral treaties. By the same token, whereas multilateral treaties are often legislative in nature—setting down general principles of applicable law and creating a legal regime binding on all members—bilateral treaties may also embody such

---

16 International Law Commission, *Analytical Guide to the Work of the International Law Commission: Crimes Against Humanity*, https://legal.un.org/ilc/guide/7_7.shtml.

17 *See generally Prosecutor v. Al Bashir*, Case No. ICC-02/05-01/09-397-Corr, Judgment in the Jordan Referral re Al Bashir Appeal (May 6, 2019).

18 *Prosecutor v. Galić*, Case No. IT-98-29-T, Judgment & Opinion, ¶¶ 124–5 (Dec. 5, 2003).

19 American Convention on Human Rights, Nov. 22, 1969, 1144 U.N.T.S. 123.

law-making provisions. In addition, multilateral treaties, as we shall see, are significantly different in their formation and operation than domestic legislation.

States generally first *sign* and then *ratify* a treaty. Signature indicates a state's acceptance of the terms of the treaty and its intent to ratify, accept, or approve the treaty. Although a state is usually not legally bound by the terms of the treaty it has only signed (unless the state so agrees), a state may not violate the object and purpose of a treaty that it has signed but not yet ratified according to the Vienna Convention. There is broad agreement that signature has the effect of creating such an obligation on the part of a state; there is little consensus on the content of this obligation or on the consequences of its violation.

A state becomes an official party to a treaty, and thus fully bound by all its terms (unless it has the right to opt out of any of them), upon ratification. When a state joins a treaty after it has come into effect, we say that the state has acceded to, rather than ratified, the treaty. Accession has the same legal effect as ratification. Ratification thus indicates a state's intent to be bound by the treaty as a matter of international law. It is important to distinguish between two types of ratification procedures—those required as a matter of international law and those required as a matter of domestic law. Internationally, ratification is usually effectuated by the state depositing a document indicating its intent to be bound by the treaty with an official depository, such as the U.N. Secretary-General. Domestically, ratification may require compliance with procedures set forth in that state's constitution or applicable legislation. In the United States, for example, the President ratifies treaties after seeking the advice and consent of the Senate.

If the treaty allows (and many do), a state may attach a reservation to its ratification. A *reservation* is a declaration that purports to alter the legal effect of a treaty provision with respect to that state. A state may agree to ratify a treaty conditional on the ability to attach reservations. Many human rights treaties, including those that permit or impose criminal liability, are often ratified with reservations. On ratifying the International Covenant on Civil and Political Rights (ICCPR), for example, the United States attached a reservation with respect to Article 20, which prohibits, among other things, hate speech. The U.S. reservation states that Article 20 cannot conflict with the right of free speech and association protected by the U.S. Constitution and other U.S. law. Alternatively, a treaty may, by its terms, forbid the use of reservations. The Rome Statute, for example, disallows reservations (although it did originally allow states to opt out of war crimes jurisdiction for a period of seven years and states can still opt out of aggression prosecutions). Where reservations are permitted, the Vienna Convention dictates that states may not attach reservations that violate the object and purpose of the treaty, thus imposing the same test, and raising the same interpretative and remedial questions, as the obligations undertaken by a state upon signing a treaty.

Very little jurisprudence exists on how to identify what constitutes the object and purpose of a treaty. The most authoritative treatment of the issue involves reservations to the Genocide Convention. In 1951, the ICJ issued an Advisory Opinion on the question of reservations to the 1948 Convention on the Prevention and Punishment of the Crime of Genocide.[20] On ratification, many states had attached reservations to Article IX of the Convention, which vests jurisdiction in the ICJ over disputes relating to the "interpretation, application or fulfillment" of the treaty "including those relating to the responsibility of a State for genocide." The ICJ determined that these reservations were not inconsistent with the object and purpose of the treaty (the prevention and punishment of the crime of genocide) and, as such, were permissible.[21]

The effect of a reservation that is not compatible with the object and purpose of a treaty remains unclear, as there is no authoritative judicial decision that has ruled on the impact of such a reservation. Borrowing from the contract law concept of severability, the Human Rights Committee (the enforcement body created by the ICCPR) has stated in a general comment that an unacceptable reservation to the ICCPR is null and void, and that the treaty will be binding on the ratifying state without the effect of the reservation.[22] This is somewhat problematic, as in most cases states agree to ratify a treaty conditional on any reservation. If the reservation is null and void, the underlying provision applies to the ratifying state despite that state's clear intent to not be bound by that provision. Thus, many states, including the United States, have formally indicated their disagreement with this approach to reservations.

In addition to reservations, the United States and other nations have attached "understandings" and "declarations" to a treaty upon ratification. *Understandings* are meant to clarify, but not alter, the legal meaning or effect of a provision. A *declaration* is normally used to indicate a state's agreement to a particular optional part of a

---

[20] Convention on the Prevention and Punishment of the Crime of Genocide, Dec. 9, 1948, 78 U.N.T.S. 277.

[21] Reservations to the Convention on the Prevention and Punishment of the Crime of Genocide, 1951 I.C.J. 15 (May 28).

[22] Human Rights Committee, *General Comment No. 24 (Issues Relating to Reservations Made Upon Ratification or Accession to the Covenant or the Optional Protocols Thereto, or in Relation to Declarations under Article 41 of the Covenant)*, U.N. Doc. CCPR/C/21/Rev.1/Add.6 (Nov. 4, 1994).

treaty—for example, allowing other state parties to bring complaints alleging a violation of the state's obligations under the treaty (as provided under Article 41(1) of the ICCPR). Collectively, reservations, understandings, and declarations are often referred to as RUDs. Notwithstanding the label a state attaches to a declaration or understanding, if the intent of the provision is to alter the legal effect of a treaty provision, then the declaration or understanding is treated as a reservation.

According to the Vienna Convention, treaty interpretation is based primarily on its plain language and the intent of the drafters. Thus, a treaty clause is to be interpreted based on its "ordinary meaning . . . in [its] context and in the light of [the treaty's] object and purpose" (Article 31(1)). The overall approach is to discern the intent of the state parties. For context, the Convention directs us to the following: (1) the preamble and any annexes to the treaty; (2) other written agreements related to the treaty, either entered into among the state parties or accepted by others as related to the treaty; (3) any subsequent agreements concerning the interpretation or application of the treaty; (4) any subsequent practice of the parties concerning the application of the treaty that reflects agreement among the parties concerning the treaty's interpretation; and (5) any applicable rules of international law that apply to the parties (see Article 31(2)–(3)). In addition to this contextual guidance, it is generally accepted at the international level that treaties are to be treated as living documents. In other words, they are to be interpreted in the context of the time in which they are being applied, and not as they would have been interpreted at the time of their drafting. Compare this to U.S. constitutional law, where "originalists" argue that the U.S. Constitution should be interpreted in keeping with the expectations of the Framers at the time of its drafting without taking into account subsequent cultural, legal, and political developments.

In addition to the primary means of treaty interpretation, the Vienna Convention lists the treaty's *travaux préparatoires* (drafting history) as a supplementary means of interpretation where a textual interpretation leads to ambiguity, obscurity, or unreasonable results (Article 32). All ICL treaties have published drafting histories that can be useful for understanding the intentions of the parties, the meaning of particular treaty terms, and the reach of the treaty. These records are particularly valuable in historical justice cases adjudicating crimes committed well in the past, because they can elucidate the state of ICL at the time historical abuses occurred. The ICC Statute in particular has generated a small library of works aimed at explaining the origins and meanings of its many provisions.[23] A tension often arises, however, in effectuating the apparent intentions of treaty drafters—primarily states that may engage in political compromises to protect themselves from any potential treaty liability—and the higher purposes of a treaty, which may undermine sovereign interests.

Some scholars have raised the question of whether the basic canons of treaty law should be modified in the case of international human rights treaties, given the fact that the beneficiaries of such treaties tend to be individuals and not states. The argument is that because treaties are meant to benefit individuals directly, they should be interpreted with that overarching purpose in mind. This argues for a mode of interpretation less focused on the intentions of the state parties (which may be to protect state sovereignty) and more on the overall or articulated purpose of the treaty, as may be gleaned from its preamble, for example. Similar arguments have been raised with respect to ICL treaties, although as noted earlier, the fact that ICL treaties may be applied in the penal context raises special concerns with respect to the principle of NCSL and the imperative of specificity in criminal law.

An example of a tribunal taking a purposive approach to treaty interpretation is the ICTY's interpretation of the term "national" found in the 1949 Geneva Conventions, which govern international armed conflicts and protect the nationals of a belligerent's opponents. Article 4 of the Fourth Geneva Convention, which is dedicated to protecting civilians, defines the class of people it protects as "those who, at a given moment and in any manner whatsoever, find themselves, in case of a conflict or occupation, in the hands of a Party to the conflict or Occupying Power *of which they are not nationals*."[24] The ICTY was faced with the prosecution of members of one ethnicity (Bosnian Muslims) for alleged war crimes committed against individuals of the same nationality (Bosnia-Hercegovina) but of different ethnicity (Bosnian Serbs). The defendants challenged the prosecution, arguing that because all of the parties were of the same nationality, the Geneva Conventions did not apply and the charges needed to be dismissed. The Appeals Chamber rejected this argument, noting that the object and purpose of the Geneva Conventions is to protect civilians who are captured by a party to which they owe no allegiance and that owes them no duties of

---

[23] *See, e.g.*, THE LEGISLATIVE HISTORY OF THE INTERNATIONAL CRIMINAL COURT (M. Cherif Bassiouni & William A. Schabas eds., 2016); FANNY BENEDETTI, KARINE BONNEAU, & JOHN L. WASHBURN, NEGOTIATING THE INTERNATIONAL CRIMINAL COURT: NEW YORK TO ROME, 1994–1998 (2014); COMMENTARY ON THE ROME STATUTE OF THE INTERNATIONAL CRIMINAL COURT: OBSERVERS' NOTES, ARTICLE BY ARTICLE (Otto Triffterer & Kai Ambos eds., 3d ed. 2016).

[24] Geneva Convention Relative to the Protection of Civilian Persons in Time of War art. 4, Aug. 12, 1949, 76 U.N.T.S. 287 (emphasis added).

protection based on citizenship. The fact that the parties in the conflict in the former Yugoslavia divided along ethnicity rather than nationality should not, the tribunal reasoned, result in the inapplicability of the Geneva Conventions.[25] In this way, the ICTY ignored the plain text of the treaty and instead resorted to its object and purpose to redefine a key term that is the lynchpin of the Conventions' grave breaches regime.

Although treaties have the benefit of offering relative certainty concerning the relevant rules of decision, treaties can also freeze the law in place at the time they are completed and opened for signature. For this reason, the drafters of the ICC Statute in Article 121 envisioned the possibility of amending the Rome Statute to account for the evolution of ICL. State parties have availed themselves of this opportunity several times: adding the definition of the crime of aggression; enabling certain war crimes—involving the use of specified weapons and starvation as a weapon of war—to be prosecuted in non-international armed conflicts in addition to international armed conflicts; and adding new war crimes involving weapons that cause superfluous injury. Furthermore, state parties removed Article 124 of the Statute, which had allowed states to "opt out" of war crimes jurisdiction for a period of seven years. The Article was always meant to be a transitional provision that, it was hoped, would facilitate the ability of certain states to join the Court, thus contributing to universality. The objective was to give states that considered themselves to be disproportionally vulnerable to war crimes charges (due, for example, to their high overseas troop commitments or regular involvement in sending peacekeepers into humanitarian crises) time to assess the performance of the Court before opening themselves up to potential prosecution. Ultimately, only two states availed themselves of this possibility—France and Colombia—and it was eliminated from the Statute in 2016.

The inclusion of the definition of the crime of aggression marks the most far-reaching amendment to the Statute to date. At the 2010 Review Conference held in Kampala, Uganda, states adopted a set of "Understandings" alongside the new treaty text defining the crime and setting out its jurisdictional regime.[26] The definition provides that the crime of aggression is committed when certain state officials plan, prepare, initiate, or execute "an act of aggression which, by its character, gravity, and scale, constitutes a manifest violation of the Charter of the United Nations." Two of the Understandings seek to clarify that the term "manifest" in this definition refers to "the most

[25] *Prosecutor v. Delalić, Mucić, Delić & Landžo*, Case No. IT-96-21-A, Judgment (Feb. 20, 2001).

[26] *See* U.N. Res. RC/Res.6, Annex III (June 11, 2010, https://treaties.un.org/doc/source/docs/RC-Res.6-ENG.pdf.

serious and dangerous form of the illegal use of force" and that a determination of whether an act of aggression has been committed should take into account "the gravity of the acts concerned and their consequences" as well as the character and scale of the state's conduct. This language was included at the behest of states that wanted to preserve the ability to engage in humanitarian interventions absent Security Council authorization and for the purpose of preventing the commission of other Rome Statute crimes. Two other Understandings address domestic jurisdiction and indicate that the amendments should not be interpreted as creating a right or obligation to prosecute the crime in national courts. It remains to be seen what force or effect these Understandings have, particularly given the Vienna Convention's schema for interpreting treaties.[27]

It is tempting to rely exclusively on treaties when looking for ICL because they provide a concrete text with which to work. These treaties, however, rarely mirror comprehensive criminal codes in their specificity, scope, or depth. As a result, courts and litigants engaged in the enforcement of ICL often look to customary international law as another important source of applicable law.

B. Customary International Law

Customary international law is a second major source of public international law, and is consequently an important source of applicable rules even as ICL is increasingly codified. Customary international law consists of two elements: (1) collective state practice (2) undertaken out of a sense of legal right or obligation.[28] This formula thus comprises an objective element (state practice) and a subjective element (*opinio juris* or *iuris*). State conduct—which includes the exercise of executive, legislative, judicial and other functions—undertaken out of convenience, habit, or expediency in and of itself does not give rise to customary international law.[29] Such conduct must be carried out with the perception that it is or should be required by law. Inaction may also constitute practice. As confirmed by the RESTATEMENT (THIRD) OF THE FOREIGN RELATIONS LAW OF THE UNITED STATES: "[i]naction may constitute state practice, as when a state acquiesces in acts of another state that affect its legal

---

[27] *See* Kevin Jon Heller, *The Uncertain Legal Status of the Aggression Understandings*, 9 J. INT'L CRIM. JUST. 229 (2011).

[28] *See generally* Report of the International Law Commission Seventieth Session (30 April–1 June and 2 July–10 August 2018), U.N. Doc A/73/10 (Advance), Supp. No. 10, at ¶ 65 (2018) (setting forth 16 conclusions on CIL formation).

[29] Legality of the Threat or Use of Nuclear Weapons (Advisory Opinion), 1996 I.C.J. 226, ¶ 67 (July 8) (finding that the non-use of nuclear weapons coupled with an articulated policy of holding weapons for the purpose of deterrence did not support the finding of *opinio juris* against the use of nuclear weapons).

rights."[30] That said, whether this public silence on the part of states can be deemed acquiescence, or even a demonstration of affirmative *opinio juris*, remains a doctrinal controversy in international law.[31]

When balancing these two elements, some scholars and jurists give more emphasis to the objective element, arguing that one can imply the subjective element if there is near-universal state practice (which may also include the practice of international organizations).[32] Others focus more on the subjective element, arguing that normative and aspirational statements in themselves can create law, even in the face of contrary or inconsistent state practice. This latter position becomes more defensible to the extent one can argue that discursive diplomatic practices themselves constitute state practice. Many jurists rely more heavily on apparent expressions of *opinio juris* when human rights are at issue. The prohibition against torture offers a useful exemplar. Although torture is still practiced in many parts of the world, almost no state argues that it has the right to commit torture and states will regularly deny the commission of torture when so accused. The ICJ thus determined that the prohibition against torture—even though the crime is committed and still only rarely prosecuted—is part of CIL.[33]

Customary international law, with its emphasis on states' conduct and subjective views, reflects the general international law principle of state consent. Thus, according to a doctrine that remains controversial, states may "opt out" of a rule of customary international law if they become *persistent objectors* as the rule is being formed and when it is invoked. A state persistently objects by making clear that it does not agree with an emerging rule of customary international law. More than silence is required to become a persistent objector. For example, the United States has succeeded in consistently and continuously making clear its objection to the emergence of a rule prohibiting capital punishment under international law. The U.S. objection has manifested itself through the continued legalization of capital punishment under domestic law (federal and state) and clear official statements opposing any

---

30 *See* RESTATEMENT (THIRD) OF THE FOREIGN RELATIONS LAW OF THE UNITED STATES § 102, cmt. (b) (AM. LAW INST. 1987).

31 Michael N. Schmitt & Sean Watts, *State* Opinio Juris *and International Humanitarian Law Pluralism*, 91 INT'L L. STUD. 171 (2015) (urging States to articulate *opinio juris* or risk the crystallization of norms in their silence).

32 *Prosecutor v. Fofana & Kondewa*, Case No. SCSL-2004-14-A, Judgment, ¶ 405 (May 28, 2008) (finding that three military manuals do not constitute sufficient state practice for the proposition that the war crime of pillage includes the destruction (*vice* appropriation) of property).

33 Questions Relating to the Obligation to Prosecute or Extradite (Belgium v. Senegal), 2012 I.C.J. 422, ¶ 99 (July 20).

suggestion that capital punishment is now prohibited under international human rights law. Such statements appear, for example, in reservations the United States has attached to international treaties restricting or prohibiting the use of capital punishment.

The one major exception to this general rule of state consent concerns *peremptory norms* of international law (so-called *jus cogens*), from which no state may opt out.[34] The prohibitions against some of the worst crimes under international law—such as slavery, genocide, and crimes against humanity—constitute *jus cogens* ("compelling law"). Unlike customary international law, states may not opt out of a *jus cogens* rule. Rules of *jus cogens* occupy an uneasy place in an international legal system that emphasizes positive law-making and state consent. Indeed, *jus cogens* offer the clearest manifestation of the natural law origins of international law.

As should be clear, confusion may arise concerning state action that conflicts with a rule of customary international law: Is the state objecting to an emerging rule or violating an existing rule? In the alternative, is the non-conforming conduct indicative of a weakening or evolution of the rule or the lack of a customary rule altogether? The key, of course, is whether the rule in question is emerging or established, a determination that is difficult to make, as the date at which an emerging rule of customary international law "crystallizes" is often unclear. A focus on articulations of *opinio juris*—what states say they believe the rule to be—can be of assistance in this regard. The risk, however, is that *opinio juris* can represent *lex lata* (the law as it is) or *lex ferenda* (the law as it should be).[35] In other words, an official statement about a rule of international law may be more aspirational than descriptive. The challenge, then, is to determine whether the expressions of *opinio juris* accurately reflect the state of the law, or are instead expressions of what the government in question would like the law to be.

Paradoxically, treaties can provide evidence of CIL. Indeed, as ICL treaties approach universal ratification and give rise to consistent state practice accepted as law, those rules may become binding on all states as a form of CIL (unless a state has established

---

[34] Vienna Convention, *supra*, at art. 53 ("A treaty is void if, at the time of its conclusion, it conflicts with a peremptory norm of general international law. For the purposes of the present Convention, a peremptory norm of general international law is a norm accepted and recognized by the international community of States as a whole as a norm from which no derogation is permitted and which can be modified only by a subsequent norm of general international law having the same character.").

[35] Anthea Elizabeth Roberts, *Traditional and Modern Approaches to Customary International Law: A Reconciliation*, 95 AM. J. INT'L L. 757, 763 (2001).

itself as a persistent objector).[36] The tribunals vary on whether they consider such treaties, including the Rome Statute, to be a form of state practice or evidence of *opinio juris*.[37] That said, the architects of the Rome Statute were wary of that treaty being cited as proof of CIL and so provided at Article 10 a disclaimer of sorts: "Nothing in this Part shall be interpreted as limiting or prejudicing in any way existing or developing rules of international law for purposes other than this Statute."

As you study the ICL field, consider the role that customary international law plays in the opinions you read. Because custom is not legislated *per se*, but rather forms through practice and articulations of *opinio juris*, it is often the courts that end up articulating the scope of the rule in question. In this regard, it is possible to envision customary international law being invoked in four primary ways: (1) as the source of a substantive rule criminalizing certain acts or forms of responsibility, or providing a defense to criminal liability; (2) to fill gaps in a treaty-created prohibition; (3) as a guide to interpreting an otherwise applicable rule of law; and (4) as confirmation that certain activity was criminalized at the time it was committed where an applicable treaty prohibition is silent as to the existence of individual criminal responsibility.

With respect to the first option, even though the existing international tribunals impose criminal liability pursuant to their constitutive statutes, they often invoke customary international law. For example, the ICTY was mandated to only prosecute those crimes and forms of responsibility prohibited by customary international law or by a treaty applicable to the former Yugoslavia.[38] Article 3 of the ICTY Statute accordingly granted jurisdiction over "violations of the laws or customs of war" and contained an open-ended list of war crimes (drawn from the 1909 Hague Convention, which by its own terms applies only to international armed conflicts). The ICTY

---

36 *Prosecutor v. Hadžihasanović et al.*, Case No. ICTY-01-47-AR72, Decision on Interlocutory Appeal Challenging Jurisdiction in Relation to Command Responsibility, ¶¶ 37–40 (July 16, 2003) (looking to the Rome Statute and Additional Protocol II to determine the customary law reach of the doctrine of superior responsibility in non-international armed conflicts).

37 *Compare Prosecutor v. Krnojelac*, Case No. ICTY-97-25-A, Judgement, ¶ 221 (Sept. 17, 2003) (treating the promulgation and entry into force of the Rome Statute as evidence of state practice) *with Prosecutor v. Furundžija*, Case No. ICTY-95-17/1-T, Judgement, ¶ 227 (Dec. 10, 1998) (treating the Rome Statute as "constituting an authoritative expression of the legal views of a great number of States"). *But see Prosecutor v. Orić*, Case No. ICTY-03-68-A, Partially Dissenting Opinion and Declaration of Judge Liu, ¶ 26 (July 3, 2008) (reasoning that the Rome Statute cannot be cited as evidence of CIL since it was finalized after the events under prosecution occurred).

38 Report of the Secretary-General Pursuant to Paragraph 2 of the Security Council Resolution 808, ¶ 34 (May 3, 1993).

invoked Article 3 to import the customary international law of war crimes into the subject matter jurisdiction of the ICTY across the conflict classification spectrum. It also referred to customary international law to identify forms of responsibility not listed in its statute, such as joint criminal enterprise.[39]

By contrast, the ICC Statute contains fewer open-ended provisions. A notable exception is found in Article 31(3), which allows defendants to invoke grounds for excluding criminal responsibility (e.g., excuses, justifications, and defenses) other than those provided for in the Statute "where such a ground is derived from applicable law as set forth in article 21." Otherwise, the ICC has resisted the ICTY's more liberal approach to invoking CIL and has generally applied its own Statute to the exclusion of CIL, without ruling on whether the statutory terms reflect existing custom.[40] For example, an ICC Pre-Trial Chamber refused to apply modes of criminal liability that have previously been deemed part of CIL, limiting itself to the closed list of forms of responsibility contained within the ICC Statute at Article 25. Acknowledging that the ICTY and other *ad hoc* tribunals had all followed CIL, the Chamber cautioned: "This is a good example of the need not to transfer the *ad hoc* tribunals' case law mechanically to the system of the Court."[41]

However, in a 2019 ruling involving the then-President of Sudan, Omar Al Bashir, the ICC Appeals Chamber determined that there was no impediment to member states arresting individuals indicted by the Court, including heads of state who would otherwise enjoy immunity from states' enforcement or adjudicative jurisdiction. Rather than relying upon the fact that the U.N. Security Council referred the matter to the Court, which would arguably generate Charter-based duties on the part of all U.N. member states to cooperate with the investigation, the Chamber instead determined that there was no rule of CIL affording head of state immunity before international—as opposed to domestic—courts. As such, it

---

39 *Compare Prosecutor v. Prlić et al.*, Case No. IT-04-74-T, Judgement, ¶¶ 206–10 (May 29, 2013) (finding the theory of joint criminal enterprise within customary international law), *with Co-Prosecutors v. Ieng Sary et al.*, Case No. 0002/19-09-2007-ECCC/OCIJ, Decision on the Appeals against the Co-Investigator Judges' Order on Joint Criminal Enterprise (JCE), ¶¶ 69–82 (May 20, 2010) (rejecting the argument that one form of the doctrine was part of CIL during the Khmer Rouge era (1975–79)).

40 *Prosecutor v. Katanga & Ngudjolo*, Case No. ICC-01/04-01/07-717, Decision on the Confirmation of Charges, ¶ 508 (Sept. 30, 2008) ("since the Rome Statute expressly provides for this specific mode of liability [co-perpetration through another person (indirect co-perpetration)], the question as to whether customary law admits or discards the 'joint commission through another person' is not relevant for this Court.").

41 *Id.*

determined that there was no impediment to Jordan arresting Al Bashir when he was on its sovereign territory.[42]

The ICC also found it instructive to look to what "territorial" jurisdiction encompasses within CIL—as reflected in states' assertion of jurisdiction over events committed abroad but that cause harm on their territories—to rule in 2019 that the Prosecutor can investigate acts of violence against the Rohingya people of Myanmar that result in cross border harm or otherwise have a transnational dimension. While Myanmar has not ratified the ICC Statute, neighboring Bangladesh—where upwards of a million Rohingya survivors have sought refuge—has.[43] In addition, when the Court is proceeding against a defendant whose state has not ratified the treaty or had not ratified it at the time the defendant acted (e.g., in connection with the exercise of territorial jurisdiction over a non-national), arguably the Court may be applying CIL rather than treaty law.

This direct application of customary international law is in marked contrast to domestic courts, which rarely apply customary international law directly in penal proceedings. U.S. courts, for example, have applied customary international law to impose *civil* liability on individuals who have violated international criminal law (under the Alien Tort Statute), but have not invoked customary international law to impose *criminal* liability. Indeed, the U.S. Supreme Court abolished most federal common law crimes (i.e., crimes that were not codified) in 1812.[44] One notable exception is found with the crime of piracy, which is still defined in Title 18 with reference to international law. Specifically, 18 U.S.C. § 1651 provides, "Whoever, on the high seas, commits the crime of piracy as defined by the law of nations, and is afterwards brought into or found in the United States, shall be imprisoned for life."[45]

The second way in which CIL may be invoked is to supplement and fill *lacunae* in treaty law, for example to establish the elements of an offense enumerated in a statute or treaty. In the *Čelebići* case before the ICTY, defendants moved for the dismissal of the counts that alleged the commission of "wilfully causing great suffering or serious injury to body or health," "inhuman treatment," and "cruel treatment" on the ground that they were not defined with sufficient specificity under international law to serve as the basis for a criminal

---

42 *Al Bashir, supra*, ¶¶ 1–2.

43 *Situation in the People's Republic of Bangladesh/Republic of the Union of Myanmar*, Case No. ICC-01/19-27, Decision Pursuant to Article 15 of the Rome Statute on the Authorisation of an Investigation into the Situation into the People's Republic of Bangladesh/Republic of the Union of Myanmar, ¶¶ 55–58 (Nov. 14, 2019).

44 *United States v. Hudson and Goodwin*, 11 U.S. 32 (1812).

45 *See United States v. Ali*, 718 F.3d 929 (D.C. Cir. 2013).

prosecution.[46] In rejecting the defense and convicting the defendants, an ICTY Trial Chamber added content to its Statute by relying on the Geneva Conventions' drafting history, the discussions within human rights institutions concerning analogous provisions in human rights treaties addressed to state parties and giving rise to state responsibility in their breach, and the overarching principles animating IHL. Likewise, the ICC has interpreted the provisions of Article 8 of its own Statute enumerating serious violations of the laws and customs of war "within the established framework of international law" to mandate consideration of IHL, even when no lacuna exists, to ensure that the treaty is interpreted in a way that is fully consistent with the law of armed conflict.[47] The Statute also empowers the judges to look to any other source of law to determine grounds for excluding criminal responsibility.[48]

In looking to customary international law to "fill gaps" in positive law, courts adjudicating ICL are not particularly rigorous about applying the traditional customary international law formula, which requires a showing of consistent state practice coupled with *opinio juris*. Rather, courts seem willing to overlook or discount contrary state practice and fixate on articulations of *opinio juris* as found in the pronouncements of states and other institutions, including nongovernmental or inter-governmental organizations. Courts may also "double count" discursive practices as both *usus* (practice) and *opinio juris*. Although this untethering of *opinio juris* from state practice is part of much public international law reasoning, it is particularly common in ICL, where the disjunction between the two elements is often so wide.

Third, customary international law can be used as a guide to interpretation. Thus, the ICTY has held that unless the contrary intent is clear from the text of a treaty, the presumption is that the provisions of a treaty are meant to be consistent with customary international law.[49] This interpretive doctrine is similar to that adopted in the United States with respect to international law, where the presumption is that unless the contrary intent is clearly

---

[46] *Prosecutor v. Delalić, Mucić, Delić & Landžo*, Case No. IT-96-21-T, Judgment (Nov. 16, 1998).

[47] *Prosecutor v. Ntaganda*, Case No. ICC-01/04-02/06-1962, Judgment on the Appeal of Mr. Ntaganda against the "Second decision on the Defence's Challenge to the Jurisdiction of the Court in Respect of Counts 6 and 9," ¶ 53 (June 15, 2017).

[48] Rome Statute, *supra*, at art. 31 ("At trial, the Court may consider a ground for excluding criminal responsibility other than those referred to in paragraph 1 where such a ground is derived from applicable law as set forth in article 21.").

[49] *Prosecutor v. Tadić*, Case No. IT-94-1-A, Judgment, ¶ 287 (July 15, 1999) ("in case of doubt and whenever the contrary is not apparent from the text of a statutory or treaty provision, such a provision must be interpreted in light of, and in conformity with, customary international law").

expressed by Congress, statutes are to be interpreted so as not to conflict with international law.[50]

Fourth, many treaties prohibit specific conduct, but do not clearly render that conduct criminal by mandating the imposition of individual penal responsibility in the event of a breach. The ICTY looked to customary international law to conclude that violations of common Article 3 of the 1949 Geneva Conventions—the only provision in that treaty governing non-international armed conflicts—gave rise to individual criminal responsibility, even though that provision is silent as to applicable remedies and implies only the civil responsibility of state parties to the treaty (and perhaps non-state actors involved in a non-international armed conflict).[51]

A more controversial use of customary international law to confirm an ICL prohibition can be seen in the 2004 decision involving the recruitment of child soldiers brought before the Special Court for Sierra Leone (SCSL).[52] The Statute of the SCSL penalized the enlistment, recruitment, or use of child soldiers committed during the overlapping conflicts in Sierra Leone. The question facing the SCSL was whether child recruitment was criminalized in 1996 when the acts subject to the prosecution were committed. The majority reasoned that such a CIL rule did, in fact, exist. In so concluding, it cited the existence in 1996 of rules from numerous states governing the minimum age of conscription, the drafting history of the ICC Statute, and human rights treaties aimed at prohibiting the recruitment and enlistment of child soldiers for support.

Judge Geoffrey Robertson (of the United Kingdom) in dissent disagreed, concluding that there was simply not enough evidence to support the assertion that child recruitment had been criminalized at the time asserted by the majority. He argued that the crime of enlisting or using child soldiers did not fully crystallize until the promulgation of the ICC Statute in 1998, which clearly lists such conduct as a war crime. Judge Robertson took issue with the majority for conflating abhorrent conduct with criminal conduct, arguing that "it is precisely when the acts are abhorrent and deeply shocking that the principle of legality must be most stringently applied, to ensure that the defendant is not convicted out of disgust rather than evidence, or of a non-existent crime."[53] Given that Sierra Leonean law did not prohibit child recruitment, Judge Robertson argued that there was no way for the embattled defendants to reasonably

---

[50] *The Charming Betsy*, 6 U.S. 64 (1804).

[51] *Prosecutor v. Tadić*, Case No. IT-94-1-AR92, Decision on the Defence Motion for Interlocutory Appeal on Jurisdiction, ¶ 134 (Oct. 2, 1995).

[52] *Prosecutor v. Norman*, Case No. SCSL-2004-14-AR72(E), Decision on Preliminary Motion Based on Lack of Jurisdiction (May 31, 2004).

[53] *Id.* ¶ 12 (Sep. Op. Robertson J.).

ascertain, through competent legal advice, that they were committing a crime when they enlisted and recruited child soldiers. He concluded that, however "inconvenient" the result, NCSL compelled the dismissal of the challenged charge.

As the discussion above indicates, customary international law played a very important role in the development of ICL. Its role, however, is not without controversy given the uncertainty that exists about the existence and content of any rule of CIL. CIL opens the door to creativity by advocates, judges, and others—creativity that, if taken too far, can transform from stating the law as it is into creating new law. In the context of international criminal law, with its appropriate concern for the rights of defendants, including ensuring in advance the clarity of applicable legal prohibitions, the consequences of taking this creativity too far is particularly worrisome. That said, we do not feel that the incorporation of customary international law has been abused by the international tribunals. As should be clear from the above, we think there are a number of appropriate places where customary international law can play a crucial role in supporting a just international criminal system.

C. General Principles of Law

The third source of international law identified in Article 38 of the ICJ Statute—general principles of law—is the least developed of the three. Article 38 refers to "general principles of law recognized by civilized nations." The modifier "civilized nations" has been effectively dropped as an arcane, and even offensive, qualification. Instead, the term "general principles of law" is interpreted to refer to general principles found in the major legal systems of the world. Two judges on the ICTY Appeals Chamber, explained their methodology as follows:

> Our approach will necessarily not involve a direct comparison of the specific rules of each of the world's legal systems, but will instead involve a survey of those jurisdictions whose jurisprudence is, as a practical matter, accessible to us in an effort to discern a general trend, policy or principle underlying the concrete rules of that jurisdiction which comports with the object and purpose of the establishment of the International Tribunal.[54]

The ICTY identified three groupings of states in discussing general principles of law concerning duress[55] as a defense against

---

[54] *Prosecutor v. Erdemović*, Case No. IT-96-22-A, Joint Separate Opinion of Judge McDonald and Judge Vohrah, ¶ 57 (Oct. 7, 1997).

[55] The defense of duress operates to excuse criminal behavior when the actor faces an immediate and well-grounded threat of death or serious injury and the actor

prosecution for war crimes and crimes against humanity: (1) civil law systems; (2) common law systems; and (3) the catch-all "criminal law of other states," under which was grouped the vastly different legal systems of Japan, China, Morocco, Somalia, and Ethiopia.[56] In practice, however, judges mostly look at common law and civil law systems to discern applicable rules, raising questions about selectivity and representation given that some legal systems do not fit neatly into these two categories.

It is important not to confuse general principles of law with customary international law, although sometimes the evidence used to prove the one may also prove the other. Customary international law requires *opinio juris*—a requirement not found in general principles of law—and customary international law consists of rules that states adopt as rules of international law. General principles of law, on the other hand, consist of commonalities found in different legal systems that are not necessarily thought of by the states adopting or relying on them as deriving from international law.

One of the earliest references in the field of ICL to the applicability of general principles of law is found in the arguments at Nuremberg justifying the inclusion of crimes against humanity as a crime within that tribunal's jurisdiction. The prosecutors at Nuremberg argued that crimes against humanity constitute, "in the last analysis, nothing less than the preparation for political ends and in a systematic manner, of common law crimes such as theft, looting, ill treatment, enslavement, murders, and assassinations, crimes that are provided for and punishable under the penal laws of all civilized states."[57] In ICL today, general principles of law encompass those principles that are common to most criminal legal systems and those principles considered inherent to the international legal system or to any system of criminal justice (e.g., the principle of equality of arms). The first concept incorporates an expressly comparative law approach; the second is deduced from the overall object and purpose of ICL.

General principles of law have been used to define the elements of the constitutive acts of crimes against humanity and war crimes, such as murder or rape, that are common to domestic legal systems. The question before the ICTY Trial Chamber in the *Furundžija* case, for example, concerned the definition of rape under international law. Furundžija had been charged with rape as a war crime for forcing a woman to engage in oral sex. The law of the former

has no reasonable opportunity for escape, except by committing the unlawful act. Duress is rarely available as a defense to the charge of murder or other serious crimes.

56 *Id.* ¶ 61.

57 *The Trial of German Major War Criminals: Proceedings of the International Military Tribunal Sitting at Nuremberg, Germany*, Part 4, p. 34.

Yugoslavia treated such conduct as sexual assault—a lesser crime—rather than rape. The Tribunal surveyed the definition of rape found in many national legal systems and discerned a trend toward broadening the definition of rape to include acts previously classified as less serious offenses. Supplementing its more empirical and comparative approach, the Trial Chamber also referred to the object and purpose of humanitarian law and human rights law (to protect and promote human dignity) to find that the charged conduct at issue constituted rape under ICL.[58]

There are times when no clear or consensus rule can be discerned from the world's legal systems. In such situations of *non liquet* ("it is not clear"), international criminal tribunals will take a more teleological (purposive) approach to discern an applicable general rule. As just noted, the Trial Chamber in *Furundžija* adopted a teleological approach to confirm the rule it derived from looking at a wide range of national legal systems. As another example, the ICTY had to determine how to address situations of concurrent convictions for the same underlying conduct. The domestic law of states (also referred to as municipal law), it turned out, dealt with this situation in a variety of ways, and no clear trend was apparent. The Trial Chamber then resorted to international practice and the object and purpose of ICL, stating: "Faced with this discrepancy in municipal legal systems, the Trial Chamber considers that a fair solution can be derived both from the object and purpose of the provisions of the Statute and from 'the general principles of justice applied by jurists and practiced by military courts' referred to by the International Military Tribunal at Nuremberg."[59] It thus adopted this more teleological approach and concluded that if by a single act or omission an accused person has perpetrated two or more distinct offenses under the ICTY Statute, the Trial Chamber can enter two separate convictions under the relevant counts of the indictment; any sentence, however, would run concurrently.

Whereas the *ad hoc* tribunals have drawn on general principles as a source of law, Article 21 of the Statute of the ICC makes clear that such general principles are a tertiary source of law within that legal system. The primary sources of law are the Court's Statute, its Elements of Crimes, and its Rules of Procedure and Evidence. Secondarily, the Court is to apply, "where appropriate, applicable treaties and the principles and rules of international law." It is presumed that the "rules of international law" include customary international law, although the precise term is inexplicably not

---

[58] *Prosecutor v. Furundžija*, Case No. IT-95-17/1-T, Judgement, ¶¶ 182–183 (Dec. 10, 1998).

[59] *Prosecutor v. Kupreškić*, Case No. IT-95-16-T, Judgement, ¶ 717 (Jan. 14, 2000).

employed. Finally, if none of the previous two categories provides a clear rule of decision, the Court is empowered to look at "general principles of law derived by the Court from national laws of legal systems of the world including, as appropriate, the national laws of States that would normally exercise jurisdiction over the crime, provided that those principles are not inconsistent with this Statute and with international law and internationally recognized norms and standards."

Although only a tertiary source, the Court has on occasion resorted to general principles of law in an effort to resolve issues before it. For example, the Appeals Chamber rejected a request to disqualify defense counsel who had previously worked for the Office of the Prosecutor, noting that the prosecution had cited only five jurisdictions in support of its claim that a general principle exists supporting such disqualification.[60] Likewise, in ruling on victims participation petitions, a Pre-Trial Chamber held that it is a general principle of law "that the burden of proof of elements supporting a claim lies on the party making the claim" and that "indirect proof" is admissible.[61]

So far, the Court has been reluctant to engage the law of the state that would normally exercise jurisdiction over the case at bar, notwithstanding that Article 21 invites it to do so as a tertiary source of law. In the Kenya situation, for example, the Court applied a presumption in the Rules and declined to allow an oral hearing on a matter even though Kenyan law would have mandated it.[62] It remains to be seen which states' laws are most relevant to any particular factual matrix. By virtue of either treaty obligations or customary international law, most ICC crimes are today subject to universal jurisdiction (either mandatory or permissive); as a result, the law of all states could arguably be relevant to this inquiry. In practice, however, it is likely that the Court would look to either the territorial or nationality state's law as most pertinent.

Other international tribunals were explicitly empowered to apply certain domestic law directly (and not as general principles of law). The SCSL had jurisdiction over some Sierra Leonean domestic crimes—including crimes of sexual violence and wanton destruction

---

[60] *Prosecutor v. Nourain & Jerbo Jamus*, Case No. ICC-02/05-03/09-252 OA, Judgment on the Appeal of the Prosecutor Against the Decision of Trial Chamber IV of 30 June 2011 entitled 'Decision on the Prosecution's Request to Invalidate the Appointment of Counsel to the Defence', ¶ 33 (Nov. 11, 2011).

[61] *Prosecutor v. Kony et al.*, Case No. ICC-02/04-01/05, Decision on Victims' Applications for Participation a/0010/06, a/006406 to a/0070/06, a/0081/06 to a/0104/06 and a/0111/06 to a/0127/06, ¶¶ 13–15 (Aug. 10, 2007).

[62] *Prosecutor v. Muthaura, Kenyatta, and Hussein Ali*, Case No. ICC-01/09-02/11 OA 4, Decision on the 'Request to Make Oral Submissions on Jurisdiction under Rule 156(3).' ¶ 11 (May 1, 2012).

of property—by virtue of its statute.[63] The SCSL, ICTY, and International Criminal Tribunal for Rwanda (ICTR)—which all exercised jurisdiction over a sovereign territory—also had "recourse to the general practice regarding prison sentences" in the relevant national courts of those territories.[64] National courts will ordinarily apply their own national law to the extent that international crimes have been specifically incorporated into their penal codes.

D. Judicial Decisions

International law generally does not follow the doctrine of *stare decisis*—the doctrine or policy of following rules laid down in previous judicial decisions except under extraordinary circumstances. The Statute of the ICJ, for example, clearly states at Article 59: "[T]he decision of the Court has no binding force except between the parties and in respect of that particular case." ICL is no different. Although trial chambers (the courts of first instance) must follow the rulings of their corresponding appellate chambers, they need not necessarily follow their own prior rulings or the rulings of their sister chambers. Moreover, judicial decisions are not formally binding across international criminal tribunals. Thus, the different ICL systems (e.g., the ICTY, the ICTR, and the ICC) are not bound by each other's precedent except insofar as the ICTY and ICTR shared an Appeals Chamber. The Statute of the SCSL was generally consistent with this, though it did provide at Article 20(3) that "[t]he judges of the Appeals Chamber of the Special Court shall be guided by the decisions of the Appeals Chamber of the International Tribunals for the former Yugoslavia and for Rwanda." Likewise, domestic tribunals are not bound, as a formal matter, to the rulings of international tribunals and *vice versa* except insofar as those rulings are deemed CIL and CIL is directly applicable within the domestic system.

In rejecting *stare decisis*, the international system is more akin to a civil, rather than common, law system. As the ICTY noted in one decision, "generally speaking, and subject to the binding force of decisions of the Tribunal's Appeals Chamber upon the Trial Chambers, the International Tribunal cannot uphold the doctrine of binding precedent (*stare decisis*) adhered to in common law countries."[65] Civil law systems eschew the rigid version of *stare decisis* on the ground that it is for the legislature, and not the courts, to make law. That said, even civil law systems privilege uniformity,

---

[63] Statute of the Special Court for Sierra Leone art. 5, annex, Special Court Agreement 2002 (Ratification) Act (2002), Supp. to the Sierra Leone Gazette Vol. CXXXIII, No. 22 (Apr. 25, 2002).

[64] *Id.* at art. 19.

[65] *See, e.g., Prosecutor v. Kupreškić*, Case No. IT-95-16-T, Judgment, ¶ 540 (Jan. 14, 2000).

judicial efficiency, and predictability in judicial pronouncements, and some systems recognize that legal rulings can become binding "jurisprudence" if they are followed on a sufficient number of occasions.

Despite the fact that *stare decisis* is not formally recognized in ICL, both the *ad hoc* international criminal tribunals drew heavily on their previous jurisprudence for identifying rules of decision. The ICTY and ICTR regularly cited to their earlier decisions for general principles of law, thus creating a consistent and coherent jurisprudence. Indeed, a whole range of judicial decisions emerging from domestic and international tribunals are regularly cited by ICL tribunals as persuasive authority, and observers would be forgiven for mistaking these citations as operating like formal precedent in a common law system. This no doubt reflects the fact that *stare decisis* is deemed critical for establishing the legitimacy, predictability, and consistency of the law.

For example, as noted above, the Statute of the SCSL required the Special Court to be "guided" by the jurisprudence of the ICTY/ICTR Appeals Chamber. In fact the SCSL appears to have generally followed, and regularly cited to, both the Appeals Chamber and many Trial Chamber decisions of the ICTY and ICTR. One notable exception was the SCSL's rejection of the controversial "specific direction" jurisprudence of the ICTY Appeals Chamber in the *Perišić* case (concerning aiding and abetting liability). In rejecting this jurisprudence, the SCSL noted:

> In examining this reasoning in terms of its persuasive value, however, the Appeals Chamber notes that the ICTY Appeals Chamber's jurisprudence does not contain a clear, detailed analysis of the authorities supporting the conclusion that "specific direction" is an element of the *actus reus* of aiding and abetting liability under customary international law.[66]

Another example is the SCSL's rejection of the ICTY Appeals Chamber decision in *Hadžihasanović* restricting superior responsibility to those subordinates who were under the superior's effective control at the time of the criminal act. Instead, the SCSL concluded that this interpretation was inconsistent with the provisions of Additional Protocol I to the Geneva Conventions that governed the issue.[67] In addition to mostly adopting and following

---

[66] *Prosecutor v. Charles Ghankay Taylor*, Case No. SCSL-03-01-A, Judgment, ¶ 477 (Sept. 26, 2013),

[67] *Prosecutor v. Issa Hassan Sesay, Morris Kallon, and Augustine Gbao*, Case No. SCSL-04-15-T, Judgment ¶ 304 (March 2, 2009). In doing so, the SCSL cited the subsequent ICTY Appeals Chamber decision in *Orić* which criticized the Appeals Chamber decision in *Hadžihasanović*.

the jurisprudence of the ICTY/ICTR Appeals Chamber, the SCSL was also guided by, and generally followed, the jurisprudence of the Special Tribunal for Lebanon (STL) and the Extraordinary Chambers in the Courts of Cambodia (ECCC). For example, the SCSL rejected the ICTY jurisprudence that allows convictions for specific intent crimes like genocide and persecution as a crime against humanity under the third version of joint criminal enterprise (JCE III).[68] In so doing, the SCSL adopted the jurisprudence of the STL, which rejected JCE III liability for specific intent crimes.[69]

Under the ICC Statute, the Court "*may* apply principles and rules of law as interpreted in its previous decisions" (Article 21(2), emphasis added). The ICC has acknowledged that "while the Appeals Chamber has discretion to depart from its previous jurisprudence, it will not readily do so, given the need to ensure predictability of the law and the fairness of adjudication to foster public reliance on its decisions."[70] Nonetheless, the Chamber dramatically deviated from its prior jurisprudence—and arguably the CIL and general principles of law devoted to the standard of review on appeal and the degree of deference owed to trial chambers—when it ruled that it could "interfere with the factual findings of the first-instance chamber whenever the failure to interfere may occasion a miscarriage of justice."[71] The Appeals Chamber thus substituted its own judgment for that of the Trial Chamber and acquitted the defendant—an outcome that generated sharp controversy.

The ICC judges have also made clear—not without controversy—that they are not bound or even persuaded by the rulings of the *ad hoc* tribunals that preceded them. They have, however, on occasion cited to those decisions without always clearly indicating where they fit within the ICC's sources doctrine. For instance, in determining the meaning of "sufficient gravity" as part of an admissibility consideration under Article 17, a Pre-Trial Chamber of the ICC looked to the rules and practice of the *ad hoc* tribunals concerning case selection. The Chamber did not treat this precedent as evidence of CIL but rather as "principles and rules of international law" derived from the nature of the ICL legal system,

---

68 JCE III was the most expansive form of the doctrine, allowing for individuals to be prosecuted for foreseeable crimes within the scope of the common plan. We discuss the three different versions of Joint Criminal Enterprise developed by the ICTY in Chapter 10 on Forms of Responsibility.

69 *Prosecutor v. Charles Ghankay Taylor*, Case No. SCSL-03-01-T, Judgment, ¶ 468 (May 18, 2012).

70 *Prosecutor v. Gbabgo & Goudé*, Case No. ICC-02/11-01/15-172 OA 6, Reasons for Recognition of Victims to Participate in Interlocutory Appeal, ¶ 14 (July 31, 2015).

71 *Prosecutor v. Bemba*, Case No. ICC-01/05-01/08-3636-Red, Judgment on the Appeal of Mr. Jean-Pierre Bemba Gombo Against TC III's "Judgment Pursuant to Article 74 of the Statute," ¶ 40 (June 8, 2018).

which suggests that international courts should prosecute only senior leaders responsible for widespread or systematic criminality.[72] In other opinions, jurisprudence from other courts was considered either a source of CIL or evidence of CIL:

> Where the founding texts do not specifically resolve a particular issue, the Chamber must refer to treaty or customary humanitarian law and the general principles of law. To this end, the Chamber may, for example, be required to refer to the jurisprudence of the *ad hoc* tribunals and other courts on the matter.[73]

ICL tribunals also look to domestic court decisions as a source of ICL. With the more frequent assertion by states of universal and other bases of jurisdiction over international crimes, domestic courts are becoming a richer source of ICL jurisprudence. Such decisions are, of course, not binding on international tribunals, but they can be used in a number of ways. First, domestic decisions interpreting ICL may be used as persuasive authority. Second, such decisions are a rich source of general principles of law, which provide an independent source of international law as noted earlier. Third, such decisions provide evidence of state practice and *opinio juris*, and thus can be used as evidence of an emerging or existing principle of customary international law.

E. The Works of Scholars and Publicists

Article 38 of the ICJ Statute also lists "the teachings of the most highly qualified publicists of the various nations" as a subsidiary means for determining rules of international law. Although your law professor may argue otherwise, the works of legal scholars are not sources of law *per se*. Nonetheless, courts may rely on legal scholarship, expert testimony, treatises, and the work of the International Law Commission—itself empowered by states to codify and progressively develop the law[74]—to identify applicable rules of law, especially rules of customary international law or general principles of law that require significant comparative and empirical research to identify and catalog applicable state practice, domestic law, and evidence of *opinio juris*. The U.S. Supreme Court has confirmed the value of "the works of jurists and commentators who by years of labor, research and experience, have made themselves

[72] *Prosecutor v. Lubanga Dyilo*, Case No. ICC-01/04-01/06-8-US-Corr, Decision Concerning Pre-Trial Chamber I's Decision of 10 February 2006 and the Incorporation of Documents into the Record of the Case against Mr. Thomas Lubanga Dyilo, ¶¶ 55–60 (Feb. 24, 2006).

[73] *Prosecutor v. Katanga*, Case No. ICC-01/04-01/07, Judgement Pursuant to Art. 74 of the Statute, ¶ 47 (Mar. 7, 2014).

[74] Statute of the International Law Commission, Article 1(1), annexed to G.A. Res 174 (II) (1947).

peculiarly well acquainted with the subjects of which they treat. Such works are resorted to by judicial tribunals, not for the speculation of their authors concerning what the law ought to be, but for trustworthy evidence of what the law really is."[75] Particularly influential in the ICL realm have been the International Committee of the Red Cross's commentaries on the Geneva Conventions and their Protocols and its CIL Study.[76] That said, as international law becomes increasingly codified, and as courts issue more guiding jurisprudence, there is no question that the influence of publicists has declined over the years.

F. "Soft Law"

The resolutions, declarations, statements, codes of conduct, and records of human rights institutions and other multilateral bodies—such as the U.N. General Assembly, the International Law Commission, or the Committee Against Torture—do not fit squarely in the sources schema contained in the ICJ or ICC Statutes. Indeed, according to the U.N. Charter, General Assembly resolutions do not have the force of law; they are merely recommendatory. These institutions thus do not play any formal role in law generation under the traditional understanding of how international law is made. And yet, they have often been empowered by states to codify international crimes, generate and interpret treaty texts, and hold states accountable for breaches of international law.

Because they are contained within non-binding texts, such pronouncements are not law *per se*. However, they can provide another source of legal or normative principles, especially when they receive unanimous approbation, are passed with a high degree of multilateral consensus, or are declarative of the law. Even if non-binding, such articulations have legal consequences and a compliance pull, because they shape states' expectations as to what constitutes appropriate behavior.

Accordingly, such "soft law" has been relied on by ICL tribunals, either as evidence of state practice, *opinio juris*, or both, or as embodying general principles of law. For example, the post-WWII tribunal in the *Justice Case*, prosecuting Nazi jurists within the U.S. zone of occupation, noted the importance of General Assembly Resolution 96(I) declaring genocide to be an international crime as an expression of an already developed international prohibition of genocide. In this regard, it stated: "The General Assembly is not an

---

[75] *The Paquete Habana*, 175 U.S. 677, 700 (1900).

[76] *See, e.g.*, *Prosecutor v. Martić*, Case No. IT-95-11-T, Judgment, ¶ 71 (June 12, 2007); *Prosecutor v. Stakić*, Case No. IT-97-24-A, Judgment, ¶ 305 (Mar. 22, 2006); Eritrea Ethiopia Claims Commission, Partial Award, Prisoners of War, Eritrea's Claim 17, ¶ 68 (July 1, 2003).

international legislature, but it is the most authoritative organ in existence for the interpretation of world opinion. Its recognition of genocide as an international crime is persuasive evidence of the fact."[77] Likewise, the ICTY cited to the U.N. Declaration on the Protection of all Persons from Enforced Disappearances[78] (and the Inter-American Convention on Enforced Disappearances) in holding that the crime of enforced disappearances could be charged as a crimes against humanity under the rubric of "other inhumane acts."[79] In this way, pronouncements that began as soft law can harden into more binding norms through the work of international and domestic tribunals.

G. Conclusion

ICL litigants and jurists regularly make use of the multiplicity of sources of international law set forth in Article 38 of the ICJ Statute—multilateral treaties, international custom, general principles of law, judicial decisions, and even the writings of publicists and soft law—to identify applicable rules of decision and to resolve interpretive questions. Indeed, jurists seem quite comfortable cobbling together the applicable law from these various sources, notwithstanding that no one source may provide all the necessary ingredients to address the legal question at hand.

International tribunals frequently start with the relevant state's treaty obligations to determine the rules to which defendants were bound at the time in question. Beyond treaty law, courts adjudicating ICL also resort to customary international law, especially when there is no complete rule of decision available in an applicable treaty. Indeed, in many cases, customary international law appears to "come to the rescue" where treaty provisions are either silent as to a particular issue (e.g., whether conduct constitutes a prosecutable crime), ambiguous or incomplete in application (e.g., with regard to the elements of a crime that must be proven by a prosecutor to secure a conviction), or even when they are more constrained in their articulations of a legal principle. Although purporting to apply customary international law, international criminal tribunals are not always rigorous about applying the traditional customary international law formula of state practice coupled with *opinio juris*. At times, tribunals are content to look at what states say and overlook what states actually do.

---

77 *United States v. Altstötter*, 3 TRIALS OF WAR CRIMINALS BEFORE THE NUREMBERG MILITARY TRIBUNALS UNDER CONTROL COUNCIL LAW NO. 10 at 3, 983 (1951).

78 G.A. Res. 47/133, U.N. Doc. A/RES/47/133 (Feb. 12, 1993).

79 *Prosecutor v. Kupreškić*, Case No. IT-95-16-T, Judgment, ¶ 566 (Jan. 14, 2000).

As you review ICL cases, pay particular attention to the way in which litigants and judges identify the applicable law and consider to what extent the methodology employed is consistent with your understanding of the formal rules governing international law sources. In addition, consider to what extent ICL has adapted the traditional hierarchy of sources set forth in Article 38 of the ICJ Statute. To the extent that tribunals are departing from the standard sources doctrine, query why they have done so and whether the results remain legitimate under the circumstances.

Chapter 4

THE INTERNATIONALIZATION OF CRIMES

This chapter is concerned with the question of how violent conduct becomes prosecutable as an *international* crime, subject to international or extraterritorial jurisdiction. As you will see when you start looking more closely at substantive international criminal law (ICL), many international crimes actually encompass a constellation of individual criminal acts. Some of these predicate crimes are unique to ICL or international humanitarian law (IHL), such as the crime of perfidy—killing or wounding someone treacherously by making the victim believe the perpetrator is entitled to protected status under the laws of war (e.g., by feigning surrender).[1] Other predicate crimes have domestic law analogs in the familiar offenses of assault, mayhem, rape, and murder. These domestic crimes are considered international crimes when certain attendant circumstances are present. As a matter of definitional structure, these attendant circumstances usually appear in the *chapeau*[2] of the crime's formulation.

A major challenge to developing and codifying the field of ICL has been to identify which attendant circumstances fully distinguish international crimes from domestic ones. For example, what attributes make an act of murder a crime against humanity, a war crime, or the crime of genocide? A clear demarcation of which crimes fall within international jurisdiction is important, not only for academic or doctrinal reasons. For one, the complete collapse of the distinction between international and domestic crimes would be worrisome to states. It would occasion the ceding of a high degree of jurisdictional sovereignty, as international crimes are often subject to international and extraterritorial jurisdiction. If every act of murder could be prosecuted anywhere in the world under expansive jurisdictional bases, a certain degree of juridical chaos might result.

---

1 *See* Rule 65, ICRC Customary International Law Database, https://ihl-databases.icrc.org/customary-ihl/eng/docs/v1_rul_rule65. The ICC's Elements of Crimes defines perfidy in keeping with Additional Protocol I to the Geneva Conventions as: "acts inviting the confidence of an adversary to lead him to believe that he is entitled to, or obliged to accord, protection under the rules of international law applicable in armed conflict, with intent to betray that confidence." *See* Article 8(2)(e)(ix), War crime of treacherously killing or wounding, ICC Elements of Crimes, Resolution RC/11 (June 10, 2010).

2 *Chapeau* elements are circumstantial or contextual elements that apply uniformly to a subsequent list of prohibited acts. The phrase comes from the French word for "hat," as the contextual elements are usually found at the top, or "hat," of the definition of an international crime.

These concerns could result in the withdrawal of support for, and consent to, the regime of ICL, which would be a major reversal of global policy trends. The distinction between international and ordinary crimes also carries certain expressive implications—calling the imprisonment of an individual the crime against humanity of unlawful detention carries greater stigma than a mere kidnapping or false imprisonment allegation. Preserving a notion of international crimes protects them from the semantic inflation that might result if every abhorrent act were designated an international crime. Notwithstanding the importance of retaining a distinction between international and domestic crimes, no grand analytic theory exists. Instead, several different approaches are apparent in distinguishing these two bodies of penal law, as discussed in the remainder of this chapter. Keep these ideal types in mind as you study the definitions of the various substantive crimes.

A. The Jurisdictional Approach

A primary, and facile, explanation for differentiating between international and domestic crimes is jurisdictional: International crimes are those crimes that can be (and often are) prosecuted before international tribunals or in domestic courts pursuant to extraordinary jurisdictional bases. There is no doubt that the distinction between international crimes and "ordinary" crimes has jurisdictional implications. For example, when an act rises to the level of an international crime, it may be prosecuted before an international tribunal if one exists with jurisdiction over the act. Additionally, such an act may be subject to certain extraordinary forms of extraterritorial jurisdiction by states with no tangible nexus to the crime with respect to the nationality of the perpetrator or victim or the place of commission. The authorization to exercise international or extraterritorial jurisdiction may be a function of customary international law or a treaty obligation. This jurisdictional explanation, however, raises a chicken-and-egg problem: Are international crimes dubbed international because they can be, or are, prosecuted before international tribunals, or are these crimes prosecuted before international tribunals because they are international crimes? Given this tautology, this internationalization theory does not provide an independent justification for the exercise of jurisdiction over a suspect (including the power to restrain their liberty) by an international tribunal or a state with no nexus to the crime.

B. The Inter-National Approach

The second approach we call the "inter-national" approach. Put simply, this approach defines as "international" those crimes that transcend national boundaries and thus involve the interests of more than one state. Implicit in this approach is the recognition that the state with the strongest nexus to the crime—the state on whose territory the crimes are being committed or initiated—is either unable or unwilling to adequately address those crimes. The relevant transnational dimensions may relate to the nationality of the participants; the place, or places, where the crime was committed or consummated; or the place where the effects of the crime are felt. An interesting example of the latter is found in the proceedings currently pending before the ICC involving international crimes being committed against the Rohingya Muslim minority in Myanmar, which is not an ICC state party. Jurisdiction is premised on the fact that essential elements of some of the crimes underway (such as deportation as a crime against humanity) and the dire effects of others (such as persecution) have taken place on the territory of Bangladesh, an ICC state party.

There are "thin" and "thick" versions of the inter-national approach. The thin interpretation is premised on the literal crossing of an international boundary, or the direct interaction between the nationals of one state with the nationals of another. The clearest example of this thin version is found in the crime of aggression, which became actionable before the ICC in 2017. Although not requiring proof of the existence of a full-scale armed conflict, the crime of aggression, as currently conceptualized, requires some transnational element; there is no notion of purely domestic acts of aggression as might be charged in connection with an unconstitutional change of government. One element of the crime is the commission of an "act of aggression," defined at Article 8*bis* of the Rome Statute as "the use of armed force by a State against the sovereignty, territorial integrity or political independence of another State, or in any other manner inconsistent with the Charter of the United Nations."[3] The text then goes on to list a number of acts that qualify as acts of aggression, including the invasion by the armed forces of one state of the territory of another; a military occupation, however temporary, resulting from such invasion or attack; the annexation by the use of force of the territory of another state or part thereof; bombardment by the armed forces of one state against the territory of another or the use of any weapons by a state on foreign territory; the blockade of the ports or coasts of a state by another state's armed forces; and an attack by the armed forces of a state on the land, sea or air forces, or marine and air fleets of another state.

The historical development of IHL offers another useful example of this thin interpretation. Historically, IHL addressed international

---

[3] Rome Statute of the International Criminal Court art. 8*bis*, Jan. 16, 2002, 2187 U.N.T.S. 90. Articles denominated with *-bis* or *-ter* are those added to an existing instrument that already contains enumerated items.

armed conflicts when the troops of more than one nation state were engaged in battle with each other—events that would necessarily transcend international boundaries. War crimes were thus conceptualized solely in terms of inter-national criminal conduct committed (a) against nationals of an opposing belligerent (b) in the context of an international armed conflict, or (c) during an occupation.[4] Today's law, by contrast, recognizes a notion of war crimes committed in non-international armed conflicts; as such, another theory is needed to explain the exercise of international jurisdiction over war crimes committed entirely within the borders of a single state (as in a classic civil war scenario).

What is left out of this thin version of the inter-national approach are atrocities that occur solely within the borders of a single state but that have spillover effects in the region or more globally. Such circumstances implicate "global stability" and suggest that a crime rises to the level of international concern because of its effect on international public order and its ability to jeopardize the peace and security of the international community as a whole (recognizing, of course, that the international community is far from monolithic). This thick interpretation of the inter-national approach explains much of the expansion of international criminal law in the post-World War II era. For example, the positive law addressing non-international armed conflicts (which include, but are not limited to, classic civil wars that pit compatriots against each other) does not include any penal component. This lacuna in the early development of IHL can be explained by the fact that such conflicts do not cross an international boundary and do necessarily feature conflict between people of different nationalities. In other words, classic civil wars do not fit within the thin version of the inter-national approach that dominated the early decades of the development of IHL. It is only through the jurisprudence of the modern ICL tribunals that IHL now recognizes that customary international law criminalizes violations that take place in the context of non-international armed conflicts. Indeed, the law governing war crimes is now almost co-extensive as between the two categories of conflict. The thick variety of the inter-national approach at least partially explains this expansion of international criminalization to conflicts that are limited to the territory of one state.

The thick interpretation of the inter-national approach also explains the international criminalization of genocide and crimes against humanity even if the constitutive acts are confined to the

---

4 Geneva Convention Relative to the Protection of Civilian Persons in Time of War (Geneva Convention IV) arts. 146–48, Aug. 12, 1949, 75 U.N.T.S. 287 (setting forth "grave breaches" that state parties are obliged to punish when committed within an international armed conflict).

territory of one state. Indeed, crimes against humanity emerged as a new international crime at Nuremberg precisely to reach conduct that would not constitute war crimes because the victim and the perpetrator shared the same nationality or hailed from allied nations. The crime of genocide, and the evolution of crimes against humanity to no longer require even a connection to an international armed conflict (see our discussion below under the Nexus approach), are examples of international crimes that do not require any cross-border conduct by the perpetrators or perpetrator state. Their inclusion within the ICL canon can thus only be explained by the regional and global effects they invariably produce. Efforts to exterminate entire populations, and widespread or systematic attacks against a civilian population, can destabilize entire regions, generate large refugee migrations, and lead to international intervention and conflict, thus justifying a collective and coordinated penal response. This is true even when the immediate effects are exclusively internal. When such crimes are underway—either at the hands of, with the acquiescence of, or in spite of, the state—they threaten to, and often do, destabilize a region (or beyond).

C. The Failed State Approach

As noted above, the inter-national theory does not adequately explain all the atrocity crimes that are criminalized internationally. Another justification for the internationalization of violent conduct is premised on evolving notions of state sovereignty. As first conceptualized, sovereignty operated as a bar to almost any form of international intervention and states were entitled to full autonomy within their territorial borders. Over time, the notion of state sovereignty—and its underlying normative principles—have evolved considerably, in part due to the influence of the international human rights system. Whereas the concept of sovereignty once signaled the state's right to exercise exclusive control over a defined territory and the corresponding power to exclude outside interference within, or scrutiny of, matters internal to the state, it now embodies an obligation to protect individuals within the state's territory and to promote their social welfare and basic human rights.[5]

This notion of sovereignty-as-responsibility finds expression in the United Nations' Responsibility to Protect (R2P) doctrine.[6] This initiative has its roots in a plea by then Secretary-General Kofi Annan following the North Atlantic Treaty Organization (NATO)'s humanitarian intervention in Kosovo ("Operation Allied Force"), which proceeded without Security Council approval in order to

---

[5] Amitai Etzioni, *Sovereignty as Responsibility*, 50(1) ORBIS 71 (Winter 2006).

[6] *See* 2005 World Summit Outcome, GA Res. 60/1, ¶ 138, U.N. Doc. A/RES/60/1 (Oct. 24, 2005).

protect Kosovo Albanians from imminent harm at the tail end of the wars of succession in the former Yugoslavia. The Secretary-General called upon the international community to craft consensus principles governing humanitarian interventions. In response, the International Commission on Intervention and State Sovereignty (ICISS), convened by Canada, prepared a report on "The Responsibility to Protect" to promote a global debate on the relationship between humanitarian intervention and state sovereignty.[7] ICISS recognized two core principles:

1. State sovereignty implies responsibility, and the primary responsibility for the protection of its people lies with the state itself.
2. Where a population is suffering serious harm, as a result of internal war, insurgency, repression or state failure, and the state in question is unwilling or unable to halt or avert it, the principle of non-intervention yields to the international responsibility to protect.[8]

The ICISS informed a larger initiative to reconsider the role of the United Nations in light of new threats posed by terrorism, poverty, war, and violence within states, and changing conceptions of sovereignty, collective security, and the use of force. As part of that process, a High-level Panel of the United Nations, and later the full General Assembly, endorsed:

> [T]he emerging norm that there is a collective international responsibility to protect, exercisable by the Security Council authorizing military intervention as a last resort, in the event of genocide and other large-scale killing, ethnic cleansing or serious violations of international humanitarian law which sovereign Governments have proved themselves powerless or unwilling to prevent.[9]

The modern R2P framework consists of three pillars: (1) states bear the primary responsibility to protect their population from genocide, war crimes, crimes against humanity, and ethnic cleansing (and incitement thereto); (2) the international community must assist states in fulfilling these protection obligations; and (3) when a state manifestly fails in its obligations (including when it is itself a perpetrator of these crimes), the international community has a

---

[7] INT'L COMM. ON INTERVENTION & ST. SOVEREIGNTY, THE RESPONSIBILITY TO PROTECT (Dec. 2001).

[8] *Id.* at xi.

[9] *A More Secure World: Our Shared Responsibility, Report of the High-level Panel on Threats Challenges and Change*, U.N. Doc. A/59/565, ¶ 203 (Dec. 2, 2004).

responsibility to take appropriate collective action "in a timely and decisive manner" through the Security Council.[10]

This evolving notion of sovereignty underlines an alternative theory for internationalizing atrocity crimes and allowing for the exercise of universal jurisdiction on the part of all sovereign members of the international community. Where the sovereign has failed in its fundamental duty to protect individuals within its territory—either because it is unwilling or unable to do so—international or transnational judicial intervention is justified, including through the exercise of foreign or international criminal jurisdiction over perpetrators.[11] Responding appropriately to prevent and repress the commission of international crimes of global significance becomes the responsibility of the entire international community, even if the failure of state governance does not create any cross-border effects. This theory, premised on this globalized obligation to prevent atrocities, can be justified by reference to the state's responsibility to ensure the rights and dignity of the people within its territory, as well as by reference to more traditional concerns about global stability.

D. The Nexus Approach

The fourth approach we call the "nexus" approach, which finds affinity in the two prior theories. Under this hypothesis, a crime becomes international because of its relationship to a set of circumstances with international implications, such as an armed conflict. In other words, acts that might otherwise not give rise to international criminal liability do so when they are committed in connection with an international event, such as an international armed conflict, or another international crime. This bootstrapping is nicely illustrated with the definition of crimes against humanity adopted by the architects of the World War II tribunals. Much of the Nazi Holocaust involved acts that, traditionally, would not have implicated international law because it primarily (although not exclusively) involved perpetrators and victims of the same nationality or of allied nationality, and occurred within the territorial jurisdiction of the state of which those individuals were nationals. The Allies conceived of the concept of crimes against humanity to find a way to charge harmful conduct that would not be considered war crimes under the prevailing understanding of that crime. They gave a nod to then-existing international law by requiring that acts prosecuted as crimes against humanity have a nexus to another

---

[10] Report of the Secretary General, *Implementing the Responsibility to Protect*, U.N. Doc. A/63/577 (Jan. 12, 2009), at 8–9.

[11] *See* Ryan Liss, *Crimes Against the Sovereign Order: Rethinking International Criminal Justice*, 113 AM. J. INT'L L. 727 (2019).

crime within the jurisdiction of the Tribunal, namely either crimes against peace (what today we would call the crime of aggression) or war crimes. As a result of this definition of crimes against humanity, the Nuremberg Tribunal expressly refused to prosecute individuals for acts that occurred prior to September 1, 1939, the year in which Germany launched World War II by invading Poland.

It is now well settled that crimes against humanity are entirely autonomous from, and may be prosecuted absent, a state of war, although it is unclear exactly when this development occurred. By 1995, the ICTY was able to conclude: "[T]here is no logical or legal basis for this requirement [of an armed conflict nexus] and it has been abandoned in subsequent State practice."[12] This comment is striking because the ICTY Statute—created by the U.N. Security Council—contained a definition of crimes against humanity that included a nexus to an armed conflict. The Extraordinary Chambers in the Courts of Cambodia (ECCC) were forced to address this issue head-on since they prosecuted crimes committed in 1975–79, well before the *ad hoc* tribunals confirmed the demise of the war nexus. Not surprisingly, perhaps, defendants before the ECCC initially argued that the war nexus remained an element of the offense of crimes against humanity at that time, even though it was not incorporated into the ECCC Statute. This requirement would have precluded many crimes against humanity charges before a full-scale armed conflict existed in the country starting around 1977. A Pre-Trial Chamber of the ECCC initially addressed this issue by reference to a rule of interpretation that requires all doubts to be resolved in favor of the accused (*in dubio pro reo*). Later ECCC Trial Chambers disagreed, reasoning that the war nexus was no longer an element of the offense by 1975.[13]

All that said, when more modern definitions of crimes against humanity were formulated, drafters struggled with identifying internationalizing elements to replace the so-called "war nexus." Relying upon national and international jurisprudence, the drafters of the ICC Statute landed on the concept of a widespread or systematic attack upon a civilian population. So long as the individual criminal act of murder or torture is committed within that context, and with knowledge of the existence of such an attack (a *mens rea* element), then the individual act can be charged as a crime against humanity. Thus, the explanation for the internationalization

---

[12] *Prosecutor v. Tadić*, Case No. IT-94-1-AR72, Decision on Defence Motion for Interlocutory Appeal on Jurisdiction, ¶ 140 (Oct. 2, 1995).

[13] *Co-Prosecutors v. Kaing Guek Eav* alias *Duch*, Case No. 001/18-07-2007/ECCC/TC, Judgement, ¶¶ 291–92 (July 26, 2010); *Co-Prosecutors v. Ieng Sary et al.*, Case No. 002/19-09-2007/ECCC/TC, Decision on Co-Prosecutors' Request to Exclude Armed Conflict Nexus Requirement from the Definition of Crimes against Humanity, ¶ 33 (Oct. 26, 2011).

of crimes against humanity shifted from the nexus approach to other approaches, including the global stability approach discussed above.

A less radical version of the nexus approach is illustrated with war crimes, which require as a threshold element some link to an armed conflict, either international or non-international. Internal disturbances, riots, and the like, which exhibit either an inadequate degree of intensity or whose opposing parties are insufficiently organized, do not trigger IHL or, by extension, the war crimes prohibitions. By contrast, where a state of armed conflict exists, either international or non-international, crimes committed in connection therewith can be classified as war crimes. The law continues to grapple with exactly what sort of nexus between the crimes and the armed conflict is required—for example, is mere temporality enough, or must the acts be committed in furtherance of the armed conflict or by actors who are also involved in the conflict?

The international criminal tribunals have taken multiple approaches to this question. Some speak of the acts being "closely related to"[14] or exhibiting an "obvious link with"[15] the armed conflict. The ICTR in one case ruled as follows:

> In addition to the offence being committed in the context of an armed conflict not of an international character satisfying the material requirements of Common Article 3 and Additional Protocol II, there must be a nexus between the offence and the armed conflict for Article 4 of the Statute to apply. By this it should be understood that the offence must be closely related to the hostilities or committed in conjunction with the armed conflict.[16]

For its part, the ICC follows its Elements of Crimes, which require a showing that the conduct in question "took place in the context of and was associated with" an international or non-international armed conflict.

By contrast and somewhat counterintuitively, the crime of aggression can be committed absent a full-scale armed conflict. Nonetheless, the *actus reus* of the crime—which encompasses acts such as invasion, attack, occupation, bombardment, blockade, and so on—often leads to, or occurs in connection with, an armed conflict.

---

[14] *Prosecutor v. Tadić*, Case No. IT-94-1-T, Opinion and Judgment, ¶ 573 (May 7, 1997).

[15] *Prosecutor v. Delalić et al.*, Case No. IT-96-21-T, Judgment, ¶ 193 (Nov. 16, 1998).

[16] *The Prosecutor v. Rutaganda*, Case No. ICTR-96-3, Judgement & Sentence, ¶ 104 (Dec. 6, 1999).

E. Identity Approaches: Sovereign Perpetrators and the Importance of State Action

Other approaches to delineating international from domestic crimes focus on the identities of the perpetrators or victims rather than more geopolitical impacts. A fifth theory may be called the "state perpetrator" approach, which finds affinity in the aforementioned idea of sovereignty-as-responsibility. State action—shown either by way of a governmental policy or through the conduct of actors enjoying the support, authorization, direction, or acquiescence of a state—has often been cited as a potential defining element of international crimes. Some historical definitions of crimes against humanity included a state action requirement, although contemporary definitions are broader in that they encompass crimes committed by non-state actors. Such a limitation was specifically rejected in the case of genocide from the beginning, however, as Article IV of the Genocide Convention makes clear that genocide may be committed by private actors with no state involvement.

Although the definitions of crimes against humanity in the statutes of most of the *ad hoc* tribunals do not include reference to state action, the ICC at Art. 7(2)(a) specifically refers to state action, though it also recognizes that non-state actors can commit the crime. The ICC Statute defines crimes against humanity as a constellation of acts (i.e. murder, torture, etc.) committed within the context of a widespread or systematic attack against a civilian population. Article 7 defines the element "attack against any civilian population" as a course of conduct "involving the multiple commission of acts . . . against any civilian population, pursuant to or in furtherance of a State or organizational policy to commit such attack." The reference to "organizational policy," as distinct from state policy, led the late Judge and German jurist Hans Peter Kaul to argue in dissent in the Kenya cases that only those organizations that are "state-like" are capable of committing crimes against humanity. While the ICC jurisprudence has adopted a broader interpretation than that advocated by Judge Kaul (see the below discussion on the policy approach to defining international crimes), the push to rationalize the reference to organization by comparing it to a state is an illustration of the pull of the "state perpetrator" identity approach to international criminality.

In contrast to its definition of crimes against humanity, the ICC Statute's definition of aggression is formulated exclusively in terms of state action. Indeed, not just any state actor will fall within the Court's personal jurisdiction when it comes to this crime. Only individuals who are "in a position effectively to exercise control over or to direct the political or military action of a State" may be prosecuted for the crime of aggression before the ICC. This would exclude members of the rank-and-file, who might be prosecuted for war crimes committed following an act of aggression, but not for the act of aggression itself.

The conventional definition of torture includes a state-action requirement, although one that has some flexibility in application. Specifically, the Convention Against Torture and Other Cruel, Inhuman and Degrading Treatment or Punishment requires a showing that the pain or suffering inflicted was done so "by or at the instigation of or with the consent or acquiescence of a public official or other person acting in an official capacity."[17] Nonetheless, jurisprudence developed by a number of bodies, including the Committee Against Torture which interprets and addresses claims of torture brought under the Torture Convention, has significantly weakened this requirement. First, the Committee's views support the idea that severe acts of violence committed by members of a non-state organization can qualify as torture. For example, in a case involving Australia's decision to return a Somali citizen back to Somalia, the Committee Against Torture found that the applicant's fear of severe ill treatment at the hands of *de facto* groups that have the attributes of a government triggered the treaty's non-refoulement provision, which states: "No State Party shall expel, return ("refouler") or extradite a person to another State where there are substantial grounds for believing that he would be in danger of being subjected to torture."[18]

Second, there is also authority for the assertion that a state is liable for torture for failing to "exercise due diligence to prevent, investigate, prosecute and punish" non-state actors, including private individuals, for committing acts of severe violence.[19] The move away from requiring more direct state action to qualify as torture has been advocated for by, among others, feminist legal scholars for decades. Feminist scholars have long challenged the traditional distinction between public or state action, on the one hand, and private or non-state action, on the other. In the case of torture, the issue is whether acts of violence committed, for example, by men in a domestic setting should be treated in the same way as similar acts of violence committed by state authorities. Just as international human rights and international criminal law have pierced the veil of sovereignty to address atrocities committed solely within the territory of a state, so feminists argue that the veil

---

[17] Convention Against Torture and Other Cruel, Inhuman and Degrading Treatment or Punishment art. 1(1), Dec. 10, 1984, 1465 U.N.T.S. 85.

[18] *Elmi v. Australia*, CAT/C/22/D/120/1998 (1999).

[19] Committee Against Torture, *General Comment 2, Implementation of Article 2 by State Parties*, U.N. Doc. CAT/G/GC/2/CRP.1/rev. 4 (2007).

separating private from public action should be similarly retracted. Regardless of the definition under the Torture Convention, when torture also constitutes a crime against humanity or a war crime, no showing of state action is required.

This focus on the state, and state actors, as perpetrators reflects the pragmatic consideration that crimes committed by, or at the behest of, a state will not likely be adequately or uniformly punished within the applicable domestic criminal system (absent a change of regime) and so must be penalized and prosecuted at the international level. Likewise, it is states that undertake obligations under the constellation of human rights and ICL treaties. Indeed, ICL developed in part because states were unwilling (or unable) to prosecute breaches of international law committed by state agents, often pursuant to a state policy. The abortive Leipzig Trials at the close of World War I and the auto-amnesties put in place by authoritarian regimes throughout Latin America in the 1980s provide apt examples of the ways in which states can institutionalize impunity through inaction and sham proceedings. Concerns about limiting international jurisdiction to those crimes that are the least likely to be pursued by an individual state partially explains the absence in the ICC Statute of several crimes that are the subject of well-subscribed-to multilateral treaties—such as terrorism crimes, drug trafficking, and counterfeiting. The ICC's drafters assumed that such crimes are likely to be aggressively prosecuted in domestic proceedings since they are usually committed by non-state actors and threaten sovereign values and national security.

F. Identity Approaches: Victims

A sixth approach for defining a crime as international focuses on the identity of the victims, what we sometimes call the "protected group" approach. Many international crimes involve group-based persecution in a way that denies the victims their individuality and targets them because of their race, ethnicity, or religion. The collective nature of these crimes may serve to enhance their egregiousness and the culpability of the perpetrator, especially where groups are targeted on the basis of "suspect" and immutable classifications, like race or ethnicity. Most saliently, the crimes of genocide and persecution (an enumerated crime against humanity) require that the victim be targeted on the basis of his or her membership in a particular group or on discriminatory grounds. This approach does not explain all crimes defined as international, as acts other than persecution can constitute crimes against humanity if they are committed in the context of a widespread or systematic attack against a civilian population, however defined. Interestingly, in its first case, a Trial Chamber of the International Criminal

Tribunal for the former Yugoslavia (ICTY) attempted to narrow the definition of crimes against humanity by requiring discriminatory intent for all of its constituent acts.[20] This ruling was overturned on appeal[21] on the ground that a showing of discriminatory intent is required only for the crime of persecution.[22] The ICC has muddied the waters a bit by identifying the targeted civilian population by its political affiliation (in the Kenyan and Côte d'Ivoire cases), though it is not clear if these are just descriptive flourishes or legal requirements for the definition of a civilian population for purposes of a crime against humanity prosecution.

The definition of war crimes within the Geneva Conventions also incorporates this group-based approach. The penal provisions of the Geneva Conventions are implicated only when the victims fall within one of various categories of "protected person." The Fourth Geneva Convention, for example, recognizes certain acts (so-called grave breaches) as war crimes only when they are committed against individuals who are not protected by the other three Conventions (addressing the wounded, the shipwrecked, and prisoners of war), but who are of a nationality different than that of the perpetrators. Specifically, protected persons are those persons who find themselves "at a given moment and in any manner whatsoever . . . in the hands of a Party to the conflict or Occupying Power of which they are not nationals."[23]

The need to prove a nationality distinction between victim and perpetrator has relaxed considerably in the modern jurisprudence. In a case involving individuals of different group identity (Serb and Muslim) but of the same nationality (Bosnian), the ICTY Appeals Chamber held that a key purpose of the Geneva Conventions is to protect victims who are "different" from the perpetrators, and thus interpreted "nationality" expansively to include ethnicity and other forms of group identification even when the individuals were all of the same formal nationality in terms of which passport they carried. The ICTY Appeals Chamber thus effectively redefined "protected persons" in terms of the party to the conflict with which the victims

---

[20] *Tadić* Judgment, *supra*, ¶¶ 650–652.

[21] *Prosecutor v. Tadić*, Case No. IT-94-1-A, Judgment, ¶¶ 273–305 (July 15, 1999) (hereinafter "*Tadić* Appeals Judgment").

[22] The Statute of the International Criminal Tribunal for Rwanda (ICTR) was an exception to this approach. That statute required a showing of discriminatory intent (recognizing national, political, racial, or religious grounds) for all crimes against humanity, not just persecution. In the ICTR, persecution as a crime against humanity could only be prosecuted on narrower (political, racial, and religious) grounds. This peculiar discrepancy was probably a drafting oversight, or an effort to conform the statute to the reality of the violence in Rwanda, rather than an attempt to modify the definition of crimes against humanity under international law.

[23] Geneva Convention IV, *supra*, at art. 4.

had "substantial relations more than ... formal bonds" of citizenship.[24] The Appeals Chamber thus reasoned:

> While previously wars were primarily between well-established States, in modern inter-ethnic armed conflicts such as that in the former Yugoslavia, new States are often created during the conflict and ethnicity rather than nationality may become the grounds for allegiance. Or, put another way, ethnicity may become determinative of national allegiance. Under these conditions, the requirement of nationality is even less adequate to define protected persons. In such conflicts, not only the text and the drafting history of the Convention but also, and more importantly, the Convention's object and purpose suggest that allegiance to a Party to the conflict and, correspondingly, control by this Party over persons in a given territory, may be regarded as the crucial test.

Premising the definition of crimes against humanity upon an attack against a *civilian* population has led to the question of whether crimes against humanity can be committed against combatants or members of an armed group. In other words, can combatants or members of an armed group qualify as a group protected by the prohibition against crimes against humanity? An answer in the affirmative would encompass, for example, crimes committed against members of an organized resistance force as in occupied France in World War II, the Khmer Rouge's internal purges of cadre suspected of being treasonous, or the crimes committed against girl soldiers in the Democratic Republic of Congo, discussed below. The tribunals have taken different approaches to this question. The ICTR held that the assassination of U.N. peacekeepers as the genocide in Rwanda was unfolding could be charged as a crime against humanity given that their mandate was exclusively defensive. The fact that individual peacekeepers took up arms in self-defense did not change this conclusion.[25] The ICTY, wary of blurring the distinction between combatants and civilians, held that the term civilian "does not include combatants or fighters *hors de combat*."[26] In so holding, the ICTY acknowledged the risk that this would create a "protection gap" in the law:

> It is important to observe that failing to consider atrocities against fighters *hors de combat* as crimes against humanity does not mean that these acts will go unpunished. If

---

[24] *Tadić* Appeals Judgment, *supra*, ¶ 166.

[25] *Prosecutor v. Bagosora et al.*, Case No. ICTR-98-41-T, ¶¶ 2174–77 (Dec. 18, 2008).

[26] *Prosecutor v. Mrkšić et al.*, Case No. IT-95-13/1-T, ¶ 461 (Sept. 27, 2007).

> committed in the context of an armed conflict, they are likely to qualify as war crimes. . . . If committed in peacetime, they will be punishable under national law. There may perhaps be a "protection gap" in those situations, as crimes of this nature would fall outside the jurisdiction of international criminal courts and national authorities may not always be willing to prosecute.[27]

The ICTY thus dismissed the crimes against humanity charges on the theory that the crimes in question did not form part of an attack on the civilian population. Rather, the victims were selected because of their known, or believed, involvement in armed forces, and the Serb forces who mistreated the victims acted on the understanding that the victims were prisoners of war.[28] The ICC, for its part, has determined that the prohibition against crimes against humanity is implicated so long as the "attack" is *primarily* directed against civilians, even if there are some non-civilians in their midst.[29] This jurisprudence reflects the fact that a particular crime base may involve harm to combatants and civilians. Rather than parsing these acts between different international crimes, the concept of crimes against humanity provides a useful umbrella charge to prosecute a range of conduct by a range of actors against a range of victims.

The ICC has also expanded the concept of war crimes to include intra-group harm. This approach is demonstrated in the case against Bosco Ntaganda, who held leadership positions in multiple rebel movements within the Democratic Republic of Congo. Ntaganda was charged with various forms of sexual violence, including rape and sexual slavery, among other crimes. What made the charges unprecedented is that many of the victims were members of Ntaganda's own militia group, including girl soldiers. Not surprisingly, the defense argued that the charges should be dismissed because the "status requirements" of war crimes were not met. The theory was that members of an armed force cannot commit war crimes against their collaborators and that only those taking no active part in hostilities can be the victims of war crimes.

The ICC disagreed and ruled that the intra-force charges were proper. It reasoned that so long as there was a nexus to the armed conflict, the rape and sexual slavery of *any* person is prohibited by IHL; as such, members of the same armed force are not *per se* excluded as potential victims of the war crimes of rape and sexual

---

27 *Id.* ¶ 460.

28 *Id.* ¶¶ 474–481.

29 *Prosecutor v. Bemba*, Case No. ICC-01/05-01/08, ¶ 153 (Mar. 21, 2016).

slavery.[30] The Appeals Chamber gave a close read to the sub-components of Article 8, prohibiting war crimes, in concluding that only certain enumerated war crimes expressly circumscribe the group of potential victims, while others do not. Holding that IHL is also concerned with protecting vulnerable persons during armed conflicts, it concluded that it is the nexus to armed conflict requirement, and not the purported status requirements, that "sufficiently and appropriately delineates war crimes from ordinary crimes."[31] Ntaganda was ultimately convicted and sentenced to 30 years' imprisonment.[32]

G. The Policy or Organizational Approach

Related to the state action requirement, and as a seventh approach, criminal conduct implicates international law when it is committed pursuant to an over-arching policy, articulated either by a state or by some other sufficiently organized group. Such a policy element would ensure that random crime waves consisting of unconnected criminal conduct are not deemed crimes against humanity. This approach is reflected in the fact that certain definitions of international crimes include a policy element as a way to distinguish international crimes from domestic ones. These formulations, however, are not found in other ICL definitions, and proof of an explicit policy is not generally considered an element of most international crimes under customary international law.

The ICC Statute, for example, contains some references to crimes committed pursuant to an organized policy. Starting with crimes against humanity, the ICC Statute defines the element of a "widespread or systematic attack against a civilian population" as including evidence of a state or organizational policy to commit the attack. The ICC definition thus seems to require proof of a policy by virtue of the operative definition of "attack." Customary international law, by contrast, does not, although proof of a policy is often valuable as an evidentiary matter. The ICC continues to grapple with what showing will satisfy the requirement of an "organizational policy" before the ICC. In the Republic of Kenya situation, for example, the Prosecutor's theory of the case was that ethnically-oriented political parties, with the tacit complicity of the police, had enlisted the *Mungiki*—a shadowy criminal network—to attack political rivals during the 2007 elections. Judge Kaul insisted in several dissents that the ICC lacked jurisdiction *ratione materiae*

---

[30] *Prosecutor v. Ntaganda*, Case No. ICC-01/04-02/06-1962, Judgment on the Appeal of Mr. Ntaganda against the "Second decision on the Defence's Challenge to the Jurisdiction of the Court in Respect of Counts 6 and 9," ¶¶ 46–69 (June 15, 2017).

[31] *Id.* at 68.

[32] *Prosecutor v. Ntaganda*, Case No. ICC-01/04-02/06, Judgment (July 8, 2019).

(subject matter jurisdiction) in Kenya because, in his estimation, the post-election violence of 2008 was not committed pursuant to the policy of a state-like organization within the meaning of Article 7(2)(a) of the Statute.[33] The majority, by contrast, looked to whether the organization in question possessed the internal capacity to orchestrate crimes against humanity. In the end, all the cases collapsed amidst rampant witness intimidation.

With respect to war crimes, individual breaches of the law of armed conflict may be prosecuted under IHL even absent proof of a formal policy on the part of the relevant warring party. At the same time, the architects of the Rome Statute were concerned about granting jurisdiction to the ICC for one-off war crimes. Accordingly, in addition to including an idiosyncratic gravity threshold, Article 8 of the ICC Statute suggests a preference for prosecuting crimes "in particular" when committed "as part of a plan or policy . . . ." This requirement is unique to the ICC. Furthermore, it serves as a non-binding guide to prosecutorial discretion (and complementarity) rather than as an element of any particular war crime.

The Convention on the Prevention and Punishment of the Crime of Genocide does not include any reference to policy; what distinguishes genocide from other international crimes is the *mens rea*, or mental element, of that crime, which requires a showing that the defendant acted with the specific intent to destroy a protected group in whole or in part. This approach has been adopted by the *ad hoc* tribunals adjudicating individual criminal responsibility. In fact, the ICTY Appeals Chamber in the *Jelisić* case concluded that an individual with genocidal intent acting on his own could be convicted of genocide without reference to whether the state on whose behalf he was acting had developed a genocidal policy.

When considering *state* responsibility for the crime of genocide under the Genocide Convention, however, the International Court of Justice (ICJ) has required a showing of the existence of a concerted plan to commit genocide, or a consistent pattern of conduct that could only point to the existence of genocidal intent, on the part of the state itself, which all but implies the existence of a policy. (In addition, the Court held that the conduct of individual state actors acting with individualized genocidal intent could be attributed to the state under established principles of state responsibility).[34] This ruling emerged

---

[33] *Prosecutor v. Muthaura, Kenyatta & Ali*, Dissenting Opinion by Judge Hans-Peter Kaul to Pre-Trial Chamber II's "Decision on the Prosecutor's Application for Summonses to Appear for Francis Kirimi Muthaura, Uhuru Muigai Kenyatta and Mohammed Hussein Ali," Case No. ICC-01/09-02/11 (Mar. 15, 2011).

[34] Application of the Convention on the Prevention and Punishment of the Crime of Genocide (Bosn. & Herz. v. Serb. & Mont.), Judgment, 2007 I.C.J. 43, ¶ 376 (Feb. 26).

in a case brought by Bosnia-Herzegovina against Serbia and Montenegro under the Genocide Convention. Incidentally, in the Bosnia case, the ICJ found that while genocide was committed during the massacre at Srebrenica in Bosnia-Herzegovina (but not elsewhere during the war), the acts in question could not be attributed to Serbia-Montenegro; the latter did, however, fail in its conventional obligation to prevent the crime of genocide being committed by armed actors over which it exercised considerable influence and to cooperate with the ICTY in its efforts to punish the perpetrators.[35]

This jurisprudence reveals that the existence of a formal policy to commit atrocity crimes can be a useful way to distinguish between international crimes and criminal conduct that might not implicate international law.

H. The Subjective Intent Approach

An eighth theory for delineating international crimes focuses on the existence of something distinct about the motive or intent of the perpetrator. As noted above in connection with the *Jelisić* case, the specific intent required for a finding of genocide has led at least one international tribunal to conclude that even the criminal acts of one person acting with the requisite intent rises to the level of an international crime. Likewise, the definition of crimes against humanity contains two *mens rea* elements. The first is the *mens rea* element associated with the constitutive crime, such as the intent to kill with respect to murder. The second is found in the definition's *chapeau* and requires a showing that the individual knew that the act of intentional murder was part of a widespread or systematic attack against a civilian population. This second-order *mens rea* element helps to internationalize the crime by connecting the act to a larger campaign of violence or persecution. An individual who commits a crime without knowing that it is part of a larger attack could not be prosecuted for crimes against humanity, but rather for the relevant domestic crime.

Terrorism crimes are also often defined in terms of the perpetrator's subjective motive in committing the crime, with motive being defined as the reason that a person engages in crime. Many terrorism definitions focus on the perpetrator's goal of terrorizing the civilian population; coercing or inducing a government to do or abstain from doing some act; disrupting public services; or otherwise achieving some political, military, ethnic, ideological, or religious goal. The International Convention for the Suppression of the Financing of Terrorism, for example, indicates that

---

[35] *Id.* ¶¶ 438, 449.

> Any person commits an offence within the meaning of this Convention if that person by any means, directly or indirectly, unlawfully and wilfully, provides or collects funds with the intention that they should be used or in the knowledge that they are to be used, in full or in part, in order to carry out: . . . [any act] intended to cause death or serious bodily injury to a civilian, or to any other person not taking an active part in the hostilities in a situation of armed conflict, when the purpose of such act, by its nature or context, is to intimidate a population, or to compel a government or an international organization to do or to abstain from doing any act.[36]

Criminal acts that do not involve these particular motives are not prosecutable as acts of terrorism. This reliance on motive as an internationalizing element is somewhat unique in the penal law, as most domestic offenses do not include motive as a substantive element of the crime.

In contrast, the architects of the definition of torture in the Torture Convention added a specific intent element to convert what would be a domestic act of police brutality into the international crime of torture. As set forth in the Torture Convention, an act by a state official (or someone acting in an official capacity) that inflicts severe pain or suffering on an individual qualifies as torture if the act is committed for the purpose of "obtaining from [the victim] or a third person information or a confession, punishing [the victim] for an act he or a third person has committed or is suspected of having committed, or intimidating or coercing him or a third person, or for any reason based on discrimination of any kind. . . ." The requirement that the act be committed by a state official or someone acting under state authority means that the internationalization of the crime of torture can also be explained by the identity-of-the-perpetrator approach.

I. The Human Dignity, or "Shocks the Conscience," Approach

This brings us to the ninth, and final, approach to defining international crimes and the one that comes closest to explaining the internationalization of the entire corpus of ICL.[37] A crime becomes of international concern if it exceeds a minimum gravity threshold with respect to the extent to which it violates human dignity on a widespread or systematic scale, breaches certain fundamental values

---

[36] International Convention for the Suppression of the Financing of Terrorism art. 2(1)(b), De. 9, 1999, 2178 U.N.T.S. 197.

[37] *See* MARGARET DE GUZMAN, SHOCKING THE CONSCIENCE OF HUMANITY: GRAVITY AND THE LEGITIMACY OF INTERNATIONAL CRIMINAL LAW (2020).

of the global community, or otherwise infringes upon the fundamental rights and dignity that all members of humankind deserve. Such crimes are considered to be of international concern even if they do not formally transcend any international borders, even if they do not immediately threaten the stability of the international community, and regardless of the characteristics of the perpetrators or victims. Rather, because of their enormity, such crimes are moral wrongs against—and an assault on—all of humanity and our innate social and political nature,[38] and not just the immediate victims or even a single polity.[39] In other words, such crimes "signal a larger constituency."[40]

In the ICC context, the idea of such global societal concern is expressed in the concept of gravity, which emerges at multiple stages: when ICC actors are determining whether a situation or case is admissible under Article 17, and when the Prosecutor is determining whether to exercise her discretion to initiate an investigation under Article 53. Gravity encompasses both quantitative and qualitative components. Elements of both approaches can be found in justifications for internationalizing certain criminal activity. For example, the threshold requirement of whether a riot or insurrection rises to the level of an armed conflict is premised on a quantitative assessment of the size of the conflict. The specific intent of genocide illustrates a qualitative approach to gravity—the extent of the actual destruction is, at least as a legal matter, irrelevant; what matters is that the perpetrator aims to eliminate the victim's community in whole or in part.

The concept of a wrong committed against the entire global community was expressed in the Moscow Declaration in which the United States, the United Kingdom, and the Soviet Union first articulated their two-part prosecutorial strategy for Nazi officers and party members: trials in the *locus delicti* for lower-level defendants and some sort of joint prosecution of those individuals whose offenses had no particular geographical localization. A commentator at the end of the Nuremberg and Tokyo proceedings justified the internationalization of those prosecutions drawing upon both the quantitative and qualitative conceptions of gravity:

> As a rule systematic mass action, particularly if it was authoritative, was necessary to transform common crime,

---

[38] David Luban, *A Theory of Crimes Against Humanity*, 29 YALE J. INT'L L. 85–167 (2004).

[39] Antony Duff, *Authority and Responsibility in International Criminal Law*, *in* THE PHILOSOPHY OF INTERNATIONAL LAW 589, 595–601 (Samantha Besson & John Tasioulas eds., 2010).

[40] LARRY MAY, CRIMES AGAINST HUMANITY: A NORMATIVE ACCOUNT 110 (2004).

> punishable under municipal law, into a crime against humanity, which thus became also a concern of international law. Only crimes which either by their magnitude and savagery or by their large number or by the fact that a similar pattern was applied at different times and places endangered the international community or shocked the conscience of mankind, warranted intervention by States other than that on whose territory the crimes had been committed, or whose subjects had been their victims.[41]

Early definitions of crimes against humanity drafted by the International Law Commission in its effort to promulgate a Draft Code of Offences Against the Peace and Security of Mankind used terms such as "widespread," "massive," or "systematic" to modify the *actus reus* of the crime and distinguish international crimes from their domestic counterparts. More recently, Article 1 of the ICC Statute limits the exercise of jurisdiction to "the most serious crimes of international concern." In addition, particular Rome Statute provisions contain their own gravity thresholds; for example, the war crimes provision (Article 8) focuses the jurisdiction of the Court with respect to war crimes "in particular" when they are committed "as part of a large-scale commission of such crimes."

Under this approach to internationalization, the principle of universal jurisdiction can be conceptualized as the delegation of jurisdictional authority to any state that is able to obtain jurisdiction over a *hostis humani generis*—enemy of all humankind. This invective was first deployed with respect to pirates but has now been applied to the *génocidaire* and the war criminal. This idea is also contained in the very lexicon of one of the central ICL crimes: the crime against humanity. Thus, genocide or crimes against humanity committed exclusively within the territorial jurisdiction of one state now triggers the ICL regime because of their innate gravity.

Defining a crime as international because of its gravity does, however, present certain challenges. Using a concept of gravity to identify international crimes is somewhat subjective where harm caused by criminal action may be incommensurable. The ICC jurisprudence on gravity embraces both qualitative as well as quantitative elements. In a case arising out of the Mali situation before the ICC, the defendant (a member of Ansar Dine/Al Qaeda in the Islamic Maghreb's Islamic Police) argued that the allegations against him did not meet the ICC's gravity threshold, as set forth in Article 17(1)(d), in terms of the number of incidents, the temporal

---

[41] UNITED NATIONS WAR CRIMES COMMISSION, HISTORY OF THE UNITED NATIONS WAR CRIMES COMMISSION AND THE DEVELOPMENT OF THE LAWS OF WAR 179 (1948).

duration of the incidents, and the number of identified victims. The Prosecutor had charged torture and other inhumane acts as war crimes and crimes against humanity in connection with the flogging of women and men in Timbuktu for being immodestly dressed. In a 2020 decision, the ICC Appeals Chamber confirmed that "both quantitative (in particular, the number of victims) and qualitative criteria (such as nature, scale and manner of commission of the alleged crimes, including the human rights violated as a result, their impact on victims, the role and degree of participation of the accused, and whether the acts were committed on the basis of discriminatory motives) are relevant to assessing the gravity requirement in a given case."[42]

In addition, gravity alone may not be sufficient to exclude certain domestic crimes from the purview of international law (such as serial murders or rapes), which can be horrific in their scale and effects. In any case, most modern definitions of international crimes allow for the prosecution of single or isolated criminal acts (e.g., a single act of pillage), so long as they are committed within the context required by the definition of the offense (thus evoking the nexus approach to international crimes). As discussed, to prosecute an individual for crimes against humanity, the criminal act must have been committed within the context of a widespread or systematic attack against a civilian population with knowledge of the attack. These threshold concepts of "widespread" and "systematic" now modify the attendant attack rather than the constitutive offense, the effects of which may be more modest in their impact. The prohibition against war crimes requires only the existence of an armed conflict, and a single war crime can constitute an international crime, even absent any serious impact. Even with the crime of genocide, a single act of violence against a protected group may constitute genocide at a theoretical level. As such, threshold provisions like those in Articles 1 and 8 of the ICC Statute are more jurisdictional than definitional and assist the Prosecutor in the discretionary process of selecting situations and cases to pursue.

J. Conclusion

In the end, one is left with the impression that the different international crimes have been designated as such for different reasons over time. This heterogeneity in many ways reflects the fact that ICL has historically evolved along disparate strands that are only today converging in a handful of centralized institutions, most

[42] *Prosecutor v. Al Hassan Ag Abdoul Aziz Ag Mohamed Ag Mahmoud*, Case No. ICC-01/12-01/18 OA, Judgment on the Appeal of Mr. Al Hassan Against the Decision of Pre-Trial Chamber I entitled 'Décision Relative à l'exception d'irrecevabilité pour Insuffisance de Gravité de l'affaire Soulevée par la Défense,' ¶ 92 (Feb. 19, 2020).

notably the ICC, and in the world's domestic penal codes. In general, the *chapeau* of each crime's definition is where one often finds clues to a justification for internationalization. For war crimes, the key overarching element is the existence of an armed conflict. Crimes against humanity have occurred where there is a widespread or systematic attack against a civilian population. The unifying theme for the crime of genocide is the targeting of a protected group. Both crimes against humanity and genocide also include second-order *mens rea* elements that apply to the attendant circumstances rather than to the enumerated crimes. For crimes against humanity, it must thus be shown that the perpetrator acts with the knowledge that their conduct is part of the attendant attack. As a result of these additional elements, the prosecution of an international crime requires the introduction of evidence that satisfies more elements than would normally be required for a domestic prosecution. This, in turn, contributes to the length and complexity of modern international trials.

Chapter 5

THE PRINCIPLE OF LEGALITY IN INTERNATIONAL CRIMINAL LAW

As a species of criminal law, international criminal law (ICL) implicates the principle of legality (*nullum crimen sine lege*, or NCSL),[1] which embodies the *ex post facto* prohibition that conduct must be criminalized and penalties fixed in advance of any criminal prosecution. It also contains two corollary legislative and interpretive principles compelling criminal statutes to be drafted with precision (*lex stricta* or the principle of specificity) and interpreted in favor of the accused (*in dubio pro reo* or the rule of lenity).[2] The principle of NCSL serves two key purposes: It ensures that individuals have fair notice of prescribed conduct so they can rationally adjust their behavior to avoid sanction, and it protects the citizenry from arbitrary state action in the face of ambiguities and gaps in the law. NCSL thus embodies an essential element of the rule of law by speaking to the very legitimacy of a legal rule and providing a check on the power of government over individuals and preserving a zone for individual liberty.[3] At the global level, NCSL also provides a check against international judicial overreach that might otherwise undermine state sovereignty, and thus state support, for the entire project of ICL.

The principle of legality finds expression in a number of human rights instruments. Some express the concept as an absolute prohibition. For example, the Universal Declaration of Human Rights states unequivocally at Article 11(2) that "[n]o one shall be

---

1 Although not unknown in ancient Roman or Greek law, the NCSL principle experienced a resurgence in the Enlightenment period, when the prevailing political ideology was one of reaction against oppressive government and judicial arbitrariness. German jurist Paul Johann Anselm Ritter Von Feuerbach (1775–1833) is credited with coining the maxim.

2 *See Prosecutor v. Blagojević*, Case No. IT-02-60-T, Judgement, ¶ 642 n.2057 (Jan. 17, 2005) (noting that "[i]n accordance with the general principle of interpretation *in dubio pro reo*, the Tribunals' case law has opted for the interpretation most favourable to the accused and found that the term 'killings', in the context of a genocide charge, must be interpreted as referring to the definition of murder, i.e. intentional homicide"). Later, a Trial Chamber argued that *in dubio pro reo* applies only to findings of fact and not conclusions of law. *Prosecutor v. Stakić*, Case No. IT-97-24-T, Judgement, ¶ 416 (July 31, 2003) ("The Trial Chamber explicitly distances itself from the Defence submission that the principle *in dubio pro reo* should apply as a principle for the interpretation of the substantive criminal law of the Statute. As this principle is applicable to findings of fact and not of law, the Trial Chamber has not taken it into account in its interpretation of the law.").

3 This chapter is adapted from Beth Van Schaack, Crimen Sine Lege*: Judicial Lawmaking At The Intersection of Law And Morals*, 97 GEORG. L. J. 119 (2008).

held guilty of any penal offense on account of any act or omission which did not constitute a penal offense, under national or international law, at the time it was committed. Nor shall a heavier penalty be imposed than the one that was applicable at the time the penal offence was committed."[4] The latter clause embodies the concept of *nulla poena* [punishment] *sine lege*. The International Covenant on Civil and Political Rights (ICCPR) builds on this prohibition with the admonition at Article 15 that "[n]or shall a heavier penalty be imposed than the one that was applicable at the time when the criminal offense was committed. If, subsequent to the commission of the offense, provision is made by law for the imposition of the lighter penalty, the offender shall benefit thereby." This provision goes on, however, to emphasize that there is no violation of the principle if the act in question has already been criminalized at the international level: "Nothing in this article shall prejudice the trial and punishment of any person for any act or omission which, at the time when it was committed, was criminal according to the general principles of law recognized by the community of nations."[5] Similarly, the European Convention for the Protection of Human Rights and Fundamental Freedoms includes the right to be spared from *ex post facto* prosecutions at Article 7, which also creates an exception for "the trial and punishment of any person for any act or omissions which, at the times when it was committed, was criminal according to the general principles of law recognized by civilized nations."[6] This language was put in place to vindicate the Nuremberg and Tokyo Charters and proceedings, which featured novel international crimes, but has also been invoked in connection with more recent abuses, as when German border guards were ordered to kill people attempting to cross the Berlin Wall, acts that were lawful under German law but unlawful under international law.[7]

Although the principle of NCSL appears in all of the omnibus human rights treaties (albeit in slightly different formulations), the International Criminal Court (ICC) is the only ICL tribunal whose constitutive statute contains an express articulation of the NCSL principle. Specifically, the ICC Statute provides at Article 22(1): "A person shall not be criminally responsible under this Statute unless the conduct in question constitutes, at the time it takes place, a crime within the jurisdiction of the Court." Article 24(2) continues: "[i]n the event of a change in the law applicable to a given case prior to a final

---

[4] Universal Declaration of Human Rights, G.A. Res. 217A (III) (Dec. 10, 1948).

[5] International Covenant on Civil & Political Rights art. 15, 999 U.N.T.S. 171 (Dec. 16, 1966).

[6] European Convention for the Protection of Human Rights and Fundamental Freedoms art. 7, Nov. 4, 1950, 213 U.N.T.S. 221.

[7] *Streletz, Kessler & Krenz v. Germany*, Applications Nos. 34044/96, 35532/97 & 44801/98, Grand Chamber (Mar. 22, 2001).

judgement, the law more favourable to the person being investigated, prosecuted or convicted shall apply." Likewise, the principle of strict construction, the ban on ruling by analogy, and the rule of lenity are specifically mandated at Article 22(2), which states with some redundancy: "The definition of a crime shall be strictly construed and shall not be extended by analogy. In case of ambiguity, the definition shall be interpreted in favour of the person being investigated, prosecuted or convicted."[8] It has been presumed that this set of admonitions applies to forms of responsibility and not just substantive law.[9] Although their statutes do not contain an articulation of NCSL, the *ad hoc* tribunals generally considered themselves bound by the principle nonetheless. The International Criminal Tribunal for the former Yugoslavia (ICTY), for example, determined that NCSL dictates that

> "penal statutes must be strictly construed" and that the "paramount duty of the judicial interpreter [is] to read into the language of the legislature, honestly and faithfully, its plain and rational meaning and to promote its object" and that ambiguities that cannot be resolved with resort to canons of construction instead should be resolved in favor of the accused.[10]

Despite its absence in the majority of international tribunal statutes, the principle of NCSL remains acutely relevant, and particularly compelling, in the field of ICL. Indeed, the principle of NCSL goes to the very heart of how international crimes are developed, interpreted, and applied. Yet, even as ICL reaches its peak in terms of codification and available precedent, defendants still argue that the acts for which they are being prosecuted were not criminal at the time they acted. This is largely because international, and to a certain extent domestic, courts have been perceived as applying new ICL norms to past conduct and engaging in a full-scale—if unacknowledged—refashioning of ICL through their jurisprudence, transforming the *lex ferenda* (the law as it should be) into the *lex lata* (the law as it is). Along the way, courts have updated and expanded historical treaties and prohibitions, upsetting arrangements carefully negotiated between states, rejecting political compromises made by states during multilateral drafting conferences, and adding content to vaguely worded provisions that

---

[8] *See Prosecutor v. Katanga*, Case No. ICC-01/04-01/07, Judgement Pursuant to Art. 74 of the Statute, ¶¶ 52–53 (Mar. 7, 2014).

[9] *Prosecutor v. Chui*, Case No. ICC-01/04-02/12, Judgement Pursuant to Article 74 of the Statute Concurring Opinion of Judge Wyngaert, ¶ 18 n.27 (Dec. 18, 2012).

[10] *Prosecutor v. Galić*, Case No. IT-98-29-T, Judgement & Opinion, ¶ 93 (Dec. 5, 2003) (citing *Prosecutor v. Delalić*, Case No. IT-96-21-T, Judgement, ¶¶ 408, 413 (Nov. 16, 1998)).

were conceived more as retrospective condemnations of past horrors than as codes for prospective penal enforcement. In these circumstances, the trade-off is clear: should the principle of legality be relaxed, in order to bring perpetrators to justice, or strictly applied, even at the expense of allowing impunity to prevail? Although ICL tribunals may achieve substantive justice with these outcomes, they also risk undermining the legitimacy of ICL as a field of criminal law by violating the human rights of criminal defendants appearing before them.

Why has the NCSL defense been so ubiquitous in ICL? Have the ICL tribunals adequately protected the interests served by the principle of NCSL in proceedings before them? Because of the importance of these questions to the field of ICL, this book devotes a chapter to the recurring themes, analytical claims, and arguments employed by ICL tribunals to address the dictates of NCSL. As you read the opinions issued by these institutions, consider whether the opinions adhere to the principle of legality as you understand it, or whether ICL judges have compromised the fundamental rights embodied in the principle of NCSL in their efforts to ensure accountability and advance the law in the face of deficiencies.

Although NCSL defenses were very common during the early years of the ICL renaissance, they are tapering off in modern proceedings. With the promulgation of the ICC Statute and its detailed definitions and elements of crimes, and with domestic legal systems rigorously incorporating international crimes in their penal codes, it is increasingly difficult for defendants to argue that they did not have fair notice of the fact that their conduct constituted an international crime subject to criminal prosecution. As such, the NCSL defense has waned in prevalence and importance, but it still makes the occasional cameo appearance.

A. NCSL in International Criminal Law

First, we address the question of why the defense of NCSL has been so ubiquitous in ICL proceedings. For one, the ICL applied by the *ad hoc* international tribunals was an incomplete and rapidly evolving area of law. Although adjudication and codification have proceeded at an aggressive pace since the end of the Cold War, there were still large gaps in positive law. Many of the primary sources of ICL rules, especially those dealing with the law of armed conflict, originated in an era during which war was waged differently. This has led skeptics to critique such treaties as being outmoded and even "quaint." Modern tribunals had to apply these antiquated provisions in the context of modern belligerency.

Second, the international system lacks a standing world legislature that can fill interstices and lacunae, modernize ancient prohibitions, or fix faulty formulations. In the domestic arena, there is the expectation that the legislature will rectify problems in the law if they are revealed through the exoneration of individuals who committed bad acts. The only way ICL treaties can be amended is through the sporadic and sluggish multilateral treaty drafting process. Indeed, states are loath to renegotiate existing treaties, not only because of the transaction costs inherent in such endeavors, but also because of the confusion wrought in trying to keep track of which states have ratified which version of which treaty, although occasionally new protocols do emerge to update earlier efforts.

Third, modern tribunals have also been asked to interpret treaties that were drafted without the precision we now expect from modern penal codes. The crimes themselves are rarely drafted in terms of the basic elements of criminal law—*mens rea, actus reus,* attendant circumstances, and so on. This is due, in part, to the fact that most treaty drafting is done by diplomats lacking technical drafting skills (rather than specialists in comparative criminal law) who are working in the context of political, and often politicized, multilateral negotiations. Moreover, it was probably not contemplated by their drafters that ICL treaty provisions would be applied directly as rules of decision in criminal prosecutions. Rather, it was expected that states would incorporate the general prohibitions contained in these treaties into their domestic penal codes and then apply these, presumably more precise, criminal definitions in their own courts when they had custody of an accused. The establishment of the international criminal tribunals forced, for the first time, the direct applicability of these provisions.

Fourth, many international treaties are open-textured, such as those prescribing the war crimes of "willfully causing great suffering," committing "inhumane and degrading treatment or punishment," or causing the destruction of property "not justified by military necessity." This is at times by design, as drafters indicated that it would be impossible to envision every type of conduct that deserved prohibition or where drafters sought to establish a general standard against which particular actions would be judged. In other circumstances, these pockets of vagueness reflect the concerted ambiguity that results from difficult interstate negotiations in which certain states have been known to jealously guard the prerogatives of state sovereignty. It is thus left to the courts to add content to these provisions. This is so even though domestic principles of statutory construction would often counsel against courts filling deliberate omissions in legislation. Although the ICC Statute, with its Elements of Crimes, better approximates the penal code ideal, key terms remain undefined even in that treaty.

Fifth, in the absence of an applicable textual provision, modern criminal tribunals have been asked to glean genuine international custom from divergent state conduct and self-serving rhetoric. Finding the relevant state practice contemporaneous to when a defendant acted may be a challenge where domestic codification was incomplete and domestic prosecutions episodic, particularly if considerable time has passed. On the international plane, the adjudication of ICL is decentralized. Since the establishment of the ICTY, the first modern *ad hoc* tribunal, additional international, hybrid, and domestic fora have proliferated that are not, as a technical matter, generally bound by the precedent generated by sister courts. Many courts must essentially start from scratch in identifying the applicable law.

At the time the *ad hoc* tribunals began their work, ICL was thus characterized by a certain degree of systemic indeterminacy. It was difficult to identify positive law, and what law existed was incomplete. Moreover, states were not inclined to develop new rules or clarify the old ones. These circumstances generate a temptation toward judicial legislation to avoid situations of *non liquet* ("it is not clear") that would exonerate a defendant who has allegedly committed heinous acts. The various ways in which, and arguments with which, the ICL tribunals have addressed these dilemmas is the topic of the rest of this chapter.

B. Responses to NCSL Defenses

1. The Applicability of NCSL in International Criminal Law

A recurring argument in the face of the defense of NCSL is that the principle simply does not apply to ICL with the same force and effect as it does in the domestic penal order. This was certainly true in the proceedings following World War II, when the two international military tribunals made quick work of the defendants' NCSL arguments. This led the late Professor and Judge Antonio Cassese—himself an ICL judge—to opine that in the postwar period, "[t]he strict legal prohibition of *ex post facto* law had not yet found expression in international law."[11] As recently as 1998, more than fifty years after Nuremberg, one ICTY Trial Chamber reasoned "[i]t is not certain to what extent [the principle of legality and its components] have been admitted as part of international legal practice, separate and apart from the existence of the national legal system. This is essentially because of the different methods of criminalisation of conduct in national and international criminal justice systems."[12]

---

11 ANTONIO CASSESE, INTERNATIONAL CRIMINAL LAW 72 (2003).

12 *Prosecutor v. Delalić*, Case No. IT-96-21-T, Judgment, ¶ 403 (Nov. 16, 1998).

The argument that NCSL does not apply, or applies with much less force, to ICL has several facets to it. Some jurists explain it with reference to the difference between international and national legal processes. They note in particular that because the different states of the world approach the NCSL principle somewhat differently, no precise or even strict formulation of the principle has emerged that would be applicable to international courts. By this reasoning, international tribunals may relax the notion of NCSL in their proceedings even though domestic courts remain constrained by their own particular constitutional, statutory, or treaty obligations with respect to the principle.

The principle's frequent invocation by modern international criminal tribunals suggests that this position is overstated. To be sure, human rights treaties technically bind the states that ratify them, and none of the statutes of the *ad hoc* tribunals specifically contained the NCSL principle. Nonetheless, many of the fair trial dictates within those treaties, including the NCSL principle, may now be binding on international judicial institutions like the *ad hoc* tribunals, either as customary international law or as a general principle of law. Indeed, the modern *ad hoc* international tribunals on the whole accepted the applicability of the principle and the values it protects to proceedings before them, reasoning that NCSL is a general principle of criminal law.

A different facet of this argument about the limited applicability of NCSL in ICL is premised on characterizing NCSL as a flexible principle of justice that can yield to competing imperatives. As the ICTY once noted: "[T]he principle *nullum crimen sine lege* is, as noted by the International Military Tribunal in Nuremberg, first and foremost, a 'principle of justice.' "[13] Convicting a defendant in breach of the principle of NCSL is one form of injustice. Allowing "loopholes" in the law to exonerate an accused found to have committed unquestionably bad acts, caused serious harm, or acted immorally results in an injustice of an altogether different, perhaps more profound, kind. By subordinating the principle of NCSL to a vision of substantive justice, tribunals have determined that the former injustice is less problematic than the latter. Thus, in explaining the outcome at Nuremberg, Cassese noted that, at the time, "the *nullum crimen sine lege* principle could be regarded as a moral maxim destined to yield to superior exigencies whenever it would have been contrary to justice not to hold persons accountable for appalling atrocities."[14]

---

[13] *Prosecutor v. Milutinović*, Case No. IT-99-37-AR72, Decision on Dragoljub Ojdanić's Motion Challenging Jurisdiction—Joint Criminal Enterprise, ¶¶ 37, 38 (May 21, 2003).

[14] CASSESE, *supra*, at 72.

In the alternative, it is argued that NCSL is not a principle of justice but of policy, easily overridden where inexpedient in application. Thus, courts balance considerations of the rights of the accused against the needs of the international community for security, accountability, and the preservation of world order. Most important in this line of reasoning, perhaps, has been the belief that a vigorous system of international justice will create a more robust system of deterrence that will prevent such abuses in the future. International courts are confronted with the need to strike the right balance between these two sets of imperatives, and NCSL is only one factor in the equation.

2. Filling Gaps in the Law

The least controversial side-stepping of NCSL involves situations in which an international tribunal provides minor clarification to law that is incomplete or unclear. Several international tribunals argued that NCSL does not prevent courts from interpreting or clarifying the elements of crime or even progressively developing the law,[15] so long as this does not go "beyond reasonable limits of clarification" and the very essence of the original crime.[16] The ICL judges have thus added content to vaguely worded treaties and other international instruments in ways that might not have been easily anticipated by potential defendants. More controversial are situations where there was no extant law to build upon.

3. Acts as *Malum In Se*

Jurists also tend to deemphasize NCSL in the face of an act that is *malum in se*—inherently bad or "wrong in itself." NCSL was at the heart of the defendants' defense before the Nuremberg and Tokyo Tribunals following World War II, particularly with respect to the novel charge of crimes against the peace (the crime of aggression in today's lexicon). The Nuremberg Tribunal rejected the NCSL defense based on the notion that it is not unfair to prosecute individuals for conduct that is *malum in se*:

> To assert that it is unjust to punish those who in defiance of treaties and assurances have attacked neighboring states without warning is obviously untrue, for in such

[15] *See Prosecutor v. Delalić*, Case No. ICTY-96-21-A, Judgement, ¶ 173 (Feb. 20, 2001) (interpretation and clarification of elements of a crime under common Article 3 does not violate *nullum crimen sine lege*); *Prosecutor v. Aleksovski*, Case No. ICTY-95-14/1-A, Judgement, ¶¶ 126–127 (Mar. 24, 2000) (noting that the principle of *nullum crimen sine lege* does not prohibit "the interpretation of the law through decisions of a court and the reliance on those decisions in subsequent cases in appropriate circumstances").

[16] *Milutinović, supra*, ¶¶ 37–38.

> circumstances, the attacker must know that he is doing wrong, and so far from it being unjust to punish him, it would be unjust if his wrong were allowed to go unpunished.[17]

In other words, it was argued, no innocents were ensnared at Nuremberg. Formal notice of the penal consequences of such conduct is deemed unnecessary when the acts in question shock the collective conscience of the international community. In such circumstances the suspects "must have known" that their acts were wrongful, and thus it would be unjust to exonerate them. This rhetoric retains contemporary currency. As one ICTY Trial Chamber argued, "[t]he purpose of this principle [NCSL] is to prevent the prosecution and punishment of an individual for acts which he reasonably believed to be lawful at the time of their commission. It strains credibility to contend that the accused would not recognize the criminal nature of the acts alleged in the Indictment."[18]

These statements, which elide the morally wrong and the legally criminal, invoke the natural law tradition found in all of public international law. This tradition is particularly cogent in ICL, which has as its origins the belief that the law must conform to a universal transnational morality and conception of justice. Because such moral rules are considered universally and intrinsically knowable in advance, prior articulation and actual notice are deemed unnecessary. Courts adjudicating serious violations of ICL thus envision themselves as operating in a realm of greater moral certainty that, it is argued, justifies overlooking a strict application of NCSL. It is perhaps not surprising that jurists would resort to ideas of natural law in the face of atrocity, when a desire to ensure the confluence of law and morality is likely to be at its strongest. In this way, tribunals appear compelled to respond to innovations in atrocity where positive law is silent.

This reasoning is most palatable when applied to heinous conduct that, for whatever reason, falls outside of positive law. Tribunals limited to adjudicating only the most "serious" of ICL violations can perhaps more easily execute this leap from *contra bonos mores* ("against good morals") to prosecutable crime. This move is increasingly difficult with respect to acts that are more morally contested or for which there is no global consensus. Such acts—including some more technical war crimes such as mis-using the red

---

17 Judgment, 22 TRIAL OF THE MAJOR WAR CRIMINALS BEFORE THE INTERNATIONAL MILITARY TRIBUNAL, Nuremberg 14 November 1945–1 October 1946 at 462 (1948) [hereinafter *Nuremberg Judgment*].

18 *Delalić*, *supra*, ¶ 313.

cross emblem—are merely *malum prohibitum* (wrong because it is prohibited) and may not generate fair notice.

4. Illegality = Criminality

In his dissenting opinion in *Prosecutor v. Norman*,[19] Justice Geoffrey Robertson made the point that, at the time of the conflict in Sierra Leone, the recruitment of child soldiers by states may have been prohibited by international law, but had not yet risen to the level of an international crime. NCSL defenses are frequently asserted in situations in which there is a norm governing state behavior that does not, on its face, govern individual behavior or render such behavior subject to penal consequences. Many historical ICL and international humanitarian law (IHL) treaties are silent as to individual criminal responsibility precisely because they were drafted at a time when the international community only conceived of collective (state) responsibility for breaches. This meant that injured states could resort to reprisals or seek reparations from responsible states in the event of a breach. Nonetheless, starting with the Nuremberg Tribunal, modern tribunals quite easily equate the international condemnation of a practice with its criminalization.

At Nuremberg, for example, the Tribunal argued that because the Kellogg-Briand Pact and various bilateral treaties of neutrality and nonaggression prohibited the acts of aggression undertaken by Germany, defendants' conduct was unquestionably "wrong" and thus punishable. It reasoned that the Pact with its "solemn renunciation of war as an instrument of national policy necessarily involves the proposition that such a war is illegal in international law; and that those who plan and wage such a war, with its inevitable and terrible consequences, are committing a crime in so doing."[20] In so arguing, the Tribunal transformed a treaty devoted to the regulation of state conduct (providing as a sanction that the state in question would "be denied the benefits furnished by" the Pact and thus render itself vulnerable to reprisals, countermeasures, retorsion, and claims for reparations) into one regulating individual conduct. By this reasoning, the treaty's renunciation of war *ipso facto* rendered war unlawful under general international law, and the illegality of war under general international law *ipso facto* rendered the pursuit of war a crime under international law. The Tribunal concluded, "On this view of the case alone, it would appear that the maxim [NCSL] has no application to the present facts."[21] In this way, the launching of aggressive war in Europe became an international crime over and

[19] *Prosecutor v. Norman*, Case No. SCSL-2004-AR72(E), Separate Opinion of Justice Geoffrey Robertson (Mar. 13, 2004).

[20] Nuremberg Judgment, *supra*, at 463.

[21] *Id.* at 642.

above a breach of a contractual obligation *inter se* ("among [the states] themselves").

Similar arguments have been made with respect to acts that were clearly criminalized in one context but not so clearly in another. Duško Tadić, the first defendant to come before the ICTY, contested *inter alia* the legality of the charges against him under Article 3 of the ICTY Statute (criminalizing "The Laws and Customs of War"). His argument was based on the premise that the conflict in the former Yugoslavia was a civil—rather than international—war. He contended (accurately) that neither the 1949 Geneva Conventions nor the 1907 Hague Convention regulated non-international armed conflicts in any detail and, to the extent that they did, any such rules did not give rise to individual criminal responsibility. In upholding the Article 3 charges against Tadić, the Appeals Chamber identified four factors that must be met for an offense to be charged as a violation of Article 3 of the ICTY Statute:

(a) the act must infringe a rule of IHL;

(b) the rule must be customary in nature or, if contained in a treaty, the treaty must be applicable;

(c) the violation must be "serious," which is to say the rule must protect "important values" and "the breach must involve grave consequences for the victim;" and

(d) the violation must entail, under customary or conventional law, individual criminal responsibility.[22]

With respect to the applicability of individual criminal responsibility, point (d), the Appeals Chamber noted that the Nuremberg Tribunal had concluded that individual criminal responsibility could exist in the absence of an explicit treaty provision to that effect. The Appeals Chamber surveyed state practice—in the form of national prosecutions, military manuals, and legislation criminalizing IHL violations in internal conflict—to conclude that although common Article 3 and Protocol II are silent as to criminal enforcement, certain breaches of the law of armed conflict committed in non-international armed conflicts nonetheless constitute international crimes as a matter of customary international law.

Tribunals justify the elision of illegality into criminality with three strands of argument. One postulates that a treaty's silence as to the penal consequences of a breach does not mean treaty breaches are not crimes. This position is articulated even where a related treaty expressly provides for criminal penalties such that a strict

---

22 *Prosecutor v. Tadić*, Case No. IT-94-1-AR92, Decision on the Defence Motion for Interlocutory Appeal on Jurisdiction, ¶ 94 (Oct. 2, 1995).

application of the *a contrario*[23] principle would dictate an interpretation of the primary treaty's silence to preclude criminal enforcement. When forced to explain these treaty silences, tribunals reason that states intended to leave details of enforcement to state parties and the international community rather than mandate any particular enforcement regime. This approach disregards an obvious counter-explanation that drafting states made a deliberate choice *not* to criminalize such behavior and instead to leave enforcement at the level of state responsibility, or leave it to individual states to decide whether to impose criminal liability as a matter of domestic law. The second strand of this argument concedes the lack of criminalization, but argues that the application of such laws is only marginally retroactive insofar as the wrongfulness of the act is clear and it is only the remedy for breach (penal consequences rather than collective responsibility) that is at issue. Tinkering with the remedy, it is argued, does not generate a full-fledged *ex post facto* problem. Third, it is argued that assigning individual rather than collective responsibility is a more progressive and fair form of enforcement, even where the applicable law is silent as to such sanctions. Collective responsibility implicates both responsible and non-responsible individuals, and may result in sanctions that draw on the resources of the state that might otherwise go towards providing services to those within its jurisdiction. Individual responsibility, the argument goes, places the cost of non-compliance squarely on those most responsible.

5. Notice Anywhere Is Notice Everywhere

In filling gaps in positive law, jurists often make use of the multiplicity of sources of international law set forth in Article 38 of the International Court of Justice (ICJ) Statute: multilateral treaties, international custom, "the general principles of law recognized by civilized nations," and (as subsidiary means) judicial decisions and the writings of publicists. These disparate sources of law may articulate different or even contradictory standards with respect to the same subject matter, and international law has only rudimentary rules for reconciling competing sources of authority. Tribunals have ruled that so long as a defendant has notice of prohibited conduct in one of these various sources of law, then the principle of NCSL is satisfied and the prosecution can proceed.

Tribunals adjudicating ICL will look to whether a state has ratified the relevant ICL or IHL treaty to determine whether defendants had sufficient notice that they may be prosecuted for acts

[23] The *a contrario* principle of interpretation states that "the fact that a provision expressly provides for one category of situations is said to justify the inference that other comparable categories are excluded."

that run afoul of particular treaty provisions, even if the acts are not denominated as crimes *per se* in those instruments. For example, in the first prosecution for the crime of terrorizing the civilian population, the ICTY on its own motion confirmed that the charge was consistent with the dictates of NCSL.[24] The judges canvassed the treaties ratified by the various breakaway republics—including a May 22, 1992, treaty in which the signatories agreed to the applicability of a number of IHL treaties to the underlying conflict—to determine that the prohibition on "acts or threats of violence the primary purpose of which is to spread terror among the civilian population"—was binding on the warring parties as a matter of treaty law. (The tribunal found support in domestic terrorism proceedings as well).[25]

Courts adjudicating ICL often resort to customary international law in particular when an otherwise applicable treaty or piece of legislation is silent, ambiguous, or more constrained in its articulation of a legal principle. The *Scilingo* case before the Spanish *Audiencia Nacional*, a national court with special jurisdiction over international crimes, provides a good—if controversial—example of this reasoning.[26] Adolfo Scilingo was prosecuted for his complicity in crimes committed during the reign of the Argentine military *junta*. Although the investigating judge had charged him with terrorism, torture, and genocide—three crimes that had long existed in the Spanish *Código Penal*—the Audiencia Nacional (the court of first instance) convicted him of crimes against humanity, which had only been codified in Spanish law in 2004, well after the acts of which Scilingo was accused. The Audiencia rejected the defendant's argument that the prosecution was *ex post facto*, reasoning that crimes against humanity were prohibited by customary international law at the time of the events in question. The court ruled that the *jus cogens* and *erga omnes* nature of the customary international law prohibition against crimes against humanity was implicitly incorporated into, and thus directly applicable in, the Spanish domestic legal system. The court also cited analogous provisions in Argentine domestic law, which it ruled were sufficient to put the defendant on notice of potential penalties for his conduct. This ruling is significant, because the Spanish Constitution specifically incorporates the principle of legality in several places.

---

[24] *Prosecutor v. Galić*, Case No. IT-98-29-T, Judgment & Opinion, ¶¶ 87, 93 (Dec. 5, 2003.

[25] *Id.* ¶¶ 97–98.

[26] *Caso Scilingo*, Sentencia Audiencia Nacional, No. 16/2005 (Apr. 19, 2005) (Sp.). *See generally* Christian Tomuschat, *Issues of Universal Jurisdiction in the* Scilingo *Case*, 3 J. INT'L CRIM. J. 3 (2005); Alicia Gil Gil, *The Flaws of the* Scilingo *Judgment*, 3 J. INT'L CRIM. J. 1082 (2005); Giulia Pinzauti, *An Instance of Reasonable Universality: The* Scilingo *Case*, 3 J. INT'L CRIM. J. 1092 (2005).

On appeal, the *Tribunal Supremo* (Supreme Court) upheld the conviction, but rejected the Audiencia's reasoning.[27] In particular, it ruled that customary international law was not directly applicable within the Spanish system. Instead, it ruled that it could substitute a conviction for the well-established domestic crimes of murder and illegal detention. That Spanish law did not provide universal jurisdiction over such crimes was of no moment, because given the context in which Scilingo committed his crimes—in furtherance of a state-sponsored policy to eradicate subversion—they constituted crimes against humanity under ICL and thus were subject to universal jurisdiction. Crimes against humanity thus did not provide the appropriate substantive charge against the defendant, but the fact that the acts in question constituted crimes against humanity gave the Spanish courts universal jurisdiction over them as a matter of customary international law. The Supreme Court then sentenced Scilingo based on the Spanish penal code, which was more lenient than the Argentine code, because the former provided maximum penalties for the crimes in question.

The opinions discussed above reveal that tribunals will also cite applicable domestic law as a source of advance notice that certain conduct is prohibited, if not criminal. As we have discussed, many international crimes have domestic criminal analogs with definitions that differ only in that they lack the *chapeau* elements that internationalize such crimes and render them prosecutable before an international tribunal. For example, an act of murder becomes a crime against humanity when it is committed in the context of a widespread or systematic attack against a civilian population with knowledge of that attack. In this way, domestic crimes serve as predicate acts for their international analogs. International tribunals have reasoned that the prohibition in domestic law of the predicate acts can provide notice of the wrongfulness and criminality of the underlying conduct. Courts have reasoned that if an act is criminal under domestic law, there is no NCSL problem where the act is simply prosecuted under an international law analog.

As discussed in the context of the *Scilingo* prosecution in Spain, this same reasoning applies to domestic prosecutions. Another example of this reasoning in the context of a national prosecution involved Estonia's prosecution of two men accused of committing the crime of deportation immediately following World War II. The two were responsible for forcibly sending a dozen families to the Union of Soviet Socialist Republics, which occupied Estonia until 1991. Crimes against humanity, however, were not codified in Estonian law until 1994; as such, the defendants argued that the charges

---

27 *Case Scilingo*, STS No. 789/2007 (Nov. 8, 2007) (Sp.).

violated the *ex post facto* prohibition. In addition, they argued that the acts alleged did not constitute crimes against humanity under international law at the time, because the deportations were not carried out in execution of, or in connection with, any crime against the peace or war crime as required by the Nuremberg Charter. The Estonian courts, however, ignored this element of the offense and determined that the deportations qualified as a crime against humanity and thus were not subject to any statute of limitation, citing the U.N. Convention on the Non-Applicability of Statutory Limitations to War Crimes and Crimes Against Humanity (which both Estonia and the then-Soviet Union had ratified), and convicted the pair.[28] The European Court of Human Rights upheld the convictions, finding no violation of the prohibition against *ex post facto* prosecutions articulated in Article 7 of the European Convention and agreeing with the Estonian courts that deportation as a crime against humanity had clearly been established at the time of the acts in question.[29]

Even so-called soft law sources and academic scholarship have been found to provide sufficient constructive notice to defendants, even though it is hard to imagine such sources providing actual notice. The German case against Nikola Jorgić, a Bosnian Serb, marked one of the first universal jurisdiction cases to be brought and the first German prosecution for genocide since ratification of the Genocide Convention in 1954. Jorgić had fled back to Germany after the war in the former Yugoslavia. German officials later charged him with participating in assaults and massacres of Bosnian civilians in his home region of Doboj. Jurisdiction in Germany was premised on Germany's then universal jurisdiction provision, Article 6 of the *Srafgesetzbuch* (the German Criminal Code).[30] The crime of genocide was defined in Article 220a of the German Criminal Code in a way that was virtually identical to the Genocide Convention definition. Nonetheless, the German Constitutional Court expanded the notion of genocide to include cultural genocide, which was specifically excluded from the Genocide Convention. It reasoned that the intent to destroy the group "includes the annihilation of a group as a social unit with its special qualities, uniqueness and its feeling of togetherness, not exclusively their physical-biological

---

[28] United Nations Convention on the Non-Applicability of Statutory Limitations to War Crimes and Crimes against Humanity art. 1, 754 U.N.T.S. 73 (Nov. 26, 1968).

[29] *Kolk & Kislyiy v. Estonia*, App. No. 23052/04 & 24018/04 (Jan. 17, 2006).

[30] Germany's new Code of Crimes Against International Law of June 26, 2002 (*Völkerstrafgesetzbuch*), enacted to systematically codify the Rome Statute crimes, has replaced Article 220a and other piecemeal enactments of international crimes within the federal penal code.

annihilation."[31] Citing a General Assembly resolution equating ethnic cleansing in the former Yugoslavia with genocide, the German court held that prohibited acts could include destroying or looting houses or buildings of importance to the group or the expulsion of members of the group. The court reasoned that the prohibition against genocide protects legal interests that "lie[] beyond the individual, namely the social existence of a group." This, it noted, "has a broader meaning than physical-biological annihilation."[32] The court concluded that this interpretation was "within the margins of the possible interpretation of the international law elements of the crime of genocide."[33] In so ruling, the court rejected contrary language in the *Krstić* case before the ICTY, which rejected the criminality of cultural genocide.[34] Jorgić was convicted of genocide and sentenced to life imprisonment.

Jorgić challenged his prosecution and conviction before the European Court of Human Rights (ECHR),[35] claiming that his prosecution violated several provisions of the European Convention, including Article 7. Jorgić argued that the German courts had expansively construed the genocide prohibition beyond the contours of positive law. The ECHR ruled that the German courts' interpretation was both in keeping with the "essence of the offense" and could reasonably have been foreseen at the material time by the applicant with the assistance of counsel. The ECHR determined that several aspects of the *actus reus* of genocide do not require the physical or biological destruction of the group, so the German court's interpretation found support in the text of the law. In addition, the ECHR determined that Jorgić could have foreseen the more expansive interpretation of the provision, especially in light of the work of several German scholars advancing such an interpretation and a degree of uncertainty in the law on this point. Thus, the ECHR determined that the German courts enjoyed discretion under the European Convention to adopt the interpretation of the genocide prohibition that they saw fit.

So long as notice was available to the defendant from some source of law—and not even necessarily one binding on the defendant at the time he acted—and so long as the defendant could reasonably ascertain in advance that the particular conduct was prohibited, even

---

[31] Bundesverfassungsgericht [BVerfG] [Federal Constitutional Court] Dec. 12, 2000, 2 BvR 1290/99, NJW 2001, S. 1848 [1849], (F.RG.), English translation available at https://www.bundesverfassungsgericht.de/SharedDocs/Entscheidungen/EN/2000/12/rk20001212_2bvr129099en.html.

[32] *Id.* ¶ 7.

[33] *Id.* ¶ 10.

[34] *Prosecutor v. Krstić*, Case No. IT-98-33-T, Judgment, ¶¶ 576–580 (Aug. 2, 2001) (rejecting notion of cultural genocide).

[35] *See Jorgić v. Germany*, Application no. 74613/01, Judgment (July 12, 2007).

if the assistance of counsel would be necessary to do so, tribunals—including human rights courts—have found no breach of the NCSL principle.[36] Tribunals thus assume defendants' ability to undertake virtually global legal research to determine the scope and content of ICL. This is especially true with respect to individuals to whom ICL is directly addressed—soldiers and statesmen. As such, "ignorance of ICL is no excuse," a legal fiction familiar from ordinary domestic law.

6. The Object and Purpose of ICL

NCSL defenses often arise in situations in which tribunals must add content to vaguely worded prohibitions. To do so, tribunals will often look to the object and purpose of the relevant prohibition, treaty, or body of law. This approach is well established within the jurisprudence of the various human rights institutions, which quite self-consciously interpret their constitutive treaties as "living" instruments that must adapt to modern needs to advance fundamental human rights. For example, in *Loizidou v. Turkey*, the European Court of Human Rights held:

> That the Convention is a living instrument which must be interpreted in the light of present day conditions is firmly rooted in the Court's case-law [. . .]. It follows that these provisions cannot be interpreted solely in accordance with the intentions of their authors as expressed more than forty years ago.[37]

As these institutions see it, the goal of human rights treaty regimes is not to enforce reciprocal obligations adopted by contracting states *inter se*, but to create and sustain a protective public order applicable to all those within the *espace juridique* of signatory states.

International criminal tribunals have adopted a similar approach, endeavoring to effectuate the object and purpose of ICL and IHL in interpreting substantive norms. At least in the realm of IHL, a teleological approach is also permitted, if not mandated, by the Martens Clause, a familiar component of many IHL treaties, which reads:

> Until a more complete code of the laws of war is issued, the High Contracting Parties think it right to declare that in cases not included in the Regulations adopted by them, populations and belligerents remain under the protection and empire of the principles of international law, as they

---

36 In the context of domestic law, *see SW v. United Kingdom*, 21 Eur. Ct. H.R. 363, (ser. A) ¶ 36, 49 (1996); *C.R. v. United Kingdom*, 1995 Eur. Ct. H.R. 51, ¶ 42 (1995) (finding no legality deficit where defendants had notice of the offense).

37 *Loizidou v. Turkey*, App. No. 40/1993/435/514, European Court of Human Rights, ¶ 71 (Feb. 23, 1995).

> result from the usages established between civilized nations, from the laws of humanity and the requirements of the public conscience.[38]

The clause suggests a reservoir of uncodified law applicable in armed conflict. It allows courts to go beyond the written text and refer not only to customary international law ("the usages established between civilized nations") but also to the moral bases of humanitarian obligations by making reference "to pre-juridical principles [and] to the sentiments of humanity."[39] As such, the Martens Clause also provides a principle of interpretation that is in keeping with the principles of humanity and moral standards. The clause, however, was drafted at a time when individual criminal responsibility—with its attendant concerns with adhering to the principle of legality—was not yet established as an expected response to treaty breaches. Courts cite it nonetheless in penal proceedings.

An example of the use of the Martens clause to support a teleological approach to the ICTY Statute is found in *Prosecutor v. Hadžihasanović*. The ICTY defendants in that case argued that IHL did not allow superiors to be prosecuted for the acts of their subordinates in internal armed conflicts, primarily because Protocol I, applicable in international conflicts, is the first and only IHL treaty to set out the elements of the superior responsibility doctrine.[40] Taking an expansive teleological approach, an ICTY Trial Chamber relied on the *Tadić* framework referenced earlier to rule that the defendants could be prosecuted under the superior responsibility doctrine in an internal armed conflict. To start, it looked to the object and purpose of the Security Council in creating the ICTY. It cited statements made by states during the drafting of the ICTY Statute showing an expectation that the doctrine of command responsibility would be applicable before the Tribunal without reference to the nature of the conflict, although this survey revealed that no state specifically argued for, or acknowledged, the applicability of the doctrine in non-international armed conflicts. The Trial Chamber then went further to examine the object and purpose of IHL writ large, separate and apart from the intentions of particular members of the Security Council. It identified IHL's object and purpose to be the "regulat[ion of] the means and methods of warfare and [the protection of] persons not actively participating in armed conflict

---

38 *See* Rupert Ticehurst, *The Martens Clause and the Laws of Armed Conflict*, 317 INT'L REV. RED CROSS (1997).

39 *The Attitude of States Toward the Development of Humanitarian Law*, *in* THE NEW HUMANITARIAN LAW OF ARMED CONFLICT: PROCEEDINGS OF THE 1976 AND 1977 CONFERENCES 221, 257 (Antonio Cassese ed., 1980) (emphasis omitted).

40 *Prosecutor v. Hadžihasanović*, Case No. IT-01-47-PT, Decision on Joint Challenge to Jurisdiction, ¶ 62 (Nov. 12, 2002).

from harm" and the "respect for human dignity."[41] The Trial Chamber invoked the Martens Clause, contained in Protocol II governing non-international armed conflict, as inspiration to consider the fundamental principles underlying IHL. The Chamber noted that the doctrine of superior responsibility promotes two such principles: the existence of individual criminal responsibility for violations, even where treaties are silent on enforcement, and the principle of responsible command.

The precise framing of the overarching object and purpose of ICL has contributed to the tribunals' more relaxed approach to the dictates of the strict version of NCSL. A fundamental assumption underpinning the principle of legality is that it will deter crime by ensuring fair notice of proscribed conduct. This assumes known—or knowable—law and rational actors who will structure their conduct to avoid anticipated censure. To date, specific deterrence has not been a primary motivation of existing ICL tribunals. Many modern tribunals were established (or have asserted jurisdiction) after the horrific events in question; the ICTY and ICC are two exceptions. Being *ex post*, these other tribunals were unable to exert any deterrent effect on defendants within their personal jurisdiction and had to settle for contributing to the general deterrence of future perpetrators. Even scholars devoted to the field doubt whether ICL can provoke deterrence under contemporary circumstances where international justice remains sporadic and random and cannot yet create consistent expectations of capture and punishment. Until legal censure is more certain, the narratives that explain why seemingly ordinary people do evil things in the context of war or state-sponsored repression—because they are beset by prejudices, intoxicated by power, manipulated by elites, terrified into submission by superior orders or threats of retaliation for their inaction, or caught up in a maelstrom of violence—likely still overwhelm any cost-benefit analysis in which individual perpetrators may engage.

Where deterrence is de-emphasized, other goals of criminology—retribution, the incapacitation of perpetrators, the rehabilitation of victims, and the public condemnation of injurious behavior—become more salient. These goals (and retribution and rehabilitation in particular) are often cited to justify moves away from the strict dictates of NCSL. Although we may decry retribution as a primitive and unenlightened motivation for criminal law, its enduring potency cannot be denied. Ending impunity is often cited as a key object and purpose of ICL. In the face of centuries, if not millennia, of impunity for what we now consider human rights atrocities, retributive

---

[41] *Id.* ¶ 64. *See also Prosecutor v. Aleksovski*, Case No. IT-95-14/1-A, Judgment, ¶ 146 (Mar. 24, 2000) (noting that the object and purpose of the Fourth Geneva Convention is to ensure the "protection of civilians to the maximum extent possible").

impulses may exceed concerns for the strict adherence to the legality principle as courts are unwilling to let bad behavior continue to go unpunished under international law. In ICL, where the problem historically has been chronic underenforcement of the law, there is still little concern for overdeterrence and a concomitant willingness to overlook legalisms that would lead to impunity in an effort to jumpstart a system of greater accountability. Likewise, ICL judges have also seen themselves as providing a voice for victims, which might push them to identify a set of concrete legal standards within the more amorphous *lex ferenda*.

C. Conclusion

Innovative judges and expansive legal interpretations are not unique or endemic to ICL. Although the codification of ICL will probably never be complete, the rate of change is slowing significantly. Early cases addressed important open areas in legal doctrine. Today's cases address issues that are more nuanced, involving the resolution of more micro inconsistencies and the filling in of increasingly smaller gaps in the law. As a result, there is less and less space for judges to build on the ICL edifice. Although there will always be a need to elucidate hazy points and adapt to changing circumstances through the progressive development of the law through judicial law-making, like any maturing system of law, most of the next phase of the evolution of ICL will happen at the outer edges of doctrine, where the implications of new ideas are perhaps less dramatic.

As the *ad hoc* tribunals continue to wind down their work, international prosecutions are increasingly proceeding before the ICC, unless the international community creates more *ad hoc* and hybrid courts. The ICC is governed by a robustly-worded NCSL provision that not only prohibits the retroactive application of law, but also mandates strict construction in favor of defendants. As the jurisdiction of the Court is expressly proscriptive, there is less space for the NCSL defense. That said, there are "legality deficits" within the statute, as many crimes remain vaguely or sparingly worded. As the ICC issues more substantive decisions and judgments, the Court will undoubtedly be faced with the pressure to innovate. It remains to be seen to what extent the NCSL provisions will truly cabin the ability of the Court to adopt expansive or novel interpretations to crimes within its jurisdiction.

Given all this, it is tempting to conclude that the dilemma posed by the NCSL principle in ICL had a relatively short shelf life. To a certain degree, it did. Nonetheless, areas remain in which innovation is possible and will be tempting. Where the defense of NCSL will retain great currency going forward will be in domestic proceedings, especially where courts adjudicating historical justice cases must decide what law to apply to events that preceded the ICL renaissance. In connection with their ratification of the ICC Statute, states are increasingly incorporating international crimes into their domestic penal codes. Such crimes are often subject to universal jurisdiction, granting domestic courts an expansive extraterritorial reach. As was the case in *Scilingo*, there will undoubtedly be additional efforts to apply these new statutes to conduct that predates codification. Such retroactive justice is enabled by the trend among national courts and legislatures to extend, toll, or abolish altogether statutes of limitation for international crimes. The NCSL dilemma also remains relevant for idiosyncratic or expansive interpretations of established law, as seen in the *Jorgić* case.

The line of cases discussed in this chapter reveals a series of interpretive devices and rhetorical moves employed by criminal tribunals to—at a minimum—fill lacunae and interstices within positive law and—at a maximum—extend the reach of ICL beyond what extant positive law provides. In many of the decisions, tribunals have departed from, expanded on, or outright rejected rules carefully negotiated by states during treaty drafting processes. This has the potential to upset the "constitutional" balance—if it can be called that—between states and the adjudicative institutions they create in the international system. As you review ICL opinions, be conscious of the arguments tribunals are using as they interpret or expand extant treaty language and consider the legitimacy of the case outcomes along the two key dimensions of respect for state sovereignty and the rights of defendants.

Part II

INTERSECTIONS

In this part, we shift gears to consider the core international crimes—war crimes, crimes against the peace or aggression, crimes against humanity, and genocide—alongside the primary international criminal law (ICL) defenses and forms of responsibility. This part focuses on crimes within the jurisdiction of the International Criminal Court (ICC) and other international, or quasi-international, tribunals. The terrorism crimes are addressed as stand-alone crimes because they are closely related to the core crimes and are the subject of active prosecution by states under extraterritorial forms of jurisdiction, particularly with respect to crimes being committed in the overlapping conflicts in Syria and Iraq. In addition, the international crime of torture (which is also an enumerated war crime and crime against humanity) is introduced with reference to the defense of necessity. Largely excluded from this discussion are other transnational crimes—such as money laundering, trafficking in people and narcotics, and international arms dealing—on the theory that such crimes are primarily (but not exclusively) defined by domestic law and prosecuted before domestic tribunals. Some of these transnational crimes were originally contemplated within the subject matter jurisdiction of the ICC. Indeed, Trinidad and Tobago first proposed reopening discussions on a permanent international criminal court after years of Cold War quiescence because they wanted an international forum to prosecute transnational drug crimes that were overwhelming smaller transit states. As negotiations for the ICC progressed, however, these crimes fell away and states focused on the core atrocity crimes.

As the following chapters indicate, the elements of international law offenses overlap considerably. For one, a single act may implicate multiple international crimes. For example, an act of murder can constitute a war crime (when a protected person is intentionally killed within the context of an armed conflict), a crime against humanity (when a person is intentionally killed within the context of a widespread or systematic attack against a civilian population), or an act of genocide (when a member of a protected group is killed with the specific intent to destroy the person's group, in whole or in part). Similarly, consider the multiple counts the following event could generate: A protected person from a minority ethnic group is intentionally killed using a prohibited weapon in the context of the bombardment of an undefended town involving excessive force out of proportion to any military advantage. The victim could be considered the victim of multiple crimes, including a whole range of different war crimes, crimes against humanity, and genocide.

Forms of responsibility add another layer of complexity to international crimes. Jurisprudence arising out of World War II (including the *Yamashita* case, which proceeded before a military commission in the field and then made its way to the U.S. Supreme Court on a petition for *habeas corpus*) began to establish the contours of the responsibility of superiors for the criminal acts of their subordinates. The jurisprudence on superior responsibility has become increasingly sophisticated through the decisions of the *ad hoc* tribunals and now the ICC. This is equally true for the other forms of responsibility: committing, ordering, inciting, instigating, permitting, failing to prevent or punish, and being complicit in the international crimes committed. While some of these forms of responsibility will be familiar to students of domestic criminal law (i.e. aiding and abetting as a form of complicity), others are either non-existent or play a very minor or peripheral role in domestic systems (i.e. superior responsibility).

The overlap of international crimes and the multiple forms of responsibility raises multiple questions about the administration of justice. These include questions about how a prosecutor should charge defendants whose conduct implicates multiple prohibitions and forms of responsibility, how a tribunal should construct its verdict in light of multiple and overlapping counts in an indictment, and how a defendant should be sentenced when the prosecutor proves the commission of multiple crimes. Resolving these questions of charging and sentencing may hinge on whether the crimes charged constitute lesser included offenses of each other. In this regard, the international criminal tribunals have largely adopted the approach articulated by the U.S. Supreme Court in *Blockburger v. United States*, 284 U.S. 299, 304 (1932):

> The applicable rule is that where the same act or transaction constitutes a violation of two distinct statutory provisions, the test to be applied to determine whether there are two offences or only one, is whether each provision requires proof of an additional fact which the other does not.

The test thus requires a determination of whether each offense contains an element not required by the other. If so, the crime that is fully encompassed is a lesser included offense of the crime containing the additional element.

As you review these materials, consider the way in which the various atrocity crimes overlap and intersect with each other. Do the various crimes "cover the field" or are there gaps that might be filled by normative development? It is also worth considering why certain international crimes have not been made subject to international jurisdiction, such as human trafficking, piracy, corruption, or terrorism. Once you are familiar with the ICC's subject matter jurisdiction, you might consider whether the ICC could or should prosecute crimes that were purposefully excluded from its subject matter jurisdiction in situations in which the acts can also be characterized as war crimes or crimes against humanity.

Chapter 6

THE LEGAL REGULATION OF WAR

As discussed in more detail in Chapter 1, the law of war has historically encompassed two main foci: the *jus ad bellum* and the *jus in bello*. The former addresses the legality of going to war and historically took the form of theological and then secular "just war" theories; the latter concedes the *de facto* existence of a conflict and seeks to regulate belligerent conduct within it, regardless of the origins of the violence in the first place. Although some of the world's greatest minds have grappled with establishing standards for determining when states had the right to go to war, by the late nineteenth century, the right to wage war began to be viewed as an inherent, if not inevitable, incident of state sovereignty. Further development of the *jus ad bellum* was all but eclipsed by prolific developments in *jus in bello*. Nonetheless, these two approaches to regulating warfare converged in the charters of the World War II international tribunals, which adjudicated violations of both bodies of law as crimes giving rise to individual criminal responsibility—even though neither body of law was necessarily designed to be applied in a courtroom.

In the postwar period, violations of *jus ad bellum* (referred to as "crimes against the peace" at Nuremberg and Tokyo) all but disappeared from the pantheon of international criminal law (ICL). Instead, Article 2(4) of the U.N. Charter addressed states—rather than individuals—and prohibited the "threat or use of force against the territorial integrity or political independence of any state, or in any other manner inconsistent with the Purposes of the United Nations." Under the U.N. Charter regime, breaches of this provision give rise to state, rather than individual criminal, responsibility. For their part, war crimes were further codified in the 1949 Geneva Conventions.

Contemporary international law now views the conceptual distinction between the *jus ad bellum* and the *jus in bello* as axiomatic: The legal evaluation of the conduct of hostilities is an inquiry entirely independent from the legal evaluation of the lawfulness of the resort to armed force. Accordingly, a just (or lawful) war may be fought unlawfully, and an unjust (or unlawful) war may be fought lawfully. Under the *jus in bello,* by consequence, all parties are treated equally, regardless of who initiated the armed conflict and their reasons for doing so. The belligerents of all sides are entitled to humane treatment if captured and the civilians on all sides are immune from direct targeting. Indeed, the International

Committee of the Red Cross (ICRC) remains strictly agnostic about the cause(s) of any armed conflicts in which it operates while carefully scrutinizing their consequences. That said, there is an intuitive appeal to the position, still advocated by some, that any act of armed force committed within the context of an unlawful war should *ipso facto* be treated as a war crime. On the flip side, many groups fighting against what they consider to be oppressive, racist, or occupier states continue to argue that any act committed in furtherance of such a just war must itself also be deemed just and lawful.

Although crimes against the peace have to date merited only a short chapter in the annals of ICL, the idea that the resort to war itself is a criminal act has become more than a historical footnote. In 2017, the International Criminal Court's (ICC) Assembly of States Parties activated amendments adding the crime of aggression—the modern lexicon for crimes against the peace—to the subject matter jurisdiction of the Court, although the crime has yet to be adjudicated. As such, the *jus ad bellum* and *jus in bello* have now been reunited in the Statute of the ICC. This chapter briefly traces some high points in the development of the penal components of these two bodies of law. It then presents the basic framework for understanding the contemporary law of aggression and then war crimes, noting areas in the law that remain in flux. Underlying this chapter is a rich legacy of legal rules aimed at the regulation of hostilities that belies the claim by Cicero that *silent enim leges inter arma*—the laws are silent among those at war.

A. *Jus Ad Bellum*

1. Crimes Against Peace: The Original Crime of Aggression

The charters for both the Nuremberg and Tokyo Tribunals contained the charge of "crimes against the peace" alongside the charges of war crimes and crimes against humanity. The postwar architects of international justice defined crimes against the peace somewhat tautologically at Article 6(a) as "planning, preparation, initiation or waging of a war of aggression, or a war in violation of international treaties, agreements or assurances."[1] In addition, the two tribunal charters allowed for the prosecution of individuals for their "participation in a common plan or conspiracy" to commit aggression. Count One of the Nuremberg Indictment charged all the defendants with conspiring to commit crimes against the peace. Count Two charged all but five defendants with actually committing crimes against the peace. All but four defendants were charged with

[1] Charter of the International Military Tribunal art. 6(a), Aug. 8, 1945, 59 Stat. 1546, 82 U.N.T.S. 279.

war crimes in Count Three. At Tokyo, all the defendants were charged with so-called Class A crimes—the crime of executing a common plan or conspiracy to wage aggressive war or wars in violation of international law—as a jurisdictional prerequisite.

Although the World War II defendants did not submit to the equally novel crimes against humanity charge without objection, the crimes against the peace charge was the most controversial element of the Charters at the time. Both sets of defendants argued that the concept of crimes against the peace violated the principle of legality, because war had never before been criminalized in international law, so the prohibition against crimes against the peace in the two charters was, in effect, *ex post facto* legislation. As is discussed more fully in Chapter 5 on the defense of *nullum crimen sine lege*, the tribunals ruled that the acts of aggression proven at trial were unlawful, and thus criminal, under extant treaties and customary norms, although none of these sources expressly provided for criminal penalties in the event of a breach. The Indian judge at Tokyo, Justice Radhabinod Pal, articulated a different critique: that the victorious allies sought suddenly to criminalize the very acts that had brought them to power in the first place during the age of imperialism and colonialization (with India gaining independence only in 1947). In his dissent, he noted:

> Certainly dominated nations of the present day *status quo* cannot be made to submit to eternal domination only in the name of peace. . . . The part of humanity which has been lucky enough to enjoy political freedom can now well afford to have the deterministic ascetic outlook of life, and may think of peace in terms of political *status quo*. But every part of humanity has not been equally lucky and a considerable part is still haunted by the wishful thinking about escape from political dominations. . . . To them the present age is faced with not only the menace of totalitarianism but also the actual plague of imperialism.[2]

Justice Pal's dissent, which until recently was relatively obscure and even difficult to find, has enjoyed increased interest from, among others, critics from the Global South, who challenge the history and power imbalances embedded in the current international legal system.[3]

---

[2] *U.S.A. v. Araki, Sadai et al.*, Judgment of the Honorable Mr. Justice Pal, *in* DOCUMENTS ON THE TOKYO INTERNATIONAL MILITARY TRIBUNAL 809, 910 (Neil Boister & Robert Cryer eds., 2008).

[3] Some of these critics are loosely organized under the banner of TWAIL (Third World Approaches to International Law). For a good introduction to TWAIL and its critique of international criminal law, *see Symposium on TWAIL Perspectives on ICL, IHL, and Intervention*, 109 AJIL UNBOUND 252 (2015). *See also* Luis Eslava,

The crime of aggression was the centerpiece of the Charter and the Nuremberg Trial, which was to be "the Trial to end all wars." Indeed, a majority of the Nuremberg Tribunal's judgment consists of describing the aggressive acts of Germany, including the invasions of (*inter alia*) Poland, Austria, what was then Czechoslovakia, and Belgium in violation of the Kellogg-Briand Pact, various bilateral treaties and assurances of nonaggression, and declarations of neutrality. In its final judgment, the Nuremberg Tribunal reasoned that belligerency was the proximate cause of all the other crimes alleged: "To initiate a war of aggression, therefore, is not only an international crime; it is the supreme international crime differing only from other war crimes in that it contains within itself the accumulated evil of the whole."[4] Given the importance of this crime in the proceedings of the immediate postwar period, it is noteworthy that none of the statutes of the contemporary *ad hoc* tribunals contains the crime of aggression, even though it would have arguably been relevant in the conflicts in the former Yugoslavia, East Timor, and Sierra Leone.

The post-WWII tribunals laid the foundation for the recognition of the crime of aggression. With the formal end of World War II, states immediately turned to the creation of the United Nations, an institution primarily concerned with the maintenance of international peace and security. Article 2(4) of the U.N. Charter, quoted above, sets forth a presumption against the use of force internationally. The U.N. Security Council bears the primary responsibility for maintaining international peace, through identifying threats to the peace and acts of aggression (Article 39) and deciding on measures, including the use of armed force, in response (Articles 41 and 42). The U.N. Charter recognizes only two scenarios in which the use of force by a state is potentially lawful: in response to Security Council authorization and in self-defense (Article 51).[5] Ancient doctrines of humanitarian intervention, and

---

TWAIL Coordinates, Critical Legal Thinking (https://criticallegalthinking.com/2019/04/02/twail-coordinates/) (Apr. 2, 2019).

4 Judgment, 1 TRIAL OF THE MAJOR WAR CRIMINALS BEFORE THE INTERNATIONAL MILITARY TRIBUNAL, NUREMBERG 14 NOVEMBER 1945–1 OCTOBER 1946 at 186 (1947), *reprinted in* 41 AM. J. INT'L L. 172 (1947) [hereinafter *Nuremberg Judgment*].

5 Article 51 reads: "Nothing in the present Charter shall impair the inherent right of individual or collective self-defence if an armed attack occurs against a Member of the United Nations, until the Security Council has taken measures necessary to maintain international peace and security. Measures taken by Members in the exercise of this right of self-defence shall be immediately reported to the Security Council and shall not in any way affect the authority and responsibility of the Security Council under the present Charter to take at any time such action as it deems necessary in order to maintain or restore international peace and security." The conditions under which states may claim preemptive or anticipatory self-defense remain contested under international law.

the United Nations' Responsibility to Protect concept, suggests a third scenario justifying the use of force: military intervention that does not threaten the territorial integrity or political independence of a state but is rather deployed to prevent the commission of atrocity crimes.[6] Collectively, these restrictions largely invalidate the use of armed force as a legitimate policy choice and, as such, run counter to von Clausewitz's claim that "war is a mere continuation of policy by other means."[7]

The Charter addresses potential state responsibility for acts of aggression; it is silent as to potential individual criminal responsibility. In the postwar period, the international community failed to draft a comprehensive treaty setting forth the elements of the crime of aggression as it did with genocide and war crimes. In taking up the proposal to establish a permanent international criminal court, the International Law Commission (ILC) promulgated a Draft Code of Crimes Against the Peace and Security of Mankind that was to provide the substantive law to be adjudicated before the proposed court. Early versions of the Draft Code designated the crime of aggression as a crime against the peace and security at Article 2 and defined the crime with reference to the use of armed force by one state against another for any purpose other than in national or collective self-defense or pursuant to a decision or recommendation of a competent organ of the United Nations.[8] Reaching a consensus definition of the crime of aggression proved to be an insurmountable impasse, however; as such, during the Cold War, the Draft Code project went into quiescence, not to be fully revived until the 1990s.

In 1974, the U.N. General Assembly unanimously passed Resolution 3314 to "guide" the Security Council in determining the occurrence of aggression in the exercise of its Chapter VII power.[9] Article 1 provides that aggression is the "use of armed force by a State against the sovereignty, territorial integrity or political independence of another State, or in any other manner inconsistent with the Charter of the United Nations." The Resolution contains in Article 3 a list of acts that constitute aggression, regardless of the existence of a declaration of war, including:

---

6 *See* INT'L COMM. ON INTERVENTION & ST. SOVEREIGNTY, THE RESPONSIBILITY TO PROTECT (Dec. 2001); 2005 World Summit Outcome, G.A. Res. 60/1, ¶¶ 138–139, U.N. Doc. A/RES/60/1 (Sept. 16, 2005); Report of the Secretary-General, *Implementing the Responsibility to Protect*, U.N. Doc. A/63/677 (Jan. 12, 2009).

7 CARL VON CLAUSEWITZ, ON WAR 101 (1968).

8 *See* 1985 YEARBOOK OF THE INTERNATIONAL LAW COMMISSION (Vol. II), at 8 (reproducing the 1954 Draft Code).

9 G.A. Res. 3314 (XXIX), U.N. Doc. A/RES/3314 (Dec. 14, 1974).

(a) The invasion or attack by the armed forces of a State of the territory of another State, or any military occupation, however temporary, resulting from such invasion or attack, or any annexation by the use of force of the territory of another State or part thereof;

(b) Bombardment by the armed forces of a State against the territory of another State or the use of any weapons by a State against the territory of another State;

(c) The blockade of the ports or coasts of a State by the armed forces of another State;

(d) An attack by the armed forces of a State on the land, sea or air forces, or marine and air fleets of another State;

(e) The use of armed forces of one State which are within the territory of another State with the agreement of the receiving State, in contravention of the conditions provided for in the agreement or any extension of their presence in such territory beyond the termination of the agreement;

(f) The action of a State in allowing its territory, which it has placed at the disposal of another State, to be used by that other State for perpetrating an act of aggression against a third State;

(g) The sending by or on behalf of a State of armed bands, groups, irregulars or mercenaries, which carry out acts of armed force against another State of such gravity as to amount to the acts listed above, or its substantial involvement therein.[10]

Article 5(2) states that a "war of aggression is a crime against international peace," but the remainder of the resolution is geared toward state, rather than individual, responsibility. Notwithstanding this consensus definition of aggression, only a few states incorporated the crime of aggression into their penal codes.[11] Nonetheless, when the international community again turned to the drafting of a statute for a permanent international criminal court in the 1990s, many state delegates argued for the revival of the crime

[10] Article 3(g) was declared customary international law by the I.C.J. in the Nicaragua case. *See* Military and Paramilitary Activities in and against Nicaragua (Nicar. v. U.S.), Merits, 1986 I.C.J. 14, 103 (June 27).

[11] For a discussion of the handful of domestic proceedings involving the crime of aggression, *see* Antonio Cassese, *On Some Problematical Aspects of the Crime of Aggression*, 20 LEIDEN J. INT'L L. 841, 842–843 (2007). In particular, *see R. v. Jones et al.*, (2006) UKHL 16 (Mar. 29, 2006) (U.K.) (finding that aggression was criminalized under customary international law, but not U.K. law).

of aggression in keeping with the Nuremberg and Tokyo legacy. Resolution 3314 was dusted off as a point of departure; it ended up informing the final destination.

2. The Modern Crime of Aggression

When the Rome Treaty was finalized, Article 5(1) listed the crime of aggression as a crime over which the ICC has jurisdiction. Delegates to the Rome Conference, however, were unable to agree on the crime's definition or on any applicable jurisdictional preconditions, and so they punted. Article 5(2) promised that the Court "shall exercise jurisdiction over the crime of aggression once a provision is adopted in accordance with articles 121 and 123 defining the crime and setting out the conditions under which the Court shall exercise jurisdiction with respect to this crime. Such a provision shall be consistent with the relevant provisions of the Charter of the United Nations." This seemingly innocuous phrase at the end of the placeholder text pinpoints one of the most highly contentious issues of defining the crime of aggression: what role the Security Council, or other U.N. bodies, would play in determining the existence of a sovereign act of aggression as a prerequisite to the ICC's criminal jurisdiction over an alleged suspect. Resolution F of the Final Act of the Rome Conference requested that the Preparatory Commission prepare proposals for a provision on aggression to be presented to the Assembly of State Parties (ASP).[12]

In 2002, the ASP established a Special Working Group on the Crime of Aggression, with Ambassador Christian Wenaweser of Liechtenstein serving as chair, to continue to work on the aggression amendments. The group was open to all states, including non-State Parties; the United States, however, did not begin participating in this process until the Obama Administration sent an inter-agency delegation in 2009. This prolonged absence proved to be a strategic mistake on the part of the United States. Entering the process midstream, the United States faced a difficult uphill battle in its efforts to influence the final definition of the crime. By 2008, participating states had largely agreed upon a definition of the crime of aggression, to be inserted at Article 8*bis*, based largely on Resolution 3314 and the U.N. Charter. The text read:

1. For the purpose of this Statute, "crime of aggression" means the planning, preparation, initiation or execution, by a person in a position effectively to exercise control over or to direct the political or military action of a State, of an act of aggression which,

---

[12] Final Act Of The United Nations Diplomatic Conference Of Plenipotentiaries On The Establishment Of An International Criminal Court, U.N. Doc. A/CONF.183/10 (July 17, 1998).

by its character, gravity and scale, constitutes a manifest violation of the Charter of the United Nations.

2. For the purpose of paragraph 1, "act of aggression" means the use of armed force by a State against the sovereignty, territorial integrity or political independence of another State, or in any other manner inconsistent with the Charter of the United Nations. Any of the following acts, regardless of a declaration of war, shall, in accordance with United Nations General Assembly resolution 3314 (XXIX) of 14 December 1974, qualify as an act of aggression.

The text went on to list all the acts enumerated in Resolution 3314, discussed above, as acts of aggression. This approach found favor among the African and Arab states, which rejected efforts to either amend the list of aggressive acts or exclude reference to Resolution 3314 altogether.

Although the definition of the crime resisted amendment from this point forward, the United States did manage to massage the definition during the 2010 Review Conference held in Kampala, Uganda, with several interpretive Understandings. These are contained in the final Resolution adopting the amendments and were introduced in Chapter 3 on the making of ICL. In Kampala, States Parties also adopted the following elements of the crime of aggression:

1. The perpetrator planned, prepared, initiated or executed an act of aggression.
2. The perpetrator was a person in a position effectively to exercise control over or to direct the political or military action of the State which committed the act of aggression.
3. The act of aggression—the use of armed force by a State against the sovereignty, territorial integrity or political independence of another State, or in any other manner inconsistent with the Charter of the United Nations—was committed.
4. The perpetrator was aware of the factual circumstances that established that such a use of armed force was inconsistent with the Charter of the United Nations.
5. The act of aggression, by its character, gravity and scale, constituted a manifest violation of the Charter of the United Nations.

6. The perpetrator was aware of the factual circumstances that established such a manifest violation of the Charter of the United Nations.

The majority of the negotiations during the Review Conference focused almost exclusively on the jurisdictional regime to govern the crime, which differs depending on whether the investigation has been triggered by a State Party or by the Prosecutor acting *proprio motu* (Article 15*bis*) or by the Security Council (Articles 15*ter*). One key element for the former scenario is an "opt out" clause, that allows States Parties to declare in advance that they do not accept jurisdiction over the crime of aggression; so far, Kenya and Guatemala have availed themselves of this option. In addition, the Court cannot exercise jurisdiction over the crime of aggression committed on the territory of a non-party state or by its nationals, a key concession to the United States.

The Prosecutor may be obliged to delay by six months the opening of an investigation if the Security Council has not yet determined that the situation involves an act of aggression. Several of the P-5[13] argued that such a determination should be a condition precedent for the Prosecutor proceeding with an investigation into the crime of aggression. This proposal did not prevail, in part because the Security Council has historically branded only a handful of situations as "acts of aggression" or "aggression," including acts committed by South Africa and Southern Rhodesia against its neighbors, by Israel against Tunisia, and by Iraq against Kuwait.[14] The text makes clear that a determination of an act of aggression by an organ outside the Court is without prejudice to the Court's own findings in this regard.

Finally, the decision of the Prosecutor to move forward on her own motion is contingent upon receiving approval to do so by the full Pre-Trial Division (investigations initiated by the Prosecutor in the absence of a referral go to a Pre-Trial Chamber). By contrast, a Security Council referral of a situation to the Court does not require any prior determination that a state committed an act of aggression by the Council. Nor must the Prosecutor seek recourse to the Pre-Trial Division before proceeding. Nor is any opt-out available, and the Council may refer a matter involving a non-party state.

Regardless of the trigger mechanism, aggression can only be prosecuted against "persons in a position effectively to exercise

---

[13] The phrase P-5 refers to the five permanent members of the Security Council (China, France, Russia, the United Kingdom, and the United States) that have the power to veto any Security Council resolution.

[14] *See* Niels Blokker, *The Crime of Aggression and the United Nations Security Council*, 20 LEIDEN J. INT'L L. 867, 880 (2007).

control over or to direct the political or military action of a State."[15] While this limitation on personal jurisdiction means that middle- and low-level officials, in addition to the rank-and-file, cannot be prosecuted for aggression, the focus on political and military leaders is likely to be vigorously resisted by the state itself unless it has been defeated or the government that initiated the aggression is otherwise overthrown. Prosecuting the crime of aggression thus has the potential to exacerbate critiques of the Court that it primarily (some argue exclusively) focuses on weaker states in the Global South and is unable or unwilling to take on powerful officials in the Global North. This is exacerbated by the continued military interventions by, among others, the United States and Russia, and the (well-founded) assumption that such acts will not be subject to ICC scrutiny.

Although the ASP agreed to amendments to the Rome Statute defining the crime of aggression, two conditions were required for them to come into effect. First, the crime of aggression could not be prosecuted until one year after the amendments were ratified or accepted by thirty States Parties. On June 26, 2016, the Palestine became the thirtieth state to ratify the amendments on the crime of aggression. As of 2020, thirty-nine State Parties have ratified the Kampala amendments. Second, the ASP had to decide to initiate the amendments; the resolution to this effect activated jurisdiction over the crime of aggression as of July 17, 2018—twenty years to the day of the adoption of the ICC Statute in Rome in 1998.

Notwithstanding the ICC's placeholder provision and intense work to reach a consensus definition of the crime of aggression, deep divisions remain among states, non-governmental organizations, and academics as to whether the ICC should exercise jurisdiction over the crime of aggression at all. The primary objection to the crime's inclusion was that it threatens to indelibly politicize the Court. Furthermore, it is argued that aggression is a state crime that is, by definition, committed against another state, rather than the crime of an individual that is committed against other individuals. Thus, only collective, rather than individual, culpability should be considered—a determination that belongs before the International Court of Justice not the ICC.[16] Others argue that including the crime of

[15] Rome Statute, Article 25(3)*bis*.

[16] *See, e.g.*, Military and Paramilitary Activities in and against Nicaragua, *supra* (finding that the United States had used unlawful force in violation of customary law by mining Nicaraguan ports, undertaking naval attacks, and arming and training the *Contras*); Oil Platforms Case (Iran v. U.S.), 2003 I.C.J. 161 (Nov. 6) (finding that the United States was not entitled to use armed force in self-defense pursuant to Article 51 of the Charter); Armed Activities on the Territory of the Congo (Dem. Rep. of Congo v. Uganda), Merits, 2005 I.C.J. 165 (Dec. 19) (finding Uganda guilty of an act of aggression within the meaning of Resolution 3314).

aggression within the jurisdiction of the Court will inevitably divert resources from the more traditional atrocity crimes at a time when the Court's resources are already over-stretched. Finally, it has been argued that there is no modern precedent for the crime of aggression, as none of the *ad hoc* tribunals exercised jurisdiction over the crime.

The debate over the inclusion of the crime of aggression has also touched on the potential intersection between the crime and the prohibitions against war crimes. Opponents of including the crime of aggression in the ICC Statute argued that the harms experienced by victims of war are captured by the prohibitions against war crimes (and even potentially those provisions governing crimes against humanity and genocide). They noted that the crime of aggression adds little to the subject matter jurisdiction of the Court given the Rome Statute's comprehensive *jus in bello* provisions.

Conversely, proponents argued that aggression remains the supreme global crime that often gives rise to all other international crimes, as was noted by the Nuremberg Tribunal. It was contended that a "clean" but nonetheless criminal war—that is, an act of aggression in which no war crimes are committed—still harms victims—including combatants sent to war—in a way that should be cognizable by the Court. In the words of the indomitable Ben Ferencz, a former prosecutor in the post-World War II trials and a staunch advocate for the inclusion of the crime of aggression in the ICC Statute:

> Ever since the judgment at Nuremberg, it has been undeniable that aggressive war is not a national right but an international crime. War is the soil from which the worst human rights violations invariably grow. The U.N. Charter prescribes that only the Security Council can determine when aggression by a state has occurred but it makes no provision for criminal trials. No criminal statute can expand or diminish the Council's vested power. Only an independent court can decide justly whether any individual is innocent or guilty. Excluding aggression from international judicial scrutiny is to grant immunity to those responsible for "the supreme international crime"—omission [of the crime of aggression] encourages war rather than peace.[17]

In this way, it was argued that including the crime of aggression in the ICC Statute will deter political and military leaders from resorting to military means in their relations with each other,

---

[17] Benjamin Ferencz, *Address to the Diplomatic Conference of Plenipotentiaries on the Establishment of an International Criminal Court,* 11 PACE INT'L L. REV. 341, 342 (1999).

because they will be on notice that deploying armed force without Security Council approval, or without credible claims to be acting in individual or collective self-defense, might give rise to individual criminal liability. This debate continues in the abstract. It remains to be seen whether those advancing these various positions will change their perspectives if and when the ICC has occasion to apply these new provisions.

B. *Jus In Bello*

Whereas the *jus ad bellum* govern the decision to utilize armed force, the *jus in bello* take hold once an armed conflict exists. Historically, the codification of the *jus in bello* proceeded along two tracks: one, referred to as Geneva law, is based on the four Geneva Conventions of 1949 and their two 1977 Protocols and originated under the auspices of the Geneva-based ICRC; the other, referred to as Hague law, derives from a series of conventions concluded in The Hague in 1899 and 1907. Geneva law creates interlocking legal regimes to protect classes of persons, such as prisoners of war (POWs) and non-combatants, who are particularly vulnerable in armed conflicts. By contrast, Hague law governs the means and methods of warfare. Together, these sets of treaties regulate many aspects of the conduct of hostilities, at times in great detail.

Until the promulgation of the 1949 Geneva Conventions, which now bear the distinction of being the first multilateral conventions to enjoy universal ratification, a notion that there were crimes of war that would give rise to individual criminal responsibility existed only in customary international law and domestic law, primarily within national military codes. The Geneva Conventions for the first time codified certain "grave breaches" of the *jus in bello* as war crimes, giving rise to individual criminal responsibility, when committed in an international armed conflict. The law of war crimes thus constitutes just one element of the *jus in bello,* as many applicable treaty rules give rise to state responsibility only. Because the treaty provisions governing war crimes remain limited, particularly when it comes to non-international armed conflicts, ICL jurisprudence has proven to be a strong engine in the development of the penal components of international humanitarian law (IHL).

The remainder of this chapter focuses on the penal provisions of the *jus in bello,* and the framework for understanding the current law of war crimes, because only these aspects of IHL fall under the rubric of ICL. We start with the antecedent question of the applicability of IHL altogether, because the prohibitions against war crimes apply only when IHL applies. This section next touches on the choice of law question occasioned by the requirement of conflict classification. This is followed by a discussion of how ICL distinguishes between ordinary criminal acts committed in war and war crimes—the nexus problem. We then discuss the distinguishing features of Geneva and Hague law: protected persons and the interlocking principles of necessity, proportionality, distinction, and precaution, respectively. The section concludes with a brief tour of the ICC Statute's war crimes provision, because it encompasses many—but not all—of the war crimes contained within IHL treaties, codified in nations' penal codes and military justice codes, and adjudicated by the *ad hoc* tribunals as crimes under customary international law. The next chapter continues this discussion by examining the intersections between the international criminal prohibitions against war crimes and the crime of terrorism.

1. Triggering International Humanitarian Law

Not all disturbances, acts of violence, or even uses of military force trigger the applicability of IHL and thus the prohibitions against war crimes. The Geneva Conventions themselves provide little insight into the question of their field of application, declaring at Article 2—common to all four Conventions—only that the bulk of their provisions apply to "all cases of declared war or of any other armed conflict which may arise between two or more of the High Contracting Parties, even if the state of war is not recognized by one of them." Common Article 3 of those Conventions creates a mini-regime governing armed conflicts "not of an international character occurring in the territory of one of the High Contracting Parties" without further definition. It was not until the coming into force of Protocol II in 1977, which elaborates on and expands common Article 3, that we find a clear statement that common Article 3's provisions do not apply to "situations of internal disturbances and tensions, such as riots, isolated and sporadic acts of violence and other acts of a similar nature, as not being armed conflicts."[18]

Determining when and where IHL applies in the absence of more express treaty guidance was a central conundrum of the work of the two *ad hoc* international tribunals. In both the former Yugoslavia and Rwanda, the Prosecutor charged individuals with war crimes for acts of violence committed well beyond the vicinity of active hostilities. For example, in response to a general challenge to the jurisdiction of the tribunal, the International Criminal Tribunal for the former Yugoslavia (ICTY) announced a broad test for determining when IHL is triggered within a particular situation, touching on the question of both when an armed conflict exists and the territorial scope of the prohibitions that then apply. In addition

---

[18] Protocol Additional to the Geneva Conventions of 12 August 1949, and relating to the Protection of Victims of Non-International Armed Conflicts (Protocol II), June 8, 1977, 1125 U.N.T.S. 609.

to arguing that jurisdiction failed because there was no armed conflict, Duško Tadić, a Bosnian Serb guard at a number of notorious detention camps who was the first person to be prosecuted by the ICTY, argued that the acts for which he was being prosecuted occurred outside of the area in which any such armed conflict was conducted. In its response, the ICTY ruled:

> [A]n armed conflict exists whenever there is a resort to armed force between States or protracted armed violence between governmental authorities and organized armed groups or between such groups within a State. International humanitarian law applies from the initiation of such armed conflicts and extends beyond the cessation of hostilities until a general conclusion of peace is reached; or, in the case of internal conflicts, a peaceful settlement is achieved. Until that moment, international humanitarian law continues to apply in the whole territory of the warring States or, in the case of internal conflicts, the whole territory under the control of a party, whether or not actual combat takes place there.[19]

The tribunal reached this conclusion by noting that although the Geneva Conventions are silent as to the geographical scope of international armed conflicts, they do imply that at least some of the provisions of the Conventions apply to the entire territory of the parties to the conflict, not just to the place of actual hostilities. In particular, provisions addressing the treatment of POWs and other individuals captured by opposing forces are not dependent on any proximity to actual hostilities. Likewise, the beneficiaries of common Article 3 and Protocol II governing non-international armed conflicts include those taking no active part (or no longer taking active part) in the hostilities. Further, Article 6(2) of Geneva Convention IV indicates that "[i]n the territory of Parties to the conflict, the application of the present Convention shall cease on the general close of military operations." The Tribunal ruled that all these provisions make clear that IHL applies broadly within embattled territory, such that the war crimes charges against Tadić could proceed.

Where IHL does not apply, other bodies of law may still penalize the conduct in question. For example, Tadić was concurrently charged with crimes against humanity, the prohibition of which is independent of any armed conflict (although that had not been definitively established until the Tribunal so ruled in *Tadić*). Acts of violence may also constitute acts of genocide (where protected groups

---

[19] *Prosecutor v. Tadić,* Case No. IT-94-1, Decision on the Defence Motion for Interlocutory Appeal on Jurisdiction, ¶ 70 (Oct. 2, 1995) [hereinafter *Tadić Decision on Jurisdiction*].

are targeted with the intent to destroy the group) or acts of terrorism under international law. Where international law does not criminalize particular acts of violence, recourse can always be had to extant domestic penal law. Many of the war crimes prohibitions find domestic analogs in the crimes of assault, kidnapping, murder, and mayhem.

2. Conflict Classification

Determining that IHL applies to a particular situation (because violence has reached the level of an armed conflict) immediately triggers a second inquiry: whether the conflict in question is an international or a non-international conflict. The 1949 Geneva Conventions primarily apply to international armed conflicts, defined at common Article 2 as "all cases of declared war or of any other armed conflict which may arise between two or more of the High Contracting Parties, even if the state of war is not recognized by one of them." This definition thus requires the presence of at least two embattled High Contracting Parties—i.e., states that have ratified the treaties. There is a difference, however, between an international conflict and a conflict that is internationalized or that involves multiple state parties.

Take the conflict in Afghanistan initiated after the events of September 11, 2001. It began as an international armed conflict when the United States and its coalition parties launched air strikes against the *de facto* (if illegitimate) Taliban government. This initiated a conflict between two or more nation-states and was thus "international" within the meaning of Article 2. Once the U.S.-friendly government of Hamid Karzai was installed, however, the conflict no longer pitted two sovereigns against each other. At that point, the conflict ceased to be an international armed conflict within the meaning of the Geneva Conventions, even though it remained internationalized by the presence of troops from multiple nations. Instead, it became a non-international armed conflict, pitting the new government of Afghanistan, with assistance from an international coalition of forces led by the United States, against what was left of the Taliban insurgency. Most of the articles of the Geneva Conventions thus no longer applied to this conflict as a technical matter.

Although the majority of the Geneva Conventions' provisions govern international armed conflicts (including situations of foreign occupation), the one exception is Article 3, common to all four Conventions, which applies in cases "of armed conflict not of an international character occurring in the territory of one of the High Contracting Parties." This article—called a "convention in miniature"—sets forth minimum protections that must be afforded to all individuals involved in non-international armed conflicts. The latter terminology is employed in lieu of "civil war" or "internal war" to encompass the entire range of conflicts that do not meet the somewhat technical and unintuitive definition of "international armed conflict" contained in Article 2. The only textual requirement for the applicability of common Article 3 is the occurrence of an "armed conflict" within "the territory" of a High Contracting Party, which describes the current situation in Afghanistan.

The international community adopted two protocols to the Geneva Conventions in 1977 in response to the changing nature of armed conflict, which included the shift to predominantly non-international armed conflicts, the movement of the battlefield to population centers, increased civilian involvement in armed conflicts, and the expansion of guerilla warfare. Most important, Protocol I expands the definition of international armed conflict to include "armed conflicts in which people are fighting against colonial domination and alien occupation and against racist regimes in the exercise of their right of self-determination."[20] By elevating these conflicts to the status of international armed conflicts, and granting a political advantage to certain liberation movements, the Protocol to a certain degree invokes the "just war" tradition of the *jus ad bellum*. Protocol I also provides a more detailed set of rules concerning the obligation to discriminate between military and civilian targets and to utilize proportionate force, and further defines and clarifies the rules with respect to precautions in attacks and mercenaries. It also expands the category of privileged combatants to include members of guerrilla movements or informal militias that adhere to certain rules to distinguish themselves from the civilian population. These latter rules are more relaxed than those contained within the Third Geneva Convention addressed to POWs, which has led to criticism that the Protocol provides disproportionate protections to guerilla fighters, better enables such fighters to hide among the civilian population and, in so doing, puts civilians at greater risk. Protocol I thus reflects elements of both Geneva and Hague law.

Protocol II elaborates on the minimum rules in common Article 3. Historically, states were reluctant to create legal rules governing the conduct of non-international armed conflicts, primarily out of fear of legitimizing dissident or insurrectionary groups and of submitting what had been viewed as internal matters to international rules and scrutiny. During the drafting of the four Geneva Conventions, the ICRC and some state delegates proposed more detailed rules for non-international armed conflicts. In the face

---

[20] Protocol Additional to the Geneva Conventions of 12 August 1949, and relating to the Protection of Victims of International Armed Conflicts (Protocol I), June 8, 1977, 1125 U.N.T.S. 3.

of steep resistance, all that was achieved was the laconic, yet important, common Article 3. The passage of Protocol II reflects a trend toward a greater acceptance of the need to regulate conflicts that do not fall within the bailiwick of the 1949 Geneva Conventions.

Protocol II also contains a more precise, and stricter, test for its field of application than that within common Article 3. Article 1 accordingly states:

> 1. This Protocol, which develops and supplements Article 3 common to the Geneva Conventions of 12 August 1949 without modifying its existing conditions or application, shall apply to all armed conflicts which are not covered by [Protocol I] and which take place in the territory of a High Contracting Party between its armed forces and dissident armed forces or other organized armed groups which, under responsible command, exercise such control over a part of its territory as to enable them to carry out sustained and concerted military operations and to implement this Protocol.
>
> 2. This Protocol shall not apply to situations of internal disturbances and tensions, such as riots, isolated and sporadic acts of violence and other acts of a similar nature, as not being armed conflicts.

Thus, Protocol II does not apply until the armed conflict involves armed groups under responsible command, who have sufficient control over territory to launch "sustained and concerted" military operations and also to conduct their operations in accordance with the rules of war contained in the Protocol. Moreover, Protocol II applies only to conflicts between a State's armed forces and rebel or dissident movements. Common Article 3 is broader, and covers armed conflicts between such groups competing for power within a state when the central government is not involved or has ceased to exist. Common Article 3 also applies to those civil wars in which guerilla forces lack any fixed location from which to exercise territorial control or are not led by responsible command.

A further wrinkle in the exercise of conflict classification involves conflicts that appear to be non-international armed conflicts, because they pit a state's military against rebel or insurrectionary forces, but involve the significant intervention of another nation state. The situation in the former Yugoslavia offers a prime example of such a conflict. The armed conflict there began as a classic civil war when ethnic groups within Yugoslavia took up arms against each other. Eventually, various republics declared independence, including Bosnia-Herzegovina and Croatia. Within Bosnia, the Bosnian Serbs (who favored continued union with

Yugoslavia or their own state) and the Bosnian Croats (who favored union with the nascent Republic of Croatia) came to blows with the Bosnian authorities. The two groups enjoyed significant financial, logistical, and strategic support from Belgrade and Zagreb, respectively. In situations in which this level of support rose to the level of "overall control"[21] over the Bosnian Serb and Bosnian Croat paramilitaries, the ICTY determined that the war became an international armed conflict, because two nation states were essentially set as rivals against each other, thus triggering the whole panoply of Geneva Convention rules.[22] Absent this degree of control, the conflict would have remained a non-international one, subject to fewer rules.

Viewed collectively, the Geneva treaty regime thus establishes a taxonomy of conflict classification that includes the following:

(a) situations that do not trigger IHL at all (e.g., riots, sporadic acts of violence);

(b) non-international armed conflicts that do not meet the heightened requirements of Protocol II but that still trigger common Article 3's protections;

(c) non-international armed conflicts between a state and armed groups that meet the heightened organizational and territorial control requirements of Protocol II;

(d) international armed conflicts within the meaning of Protocol I (e.g., situations in which an indigenous population is resisting colonial domination);

(e) sufficiently internationalized armed conflicts that trigger the greater part of the protections of the 1949 Geneva Conventions when a state exercises overall control over a non-state actor embattled against another state within the conflict; and

(f) traditional international armed conflicts pitting two High Contracting Parties against each other.

The latter three scenarios trigger the bulk of the 1949 Geneva Conventions, including its penal regime, as discussed in more detail below.

---

[21] Note that the International Court of Justice has articulated a different test—that of effective control—to determine whether the acts of non-state actors can be attributed to a state for the purpose of state responsibility (which would also internationalize any conflict involving another sovereign entity). *See* Military and Paramilitary Activities in and against Nicaragua *supra*.

[22] *See, e.g., Prosecutor v. Tihomir Blaškić*, Case No. IT-95-14-T, Judgment (Mar. 3, 2000) (finding Republic of Croatia exercised overall control over Bosnian Croats embattled in Bosnia-Herzegovina).

3. Choice of Law Implications of Conflict Classification

The question of conflict classification is more than academic in ICL. From the perspective of positive law, only the Geneva Conventions governing international (or sufficiently internationalized) armed conflicts contain war crimes provisions. Specifically, it is only certain "grave breaches" of those treaties that give rise to individual criminal responsibility. By their own terms, violations of other treaty provisions (including much of the four Geneva Conventions and common Article 3) and additional IHL treaties (Protocol II and the Hague Conventions) only give rise to the civil liability of states and do not set forth any individual penal sanctions.

Notwithstanding these textual realities, the *ad hoc* tribunals made quick work of dismantling distinctions between the norms applicable in international and non-international armed conflicts that were so carefully crafted by states during the IHL treaty-drafting process. As a result, much conduct prohibited or criminalized in international armed conflicts now constitutes war crimes even if committed in internal or other non-international conflicts. With respect to the ICTY, this process was enabled by the formulation of the war crimes provisions within the ICTY Statute. Article 2 of the ICTY Statute reproduced the grave breaches regime of the Geneva Conventions. Article 3 of the ICTY Statute extended the jurisdiction of the Tribunal to cover "violations of the laws and customs of war," including a non-exhaustive list of violations of the regulations contained within the Fourth Hague Convention. The Tribunal interpreted this latter provision expansively to penalize violations of common Article 3 as well as other prohibitions within the Geneva Conventions and their Protocols, finding authority for this assertion in customary international law rather than treaty law.

In penalizing violations of common Article 3 and Protocol II, the ICTY essentially merged the law governing international and non-international armed conflicts, rendering conflict classification a virtually irrelevant exercise in its proceedings. The Appeals Chamber in *Tadić* was quite self-conscious about this, having found that national practice and the inroads made by the international human rights regime into areas traditionally shrouded by state sovereignty have "blur[red] the traditional dichotomy between international wars and civil strife."[23] In addition, as most global conflicts are now internal in character, the distinction between the

[23] *Tadić* Decision on Jurisdiction, *supra*, ¶ 97 ("Why protect civilians from belligerent violence, or ban rape, torture or the wanton destruction of hospitals . . . when two sovereign States are engaged in war, and yet refrain from the same bans or providing the same protection when armed violence has erupted 'only' within the territory of a sovereign State?").

two bodies of law seemed increasingly arbitrary and outmoded to the judges of the modern tribunals. This merger—a function of the Security Council creating an opening in the ICTY Statute for judicial activism—now finds positive expression in Article 8 of the ICC Statute, indicating that this expansive approach has been largely—although not entirely—ratified by the community of states. As a result, the ICC can prosecute most—but not all—war crimes committed in any type of conflict, as can states that have harmonized their domestic penal codes with the ICC Statute. For its part, the ICRC has identified in Rule 156 of its magisterial study of customary IHL a number of war crimes that may be prosecuted, regardless of conflict classification.[24] Even this list, however, remains somewhat indeterminate when it comes to non-international armed conflicts. There are certain instances in the customary international law (CIL) study in which the ICRC identifies a prohibition under IHL as applicable across the conflict spectrum, but has not yet confirmed an international consensus in terms of state practice and *opinio juris*, the two components of CIL further discussed in Chapter 3, on whether the breach of such a prohibition constitutes a prosecutable war crime.

4. Nexus to Armed Conflict

Establishing the applicability of IHL does not end the inquiry of whether and how an individual who commits a violent act can be prosecuted for the commission of war crimes. In particular, it must still be determined whether the act in question—such as an act of murder or the theft of property—constitutes a war crime as opposed to a simple domestic crime or some other international crime. As discussed in Chapter 4 on the Internationalization of Crimes, only offenses that have some sort of a nexus to an armed conflict fall within the category of war crimes under IHL. If there is no link between the offense and the armed conflict, then the act must be charged under some other head of ICL or under domestic criminal law.

The *ad hoc* tribunals struggled with how to define this link. The ICTY Trial Chamber in *Prosecutor v. Delalić* stated that "there must be an obvious link between the criminal act and the armed conflict."[25] In *Tadić*, another Trial Chamber noted that "the offences [must be] closely related to the armed conflict as a whole."[26] In *Semanza*, the International Criminal Tribunal for Rwanda (ICTR) identified the

---

[24] Rule 156, CUSTOMARY INTERNATIONAL HUMANITARIAN LAW (Jean-Marie Henckaerts & Louise Doswald-Beck eds., 2005) ("Serious violations of international humanitarian law constitute war crimes.").

[25] *Prosecutor v. Delalić*, Case No. IT-96-21-T, Judgment, ¶ 193 (Nov. 16, 1998).

[26] *Prosecutor v. Tadić*, Case No. IT-94-1-T, Opinion and Judgment, ¶ 573 (May 7, 1997).

requirement that the act *either* be "closely related to the hostilities," *or* "committed in conjunction with them."[27] Defining this link became particularly acute in the Rwandan context, because although the genocide occurred nationwide, the actual theater of the armed conflict—which pitted Hutu government armed forces against the Tutsi-led Rwandan Patriotic Front billeted in neighboring Uganda—only engulfed part of the country. This led to a number of acquittals on war crimes counts, although most of the same defendants were convicted of genocide and crimes against humanity, which require no link to armed conflict.

In the *Akayesu* case, for example, the Trial Chamber acquitted the defendant of war crimes charges on the ground that "it has not been proved beyond reasonable doubt that the acts perpetrated by Akayesu . . . were committed in conjunction with the armed conflict."[28] Likewise, in *Kayishema,* the Trial Chamber ruled that it was insufficient to show a simple temporal concurrence between the crimes charged and the internal armed conflict occurring elsewhere in the country. Rather, the Trial Chamber required a showing that "there was a direct link between crimes committed against these victims and the hostilities" and that the defendants were connected to one of the two embattled parties.[29] The Trial Chamber also noted that the armed conflict had been used as pretext to unleash an official policy of genocide, but that these two phenomena were distinct within the region in question.

The ICTR and ICTY shared an Appeals Chamber, which *sub silentio* disagreed with this approach in the context of the Yugoslav cases. In *Prosecutor v. Kunarac*, it ruled that although the armed conflict must have "played a substantial part in the perpetrator's ability to commit [the charged crime], his decision to commit it, the manner in which it was committed or the purpose for which it was committed," it was enough if, as in the present case, "the perpetrator acted in furtherance of or under the guise of the armed conflict."[30] The Tribunal identified a nonexclusive series of factors that would help to guide this nexus inquiry:

- the perpetrator was a combatant;
- the victim was a non-combatant;

---

[27] *Prosecutor v. Semanza,* Case No. ICTR 97-20-T, Trial Chamber Decision, ¶ 14 (May 15, 2003).

[28] *Prosecutor v. Akayesu,* Case No. ICTR-96-4-T, Judgment, ¶ 643 (Sept. 2, 1998).

[29] *Prosecutor v. Kayishema & Ruzindana,* Case No. ICTR-95-1-T, Judgment, ¶¶ 603, 616 (May 21, 1999).

[30] *Prosecutor v. Kunarac,* Case No. IT-96-23-A & IT-96-23/1-A, Judgment, ¶ 58 (June 12, 2002).

- the victim was a member of the opposing party;
- the act may be said to serve the ultimate goal of a military campaign; and
- the crime was committed as part of or in the context of the perpetrator's official duties.[31]

In the ICC's Elements of Crimes, drafters settled on the following formulation: It must be shown that the charged conduct "took place in the context of and was associated with" an international or non-international armed conflict. Furthermore, the perpetrator must have knowledge of the existence of the conflict (but need not have legal knowledge of the nature or precise classification of the conflict). This formulation eases up on the strict requirements established in *Kayishema* and seems to imply the necessity only of a geographical and temporal nexus. The nexus requirement in the Rome Statute may be easier to satisfy before the ICC if, as so far appears to be the case, the ICC focuses on high-level political and military leaders; under these circumstances the link to, and knowledge of, an armed conflict may be easier to prove than with low-level offenders.[32]

5. Protected Persons

The collective goal of the Geneva treaty regime is to mitigate the effects of war by protecting four classes of persons who do not, or who can no longer, participate in hostilities. Thus, the four Geneva Conventions apply to (1) the sick and wounded on land (Geneva Convention I); (2) the sick and wounded at sea (Geneva Convention II); (3) POWs (Geneva Convention III); and (4) civilians, or more accurately, anyone who does not fall into one of the other treaties' protective regimes (Geneva Convention IV). Each treaty contains a provision defining the class of "protected persons" to whom it applies. The Fourth Geneva Convention acts as a catch-all for individuals who fall outside of the prior three regimes. For example, Article 4 of the Fourth Geneva Convention defines its protected persons as follows:

> Persons protected by the Convention are those who, at a given moment and in any manner whatsoever, find themselves, in case of a conflict or occupation, in the hands of a Party to the conflict or Occupying Power of which they are not nationals. Nationals of a State which is not bound by the Convention are not protected by it. Nationals of a neutral State who find themselves in the territory of a

---

[31] *Id.* ¶ 58.

[32] *See, e.g.*, WILLIAM A. SCHABAS, THE INTERNATIONAL CRIMINAL COURT: A COMMENTARY ON THE ROME STATUTE 207 (2010).

> belligerent State, and nationals of a co-belligerent State, shall not be regarded as protected persons while the State of which they are nationals has normal diplomatic representation in the State in whose hands they are. . . . Persons protected by [one of the other three Conventions] shall not be considered as protected persons within the meaning of the present Convention.

Key elements of this definition are the fact that the individual is "in the hands of" a party "of which they are not nationals"—that is, a different nation state—and not protected by one of the other Conventions. The definition of civilian is both broader and narrower than the common understanding of the term. Excluded from protection are individuals who are nationals of a state that is aligned with their captors' state or that is neutral. Because the definition is not centered on a characteristic of the individual, but on whether they "find themselves . . . in the hands of a Party to the conflict or Occupying Power of which they are not nationals," it also provides protection to fighters who do not meet the definition of prisoners of war in Article 4 of Geneva Convention III. This presumably includes so-called "unprivileged belligerents"—irregular combatants who are not part of a High Contracting Party's military force or who are nationals of states not formally at war—although this point remains contentious.

In connection with the global "war on terror," for example, the U.S. government argued that none of the detainees held in Guantánamo or elsewhere was entitled to claim protection under the Geneva Conventions because, under the U.S. government's reading, these individuals met neither the definition of "prisoner of war" under Geneva Convention III nor the definition of "civilian" pursuant to Geneva Convention IV. Instead, the Bush administration employed an alternative terminology, referring to these individuals as "enemy combatants" or "unlawful enemy combatants"—terms that are not found within IHL or any of its treaties. Furthermore, the Fourth Geneva Convention's definition of protected person set forth earlier does not turn on combatant or civilian status. That said, many of the individuals detained by the United States were captured within the context of a non-international armed conflict, the regulation of which by international law does not contain a POW regime. In addition, many of these individuals were not nationals of a High Contracting Party with which the United States was at war.

Under the Geneva Conventions' grave breaches regimes, only protected persons can be the victims of war crimes. This requirement has been relaxed in contemporary jurisprudence, however. For example, in the former Yugoslavia, Bosnian Muslims often found themselves "in the hands of" Bosnian Serb forces with whom they shared a nationality, but not an ethnicity or ultimate allegiance. The ICTY rejected arguments that no war crimes were committed when such individuals were harmed because the victim and the perpetrator shared a bond of citizenship. In one case, it held:

> While previously wars were primarily between well-established States, in modern inter-ethnic armed conflicts such as that in the former Yugoslavia, new States are often created during the conflict and ethnicity rather than nationality may become the grounds for allegiance. Or, put another way, ethnicity may become determinative of national allegiance. Under these conditions, the requirement of nationality is even less adequate to define protected persons. In such conflicts, not only the text and the drafting history of the Convention but also, and more importantly, the Convention's object and purpose suggest that allegiance to a Party to the conflict and, correspondingly, control by this Party over persons in a given territory, may be regarded as the crucial test.[33]

By adopting a functional and teleological approach to the treaties and to the concept of "protected persons," the ICTY significantly diminished the significance of nationality in determining protected person status. This ruling had implications for the "war on terror", suggesting that nationality alone should not be the basis for excluding individuals from the protections of the Geneva Conventions—a position never conceded by the United States.

This innovation in the interpretation of protected persons by the ICTY has taken hold at the ICC. While the Rome Statute's Element of Crimes does not remove the reference to "nationality" found in the original Geneva Conventions, it does open the door for the ICTY approach by stating that "[w]ith respect to nationality, it is understand that the perpetrator needs only to know that the victim belonged to an adverse party to the conflict."[34] At least one Pre-Trial Chamber at the ICC has expressly endorsed the ICTY approach: "Although the nexus between nationality and allegiance remains an important factor in determining protected status for persons involved in international armed conflicts, as the ICTY jurisprudence demonstrates, it is no longer the definitive test."[35]

---

[33] *Prosecutor v. Delalić,* Case No. IT-96-21-A, Judgment, ¶ 166 (Feb. 20, 2001).

[34] Elements of Crimes, War Crimes, Art. 8(2)(a).

[35] *Prosecutor v. Katanga,* Case No ICC-01/04-01/07-717, Decision on the Confirmation of Charges, ¶ 291 (Sept. 30, 2008).

6. Means and Methods of Warfare

Hague law, the principles of which are included within Protocol I, is not organized around the concept of protected persons; rather, it sets forth rules concerning the methods and means of warfare that seek to regulate what kinds of weapons are allowed, what constitutes a legitimate military target, and what type and degree of force is permissible. In particular, the following categories of conduct may give rise to individual criminal responsibility within this tradition: attacks violating the rule of distinction; the employment of means and methods of warfare violating the prohibition on unnecessary suffering; the destruction of property not required by military necessity; and violations of particular rules governing warfare, such as the prohibition on perfidy[36] or the use of starvation as a weapon of war. Hague law traditionally, and by its terms, only applied to international conflicts. Modern developments before the international criminal tribunals, within the ICC Statute, and within national military manuals and military justice codes, however, have extended many of these principles to non-international armed conflicts.

The Hague Conventions originally established basic principles and specific rules governing the means and methods of warfare and the use of force in pursuit of a military objective. Protocol I to the 1949 Geneva Conventions re-codified and expanded upon many of these principles and rules, thus signaling the convergence of the Hague and Geneva traditions. This body of law most importantly subjects the use of force within an armed conflict to the interlocking principles of necessity, distinction, proportionality, and precaution. Necessity requires that armed attacks be designed and intended to defeat the opponent militarily. Thus, Article 52(2) of Protocol I states:

> Attacks shall be limited strictly to military objectives. In so far as objects are concerned, military objectives are limited to those objects which by their nature, location, purpose or use make an effective contribution to military action and whose total or partial destruction, capture or neutralization, in the circumstances ruling at the time, offers a definite military of advantage.

The principle of distinction requires that parties to an armed conflict distinguish between legitimate military targets and illegitimate targets, such as civilians or civilian infrastructure.

[36] Perfidy refers to the act of "treacherously" killing or wounding an individual. As defined in the ICC's Element of Crimes, an individual who "invite[s] the confidence or belief of one or more persons that they were entitled to, or were obliged to accord, protection under rules of international applicable in an armed conflict," and betrays that belief or confidence by killing or injuring such person, that individual is guilty of perfidy. Element of Crimes, Art. 8(2)(b)(xi).

Article 48 of Protocol I provides that "[p]arties to the conflict shall at all times distinguish between the civilian population and combatants." Not surprisingly, interpretive problems arise with respect to so-called dual use facilities—such as bridges, power plants, or communication facilities—and war-sustaining facilities. Indiscriminate attacks are also prohibited. Article 51 of Protocol I defines indiscriminate attacks to include "[t]hose [attacks] which employ a method or means of combat the effects of which cannot be limited as required by this Protocol; and consequently, in each such case, are of a nature to strike military objectives and civilians or civilian objects without distinction." This principle has also been interpreted to prohibit certain types of weapons (such as cluster bombs and landmines) that, by their very nature, do not discriminate among lawful and unlawful targets. The international community has promulgated multilateral treaties dedicated to ending the use of such weaponry, although many of the major state-suppliers and state-consumers of these weapons have yet to sign or ratify these treaties.

The principle of proportionality states that when military force is used against a proper military objective, only that force that is proportional to the military objective to be gained may be used. If a choice of weaponry or tactics is available, the commander should choose those that will cause the least incidental harm. Civilian casualties in and of themselves are not unlawful. Rather, only those attacks that cause damage to civilian objects that is excessive in relation to the anticipated military advantage of the attack are prohibited. The greater the degree of military advantage anticipated, the more so-called "collateral damage" is allowed. Thus, civilian casualties do not indicate a violation of the laws of war where they are the result of an attack that is proportional to the military advantage sought. Warring parties are obliged under Article 57 to take feasible precautions in the choice of means and methods of attack "with a view to avoiding, and in any event to minimizing, incidental loss of civilian life, injury to civilians and damage to civilian objects."

The principle of precaution requires all parties to a conflict to take all "feasible" measures to protect civilians. There is thus an obligation on the part of an attacker to take precautions to avoid civilian casualties and civilian objects, and on the part of a party being attacked to take measures to protect the civilian population and civilian objects under their control. The latter obligation implicates, for example, the location of military installations. Placing military facilities in or near a heavily populated area may violate the duty to take precautions. The principle of precaution also requires that parties to a conflict provide, as much as possible, effective warnings to a civilian population before an attack that may affect them.

Hague law thus evaluates the legality of a course of conduct from the point of view of the military tactics employed, the targets identified, the amount of force deployed, and the collateral consequences of a belligerent's decisions. Geneva law takes a more rights-based approach, defining categories of potential victims and the protections to which they are entitled. As should be clear, however, while the focus of Hague and Geneva law is somewhat different, the rules serve to reinforce each other. Indeed, Geneva law's protection of vulnerable classes of individuals from the effects of armed conflict and the Hague rules governing the principle of distinction and the legitimate use of force during an armed conflict are in essence two sides of the same coin.

7. War Crimes Before the International Criminal Court

Given their long-standing pedigree, there was never any question that the ICC would exercise jurisdiction over violations of the *jus in bello* that give rise to individual criminal responsibility. The devil, as always, was in the details. The ICC's list of war crimes contains a partial synthesis of Geneva and Hague law, the two major strands of the *jus in bello*. Rather than adopt an open-ended provision along the lines of the ICTY Statute's Article 3, the drafters chose to specifically list chargeable crimes to better adhere to the principle of legality but also to cabin the reach of the Court. Because the ICC is governed by a strict articulation of the *nullum crimen sine lege* provision (as discussed in Chapter 5), the ICC does not have the leeway enjoyed by the ICTY to identify additional war crimes that may be prosecutable under customary international law. The entire war crimes article in the treaty is preceded by a threshold provision at Article 8(1) that emphasizes that the ICC has jurisdiction over war crimes "in particular when committed as part of a plan or policy or as part of a large-scale commission of such crimes." This is not a jurisdictional limitation *per se*, but rather is meant to guide prosecutorial discretion.

The remainder of the Article itself is quite unwieldy by virtue of the fact that it separately enumerates the crimes applicable in international armed conflicts (Article 8(2)(a) and (b)) and non-international armed conflicts (Article 8(2)(c)–(f)). The latter provisions reflect existing treaty law in the sense that they are less expansive than the former provisions. They are also subject to two different triggering prerequisites. Common Article 3 crimes can be charged under Article 8(2)(c) with respect to non-international armed conflicts that are distinct from "internal disturbances and tensions, such as riots, isolated and sporadic acts of violence, or other acts of a similar nature" (Article 8(2)(d)). In this way, the drafters essentially applied some of the standards contained in Protocol II's material field of application (Article 1(2)) to common Article 3. The other war crimes can be charged with respect to "armed conflicts that take place in the territory of a State when there is protracted armed conflict between governmental authorities and organized armed groups or between such groups" (Article 8(2)(f)). This limitation mirrors the *Tadić* test for the existence of an armed conflict, as discussed previously.

In addition to reproducing the Geneva Conventions' grave breaches provisions (Article 8(2)(a)) and common Article 3 (Article 8(2)(c)), the remainder of the article enumerates crimes that find expression in the laws and customs of war, as drawn from the Hague Conventions, Protocol II, other IHL treaties (such as those protecting cultural property or prohibiting particular weapons of war), and customary international law. In identifying these lists of crimes, the drafters were guided by two main considerations: the gravity of the acts in question, which informs whether they merit international prosecution, and whether the particular acts gave rise to individual criminal responsibility under either treaty or customary international law. Although the ICC Statute drafters often claimed that they were merely codifying existing law, it is impossible not to conclude that some progressive development in the law occurred, especially with respect to the crimes that may be committed within non-international armed conflicts.

As originally drafted, there were some noticeable differences between the list of war crimes prosecutable within international versus non-international armed conflicts in the Rome Statute. Perhaps most important, under Article 8(2)(b)(iv), disproportionate attacks—"intentionally launching an attack in the knowledge that such attack will cause incidental loss of life or injury to civilians or damage to civilian objects or widespread, long-term and severe damage to the natural environment which would be clearly excessive in relation to the concrete and direct overall military advantage anticipated"—can be prosecuted only when committed within an international armed conflict. The following acts likewise could only be prosecuted if committed within an international armed conflict: intentional attacks against civilian objects; many weapons crimes (e.g., the use of expanding dum dum bullets; poison or poisoned weapons; asphyxiating, poisonous or other gases; and all analogous liquids, materials and devices); and, the deliberate starvation of the civilian population as a tactic of war. Not without controversy, a number of weapons that cause superfluous injury—nuclear, biological, and chemical weapons—were not specifically penalized at all. These IHL rules on weapons can be particularly important because they protect combatants and other armed actors who may be the object of direct attack (indeed, that is the essence of warfare), as well as civilians, who may not be the object of attack unless they directly participate in hostilities. These limitations all reflect the preferences of states, which have generally resisted applying international law to civil wars or to means and methods that they want to preserve the ability to utilize in their armed interactions with adversaries.

As a result of these statutory features, it was originally more difficult for the ICC to adjudicate many of the brutal war crimes that have come to define modern armed conflicts—the use of chemical and improvised weaponry, sieges and starvation of civilians as weapons of war, and indiscriminate and disproportionate attacks on areas populated by civilians (unless such actions can be characterized as crimes against humanity or genocide). As discussed in Chapter 3 on the making of ICL, subsequent amendments to the Rome Statute proposed by Belgium have, however, eliminated many of these distinctions and rendered these crimes prosecutable across the conflict classification spectrum (although these changes await full ratification by ICC state parties).[37] In addition, the ASP added three new war crimes in 2017: the use of biological weapons, certain fragmentary weapons, and laser weapons that cause permanent blindness in any conflict.[38] A further proposal to criminalize the use of anti-personnel mines was dropped, for now. The inclusion of these latter three crimes drew a bit more controversy, because it was not clear if the deployment of these weapons is criminalized under customary international law or if that even mattered.

Conspicuously absent altogether from Article 8 are several important war crimes contained in Protocol I and customary international law. For example, the ICC Statute contains no provision criminalizing indiscriminate attacks—regardless of conflict classification. As such, the ICC Prosecutor can only charge intentional attacks on civilians and civilian objects (and the latter only in international conflicts). Furthermore, the ICC cannot prosecute the crime of deliberately inflicting terror among the civilian population, even though this crime has a strong treaty basis in both international and non-international armed conflicts and customary international law.[39] The ICTY Prosecutor generally

---

[37] *See* Resolution RC/Res.5, Amendments to Article 8 of the Rome Statute (June 10, 2010) (extending the criminalization of the use of certain weapons crimes to non-international armed conflicts).

[38] *See* Resolution ICC-ASP/16/Res.4, Resolution on amendments to article 8 of the Rome Statute of the International Criminal Court (Dec. 14, 2017).

[39] Article 51(2) of Protocol I states: "The civilian population as such, as well as individual civilians, shall not be the object of attack. Acts or threats of violence the primary purpose of which is to spread terror among the civilian population are

employed this prohibition to charge those responsible for attacking populated areas, particularly when there were limited civilian deaths.[40] In ruling on these charges, the ICTY confirmed that the actual infliction of death or serious bodily harm is not a required element of the crime of inflicting terror on the civilian population; what matters is that the defendant acted with the *intent* to spread terror. This crime was deemed separate and distinct from the counts alleging the commission of unlawful attacks against civilians, including direct, indiscriminate, and disproportionate attacks.[41]

Furthermore, the ASP has yet to identify additional weapons and weapons systems that cause unnecessary or superfluous suffering and, concomitantly, whose use would constitute a war crime—even when deployed against combatants who otherwise are amenable to direct attack. Article 8(2)(b)(xx) envisions the prosecution of the following war crimes:

> [e]mploying weapons, projectiles and material and methods of warfare which are of a nature to cause superfluous injury or unnecessary suffering or which are inherently indiscriminate in violation of the international law of armed conflict, provided that such weapons, projectiles and material and methods of warfare are the subject of a comprehensive prohibition and are included in an annex to this Statute, by an amendment in accordance with the relevant provisions set forth in articles 121 and 123.

Cluster munitions;[42] chemical,[43] biological, incendiary, and nuclear weapons; and landmines are obvious candidates for inclusion. The ASP has yet, however, to populate this annex. Belgium attempted to generate just such a list of prohibited munitions in time for the 2010 Kampala Review Conference; however, there was insufficient support for this amendment at the time and the provision remains a dead letter. This increasingly complex patchwork of prohibitions that depend on whether an armed conflict is international or not, and the selective list of prohibited weapons, continues to make prosecutions for war crimes some of the most difficult to bring from a technical point of view, particularly in modern armed conflicts, which are

prohibited." The treaty at Article 85(3)(a) designates this offense as a grave breach giving rise to individual criminal responsibility.

40 *Prosecutor v. Galić*, Case No. IT-98-29-T, Judgment, ¶¶ 86–138 (Dec. 5, 2003) (finding the crime of terror to have formed part of CIL at the time the defendants acted).

41 *Prosecutor v. Milošević*, Case No. IT-98-29/1-A, Appeals Chamber Judgment, ¶¶ 33–39 (Nov. 12, 2009).

42 Convention on Cluster Munitions, Dec. 3, 2008, 2688 U.N.T.S. 39.

43 Convention on the Prohibition of the Development, Production, Stockpiling and Use of Chemical Weapons and on Their Destruction art. I, Jan. 13, 1993, 1974 U.N.T.S. 45.

primarily non-international in classification. Although the conflict classification gap is narrowing, it persists. While the ICC Prosecutor could still bring a charge of war crimes involving those munitions not specifically mentioned in the statute (e.g. cluster munitions or incendiary weapons), the lack of specific reference to them increases the burden on the Prosecutor to prove that the use of such weapons in a specific situation resulted in a proportionality or distinction violation, rather than being able to rely on the use of the weapon itself.

Notwithstanding these gaps in Article 8, many of the forms of violence discussed above and being seen today may also constitute crimes against humanity, the subject of Chapter 8. An attack involving chemical weapons could be charged as the crimes against humanity of murder, extermination, or the catch-all "other inhumane acts," for example, without reference to IHL so long as the assault formed part of an attack against a civilian population. As formulated in the ICC Statute, the crime against humanity of extermination covers not only the mass killing of civilians, but also intentionally inflicting conditions of life "calculated to bring about the destruction of part of a population," including "the deprivation of access to food and medicine" so long as death results. This definition would enable the prosecution of "famine crimes"—the deliberate use of hunger as a tool of extermination and the deliberate withholding of humanitarian aid. This potentiality exemplifies one of the core features of ICL: a high degree of substantive overlap between the core international crimes, as will be discussed in the next chapters.

Chapter 7

THE CRIMES OF TERRORISM

Terrorism is a concept with a colloquial meaning that lacks a consensus definition under international law. Although particular terrorist acts are criminalized in a suite of multilateral treaties, an omnibus definition of the crime of terrorism has eluded the international community to date largely because of the now trite adage: "One person's terrorist is another person's freedom fighter." Indeed, many international instruments condemning terrorism seem to carve out exceptions for national liberation movements and groups struggling for self-determination in the context of a history of colonialism and oppression. For example, a 1991 U.N. General Assembly Resolution denounced terrorism, but in virtually the same breath, reaffirmed "the inalienable right to self-determination and independence of people under colonial and racist and other forms of alien domination and foreign occupation."[1] Nor do such instruments recognize a notion of state terrorism; rather, terrorism is seen as an affront to the state's monopoly on the deployment of "legitimate" violence. As a result of this normative ambivalence, codification efforts have yielded a number of multilateral treaties that require states to criminalize only specific terrorist acts (such as aircraft hijacking or attacks against internationally protected persons), without defining the genus crime more broadly.

Due in part to these definitional challenges, the architects of the International Criminal Court (ICC) excluded the crime of terrorism from the ICC Statute altogether. However, ever since the catastrophic attacks of September 11, 2001, and subsequent events, countering the threat of terrorism has remained high on the agendas of individual states, the Security Council, and other elements of the international community. As such, terrorism has made various appearances in ICL. For example, a unique hybrid court in Lebanon is devoted to adjudicating terrorist crimes as defined by Lebanese law, so long as they are related to the 2005 assassination of former Prime Minister Rafik Hariri. The overlapping conflicts in Syria and Iraq have led to a number of terrorism prosecutions in domestic courts around the world, including against foreign fighters who joined the fight but later returned to the comforts of Europe. And, some states continue to voice support for the crime's eventual inclusion in the ICC's subject matter jurisdiction. For these reasons,

[1] G.A. Res. 46/51, U.N. Doc. A/RES/46/51 (Jan. 27, 1992).

we include this category of crimes within the "canon" of international criminal law (ICL).

After offering a brief history of the piecemeal codification of an international prohibition against terrorism, this chapter endeavors to identify the elements of terrorism that distinguish it from other international crimes. It also considers the way in which the phenomenon of terrorism at times implicates and intersects with international humanitarian law (IHL) and the prohibitions against war crimes. Finally, it explores the extent to which terrorism crimes might be prosecutable before the ICC, notwithstanding that these crimes were purposefully excluded from the Court's subject matter jurisdiction.

A. Terrorism Under Positive International Law

Although there have been efforts to codify a global prohibition against terrorism under international law for decades, there is no universal treaty or international instrument that defines the crime of terrorism writ large. The League of Nations embarked on the first major attempt in the modern era to prohibit the crime of terrorism after the 1934 assassination by Croatian separatists of King Alexander of Yugoslavia and others. The treaty—the Convention for the Prevention and Punishment of Terrorism (1937)—defined terrorism as follows: "All criminal acts directed against a State and intended or calculated to create a state of terror in the minds of particular persons or a group of persons or the general public."[2] The treaty attracted twenty-four state signatories; only India ultimately ratified the Convention. The onset of World War II scuttled further efforts to bring the treaty into effect. After the dissolution of the League of Nations, the treaty was never revived.

From this abortive start, the international community has proceeded in a disjointed fashion by criminalizing various manifestations of terrorism (such as offenses committed on board aircraft, crimes against internationally protected persons, hostage taking, crimes involving maritime navigation or nuclear material, terrorist bombing, and the financing of terrorism), often in response to particular terrorist incidents. In addition to providing penal definitions, many of these treaties obligate state parties to incorporate the relevant prohibitions into their domestic criminal codes, to treat enumerated acts of terrorism as extraditable offenses, to grant mutual legal assistance in the investigation and prosecution of proscribed acts, and to either extradite or prosecute offenders pursuant to broad principles of extraterritorial jurisdiction, including universal jurisdiction. In this regard, the efforts to address crimes of

---

[2] Convention for the Prevention and Punishment of Terrorism, League of Nations Doc. C.94.M.47.1938.V (1937).

terrorism have been largely responsible for the greater acceptance of passive personality jurisdiction in international law, as states increasingly seek to assert jurisdiction over extraterritorial acts of terrorism committed against their nationals.

This proliferation of definitions has led courts and commentators to conclude that there is no established definition of terrorism under customary international law. Nonetheless many definitions of terrorism share certain basic structural elements:

1. The perpetration of violence by means which may or may not be enumerated depending on the instrument in which it is defined;

2. The targeting of innocent civilians or elements of the civilian or governmental infrastructure;

3. Conduct undertaken:

   (a) With the intent to cause violence or with wanton disregard for the act's consequences;

   (b) For the purpose of causing fear or terror, coercing a government, or intimidating an enemy; and

   (c) To achieve some political, military, ideological, or religious goal.

As you review the various definitions of terrorism provided in the literature, try to identify common and divergent elements. You will see that although many instruments and penal codes addressing terrorism do not list prohibited acts with specificity, most contain one or more specific intent or motive elements requiring proof of the existence of some mental state over and above the general intent to commit acts of violence.[3] In some cases, this mental element is aimed at the civilian population (the intent to cause terror) or a government

---

[3] In these formulations, it is often unclear if this mental element is the equivalent of a specific intent requirement (along the lines of the definition of genocide) or simply a required motive. Specific intent is generally defined as the ultimate objective that the perpetrator intends to accomplish by committing a specific criminal act. Specific intent is usually a special mental element that is required above and beyond any mental state associated with the underlying *actus reus* of the crime. (For example, burglary—the breaking and entering into of a dwelling of another—requires a showing of the specific intent to commit a felony therein). The concept of specific intent often elides with that of motive, which is the guiding purpose or goal behind an individual's criminal action. Our emblematic burglar, for example, may have a motive of self-enrichment. Normally, proof of motive is not required for a criminal conviction, although proving the defendant's motive is often an integral part of any prosecution and is often relevant at the time of sentencing. By contrast, the prosecution must prove the existence of specific intent if it is an element of a crime. One exception to this general rule that crimes are not defined by motive involves hate crimes, which require proof that the defendant was motivated by animosity toward a protected group.

(the intent to influence a government). This emphasis on the perpetrator's motive markedly distinguishes crimes of terrorism from other domestic and international crimes.

Many multilateral instruments limit their application to terrorism committed by nonstate actors, implicitly or explicitly failing to recognize any notion of state terrorism. Thus, some definitions—such as the one contained in the 1997 Terrorist Bombing Convention—prohibit acts committed, *inter alia*, against governmental facilities or public installations.[4] National terrorism definitions, by contrast, do not necessarily make this distinction. Indeed, there are a number of domestic prosecutions underway under penal provisions that recognize a form of "state terrorism" during the Latin American "dirty wars."[5]

Many multilateral treaties limit their application to acts of "international terrorism," thus implicitly excluding jurisdiction over acts of terrorism committed by substate actors operating solely within a state. The Nuclear Terrorism Convention, for example, provides at Article 3 that

> This Convention shall not apply where the offence is committed within a single State, the alleged offender and the victims are nationals of that State, the alleged offender is found in the territory of that State and no other State has [grounds to assert territorial, nationality, or passive personality jurisdiction].[6]

By contrast, other treaties include no specific place or manner restrictions in their definitional provisions.

The 1999 International Convention for the Suppression of the Financing of Terrorism in certain respects harmonizes and unifies the disparate definitions in these prior terrorism treaties. Article 2(1) of that treaty incorporates a number of extant treaties in its annex by providing that

---

4 International Convention for the Suppression of Terrorist Bombings, Jan. 9, 1998, S. Treaty Doc. No. 106–6, 37 I.L.M. 251 (prohibiting attacks on "a place of public use, a State or government facility, a public transportation system or an infrastructure facility with the intent to cause death or serious bodily injury or with the intent to cause extensive destruction of such a place, facility or system, where such destruction results in or is likely to result in major economic loss").

5 Spain, for example, convicted Salvadoran Colonel Inocente Orlando Montano for state terrorism for his involvement in the 1989 massacre of six Jesuit priests, their housekeeper, and her daughter during that country's dirty war. El Salvador is prosecuting former regime figures accused of masterminding and carrying out the 1981 El Mozote Massacre under a state terrorism provision within the Salvadoran penal code.

6 International Convention for the Suppression of Nuclear Terrorism, Apr. 13, 2005, 2445 U.N.T.S. 89.

> Any person commits an offence within the meaning of this Convention if that person by any means, directly or indirectly, unlawfully and wilfully, provides or collects funds with the intention that they should be used or in the knowledge that they are to be used, in full or in part, in order to carry out [any violation of an annexed treaty].

In addition, besides the terrorist acts encompassed by the treaty annex, the Terrorist Financing Convention further prohibits providing funding for:

> Any other act intended to cause death or serious bodily injury to a civilian, or to any other person not taking an active part in the hostilities in a situation of armed conflict, when the purpose of such act, by its nature or context, is to intimidate a population, or to compel a government or an international organization to do or to abstain from doing any act.[7]

This latter provision comes quite close to an omnibus definition of the crime.

Given the inability of states to negotiate a comprehensive terrorism treaty, the U.N. Security Council has adopted a number of counter-terrorism resolutions under its Chapter VII powers, which impose binding obligations on states. The Financing Convention, for example, is bolstered by a Chapter VII resolution passed in the weeks following the attacks of September 11, 2001, requiring all states to, *inter alia*, suppress the financing of acts of terrorism and freeze financial assets of persons or entities involved in terrorism.[8] Another resolution condemns the incitement of terrorist acts as well as the justification or glorification thereof, urging all states to fulfill their obligations under international law by adopting all necessary and appropriate measures to:[9]

1. Prohibit by law incitement to commit a terrorist act or acts;
2. Prevent such conduct;
3. Deny safe haven to any persons with respect to whom there is credible and relevant information giving serious reasons for considering that they have been guilty of such conduct.

---

7 International Convention for the Suppression of the Financing of Terrorism, G.A. Res. 109, U.N. GAOR 6th Comm., 54 Sess., 76th mtg., Agenda Item 160, U.N. Doc. A/54/109 (1999).

8 S.C. Res. 1373, U.N. Doc. S/RES/1373/2001 (Sept. 28, 2001).

9 S.C. Res. 1624, U.N. Doc. S/RES/1624 (Sept. 14, 2005).

Additionally, the resolution directs all states to strengthen security at international borders and passenger screening facilities, promote tolerance, and "prevent the subversion of educational, cultural, and religious institutions by terrorists and their supporters." The Security Council's fixation on violence that constitutes terrorism—versus other forms of mass violence, such as crimes against humanity or genocide, that are not necessarily seen as targeting the state—has drawn distinct criticism both from those who argue that the Security Council pays insufficient attention to these core international crimes, and from those who argue that the Security Council is reinforcing the power imbalances of the *status quo* by condemning violence against the state and turning a blind eye to violence by the state.

B. Prosecuting Terrorism

The *ad hoc* tribunals were not, in general, empowered to prosecute terrorism as a stand-alone crime. The Statutes of the International Criminal Tribunal for Rwanda (Article 4(d)) and of the Special Court for Sierra Leone (Article 3(d)) are unique in listing "acts of terrorism" as war crimes. The prohibition against inflicting terror on a population is drawn from the Additional Protocols to the 1949 Geneva Conventions at Article 51(2) in Additional Protocol I and Article 13(2) in Additional Protocol II.[10] The Fourth Geneva Convention, which is aimed at protecting civilians, also contains the following prohibition with respect its protected persons at Article 33: "Collective penalties and likewise all measures of intimidation or of terrorism are prohibited." These acts, however, are not designated as grave breaches of that treaty. These references to terror and terrorism opened the door for the prosecution as war crimes of some acts that would qualify as terrorism under many of the definitions listed above.[11]

Even though the Statute of the International Criminal Tribunal for the former Yugoslavia (ICTY) did not contain reference to the 1977 Protocols, the tribunal nonetheless read these prohibitions into Article 3 of the ICTY Statute, which provided for jurisdiction over an exemplary but not closed list of "violations of the laws and customs of war." In *Prosecutor v. Galić*, the prosecution charged the defendant with "inflicting terror on the civilian population" as a war crime, even though the Statute was silent as to this offense and neither of the IHL treaty provisions contemplates individual criminal liability or defines "spreading terror" as a criminal offense. Nonetheless, the

---

[10] These provisions identically provide that "[t]he civilian population as such, as well as individual civilians, shall not be the object of attack. Acts or threats of violence the primary purpose of which is to spread terror among the civilian population are prohibited." Article 4(2) of Protocol II also prohibits "acts of terrorism" against civilians or others *hors de combat* as a Fundamental Guarantee.

[11] *Prosecutor v. Galić*, Case No. IT-98-29-T, Judgement (Dec. 5, 2003).

ICTY convicted the defendants of the charged crime. In so doing, the ICTY identified the following elements of the crime of inflicting terror on the civilian population under customary international law:

1. Acts of violence directed against the civilian population or individual civilians not taking direct part in hostilities causing death or serious injury to body or health within the civilian population.
2. The offender willfully made the civilian population or individual civilians not taking direct part in hostilities the object of those acts of violence.
3. The above offence was committed with the primary purpose of spreading terror among the civilian population.[12]

This opinion provides an avenue for prosecuting acts of terrorism within IHL, regardless of whether the perpetrators are state or non-state actors.

Only one of the many international and hybrid criminal tribunals that have been created includes terrorism un-connected to an armed conflict in its subject matter jurisdiction. The Special Tribunal for Lebanon (STL) is a hybrid tribunal established by the United Nations and Lebanon to investigate and prosecute those "responsible for the terrorist crime which killed the former Lebanese Prime Minister Rafiq Hariri and others."[13] The Tribunal has a mandate to apply only the domestic laws of Lebanon "relating to the prosecution and punishment of acts of terrorism, crimes and offences against life and personal integrity, illicit associations and failure to report crimes and offences, including the rules regarding the material elements of a crime, criminal participation and conspiracy." Article 314 of the Lebanese Penal Code, one of several terrorism-related provisions that may be litigated before the STL, "defines 'terrorist acts' as all 'acts designed to create a state of alarm which are committed by means such as explosive devices, inflammable materials, poisonous or incendiary products or infectious or microbial agents likely to create a public hazard.' "[14] The *mens rea* element requires knowledge and a will to commit the terrorist act along with a specific intent to create a state of alarm or fear. As such, although it is interpreting Lebanese domestic law, the STL's jurisprudence will no doubt be persuasive as other tribunals consider terrorism

---

[12] *Prosecutor v. Galić*, Case No. IT-98-29-T, Judgment, ¶ 133 (Dec. 5, 2003). *See also Prosecutor v. Fofana and Kondewa*, Case No. SCSL-04-14-T, Judgment, ¶ 170 (Aug. 2, 2007).

[13] S.C. Res. 1757, U.N. Doc. S/RES/1757 (2007).

[14] *See* Nidal Nabil Jurdi, *The Subject-Matter Jurisdiction of the Special Tribunal for Lebanon*, 5 J. INT'L CRIM. J. 1125 (2007).

crimes in the future. In an important preliminary decision, the STL reasoned that the international law of terrorism, including rules embodied in treaties ratified by Lebanon, could be invoked to interpret and apply Lebanese terrorism law.[15]

C. Terrorism Within the ICC Statute

As originally envisioned, the ICC's constitutive statute was to be primarily procedural in nature, incorporating the "core" international crimes of genocide, crimes against humanity, and war crimes by reference and as defined by customary international law along with certain "treaty crimes" set forth in discrete multilateral treaties already in existence, such as treaties addressing terrorism, drug trafficking, money laundering, and the like. To that end, nine of the terrorism treaties referenced earlier (for example, those addressing terrorism against aircraft, ships, hostages, and diplomats) were included in an annex to the draft statute.

Early on, delegates expressed concern that customary international law alone would not define the relevant crimes as clearly as would be necessary to provide adequate notice to an accused pursuant to the principle of *nullum crimen sine lege*. In addition, with respect to treaty crimes, delegates anticipated that it might be necessary to confirm that the treaty was in force with respect to the relevant states (e.g., the territorial and nationality state) for a treaty crime prosecution to proceed. These concerns led states to agree to set out the operative definitions of all the crimes in the Statute (and later adopt Elements of Crimes) rather than to incorporate such crimes by reference to preexisting treaties or customary international law.

As the negotiations proceeded at the 1998 Rome Conference, the treaty crimes eventually either fell out of the Statute, as was the case with terrorism *stricto sensu* and drug trafficking, or were incorporated into the core crimes, as was the case with respect to crimes against internationally protected persons (which are enumerated as war crimes at Article 8(2)(b)(iii)) and apartheid (which is listed as a crime against humanity at Article 7(1)(j)). With respect to terrorism crimes, drafters articulated several reasons for eventually excluding them from the Statute altogether: (1) terrorism has no universally accepted definition; (2) terrorism was not considered to be one of "the most serious crimes of international concern" as contemplated by Article 1; (3) at the time, terrorism was not clearly recognized as a crime under customary international law; (4) including crimes of terrorism would unnecessarily politicize the

---

15 *The Prosecutor v. Ayyash et al.*, Case No. STL-11-01/I, Interlocutory Decision on the Applicable Law: Terrorism, Conspiracy, Homicide, Perpetration, Cumulative Charging, ¶ 62 (Feb. 16, 2011).

ICC; and (5) there were alternative domestic venues for terrorism prosecutions such that establishing international jurisdiction would be unnecessary or duplicative. In addition, delegates at the Rome Conference were committed to concluding the treaty in five weeks, and the inclusion of terrorism was proving to be a sticking point in the negotiations.

With respect to the politicization argument, states contended that the inclusion of terrorism would impede ratification of the Rome Statute for fear of politicized prosecutions and proceedings, especially in cases in which states were battling subversive groups or internal rebellions. As one scholar has noted, terrorism "is not only a phenomenon, it is also an invective, and there are many examples of States using this invective in a most subjective manner to de-legitimize and demonize political opponents, associations or other States" and to infringe civil liberties—observations that continue to ring true today.[16] This argument overlooks the fact that many of the crimes within the jurisdiction of the Court have significant political ramifications, not the least of which is the crime of aggression.

With respect to the existence of a viable alternative domestic venue, because governments are usually the direct or indirect target of terrorist acts, states are highly motivated to criminally prosecute acts of terrorism, to cooperate with each other toward this end, and to encourage the pursuit of civil actions by victims. Indeed, as compared to the "atrocity crimes," terrorism crimes are more often incorporated into domestic penal codes and are more frequently prosecuted by states. Given this observation, it was argued that the principle of complementarity would likely prevent the prosecution of acts of terrorism before the ICC in many cases.[17] While compelling, the complementarity argument is less germane when it comes to state-sponsored terrorism. Moreover, an effective counterterrorism program requires "long-term planning, infiltration into the organizations involved, the necessity of giving immunity to some individuals involved, and so forth"[18]—all functions more effectively

---

[16] Christian Munch, *The International Criminal Court (ICC) and Terrorism as an International Crime*, 14 MICH. ST. J. INT'L L. 121, 133 (2006).

[17] The principle of complementarity is fundamental to the ICC framework and provides that the Court will exercise jurisdiction only where the relevant domestic authorities (for example, the territorial and nationality states) are either unwilling or unable to prosecute offenders. Notably, complementarity is not triggered, at least according to the plain text of Article 17, where the domestic courts are overly zealous toward prosecutions or where the defendant's due process rights are potentially in jeopardy—two risks for terrorism prosecutions where the state is the target of the acts in question and has adopted vigorous counter-terrorism policies.

[18] Mahnoush H. Arsanjani, *The Rome Statute of the International Criminal Court*, 93 AM. J. INT'L L. 22, 29 (1999).

exercised by national jurisdictions than an international court far from the events in question and the relevant political milieu.

In the end, the final ICC Statute supports jurisdiction over only the four core crimes, namely genocide, crimes against humanity, war crimes, and aggression (undefined at the time the treaty was first open for signature). Some drafters remained uneasy with this result and managed to secure the adoption of Resolution E at the Rome Conference, which recommended that a review conference assemble later to consider the inclusion of the crime of terrorism in the ICC Statute.[19] Ultimately, the proposal to include terrorism in the Statute did not move forward at the Kampala Review Conference held in 2010 or during subsequent amendment processes. Nonetheless, many states and scholars continue to argue that terrorism should eventually be included within the Court's jurisdiction. In particular, these advocates question the assumption made during the Rome Conference—which occurred in 1998 prior to the attacks of September 11, 2001—that terrorism is not a serious crime of international concern. They argue that terrorism represents a substantial and growing threat, especially given the possibility of attacks with nuclear, chemical, or biological weapons of mass destruction.

While the threat of terrorism enjoys a greater level of international recognition and concern since the convening of the Rome Conference, the question of how best to address terrorist crimes as a legal matter is still very much an open one. It remains to be seen whether the more established international crimes currently within the jurisdiction of the ICC adequately provide redress for terrorist acts, or whether there is a jurisdictional lacuna that still needs to be filled.

D. The Interface Between Terrorism and War

One of the challenges to creating a penal regime for acts of terrorism stems from the fact that the crimes encompassed within the concept of terrorism sit at the intersection of the *jus ad bellum* (governing the legality of the resort to armed force *ab inicio*) and the *jus in bello* (governing the legality of the use of armed force and the conduct of hostilities once an armed conflict has been initiated). As was discussed in Chapter 6 on the legal regulation of war, contemporary international law treats these two bodies of law as conceptually distinct. Yet acts of terrorism are often defended by reference to the justness of the cause that inspired them. Indeed, there remains a deep-seated unwillingness within segments of the international community to fully relinquish the idea that certain

---

[19] The Final Act of the Rome Conference is available here: https://legal.un.org/icc/statute/finalfra.htm.

forms of otherwise prohibited violence are legitimate if they are employed in opposition to a colonial, racist, alien, occupying, or oppressive regime by a group seeking independence or self-determination. In such situations of asymmetrical power, an armed conflict fought "according to the rules" would undoubtedly result in a military victory for the dominant power; thus, those challenging dominant military powers are faced with the choice of being defeated militarily or adopting unconventional military tactics, including acts of terrorism. This also explains the rhetorical persistence of the bromide "one person's terrorist is another person's freedom fighter."

Likewise, a certain degree of uncertainty surrounds the interface between the law governing the crimes of terrorism and IHL. This is especially true where terrorists' organizational capabilities and destructive potential rival that of conventional militaries. Acts that would be criminal under domestic law, or would constitute acts of terrorism under the various treaty prohibitions against terrorism, may be lawful acts of war under IHL when committed within the context of an armed conflict (e.g., attacks on combatants in a conflict setting). This section attempts to untangle these two bodies of law based on a series of scenarios.

1. Violent Acts Committed Within an International Armed Conflict

Imagine two signatories to the 1949 Geneva Conventions and their Protocols, Alpha and Beta, at war with each other. Alpha's troops launch two attacks against Beta's troops: one on a traditional battlefield along the border between the two states and one against a military barracks within Beta's territory in the dead of night while Beta's troops are asleep. Both attacks by Alpha's combatants against Beta's combatants are legitimate acts of warfare under classic IHL.[20] Military installations and combatants are always lawful objects of attack in a conflict setting, even if the combatants are posing no threat to their opponents at the time. Indeed, the billeting of these combatants in the barracks is not dispositive; these individuals could conceivably be attacked in their homes as well, although IHL would condemn the deaths of any civilians deliberately targeted or the unintentional deaths of civilians in the vicinity of the combatants if the force used was disproportionate to any military advantage to be gained by attacking off-duty troops. It is only once they are officially *hors de combat* ("outside of combat") as a result of illness, injury, capture, or surrender that combatants may no longer be targeted. In

[20] Note that revisionist accounts of IHL have posited that there is a duty to capture, rather than kill, enemy combatants if it is feasible to do so under the circumstances. According to this view, Alpha should endeavor to capture the sleeping Beta combatants rather than kill them. This minimization of harm approach remains controversial as a matter of law but may be implemented as a matter of policy.

our scenario, Beta's combatants have certainly "laid down their arms," but that terminology is not meant to cover combatants who have simply retired for the night.

Assuming the only individuals deliberately targeted are combatants, and that appropriate levels of force and types of weaponry are utilized, this attack generates no prosecutable event by Beta, Alpha, or others within the international community. Combatants representing nation-states at war with each other are deemed "privileged belligerents," which is to say that under IHL they are entitled to use force against each other. Indeed, this is the essence of war. Presumably, if Beta attempted to prosecute either of these acts as war crimes or as violations of domestic law, the defendants would have a strong defense of combat immunity that would find support in IHL and trump domestic law as the *lex specialis*. Thus, although we often think of the laws of armed conflict as limiting the use of force, the same laws also provide legal justification for certain acts of violence that would otherwise be illegal outside of an armed conflict.

By contrast, in the same conflict scenario, imagine an attack by Alpha's troops against a civilian hospital in Beta that contained no Beta military personnel and was serving no military purpose. A deliberate attack by Alpha's combatants on Beta's medical personnel (that is, non-combatants) and on a civilian object in the context of an international armed conflict is the quintessential war crime. The perpetrators of this act remain privileged belligerents, but they become war criminals when they deliberately misuse their military might against a protected class of persons or target. Alpha's combatants may be prosecuted for the war crimes of willfully killing protected persons or the "extensive destruction and appropriation of property, not justified by military necessity and carried out unlawfully and wantonly," within the lexicon of the 1949 Geneva Conventions.[21] Under the Rome Statute (Articles 8(2)(b)(i) and (ii)), this attack could also be prosecuted as "intentionally directing attacks against the civilian population as such or against individual civilians not taking direct part in hostilities" and "intentionally directing attacks against civilian objects, that is, objects which are not military objectives."

To adapt our facts once more: imagine an attack by Alpha on a military objective—the barracks for example—that was located within a Betan civilian area. If civilians are harmed during this attack, it is necessary to conduct a close analysis of whether the attack was indiscriminate (see Article 51 of Additional Protocol I) in

[21] *See* Article 147, Convention (IV) Relative to the Protection of Civilian Persons in Time of War (Aug. 12, 1949).

the sense of being expected to cause incidental loss of civilian life that would be excessive in relation to the concrete and direct military advantage anticipated. An indiscriminate attack is a war crime in an international armed conflict; if the attack was proportionate, the resulting harm to civilians is unfortunate—but not unlawful—"collateral damage." This concept, based in part upon the doctrine of double effect, indicates that it is a war crime to intentionally kill civilians; if harm is merely accidental or incidental to an otherwise lawful attack, it is—while regrettable—no war crime. By the way, Beta's placement of the barracks in the vicinity of civilian objects may constitute a violation of IHL (notably Article 58 of Protocol I), which requires parties to avoid locating military objectives within densely populated areas and taking precautions to protect the civilian population against the dangers resulting from military operations. A breach of this requirement (which applies during peacetime) is not, however, denominated as a war crime *per se*.

2. Violent Acts Committed Outside of Armed Conflict

Now, remove the state of war between Alpha and Beta, but imagine that non-violent political tensions exist between the two states. Alphan civilians form a radical group intent on escalating the conflict. A deliberate armed attack on the Betan political leadership or a civilian market in Beta by members of the Alphan radical group, whose members are motivated by some political or ideological purpose, is the quintessential terrorist act. Under current international treaties governing terrorism, however, only the Terrorist Bombing Convention is implicated by this scenario, and even then only if a "place of public use," "state or government facility," "transportation system," or "infrastructure facility" is intentionally targeted using an "explosive or other legal device," as those terms are defined by the treaty. A small arms attack against a single government official (or on a civilian neighborhood for that matter) would likely not qualify.

Either Alpha or Beta would be entitled to prosecute this act as the crime of murder, or attempted murder, under their domestic penal codes pursuant to the nationality or territorial principles of jurisdiction, respectively. If the penal codes of Alpha and Beta codify any crimes of terrorism, the attack may also be prosecutable as such under domestic law if the elements of those crimes are met. Without the existence of an armed conflict between the two states, or between non-state actors and either state, IHL is not implicated at all and no war crimes have been committed. Likewise, the perpetrators from Alpha are not entitled to prisoner of war status, if captured, or any form of combatant immunity, if prosecuted. This scenario—when violence is committed against civilians in peacetime—suggests one gap in ICL that a comprehensive international prohibition against terrorism might fill.[22]

The distinction between war crimes and acts of terrorism seems relatively comprehensible under these two scenarios. As demonstrated below, once we start altering the operative variables, this categorization gets murkier.

3. The Initiation of an Armed Conflict, Whether International or Non-International

Going back to our original scenario, the first use of armed force by Alphan troops in Beta would initiate an international armed conflict between the two nation states within the meaning of Article 2 of the Geneva Conventions and trigger the application of the IHL governing international armed conflicts (and a right of Beta to engage in self-defense within the meaning of Article 51 of the U.N. Charter).[23] This would likely constitute the crime of aggression under the Rome Statute definition and a breach of the U.N. Charter. Likewise, when it comes to the attack by the radicalized group from Alpha, this violence may also constitute the initiation of an armed conflict and trigger the application of IHL. For this to constitute an international armed conflict, the radical group would have to be under the "overall control" of the government of Alpha—the test devised by the ICTY to establish the existence of an *international* armed conflict.[24] By contrast, an attack by an organized militia not under the overall control of Alpha might initiate a non-international armed conflict within Beta, as discussed more fully below. This would trigger the application of those more limited, though increasingly comparable, rules of IHL addressed to non-international armed conflicts.

Determining when IHL is initiated, and whether the rules governing international or non-international armed conflicts apply, returns us to a topic in Chapter 6. Recall that the ICTY in *Tadić*

---

[22] If this attack is serious enough, it might also constitute a crime against humanity, which requires as a predicate a widespread or systematic attack against a civilian population. The attacks of September 11th, for example, likely constitute a crime against humanity standing alone.

[23] The U.N. Charter recognizes the inherent right of states to respond defensively to an "armed attack" until the Security Council has taken measures necessary to maintain international peace and security.

[24] These militia might not qualify for prisoner of war treatment, however, if captured. Article 4 of Geneva III contemplates the involvement of "militias . . . belonging to a [High Contracting] Party to the conflict and operating in or outside their own territory" in addition to formal forces. To qualify as privileged belligerents, and to be entitled to prisoner of war treatment, these militia must (a) be commanded by a person responsible for his or her subordinates; (b) have a fixed distinctive sign recognizable at a distance; (c) carry arms openly; and (d) conduct their operations in accordance with the laws and customs of war.

concluded that "an armed conflict exists whenever there is a resort to armed force between States or *protracted* armed violence between governmental authorities and *organized* armed groups or between such groups within a State" (emphasis added).[25] In the same breath, the ICTY also noted that IHL applies "from the initiation of such armed conflicts and extends beyond the cessation of hostilities until a general conclusion of peace is reached." Once the IHL governing international armed conflicts applies, acts that would otherwise be criminal under international or domestic law may become legitimate acts of war (e.g., fighting between combatants). A deliberate attack on civilians, however, is always criminal and never a lawful act of war.

4. Violent Acts Committed Within Non-International Armed Conflicts

To amend our scenario again, we can entirely internalize the conflict. Imagine a civil war that qualifies as a non-international armed conflict within Beta in which citizens of Beta who practice the same religion as inhabitants of Alpha seek secession from Beta and integration within Alpha. In the dark of night, the Betan secessionists—with no assistance from or involvement of Alpha—attack a civilian hospital and a military barracks in Beta.

Common Article 3 of the Geneva Conventions[26] and Protocol II regulate military conduct in civil wars and other non-international armed conflicts. The attack on the civilian hospital is prohibited by provisions within common Article 3 and Articles 4 and 13 of Protocol II that protect persons who do not take direct part in hostilities, including members of the civilian population. Neither instrument,

---

[25] *The Prosecutor v. Tadić*, Case No. IT-94-1, Decision on the Defence Motion for Interlocutory Appeal on Jurisdiction, ¶ 70 (Oct. 2, 1995).

[26] Common Article 3 reads in relevant part:

> (1) Persons taking no active part in the hostilities, including members of armed forces who have laid down their arms and those placed "hors de combat" by sickness, wounds, detention, or any other cause, shall in all circumstances be treated humanely, without any adverse distinction founded on race, colour, religion or faith, sex, birth or wealth, or any other similar criteria. To this end, the following acts are and shall remain prohibited at any time and in any place whatsoever with respect to the above-mentioned persons:
>
> (a) violence to life and person, in particular murder of all kinds, mutilation, cruel treatment and torture;
>
> (b) taking of hostages;
>
> (c) outrages upon personal dignity, in particular humiliating and degrading treatment;
>
> (d) the passing of sentences and the carrying out of executions without previous judgment pronounced by a regularly constituted court, affording all the judicial guarantees which are recognized as indispensable by civilized peoples.

however, contains a penal regime. So, to prosecute these acts as war crimes would require a domestic statute that goes beyond Beta's IHL treaty obligations. Absent such a statute, these acts could be prosecuted within Beta as ordinary murder and mayhem (and likely treason).

By contrast, neither instrument specifically prohibits the attack on the military barracks (a military objective). Under IHL, Beta's combatants remain legitimate objects of attack even when they are not actively engaged in combat. In other words, once the fact of an armed conflict is established, members of the armed forces of a state are combatants, always considered to be taking a direct part in hostilities and thus targetable. However, the Betan separatists are not considered privileged combatants, as they are not connected to a state or participating in an international armed conflict. As such, their conduct does not give rise to combatant immunity. Although they likely cannot be prosecuted for war crimes *per se* under extant IHL, they still can be prosecuted for ordinary murder, etc. Circumstances like this can also give rise to charges of terrorism. This reveals a second area where the crime of terrorism fills a lacuna in international law: allowing for the prosecution of attacks by unprivileged combatants against privileged combatants and military objectives. In this way, a concept of terrorism can be used to distinguish "legitimate" and "illegitimate" uses of force, generally from the perspective of the state's interests and legal order.

A rather unintuitive asymmetry in IHL reveals itself if we alter our facts a bit. Imagine that as our secessionists attack government troops, the government troops advance around the perimeter and attack the secessionists from behind, causing them to disband and scatter. Under IHL, this is a lawful act of war. The secessionists are taking direct part in hostilities and, as such, are lawful objects of attack. Further imagine that during this confrontation, government troops identified particular individuals during the attack who subsequently escaped capture. Can government troops later track these individuals down and kill them in their homes? The answer according to Protocol II is no. Unlike the government troops mentioned earlier, who are always considered to be taking direct part in hostilities and are thus always targetable, our secessionists are not technically combatants because they are not representing a state. As noncombatants, they may be targeted only when they are taking a direct part in hostilities pursuant to Article 13(3) of Protocol II, which states "[c]ivilians shall enjoy the protection afforded by this part [not to be targeted], unless and for such time as they take a direct part in hostilities."

The thorny question of when precisely noncombatants "take a direct part in hostilities" has been the subject of long-running discussions between the International Committee of the Red Cross (ICRC), IHL experts, and military lawyers. If the secessionists were billeted in a rebel camp somewhere in the territory of the state, this might still qualify as "participation in hostilities." If they have returned home for the evening, it might not. According to the ICRC's interpretive guidance on this point, individuals who assume a "continuous combat function" may be targeted at any time with lethal force; however, individuals who do not serve such a function become immune from direct attack while they are not directly participating in hostilities.[27] This doctrinal asymmetry—treaty rules that render members of a state's armed forces continuously targetable but members of a rebel force only targetable when they are directly participating in hostility—has, not surprisingly, generated significant controversy within states.

5. The Initiation of a Non-International Armed Conflict

To alter our scenario somewhat again, imagine the same situation as given previously in which a group of individuals in Beta who practice the same religion as inhabitants of Alpha desire secession from Beta to join Alpha. Assume that, for the moment, this is merely a political, and not an armed, conflict, so IHL does not yet apply. Imagine that individual secessionists in Beta radicalize and decide to deploy violence within Beta to draw attention to their cause. At first, only domestic law will apply; IHL has not yet been triggered while the violence remains below a certain threshold and the group remains unorganized. Eventually, however, the group becomes more and more organized and the violence escalates in terms of the frequency and severity of attacks. At a certain point, the IHL governing a non-international armed conflict will begin to apply.

Recall from Chapter 6 that common Article 3 and Protocol II have different thresholds of applicability.[28] The former requires simply an armed conflict "occurring in the territory of one of the High Contracting Parties," with the ICTY defining "armed conflict" as "protracted armed violence between governmental authorities and organized armed groups." The latter (at Article 1(1)) requires an armed conflict within the territory of a party to the Conventions in which the nonstate actors are under responsible command and exercise a degree of control over the state's territory that enables them "to carry out sustained and concerted military operations and to implement [the] Protocol." The Protocol at Article 1(2) makes clear that it does not apply to "situations of internal disturbances and

---

[27] ICRC, INTERPRETIVE GUIDANCE ON THE NOTION OF DIRECT PARTICIPATION IN HOSTILITIES UNDER INTERNATIONAL HUMANITARIAN LAW (Dec. 21, 2010).

[28] In *Hamdan v. Rumsfeld*, 548 U.S. 557 (2006), for example, the U.S. Supreme Court determined that common Article 3 applied to the armed conflict between the United States and Al Qaeda.

tensions, such as riots, isolated and sporadic acts of violence and other acts of a similar nature." If our secessionists do not meet this standard—for example, if they possess no territory or are not under responsible command—their acts of violence will be governed only by the relatively sparse common Article 3. By contrast, Protocol II contains more detailed rules governing non-international armed conflicts that apply once its threshold of applicability has been met. The implications of this distinction is that states are less constrained by international law in common Article 3 conflicts and can address such scenarios using their domestic law, as tempered by their treaty and customary international law human rights obligations.

6. The Penal Consequences of Violent Acts Committed Within International Versus Non-International Armed Conflicts

Classic IHL, as derived from the four Geneva Conventions of 1949 and their Protocols, would treat all these events quite differently than would modern customary IHL in terms of their penal consequences. Most important, although the Geneva Conventions identify a list of "grave breaches" that constitute war crimes under IHL, neither common Article 3 nor Protocol II creates or mandates the domestic creation of a penal regime for non-international armed conflicts. As a result, if we consider only the existing treaty text, any penal liability for acts of violence committed within a non-international armed conflict would be governed by domestic law.

So, assuming that Beta has domestically incorporated the Geneva Conventions and their Protocols, but not provided for any additional penal provisions for violations of IHL in its domestic law, the killing by the Betan secessionists of civilian patients in the hospital and members of Beta's military quartered in their barracks would be treated as acts of ordinary murder or terrorism by Beta's authorities. They could not be prosecuted as war crimes. The crimes against both targets may thus be treated exactly the same; it is of no moment that the military barracks would be a lawful object of attack within the context of an international armed conflict. The classic treaty law governing non-international armed conflicts entitles states to treat secessionists as common criminals rather than privileged belligerents. Individuals who are not considered privileged belligerents under IHL are not entitled to combatant immunity for what would otherwise be lawful acts of war. Nor, for that matter, need they be treated as prisoners of war when they are captured, but the state's standard constitutional and human rights protections would still apply.

Some states have gone beyond their treaty obligations, however, and domestically penalized other violations of IHL, including common Article 3 and Protocol II governing non-international armed conflicts. The United States did so with the passage of the 1996 War Crimes Act.[29] The Act was quickly amended in 1997 to define war crimes to include acts that constitute "a violation of common Article 3 of the international conventions signed at Geneva, 12 August 1949, or any protocol to such convention to which the United States is a party and which deals with non-international armed conflict." Common Article 3(1)(a) prohibits "violence to life and person, in particular murder of all kinds" when committed against a person "taking no active part in the hostilities, including members of armed forces who have laid down their arms." If the Betan penal code mirrored U.S. law, this provision would render the secessionists' attack against the civilian hospital the war crime of violence to life and murder. (The attack could also be prosecuted as ordinary murder or as terrorism). Because common Article 3 does not prohibit the attack on the government barracks, no criminal liability would exist under this hypothetical war crimes statute. However, the operation could be prosecuted as an "ordinary" crime under the domestic penal code or as an act of terrorism.

Modern developments in customary IHL have significantly expanded the concept of war crimes beyond the treaty texts. In particular, the statutes of the two *ad hoc* criminal tribunals, and the jurisprudence thereunder, largely collapsed the distinction between international and non-international armed conflicts in terms of the penal consequences of acts of violence within the latter. In so doing, the tribunals regularly prosecuted violations of treaty provisions that are not identified as crimes by the treaties themselves. The tribunals' approach to war crimes in non-international armed conflicts was largely adopted and codified by the ICC Statute at Article 8 (although that provision still contains a longer list of war crimes for international armed conflicts as compared to non-international armed conflicts).[30] This suggests an emergent set of customary

---

[29] The original version of the War Crimes Act of 1996 criminalized all violations of common Article 3 of the Geneva Conventions so long as they were committed by or against a member of the Armed Forces of the United States or a national of the United States. 18 U.S.C. § 2441(3). Following the revelation of custodial abuses by U.S. personnel at Abu Ghraib prison and elsewhere, Congress amended this statute by way of the Military Commission Act of 2006. In so doing, Congress decriminalized certain violations of common Article 3, namely "(c) outrages upon personal dignity, in particular humiliating and degrading treatment" and "(d) the passing of sentences and the carrying out of executions without previous judgment pronounced by a regularly constituted court, affording all the judicial guarantees which are recognized as indispensable by civilized peoples." This made it more difficult to prosecute many of the custodial abuses as war crimes under U.S. law and opened the door for the convening of military commissions that did not meet ordinary due process standards.

[30] Domestic war crimes statutes are increasingly following suit as states adjust their penal codes after ratification of the ICC Statute. This suggests that customary international law now recognizes the possibility of war crimes being committed within

international law rules governing the commission of war crimes in non-international armed conflicts. However, the crime of spreading terror among the civilian population is conspicuously absent from Article 8 of the ICC Statute, limiting—but not eliminating—the ability of the ICC to prosecute acts of terrorism, as discussed below.

E. Prosecuting Acts of Terrorism Before the ICC

Despite the clear omission of terrorism *per se* from the Rome Statute, arguments exist that the Court could adjudicate certain acts that one might also consider acts of terrorism within its existing subject matter jurisdiction. This is because in certain situations, acts of terrorism may satisfy the elements of other international crimes. As exemplified above, the high degree of intersection between acts of terrorism and war crimes suggests that the former may be prosecutable before the ICC and other international tribunals with jurisdiction over war crimes.

Considering our scenarios involving states Alpha and Beta, the ICC could consider Alpha's attack on the hospital, if committed during an international armed conflict, to qualify as the following war crimes, *inter alia*, within the Rome Statute:

- Willful killing (Article 8(2)(a)(i));
- Violence to life and persons (Article 8(2)(a)(iii));
- Extensive destruction of property . . . not justified by military necessity (Article 8(2)(a)(iv));
- Intentionally attacking civilians (Article 8(2)(b)(i));
- Intentionally directing attacks against civilian objects (Article 8(2)(b)(ii)); or
- Intentionally directing attacks against hospitals (Article 8(2)(e)(iv)).

Likewise, if the attack on the hospital occurred within the context of a non-international armed conflict, the following provisions may be applicable:

- Violence to life and person, in particular murder (Article 8(2)(c)(i));
- Intentionally directing attacks against civilians (Article 8(2)(e)(i)); or
- Intentionally attacking hospitals (Article 8(2)(e)(iv)).

---

non-international armed conflicts even though the original treaties are silent in this regard.

Note that an attack undertaken for the purpose of terrorizing the civilian population, which is prohibited under Article 51(2) of Additional Protocol I and Article 13(2) of Additional Protocol II, is not included in these lists. None of the provisions of Article 8 penalizes the attack on the military barracks, whether committed in an international or non-international armed conflict. The targeting of a military objective is generally a lawful act of war; however, it becomes a war crime where disproportionate force is used such that there is an incidental loss of life, long-term or severe environmental damage, or superfluous injury.[31] Absent this, any prosecution of the barracks attack would have to occur before domestic courts under domestic law.

In addition to these war crimes, where violent acts (such as murder, torture, or kidnapping) are committed within the context of a widespread or systematic attack against a civilian population, they may constitute crimes against humanity under Article 7. The definition of crimes against humanity in the ICC Statute requires proof that the attack was "pursuant to or in furtherance of a State or organizational policy to commit such attack" (Article 7(2)(a)). Presumably, many terrorist groups could be shown to possess such a policy to attack civilians. Indeed, part of what makes terrorism so scary—and more worthy of condemnation than ordinary murder or other forms of violence—is that the victims are often apparently chosen at random. That said, terrorist attacks may also implicate the prohibition against genocide, where the acts target a protected group with the intent to destroy that group. Although there are many instances of acts of terrorism being directed against a protected group (such as those committed during "the troubles" in Northern Ireland or even the attacks of September 11, 2001), it may be difficult to prove the specific intent to commit genocide as opposed to the intent to intimidate or coerce a government—the hallmark of terrorism.

As you review the terrorism materials in your course, and the degree of normative redundancy in ICL, reflect on whether terrorism crimes should be expressly included within the Rome Statute or whether such acts are better prosecuted before domestic courts. In addition, given the clear intent of the majority of drafters to exclude crimes of terrorism from the ICC, consider to what extent the ICC should prosecute acts that would otherwise be considered acts of terrorism under the terrorism treaties or pursuant to an emerging customary international law prohibition.

---

[31] Article 8 prohibits the use of weapons that cause unnecessary or superfluous suffering, such as poison or poisoned weapons, asphyxiating gases, or so-called dum dum bullets (bullets that expand on impact). *See* ICC Statute, Articles 8(2)(b)(xvii)–(xx).

Chapter 8

GENOCIDE AND CRIMES AGAINST HUMANITY

Genocide and crimes against humanity are the criminal counterparts of many human rights prohibitions under international law. Called "atrocity crimes" by some, these two great crimes sit at the pinnacle of international criminal law (ICL). This chapter presents the history and scope of genocide and crimes against humanity, and the relationship between them, with an eye toward exploring their division of labor in ICL and whether a conceptual distinction between them should be maintained.

Although an ancient scourge, the concept of genocide as a distinct international crime arose out of the Nazi Holocaust and World War II. We think of Nazi crimes as the paradigmatic case of genocide, but treaty codification of the crime came too late to prosecute anyone for what has sometimes been called "the crime of crimes."[1] The perpetrators of the Nazi Holocaust were instead prosecuted under the Nuremberg Charter for crimes against humanity, another international crime that traces its formal origins to the World War II period. Although genocide became the subject of a dedicated multilateral treaty in 1948, additional codification of crimes against humanity beyond the charters for the two post-World War II tribunals did not happen until the U.N. Security Council created the International Criminal Tribunal for the former Yugoslavia (ICTY) in 1993. The International Law Commission (ILC) in 2019 adopted Draft Articles on the Prevention and Punishment of Crimes Against Humanity that have been shared with the U.N. General Assembly for treaty consideration. Given some resistance within the General Assembly, it will likely take several years for any treaty to be negotiated and then opened for signature.

In addition to a shared history, the two crimes are also conceptually similar. Crimes against humanity are a constellation of acts made criminal under international law when they are committed within the context of a widespread or systematic attack against a civilian population with knowledge of that attack. This crime's very name captures two important facets of the crime: Crimes against humanity are considered to be committed against all of humanity, not just the individual victims or their immediate communities, and crimes against humanity "violat[e] the core

---

1 *Prosecutor v. Kambanda*, Case No. ICTR-97-23-S, Judgement, ¶ 16 (Sept. 4, 1998).

humanity that we all share and that distinguishes us from other natural beings."[2] Genocide involves the commission of one of a set of enumerated acts against members of a protected group with the intent to destroy the group, in whole or in part. The goal of genocide is thus to eradicate a very segment of humanity, defined by race, ethnicity, religion, or nationality. Like crimes against humanity, genocide also threatens humanity as a whole, though not by directly attacking all of humanity but instead by singling out a group for destruction, and thus threatening to reduce the world's racial, ethnic, religious, or national diversity.

Notwithstanding this similarity, there are clear doctrinal distinctions between crimes against humanity and genocide. First, genocide requires that the perpetrator have the specific intent to "destroy" a protected group, in whole or in part, whereas crimes against humanity do not require any form of specific intent. Second, only acts committed against groups identified by their race, ethnicity, religion, or nationality may constitute genocide; conversely, criminal acts committed against any "civilian population" can qualify as crimes against humanity. Third, conduct rises to the level of crimes against humanity when the perpetrator acts within the context of a "widespread or systematic" attack against a civilian population; there is no similar threshold for genocide. As a result, a single isolated act (such as the killing of a handful of members of a protected group) could qualify as genocide if the perpetrator acted with the requisite specific intent,[3] whereas a single isolated act against a civilian is unlikely to qualify as a crime against humanity on its own. Debate exists over whether proof of a policy is a required element of crimes against humanity in customary international law; the ICC Statute includes it, other formulations do not.

Given the parallels between these two crimes, this chapter raises the question of whether there is a legal justification for continuing to distinguish between the two, or whether the notion of crimes against humanity encompasses the crime of genocide in all circumstances. In other words, do the unique characteristics of the crime of genocide warrant preserving the two separate crimes? To guide our inquiry, this chapter provides the basic history of the two crimes followed by a discussion of their elemental similarities and differences.

---

2 David Luban, *A Theory of Crimes Against Humanity*, 29 YALE J. INT'L L. 85, 86 (2004).

3 The Appeals Chamber of the ICTY has taken this position, although in a single opinion the facts of which were never replicated. As noted later in this chapter, the Tribunal concluded that Goran Jelisić was on "a one-man genocide mission, intent upon personally wiping out the protected group." *See Prosecutor v. Jelisić*, Case No. IT-95-10-T, Judgement, ¶ 108 (Dec. 14, 1999).

A. Crimes Against Humanity

Crimes against humanity were first codified in response to the atrocities of World War II. There were, however, some earlier references to crimes against the laws of humanity. The first use of the term "crimes against humanity" that we can find occurred in 1890 in a letter from the African-American journalist, George Washington Williams, to the U.S. Secretary of State, James Blaine, describing the atrocities committed in the Belgian Congo (present-day Democratic Republic of Congo).[4] The term was also used during the post-World War I period, when international prosecutions were first contemplated to address atrocities of global proportions. In particular, the deportation and massacre of the Armenian population of the Ottoman Empire prompted the Allied governments of France, Great Britain, and Russia to issue in 1915 a joint Declaration to the Ottoman Empire denouncing these acts as "crimes against humanity and civilization for which all the members of the Turkish Government will be held responsible together with its agents implicated in the massacres."[5] The majority of the Allies originally envisioned international trials against "[a]ll persons belonging to enemy countries, however high their position may have been, without distinction of rank, including Chiefs of States, who have been guilty of offences against the laws and customs of war or the laws of humanity."[6] The U.S. delegation dissented from the reference to crimes against humanity, however, arguing that the notion of crimes committed against all of humanity was too inchoate and contextual to underlie criminal justice processes. The U.S. position ultimately prevailed, and the 1919 Treaty of Versailles bringing World War I to a close excluded reference to "crimes against humanity" in the provisions addressing criminal responsibility (Articles 228–229).[7] In the end, the whole project of international justice was scrapped, and only a few trials before domestic tribunals were held.

---

[4] This early use of the phrase has been difficult to track down. Adam Hochschild in his well-regarded book about the Belgian Congo, KING LEOPOLD'S GHOSE: A STORY OF GREED, TERROR, AND HEROISM IN COLONIAL AFRICA 112 (2000) mentions this early use of the phrase. According to Norman Geras, George Washington Williams wrote to James Blaine, "The State of Congo is in no sense deserving your confidence or support. It is actively engaged in the slave trade and is guilty of many crimes against humanity." NORMAN GERAS, CRIMES AGAINST HUMANITY: BIRTH OF A CONCEPT 4 (2011), citing to FRANÇOIS BONTINCK, AUX ORIGINES DE L'ETAT INDÉPENDENT DU CONGO: DOCUMENTS TIRÉS D'ARCHIVES AMÉRICAINES 449 (1966).

[5] Declaration of France, Great Britain and Russia, 24 May 1915, *quoted in* Egon Schwelb, *Crimes Against Humanity*, 23 BRIT. Y.B. INT'L L. 178, 181 (1946).

[6] Commission on the Responsibility of the Authors of the War and on Enforcement of Penalties, *Report Presented to the Preliminary Peace Conference* (Mar. 29, 1919), *reprinted in* 14 AM. J. INT'L L. 95, 177 (1920).

[7] Versailles Treaty of Peace Between the Allied and Associated Powers and Germany, June 28, 1919, 225 Consol. T.S. 188.

When the prospect of international criminal justice was revived at the end of World War II, it was clear that existing ICL would be insufficient to condemn the full horror of the recent war. As philosopher Hannah Arendt wrote, the Holocaust was "a new crime, [a] crime against humanity—in the sense of a crime 'against the human status,' or against the very nature of mankind."[8] More precisely, the well-established prohibitions against war crimes did not reach the acts of international aggression committed against peaceful states or acts of violence committed against a state's own civilians or against civilians from allied countries. The framers of the Nuremberg Charter thus dusted off the previously discarded concept of crimes against humanity to address the latter phenomenon, in many ways the defining brutality of the Nazi enterprise.[9] Although the crime of aggression—deemed "the greatest menace of our times"—was the centerpiece of the Charter and the Nuremberg Trial, the notion of crimes against humanity has proven to be the real legacy of Nuremberg, albeit with chronic definitional variation.

Unlike the crimes of genocide, torture, and war crimes, crimes against humanity never became the subject of a comprehensive penal treaty in the postwar period. As a result, considerable definitional confusion has plagued the crime over its life span. During the negotiations surrounding the ILC's Draft Code of Crimes Against the Peace and Security of Mankind (1996), drafters experimented with various elements of the crime in an effort to arrive at a consensus definition. The hodgepodge of definitions produced by the ILC and national legislatures did little to satisfy the principle of legality. It was not until the promulgation of the statutes of the two *ad hoc* international criminal tribunals that an official modern definition emerged. Yet, in spite of the proximity in time and subject matter of the statutes of the two *ad hoc* tribunals—essentially Irish twins of the Security Council—their definitions of the crime contain significant variations.

The International Criminal Tribunal for Rwanda (ICTR) definition of crimes against humanity includes a requirement that the attack against a civilian population be "on national, political, ethnic, racial, or religious grounds." This addition of a discriminatory motive to the definition is an anomaly; no legal definition before or

8 HANNAH ARENDT, EICHMANN IN JERUSALEM: A REPORT ON THE BANALITY OF EVIL 268 (1965).

9 The charge of crimes against the peace, now termed the crime of aggression, was devised to address the crimes committed against the society of sovereign states—the traditional subject of public international law. Crimes against humanity addressed crimes against all of humankind, cutting across particular state affiliations. The notion that humanity itself could be the victim of an international crime in many ways undergirded the human rights movement, which also traces its broadest roots to the post-World War II period.

since has included such a requirement. The ICTY definition was also not without its unique aspects, reintroducing the nexus to armed conflict requirement that was present at Nuremberg but that all had assumed was no longer a necessary condition for an act to constitute a crime against humanity. These definitions, including their noted idiosyncrasies, were further refined in the case law of the two tribunals. These jurisprudential enhancements, with some additional modifications, are codified in a consensus definition in Article 7 of the Statute of the International Criminal Court (ICC). The ILC largely adopted this definition, in whole cloth, for their new Draft Articles dedicated to the crime. Through this iterative process of codification and interpretation, many definitional issues left open in the postwar period have been finally resolved, as discussed in greater detail in the remainder of this chapter.

The prohibition against crimes against humanity is increasingly important in ICL. It applies where the prohibition against genocide does not, such as where the group targeted is not a protected group (i.e., it is not a national, religious, ethnic, or national group) or where the defendant did not act with the specific intent to destroy the group. It also applies where the technical requirements of the war crimes prohibitions are not satisfied, such as where there is no armed conflict or where the victims do not constitute "protected persons." Finally, the crime against humanity of "persecution" is potentially far reaching, as it may "criminalize" violations of certain economic, social, and cultural rights.

It is thus fitting that the ILC has recently forwarded a set of Draft Articles on the Prevention and Punishment of Crimes Against Humanity to the U.N. General Assembly for consideration.[10] The proposed treaty would define the crime (almost identically to the ICC Statute) as well as establish a system for mutual legal assistance and extradition in favor of the crime's domestic or international prosecution. While many states have enacted a crimes against humanity statute in connection with their ratification of the ICC Statute, others have not. Widespread ratification of the treaty would encourage domestic incorporation as well as harmonize the substantive law (which in turn, facilitates enforcement efforts). Although the draft treaty is similar to other international crimes treaties, it is unique in that it explicitly envisions liability for legal persons, e.g., corporate entities, and includes a comprehensive preventative framework. It does not, at present, envision a treaty monitoring mechanism, such as the expert committees established by the core human rights treaties. However, the draft contains a

---

[10] International Law Commission, *Analytical Guide to the Work of the International Law Commission: Crimes against Humanity*, https://legal.un.org/ilc/guide/7_7.shtml.

compromissory clause granting the International Court of Justice jurisdiction over disputes relating to the interpretation, application, or fulfilment of the treaty, including those relating to the responsibility of the state for breaches.

B. Genocide

The term "genocide" occupies a singular position in the ICL lexicon. Yet a variance exists between the legal or technical definition of genocide, as embodied within the Convention on the Prevention and Punishment of the Crime of Genocide (the Genocide Convention) and its progeny, and lay conceptions of the crime.[11] The exclusion of certain instances of mass killing from the legal definition of genocide (even though such killings often qualify as a crime against humanity) generates extreme dissatisfaction among victim groups who consider themselves to have been the victim of a campaign of genocide, which they view as the supreme international crime.[12] This disjuncture is in many respects the result of a series of political compromises that occurred during the drafting of the Genocide Convention. Modern adjudications of the crime of genocide have to a certain degree begun to unravel these compromises, although the technical requirements in the definition of the crime continue to challenge international criminal lawyers.

Genocide is a modern word for an old crime. The term was originally coined by Polish jurist Raphael Lemkin, who, after learning of the Armenian massacre of World War I, campaigned tirelessly for the drafting of a multilateral treaty prohibiting the crime. Despite his efforts, it took the events of World War II to compel the international community to finally bring Lemkin's project to fruition. The charters of the Nuremberg and Tokyo Tribunals did not include genocide as an enumerated crime; instead, they provided for the prosecution of war crimes, crimes against humanity, and crimes against the peace. While no one was thus convicted of genocide by these first international criminal tribunals, the Nuremberg indictment did include a reference to genocide, which was defined as "the extermination of racial and national groups . . . in certain occupied territories in order to destroy particular races and classes of people, and national, racial or religious groups, particularly Jews,

---

[11] *See* Revised and updated report on the question of the prevention and punishment of the crime of genocide prepared by Mr. Whitaker, Commission on Human Rights, Sub-Commission on Prevention of Discrimination and Protection of Minorities, 38th Sess. U.N.Doc. E/CN.4/Sub.2/1985/6 (July 2, 1985) at 20 (" '[G]enocide' in popular modern usage covers many more cases of mass killings than those covered in the Convention.").

[12] *Id.* at 10 ("It could seem pedantic to argue that some terrible mass-killings are legalistically not genocide, but on the other hand it could be counter-productive to devalue genocide through over-diluting its definition.").

Poles, and Gypsies."[13] (Note that the Nazis' efforts to exterminate gay and lesbian persons goes unmentioned). Further, the Judgment found the Nazi defendants guilty of acts that would amount to genocide under the contemporary definition of the crime.

Following the Nuremberg Judgment in 1946, the U.N. General Assembly took up the matter of genocide and passed a resolution confirming that genocide constituted a crime under international law, the punishment of which was a matter of international concern.[14] The unanimous resolution also recommended that the United Nations draw up a draft convention on genocide to be submitted to the full General Assembly for signature and ratification. Throughout this drafting process, the provisions concerning the element of intent (*mens rea*), the enumerated protected groups, the inclusion of cultural genocide,[15] and the application of universal jurisdiction received the most intense debate. The Convention entered into force in January 1951 and, to date, it has been ratified by 152 states.[16] It envisions genocide being prosecuted by the state on whose territory the crime occurred and an international criminal court, which would not be established until decades later.

C. The Elements of the Two Crimes

Like many international crimes, crimes against humanity and genocide are characterized by two sets of elements.[17] The first set of elements is referred to as the *chapeau* ("hat") of the definition of the crime.[18] The *chapeau* elements apply to any subsequent enumeration

[13] *U.S. et al. v. Goering*, 1 TRIAL OF THE MAJOR WAR CRIMINALS BEFORE THE INTERNATIONAL MILITARY TRIBUNAL 27, 43–44 (1946).

[14] *See* G.A. Res. 96(I), U.N. Doc. A/RES/96 (Dec. 11, 1946).

[15] Lemkin's original conception of the crime of genocide encompassed all forms of destruction of a group as a distinct social entity. Accordingly, early formulations of the legal prohibition against genocide defined the crime broadly to involve coordinated actions against a protected collectivity's culture, religion, language, and social institutions as well as physical acts of violence. The drafters of the Genocide Convention, however, ultimately excluded reference to acts of "cultural genocide" on the grounds that such an offense was too vague and too far removed from physical destruction to merit inclusion in the treaty. The crime of forcibly transferring children from the protected group is the sole vestige of this notion of cultural genocide.

[16] Convention on the Prevention and Punishment of the Crime of Genocide, 78 U.N.T.S. 277 (Jan. 12, 1951).

[17] We focus here on the definitions of crimes against humanity and genocide as set forth in the Rome Statute. As noted earlier, the definition of crimes against humanity varies among the Rome Statute, the statutes of the *ad hoc* tribunals, and customary international law. All positive international law definitions of genocide mirror that found in the Genocide Convention, although some states have introduced variances in their domestic codes.

[18] In the Rome Statute, for example, these elements are found in the first paragraph under Article 6 for genocide, and Articles 7(1) and 7(2)(a) for crimes against humanity.

of prohibited acts. Thus, for an act to qualify as either a crime against humanity or genocide, it must meet the requirements of these *chapeau* elements. For genocide, the key *chapeau* element is that the perpetrator acted with "the intent to destroy, in whole or in part, a national, ethnical,[19] racial, or religious group, as such." For crimes against humanity, the key *chapeau* elements are twofold: The perpetrator's act must be "part of a widespread or systematic attack directed against any civilian population" and the perpetrator must have acted "with knowledge of the attack."

The second set of elements identifies the specific acts (such as killings) that, if committed in the context of the elements set forth in the *chapeau*, qualify as either a crime against humanity or an act of genocide. As with the *chapeau* elements, the definitions of genocide and crimes against humanity include different lists of constituent acts, although there is considerable overlap between the types of brutal conduct covered.

1. The *Chapeau* Elements

The *chapeau* elements of the definitions of crimes against humanity and genocide reveal four core differences between these two crimes. First, and most significant, is the *mens rea* requirement of each crime. Second is the definition of the victim group. Third is the question of whether either crime requires the showing of a formal policy or plan as a formal element of the offense. Fourth is the question—now largely obsolete—of whether crimes against humanity are indelibly linked to a state of armed conflict, an issue that has never arisen with respect to the definition of the crime of genocide.

2. *Mens Rea* and the Challenge of Specific Intent

The concept of *mens rea*—the mental component of criminal liability—is a fundamental precept of the criminal law, as the definitions of most crimes contain such a subjective element (with the exception of a limited quantity of strict liability regulatory crimes). To be found guilty, a defendant must have committed a criminal act (*actus reus*) with the required mental state (*mens rea*). With respect to most crimes, a prosecutor must show that the defendant acted either intentionally or with reckless disregard to the potential consequences of his or her action. It may also be sufficient if the perpetrator acts with knowledge of particular facts or circumstances.

The most significant difference between crimes against humanity and genocide is the *mens rea* element of specific intent (*dolus specialis*) required for genocide. The notion of specific intent

---

[19] The Convention uses the term "ethnical" rather than "ethnic."

indicates that the perpetrator acted with the intent to bring about a certain consequence. In the case of genocide, this consequence is the complete or partial destruction of a protected group. Accordingly, to make out a charge of genocide, the prosecutor must demonstrate that the accused acted with the specific intent to destroy a protected group in whole or in part. This mental state transforms what would otherwise be a municipal law crime (such as murder) or a crime against humanity (such as extermination) into genocide. This distinguishing feature of genocide makes it a particularly difficult crime to prove. Prosecutors may thus choose to charge someone with a crime against humanity rather than genocide if the evidence of specific intent is weak.

By contrast, the ICTY and ICTR Statutes contained no express *mens rea* element for crimes against humanity. Nonetheless, the tribunals through their jurisprudence constructed a two-tier *mens rea* for the crime: One *mens rea* requirement relates to the particular charged constitutive act and the other is essentially a *chapeau* element that applies to all crimes against humanity. With respect to the latter, it must be shown that the defendant knew that his or her actions were part of the widespread or systematic attack against the civilian population. This overarching *mens rea* is in addition to the primary *mens rea* that is required for the underlying constitutive offense, such as murder (the intent to kill) or deportation (the intent to transport someone across an international boundary). The drafters of the ICC Statute adopted this two-tiered *mens rea* approach in Article 7. The ICC's Elements of Crimes make clear that in order to satisfy the overarching *mens rea*, it need not be shown that the defendant had knowledge of all details of the attack or any underlying plan or policy.[20] Indeed, knowledge of the attack can be actual or constructive.[21]

Although proving the *mens rea* required for crimes against humanity may be challenging, it is far less onerous on its face than the specific intent required to prove genocide. Absent a guilty plea or incriminating manifesto (something that most *génocidaires* have today learned to avoid), it is difficult to ascertain whether an accused in fact acted with the necessary specific intent. The two *ad hoc* tribunals, however, developed a comprehensive jurisprudence with respect to the specific intent requirement that allows an inference to be drawn with respect to the mental state of the accused from the surrounding nature of the crimes alleged and other contextual

---

[20] Article 7, *Report of the Preparatory Commission for the International Criminal Court; Addendum: Finalized Draft Text of the Elements of Crimes*, U.N. Doc. PCNICC/2000/INF/3/Add.2 (July 6, 2000).

[21] *See Prosecutor v. Kayishema & Ruzindana*, Case No. ICTR-95-1-T, Judgement, ¶ 134 (May 21, 1999).

factors. For evidence of specific intent, the tribunals have looked at, *inter alia,* the relative proportionate scale and systematicity of the actual or attempted destruction, the status of the victims, the existence of discriminatory propaganda, the nature of the acts committed, attendant acts of violence, and statements or speeches made at the time the acts were committed. For example, a Trial Chamber of the ICTR noted that

> in the absence of a confession from the accused, his intent can be inferred from a certain number of presumptions of fact. . . . [I]t is possible to deduce the genocidal intent inherent in a particular act charged from the general context of the perpetration of other culpable acts systematically directed against that same group, whether these acts were committed by the same offender or by others. Other factors, such as the scale of atrocities committed, their general nature, in a region or a country, or furthermore, the fact of deliberately and systematically targeting victims on account of their membership of a particular group, while excluding the members of other groups, can enable the Chamber to infer the genocidal intent of a particular act. [It is also] possible to infer the genocidal intention that presided over the commission of a particular act, *inter alia,* from all acts or utterances of the accused.[22]

Can one look to the commission of acts—by the defendant or others—that would not themselves qualify for genocide as evidence of an individual's genocidal intent? In a series of judgments, the ICTY adopted a holistic approach to determining genocidal intent. For example, the Trial Chamber in the *Tolimir* case concluded that the following factors are relevant to infer genocidal intent: "the general context, the perpetration of other culpable acts systematically directed against the same group, the scale of atrocities, the systematic targeting of victims on account of their membership in a particular group, or the repetition of destructive or discriminatory acts."[23] The Trial Chamber further observed that genocidal intent is not required to be shown for each of the enumerated acts that constitute genocide; rather "consideration should be given to all of the evidence, taken together."[24] In other words, even acts that would not satisfy the *actus reus* element of genocide, such as acts of discrimination or "cultural genocide" (the destruction of the cultural

---

[22] *Prosecutor v. Akayesu,* Case No. ICTR-96-4-T, Judgement, ¶ 477 (Sept. 2, 1998).

[23] *Prosecutor v. Tolimir,* Case No. IT-05-88/2-T, Judgement, ¶ 745 (Dec. 12, 2012).

[24] *Id.* ¶ 772.

manifestations of a protected group), may support a finding that an accused was acting with genocidal intent. In the *Tolimir* case, the ICTY Trial Chamber inferred genocidal intent by citing to, among other things, "verbal abuse on account of affiliation with the Islamic faith," and the deliberate destruction of mosques.[25] The existence of acts of cultural genocide—such as the destruction of centers of learning, cultural artifacts, houses of worship, or other institutions associated with a particular group—also neutralize arguments that casualties within the protected group were merely incidental to a traditional armed conflict.

This circumstantial and inferential approach to genocidal intent does not mean that international tribunals are quick to conclude that an accused is guilty of genocide. In the case against Goran Jelisić, a Trial Chamber of the ICTY acquitted the defendant on a single count of genocide, finding no genocidal intent despite some direct evidence pointing to such an intent.[26] Jelisić had, among other things, called himself the "Serb Adolf," stated that his mission was to "kill Muslims," and admitted that he had killed a number of Muslim individuals because they were Muslims. The Trial Chamber concluded that although the defendant acted with "discriminatory intent," he did not act with the requisite specific intent to destroy the Muslim group. In particular, the Trial Chamber ruled that the evidence did not establish that there was a plan or policy in place to kill Muslim individuals. (We discuss the plan or policy issue with respect to genocide and crimes against humanity later.) The Trial Chamber implied that although it may be theoretically possible for a single person to commit genocide acting alone, it would be difficult to do so. In this case, the Chamber found that the defendant "killed arbitrarily rather than with a clear intention to destroy a group."[27]

On appeal, the Appeals Chamber reversed. It reviewed the evidence and determined that the defendant believed himself to be following a plan established by superiors to eradicate the Muslim population of Brčko and that, regardless of the existence of such a plan, Jelisić was on "a one-man genocide mission, intent upon personally wiping out the protected group."[28] Accordingly, the Appeals Chamber ruled that a reasonable finder of fact could have convicted the defendant of genocide and so the motion for acquittal should not have been granted.

---

[25] *Id.* ¶ 773.

[26] *See Prosecutor v. Jelisić*, Case No. IT-95-10-T, Judgement (Dec. 14, 1999) [hereinafter *Jelisić* Trial Judgement].

[27] *Id.* ¶ 108.

[28] *Prosecutor v. Jelisić*, Case No. IT-95-10-A, Judgement, ¶ 66 (July 5, 2001).

The *ad hoc* tribunals also lessened the difficulties associated with proving specific intent by removing it as a requirement in cases involving accomplice liability to genocide. The Genocide Convention at Article III prohibits "complicity in genocide" along with genocide, conspiracy to commit genocide, and direct and public incitement to commit genocide. The same types of liability may be prosecuted before the *ad hoc* tribunals and the ICC. With respect to cases against individuals accused of being accomplices to genocide, the *ad hoc* tribunals held that the accomplice need only act "knowingly" with respect to the primary perpetrator, thus paving the way for genocide convictions without genocidal intent. In other words, under this approach, if a defendant charged with complicity knew that the principal actor was acting with the specific intent to commit genocide, the accomplice could be liable for genocide as well, even though the accomplice did not himself or herself possess genocidal intent. If the defendant accomplice did not know the principal offender was acting with genocidal intent, however, the accomplice could only be charged as an accessory to the predicate act (for example, murder or cruel treatment).[29] This result is not without its detractors. It has been argued that genocide is—by definition—a specific intent crime such that anyone convicted of genocide must possess the special *mens rea* that sets genocide apart from other international or domestic crimes.

What about a subordinate who acts pursuant to the orders or direction of a superior? Can a subordinate who committed an enumerated act, such as the killing of members of a protected group, escape a charge of genocide by arguing that they acted under superior orders and thus did not themselves possess the requisite genocidal intent? The ICTY confirmed that under international law generally, the fact that a defendant acted under superior orders does not absolve them of liability for the acts committed, although such a defense may mitigate punishment. However, it has yet to be determined whether the fact that a subordinate acted under superior orders could negate the intent requirement to transform a municipal crime or a crime against humanity into genocide. Notably, Article 33 of the Rome Statute states that "orders to commit genocide . . . are manifestly unlawful," thereby signaling that acting under superior orders may not mitigate punishment or negate the intent requirement before the ICC. The inverse of this question also remains contentious: can a superior—who failed to properly supervise their subordinates—be convicted of genocide if their subordinates committed enumerated acts with the necessary specific intent? Most of the cases before the ICTR that involved superior

---

[29] *See Prosecutor v. Blagojević & Jokić*, Case No. IT-02-60-A, Judgement (May 9, 2007); *Prosecutor v. Krstić*, Case No. IT-98-33-A, Judgement (April 19, 2004).

responsibility also involved charges that the defendant personally committed genocide, so there was evidence that the superior possessed genocidal intent.[30] In several such cases, the judges refused to convict the defendant under both theories of liability (direct and superior), instead convicting them of direct responsibility and treating the abuse of the defendant's superior position as an aggravating circumstance at sentencing.[31]

Some of these open questions concerning the crime of genocide may be clarified through the jurisprudence of the ICC. At the moment the only major discussion of the crime of genocide by the ICC arose out of the request for an arrest warrant against the then-President of the Sudan, Omar Al Bashir. The Al Bashir case raises a number of interesting questions about how to interpret and apply the criminal prohibition against genocide. Most controversially, the ICC's Elements of Crimes for genocide include the requirement that the conduct in question was either part of a "manifest pattern of similar conduct" directed against the protected group, or "was conduct that could itself effect such destruction." It is this last version of this requirement—conduct that could bring about the destruction of a group—that controversially led the Pre-Trial Chamber to conclude that the crime of genocide only exists if the threat against the protected group "becomes concrete and real, as opposed to just being latent or hypothetical."[32] Some have criticized the decision on a technical level, arguing that the quoted language in the Elements of Crimes actually adds an element to the definition of the crime that is not present in the definition of the crime in the Statute (and in every other international articulation of the crime). As the Statute takes precedence over the Element of Crimes, any additional requirements not found in the Statute itself are thus invalid. In addition to this more technical criticism, some also argue that this interpretation fundamentally narrows the definition of the crime, and is contrary to the intent of the original drafters of the definition to provide a strong deterrent against genocide even in its early nascent stage. This line of reasoning throws into question, for example, the ICTY conviction of Jelisić who, it was argued, was alone in having genocidal intent.

---

[30] *See, e.g., Prosecutor v. Musema*, Case No. ICTR-96-13-T, Judgement, ¶ 936 (Jan. 27, 2000).

[31] *Prosecutor v. Nahimana*, Case No. ICTR-99-52-A, Judgement, ¶ 667 (Nov. 28, 2007).

[32] *Prosecutor v. Al Bashir*, Case No. ICC-02/05-01/09, Decision on the Prosecution's Application for a Warrant of Arrest Against Omar Hassan Ahmad Al Bashir, ¶ 124 (Mar. 4, 2009).

3. Protected Groups

The second major element distinguishing genocide from crimes against humanity is the definition of the victim group. The prohibition against crimes against humanity merely requires a showing that crimes took place within the context of an attack "directed against a civilian population." This element is satisfied where the civilian population is the primary object of attack and may be proven with reference to "the means and method used in the course of the attack, the status of the victims, their number, the discriminatory nature of the attack, the nature of the crimes committed in its course, the resistance to the assailants at the time, and the extent to which the attacking force may be said to have complied or attempted to comply with the precautionary requirements of the laws of war."[33]

In developing a jurisprudence around crimes against humanity, the international tribunals have given content to the notion of a *civilian population*. Although the interpretive issues with respect to the civilian population requirement are not as prominent or perhaps as consequential as those raised with respect to the closed list of protected groups within the genocide definition, international tribunals have also clarified some of the open issues and have generally interpreted the term in a way that expands, rather than contracts, the definition of crimes against humanity. An exception to this more expansive trend is found in the Kenya jurisprudence before the ICC, which in *dicta* in 2012 appeared to require that the civilian population share some other common characteristic—in those cases, political affiliation. In coming to this conclusion, the Pre-Trial Chamber in the Kenya cases appears to have misread or outright rejected previous precedent before both the ICC and the ICTY. That earlier caselaw from the ICTY made clear that the phrase "any civilian population" meant that the civilian population could be of the same nationality of the perpetrator and share no other characteristics.[34]

In an early decision on the matter, the ICC followed this more expansive approach, holding that the Rome Statute "affords rights and protections to 'any civilian population' regardless of their nationality, ethnicity or other distinguishing feature."[35] This language was then reinterpreted by the Pre-Trial Chamber in the case against Jean-Pierre Bemba Gombo (involving his actions in the

---

[33] *Prosecutor v. Kunarac,* Case No. IT-96-23&23/1, Judgement, ¶ 90 (June 12, 2002).

[34] *See, e.g., Prosecutor v. Tadić,* Case No. I-94-1-T, Judgement, ¶ 635 (May 7, 1997).

[35] *Prosecutor v. Katanga,* Case No. ICC-01/04-01/07-717, Decision on the Confirmation of Charges (Public Redacted Version), ¶ 399 (Sept. 30, 2008).

Central African Republic) in a way that appeared to require that there be some distinguishing feature common to the civilian population under attack: "the potential civilian victims under article 7 of the Statute could be of any nationality, ethnicity *or other distinguishing features*."[36] It was this language that the Pre-Trial Chamber in the Kenya cases then cited when discussing and finding that the civilian population "can include a group defined by its (perceived) political affiliation."[37] Similarly, the Pre-Trial Chamber involved in the Côte d'Ivoire matter noted in confirming the charges against Charles Blé Goudé two years later that the civilian population under attack consisted of "perceived Alassane Ouattara's supporters" (i.e. a group defined by its perceived political affiliation).[38] In contrast, the Trial Chamber in 2014 in the *Katanga* prosecution (involving the Democratic Republic of Congo) clarified that "where the commission of crimes against humanity is at issue, the nationality of the members of such a population, their ethnic group or any other distinguishing feature is immaterial to the protection that attaches to a 'civilian' character."[39] Given these divergent opinions, the issue is far from a settled one before the ICC. If the ICC embraces the requirement that the targeted civilian population must be defined by a common characteristic (whether nationality or, as in some of the earlier jurisprudence, political affiliation), the distinction between genocide and crimes against humanity will be further narrowed, and the general protection that crimes against humanity provides to civilians *qua* civilians will be lessened.

Another issue with respect to the definition of civilian population concerns the presence of combatants or other armed actors in the targeted group. In other words, if an attack is directed against combatants and non-combatants (for example, members of a guerrilla movement embedded among the civilian population), can this attack constitute a crime against humanity or is this a legitimate act of war against combatants with legally-acceptable civilian casualties? The jurisprudence of the *ad hoc* tribunals established that so long as the population is "predominantly civilian," even if it is actively involved in an armed resistance movement, the attack

---

[36] *Prosecutor v. Bemba*, Case No. ICC-01/05-01/08-424, Decision Pursuant to Article 61(7)(a) and (b) of the Rome Statute on the Charges of the Prosecutor Against Jean-Pierre Bemba Gombo, ¶ 76 (June 15, 2009) (emphasis added).

[37] *Prosecutor v. Muthaura*, Case No. ICC-01/09-02/11-382-Red, Decision on the Confirmation of Charges Pursuant to Article 61(7)(a) and (b) of the Rome Statute (Public Redacted Version), ¶ 110 (Jan. 23, 2012).

[38] *Prosecutor v. Blé Goudé*, Case No. ICC-02/11-02/11, Decision on the Confirmation of Charges against Charles Blé Goudé, ¶ 127 (Dec. 11, 2014).

[39] *Prosecutor v. Katanga*, Case No. ICC-01/04-01/07, Judgment Pursuant to Article 74 of the Statute, ¶ 1103 (Mar. 7, 2014).

qualifies as one against a civilian population.[40] Crimes against humanity may also be committed against combatants who are *hors de combat*—because they have been injured or captured, or because they have laid down their arms in surrender—thus giving rise to a potential overlap between the prohibitions against war crimes and crimes against humanity during situations of armed conflict.[41]

Although note that controversy remains as to whether combatants who are *hors de combat* count on the "civilian" side of the proportionality calculus under the laws of war when a military objective is under attack.[42] In other words, if a hospital is being used as a snipers' nest, it becomes a lawful military objective—an object that by its "nature, location, purpose, or use make[s] an effective contribution to military action and whose partial or total destruction . . . offers a definitive military advantage."[43] The military advantage to be achieved in attacking the hospital must be weighed against anticipated loss of civilian life. Potential harm to any injured civilians within the hospital would be considered in this calculus; controversy remains as to whether potential harm to any injured combatants would too.

This potential overlap has been cited as justification for the elimination of the distinction between war crimes and crimes against humanity (and even perhaps genocide). As one former ICTY prosecutor reasoned, "[i]ssues relating to classification of a conflict, the significance of the law of war to that conflict, or the jurisdiction of a tribunal over an alleged act of genocide would all fade into insignificance if they were brought within the rubric of crimes against humanity."[44] Under the current law, however, where an act is lawful under humanitarian law (for example, the killing of a combatant engaged in the armed conflict), it would not constitute the crime against humanity of murder by operation of the principle of *lex specialis derogat legi generali*, which states that when two rules are in conflict, the rule from the more specialized area of law (here, the law of war) takes precedent.

---

40 *Prosecutor v. Kordić & Čerkez*, Case No. IT-95-14/2, Judgement, ¶ 180 (Feb. 26, 2001); *Prosecutor v. Kupreškić et al.*, Case No. IT-95-16, Judgement, ¶ 549 (Jan. 14, 2000); *see also The Barbie Case*, French Court of Cassation (Criminal Chamber), Dec. 20, 1985, *available at* 78 ILR 125.

41 *Prosecutor v. Blaškić*, Case No. IT-95-14, Judgement, ¶ 214 (Mar. 3, 2000).

42 According to the International Committee of the Red Cross's customary international law study, "[l]aunching an attack which may be expected to cause incidental loss of civilian life, injury to civilians, damage to civilian objects, or a combination thereof, which would be excessive in relation to the concrete and direct military advantage anticipated, is prohibited." ICRC, *Customary International Law Database*, Rule 14.

43 *Id.* at Rule 8.

44 William J. Fenrick, *Should Crimes Against Humanity Replace War Crimes?*, 37 COLUM. J. TRANSNAT'L L. 767, 780 (1999).

By contrast to the broad notion of "civilian population" developed by the tribunals, the prohibition against genocide applies only to acts intended to destroy groups defined by four characteristics: nationality, ethnicity, religion, or race. The drafters of the Genocide Convention intentionally excluded political, social, linguistic, economic, sexual, and other groups from the list of protected groups. All subsequent international definitions of genocide have mirrored this approach (although some national definitions have expanded upon, or contracted, this list). As a result, many twentieth-century episodes of mass killings—such as the Stalinist pogroms against the kulaks (petty bourgeoisie opposed to state ownership) in the former Soviet Union in 1929–1930, the targeting of communists in Indonesia in the 1960s, the majority of the repression in Cambodia during the Khmer Rouge era of 1975 to 1979, and the dirty wars in Latin America in the 1970s and 1980s—do not cleanly satisfy the elements of the crime of genocide as it is defined by the Convention (although these crimes would satisfy the definition of crimes against humanity and, in some cases, war crimes).

The limitation on the groups to which the crime of genocide applies raises the question of whether genocide has been defined too narrowly to be useful in today's world. Proponents of maintaining a distinct crime of genocide and of resisting its expansion argue that the crime of genocide captures something distinct from more generic crimes against humanity. Unlike the latter, genocide is a crime committed with the ultimate goal of eliminating a distinct people from the face of the earth because they share some largely immutable and innate characteristic. It is argued that such a crime not only harms the targeted group, but also harms the rest of humanity by threatening to diminish the racial, religious, ethnic, or national diversity of the world's population in a way that is irreversible.

On the other hand, it can be argued that the genocide definition is artificially restrictive as it excludes the wholesale slaughter of human groups that do not happen to share one of the four characteristics listed in the genocide definition. This gives rise to two broad critiques. First is the critique that the definition excludes attacks against groups that share characteristics other than the four listed—such as political affiliation, sexual orientation, sex or gender, language, economic class, disability, and so on—and are targeted because of that characteristic. If these crimes are committed with the intent to destroy in whole or in part all communists, gays and lesbians, women, Basque speakers, or bourgeois, why should they not also fall under the moniker of genocide, the ultimate international crime? A common response to the argument to expand the list of protected groups is that the four listed characteristics are immutable and are generally present at the time each of us is born. This explanation is problematic, however, as some of the characteristics may clearly be adopted out of choice (e.g., religion or nationality), and our postmodern sensibility recognizes that attributes like "ethnicity" and "race" are more socially constructed than based on any firm, objective biological reality. In addition, sex and sexual orientation are arguably as immutable as any of the four listed groups.

The second critique is that any instance of the mass slaughter of civilians should be considered genocide, in keeping with the lay understanding of the crime. This argument is weaker than the first, as it would result in the elimination of any notion of discriminatory *animus* from the genocide definition, thus treating the killing of one million people because of their ethnicity the same as the killing of one million civilians committed without any special *animus* (although proof of discrimination could operate as an aggravating factor at sentencing much the way domestic hate crimes statutes operate). Many international lawyers would argue that there is value in the law recognizing the discriminatory motive and intent of certain episodes of mass killing, and that acts committed with a genocidal intent are different from, and perhaps worse than, the same acts committed without that intent.

Many have argued that the ICTR subtly relaxed the protected group requirement for genocide by adopting a subjective approach to defining the groups. The case against Jean-Paul Akayesu—the inaugural international genocide prosecution—is instructive. In adjudicating the genocide counts, the ICTR had to determine whether Hutu and Tutsi groups within Rwanda constitute different "ethnic groups" within the meaning of the statute's definition of genocide. The Tribunal noted at the outset that "the Tutsi population does not have its own language or a distinct culture from the rest of the Rwandan population."[45] The Tribunal conceded that the term "ethnic group is, in general, used to refer to a group whose members speak the same language and/or have the same culture. Therefore, one can hardly talk of ethnic groups as regards Hutu and Tutsi, given that they share the same language and culture."[46] The Tribunal concluded nevertheless that within the Rwandan context, the two groups should be considered separate ethnic groups: "in the context of the period in question, they were, in consonance with a distinction made by the colonizers, considered both by the authorities and themselves as belonging to two distinct ethnic groups; as such, their identity cards mentioned each holder's ethnic group."[47]

---

45 *Akayesu, supra*, ¶ 170.

46 *Id.* ¶ 122 n.56; *see also id.* ¶¶ 511–515 (defining all enumerated groups).

47 *Id.* ¶ 122 n.56.

To come to this conclusion, the ICTR identified "a number of objective indicators of the group as a group with a distinct identity."[48] The majority of these "objective indicators" stem from the colonial experience within Rwanda and not from any innate linguistic, cultural, or biological characteristic. For example, the Tribunal noted that "[e]very Rwandan citizen was required before 1994 to carry an identity card which included an entry for ethnic group."[49] Further, the Civil Code of 1988 provided that all persons are to be identified by sex and ethnic group. The ICTR also noted that the Rwandan witnesses who testified before the Chamber identified themselves by ethnic group, and generally knew the ethnic group to which their friends and neighbors belonged. Finally, the Tribunal found dispositive that "the Tutsi were conceived of as an ethnic group by those who targeted them for killing."[50] The Trial Chamber thus concluded that the identification of persons as belonging to the group of Hutu or Tutsi had become embedded in Rwandan culture. While using the language of objectivity, the ICTR firmly planted itself in the camp of acknowledging the social construction of ethnicity (and thus presumably of the other four "immutable" group characteristics protected against genocide). In the case against Kayishema and Ruzindana, a Trial Chamber noted that an ethnic group could be "a group identified as such by others, including the perpetrators of the crimes."[51] In other words, the victim group can be identified by using the "criteria of stigmatization" employed by the perpetrators of the crime on the basis of perceived national, ethnical, racial, or religious characteristics, even if the victim group shares no objective indicia of a protected group. According to this interpretive approach, protected groups can be identified within the socio-historic context in which they exist, and it is of no moment that the group in question has no "objective" existence outside of that context.

Similarly, the ICTY reasoned that this approach is warranted by the difficulty of objectively defining and identifying the four protected groups. In particular, it noted:

> Although the objective determination of a religious group still remains possible, to attempt to define a national, ethnical or racial group today using objective and scientifically irreproachable criteria would be a perilous exercise whose result would not necessarily correspond to the perception of the persons concerned by such categorisation. Therefore, it is more appropriate to evaluate the status of a national, ethnical or racial group from the

---

48 *Id.* ¶ 170.

49 *Id.*

50 *Id.* ¶ 171.

51 *Kayishema & Ruzindana, supra,* ¶ 98.

> point of view of those persons who wish to single that group out from the rest of the community. The Trial Chamber consequently elects to evaluate membership in a national, ethnical or racial group using a subjective criterion.[52]

In addition, the ICTY ruled that groups may be defined negatively, for example as non-Croats.[53] At the same time, another ICTR Trial Chamber in the case against Musema muddied the waters by noting that subjective definitions of groups alone are insufficient, because the drafters of the Genocide Convention specifically intended to exclude political and economic groups from the genocide prohibition.[54] This suggests that a group that was erroneously considered to be an ethnic group by an attacker, but was in fact more properly considered to be an economic group, could not claim to be the victim of genocide.

The ICC appears to have adopted a more objective approach. In considering the application for an arrest warrant against the former President of the Sudan, a Pre-Trial Chamber summarily concluded that the alleged targeted groups (the Fur, Masalit, and Zaghawas) "appear to have Sudanese nationality, similar racial features, and a shared Muslim religion;" however, they still qualified as distinct ethnic groups as there were "reasonable grounds to believe that each of the [targeted] groups . . . has its own language, its own tribal customs and its own traditional links to its lands."[55] Although the Pre-Trial Chamber did not consider the subjective approach, the decision did clearly state that "the targeted group must have particular positive characteristics (national, ethnic, racial or religious), and not a lack thereof."[56] In other words, it was not sufficient to say that the perpetrator was targeting only individuals *not* belonging to a particular group (e.g. Arab or Muslim).

The Khmer Rouge period (1975–79) in Cambodia offered a fundamental test of the definition of genocide. By the time a Vietnamese invasion opened the killing fields for the world to see, "a greater proportion of the population [had] perished than in any other revolution during the twentieth century."[57] The roughly two million deaths are largely considered by the general public—within

---

[52] *Jelisić* Trial Judgement, *supra*, ¶ 70.

[53] *Prosecutor v. Kvočka*, Case No. IT-98-30/1-T, Judgement, ¶ 195 (Nov. 2, 2001). *See also Prosecutor v. Stakić*, Case No. IT-97-24-T, Judgement, ¶ 512 (July 23, 2003) (noting that it is not sufficient to define the group as "non-Serb").

[54] *Prosecutor v. Musema*, Case No. ICTR 96-13-T, Judgement, ¶ 162 (Jan. 27, 2000).

[55] *Al Bashir*, *supra*, ¶¶ 136–7.

[56] *Id.* ¶ 135.

[57] Karl D. Jackson, *The Khmer Rouge in Context*, *in* CAMBODIA, 1975–1978: RENDEZVOUS WITH DEATH 3, 3 (Karl D. Jackson ed., 1989).

Cambodia and abroad—to be genocide. Indeed, Cambodia often bears the dubious distinction of being described as the first post-Holocaust genocide. Yet a close read of the Genocide Convention reveals that much of the violence committed by the Khmer Rouge in Cambodia does not technically constitute genocide, primarily because the perpetrator group and the victim group shared the same nationality, ethnicity, race, and religion. Instead, the majority of the victims were targeted on the basis of what an objective assessment would describe as their membership in an undesirable political, social, or economic group. Indeed, the term "auto-genocide" was coined to describe this violence. That said, the Khmer Rouge often reasoned that Cambodians targeted for destruction were effectively enemy "Vietnamese in Cambodian bodies," suggesting much of the killing by the Khmer Rouge would qualify as genocide under a purely subjective approach.

In the end, the Extraordinary Chambers in the Courts of Cambodia (ECCC) did find that genocide had been committed by the Khmer Rouge, but only against the Muslim Cham (on the basis of religion)[58] and people of Vietnamese descent (on the basis of nationality), who collectively made up a small proportion of the victims of the Khmer Rouge terror.[59] Ultimately, the ECCC Co-Prosecutors chose not to charge the majority of the deaths as genocide, relying instead on crimes against humanity. Given the scale of the killings in Cambodia, and the clear intent on the part of the Khmer Rouge to destroy those it perceived as being "other," the Cambodian example pointedly raises the question of whether the definition of genocide is too narrow (in that it does not capture much of what the Khmer Rouge did), or whether, as we raise above, it makes sense to distinguish between mass killings as a crime against humanity and mass killings as genocide.

4. Policy or Plan

Is it necessary to prove a formal policy or plan to establish the existence of either genocide or crime against humanity? Neither crime as ordinarily formulated contains such an element in its definition. To be sure, the existence of a policy or plan may affect the effectiveness of a genocidal attack or a crime against humanity, or may be helpful as an evidentiary matter; this, however, is separate from the question of whether adequate proof of such a plan or policy is legally required to constitute the offense. Arguably, when the attack against a civilian population is systematic (as opposed to widespread), a policy is likely at work. In fact, it is hard to imagine a

---

[58] Case 002/02, Case No. 002/19-09-2007/ECCC/TC, Judgment, ¶ 3348 (Nov. 16, 2008).

[59] *Id.* ¶ 3519.

systematic attack that is not the result of some perpetrator or entity's nefarious policy.

Although the jurisprudence suggests that a policy or plan is not required in the case of genocide, there is some conflicting authority with respect to such a requirement for crimes against humanity. The Appeals Chamber of the *ad hoc* tribunals held that a policy or plan is not required as an element of the offense.[60] In contrast, however, the ICC Statute at Article 7(2)(a) defines the phrase "attack directed against any civilian population" with reference to "a State or organizational policy to commit such attack." The Statute's Elements of Crimes clarify that the policy language "requires that the State or organization actively promote or encourage such an attack."[61] At the same time, such a policy "may, in exceptional circumstances, be implemented by a deliberate failure to take action, which is consciously aimed at encouraging such attack."[62] The failure to intervene in an attack, combined with the intention of allowing the attack to continue, may thus satisfy any policy element in the ICC Statute. When crimes against humanity are adjudicated in other fora—such as U.S. tort litigation—defendants generally cite the ICC Statute to argue that there is such a requirement, whereas prosecutors (and plaintiffs) argue that proof of a policy or plan is not an element of the offense *stricto sensu,* although it is useful as an evidentiary matter.

Related to the policy requirement is whether the entity that is implementing the policy qualifies as an "organization" within the meaning of the Rome Statute's requirement of "a State or organizational policy." This issue was presented in the Kenya cases, where the majority found that the *Mungiki*, a non-state entity that was implicated in many of the post-election attacks against the civilian population, qualified as an organization for purposes of the definition of crimes against humanity. The Pre-Trial Chamber authorizing the Prosecutor's investigation in the Kenya situation held that whether an entity qualified as an organization was to be made on a case-by-case basis, with reference to the following "considerations" that the Chamber "may take into account":

(i) whether the group is under responsible command, or has an established hierarchy;

(ii) whether the group possesses, in fact, the means to carry out widespread or systematic attack against a civilian population;

60 *Kunarac, supra,* ¶ 98.

61 ICC Element of Crimes, Art. 7(3).

62 *Id.* Art. 7(3) n. 6.

(iii) whether the group exercises control over part of the territory of a State;

(iv) whether the group has criminal activities against the civilian population as a primary purpose;

(v) whether the group articulates, explicitly or implicitly, an intention to attack a civilian population; [and]

(vi) whether the group is part of a larger group, which fulfills some or all of the abovementioned criteria.[63]

After listing these considerations, the Chamber made clear that they "do not constitute a rigid legal definition, and do not need to be exhaustively fulfilled."

In dissent, the late Judge Kaul argued that the *Mungiki* did not qualify as an organization for purposes of the Statute, reasoning that to qualify such an organization should be "state-like." Judge Kaul's concern raises the fundamental question of what triggers international jurisdiction over an otherwise domestic criminal act. Judge Kaul presumed that only crimes committed by state-like organizations should qualify, i.e. those entities that "partake of some characteristics of a State . . . eventually turn the private 'organization' into an entity which may act like a State or has quasi-State abilities."[64] To find otherwise, he argued, many common crimes, including those committed by organized criminal groups, would trigger international jurisdiction and overwhelm the international justice system.

Although there is no requirement that an act be part of a policy or plan to qualify as a crime against humanity under customary international law, a nexus is required between the attack against the civilian population and the act of the accused. This does not mean, however, that the accused must act for the purpose of furthering the overall attack. The *ad hoc* tribunals ultimately held that a defendant need not have a formal connection with the group or entity carrying out the larger attack; as such, the defendant might be acting out of purely personal motives.[65] So long as the accused has knowledge of the overall attack, and of the fact that their conduct will contribute to the attack, it does not matter if the accused intended to further the overall attack. The ICC Elements of Crimes state that it must be shown that a suspect accused of a crime against humanity "knew that

[63] *Situation in the Republic of Kenya*, Case No. ICC-01/09-19-Corr, Decision Pursuant to Article 15 of the Rome Statute on the Authorization of an Investigation into the Situation in the Republic of Kenya, ¶ 93 (Mar. 31, 2010).

[64] *Id.*, Dissenting Opinion of Judge Hans-Peter Kaul, ¶ 51 (Mar. 31, 2010).

[65] *Prosecutor v. Tadić*, Case No. IT-94-1-A, Judgement, ¶ 272 (July 15, 1999) [hereinafter *Tadić* Appeals Judgement]; *see also Blaškić*, *supra*, ¶ 257 (noting that it is not necessary to show that the defendant identified with the ideology, plan or policy).

the conduct was part of or intended the conduct to be part of a widespread or systematic attack against a civilian population."[66] This language is consistent with the jurisprudence of the *ad hoc* tribunals in that it clearly does not require that the suspect *intend* their conduct to be part of the attack so long as they are *aware* that their acts are part of that attack.[67]

In addition, because the descriptors "widespread" and "systematic" modify the term "attack," a single act may constitute a crime against humanity so long as it manifests the necessary nexus to a larger attack against a civilian population, regardless of motive.[68] For example, a U.S. district court found that the assassination of Salvadoran Archbishop Oscar Romero constituted a crime against humanity. The court reasoned that the required nexus was demonstrated where the single act was shown to be "part of an overall policy or a consistent pattern of inhumanity."[69] Thus, as a general rule, an isolated criminal act cannot be prosecuted as a crime against humanity unless the act is itself a "widespread or systematic" attack, such as the attacks of September 11, 2001.[70] A requirement that there be a policy or plan to prove genocide is absent from the jurisprudence, marking a significant distinction between the two crimes.

5. Crimes Against Humanity and Armed Conflict

One further definitional issue with respect to crimes against humanity, since resolved in modern jurisprudence, was the question of whether an armed conflict was a necessary condition for the crime. The Nuremberg and Tokyo Tribunals required the prosecution to demonstrate a "nexus" between the charged crime against humanity and the war of aggression launched by Nazi Germany and Japan. This nexus element was in part a function of the way the crime was formulated in the tribunals' constitutive charters. For example, Article 6(c) of the Nuremberg Charter (emphasis added) defined the crime as:

> [M]urder, extermination, enslavement, deportation, and other inhumane acts committed against any civilian population, before or during the war, or persecutions on

---

[66] ICC Elements of Crimes, Art. 7.

[67] *See, e.g., Prosecutor v. Katanga*, Case No. ICC-01/04-01/07-717, Decision on the Confirmation of Charges, ¶ 401 (Sept. 30, 2008).

[68] *Prosecutor v. Mrkšić*, Case No. IT-95-13-R61, Judgement, ¶ 30 (Apr. 3, 1996).

[69] *Doe v. Alvaro Rafael Saravia*, 348 F. Supp. 2d 1112, 1156 (E.D. Cal. 2004).

[70] Note, however, that the United States led the charge to prevent terrorism from being listed as a crime against humanity in the Rome Statute. If future adjudicators want to remain faithful to this original intent, they may deny jurisdiction over acts that are primarily acts of terrorism, notwithstanding that such acts may also be characterized as the crimes against humanity of murder, extermination, and so on.

> political, racial, or religious grounds in execution of or *in connection with any crime within the jurisdiction of the Tribunal*, whether or not in violation of the domestic law of the country where perpetrated.[71]

The Nuremberg Tribunal interpreted the italicized passage to preclude the prosecution of events preceding the commencement of World War II, which it pegged to Germany's invasion of Poland in 1939. This made crimes against humanity a byproduct of war rather than an autonomous offense. This ruling was only partially supported by the text, as this interpretation required the Tribunal to ignore the preceding phrase "before or during the war." Notwithstanding the war nexus requirement, the Nuremberg Tribunal was satisfied by evidence of a relatively fragile connection between the crimes against humanity charged and other war crimes or acts of aggression. For example, the Nuremberg Tribunal found a war nexus with respect to charges against defendant Baldur von Schirach (the leader of the Hitler Youth and Reich Governor in Vienna) in connection with crimes against Austrian nationals while Austria was annexed by Germany (the so-called *Anschluss*), an act that constituted a crime against the peace under the Charter. To find the required nexus for the charge of crimes against humanity, the Tribunal cited to the occupation of Austria in 1938, which occurred prior to the formal start of World War II in 1939 with the invasion of Poland; no other link was identified.

The war nexus served two important purposes in the post-World War II proceedings. First, it helped to satisfy the principle of legality by tying the new charge of crimes against humanity to the relatively well-established prohibition against war crimes. Second, it justified the intrusion of international law into the domestic affairs of a sovereign state. Crimes against humanity effectively trumped domestic authority by criminalizing acts "whether or not in violation of the domestic law of the country where perpetrated." The war nexus ensured that only after a state had already breached international peace by committing acts of aggression would crimes committed internally be susceptible to international scrutiny and prosecution. This concern has become less acute over time with the rise of the human rights movement premised on the idea that the way in which a state treats individuals within its territory and under its control is now beyond doubt a matter of international concern.

Although the purposes served by the war nexus at the founding of crimes against humanity have become largely obsolete, the U.N. Security Council nonetheless (and somewhat inexplicably) included

---

[71] The Charter of the Tokyo Tribunal included a similar definition at Article 5(c).

an armed conflict requirement in its definition of crimes against humanity in the ICTY Statute (but not the ICTR Statute). Specifically, Article 5 of the ICTY Statute required that crimes against humanity be committed "in armed conflict, whether international or internal in character," and directed against any civilian population. In the first modern prosecution for crimes against humanity, defendant Duško Tadić argued that the ICTY Statute's formulation offended the *nullum crimen sine lege* (NCSL) principle because it allowed a link to a *non international* armed conflict. He reasoned that the Nuremberg definition required a nexus to an *international* armed conflict, which—in his estimation—was not occurring in the former Yugoslavia (a position that was ultimately rejected by the ICTY). The Tribunal confirmed that NCSL was not offended by the statute's definition when it ruled that:

> the definition of Article 5 is in fact more restrictive than the general definition of crimes against humanity recognised by customary international law. The inclusion of the nexus with armed conflict in the article imposes a limitation on the jurisdiction of the International Tribunal and certainly can in no way offend the *nullum crimen* principle so as to bar the International Tribunal from trying the crimes enumerated therein. Because the language of Article 5 is clear, the crimes against humanity tried in the International Tribunal must have a nexus with an armed conflict, be it international or internal.[72]

The Trial Chamber had held that the formulation of the war nexus in the ICTY Statute "necessitates the existence of an armed conflict and a nexus between the act and that conflict." The Appeals Chamber overruled this aspect of the judgment, finding that "a nexus between the accused's acts and the armed conflict is *not* required" and that the "armed conflict requirement is satisfied by proof that *there was* an armed conflict."[73] In other words, the enumerated act must have occurred "in the course or duration of an armed conflict" (geographically and temporally), but need not form part of that conflict.[74]

The war nexus is an issue that does not arise with respect to genocide, as there was never any requirement that acts of genocide be linked to armed conflict. Indeed, in the *Al Bashir* arrest warrant opinion, the Pre-Trial Chamber noted that a counter-insurgency

---

72 *Prosecutor v. Tadić*, Case No. IT-94-I-T, Decision on the Defence Motion, ¶ 32 (Aug. 10, 1995).

73 *Tadić* Appeals Judgement, *supra*, ¶ 251 (emphasis in original).

74 *Id.* ¶ 239.

campaign can be genocidal.[75] The demise of the war nexus for crimes against humanity has thus brought the two crimes closer together definitionally.

D. Enumerated Acts

In addition to different *chapeau* elements, the crime of genocide and crimes against humanity differ with respect to their *actus rea,* or the enumerated acts that trigger individual liability. In part because of its early codification, the list of acts that constitute genocide is much shorter than the list found in the various permutations of the definition of crimes against humanity. In addition to killing members of a protected group, the Genocide Convention provides that genocide can be committed through causing serious bodily or mental harm to members of the group, inflicting adverse conditions of life on the group, interfering with the group's ability to procreate, and transferring children from the group. The theory is that these acts, although not directly amounting to the full or partial destruction of a group, have the potential to bring about this destruction through a process of "slow death."[76]

1. Sexual Violence

The Genocide Convention does not list sexual violence, *per se*, as the *actus reus* of genocide, although the prohibition on "imposing measures intended to prevent births within the group" has a gender component. In the *Akayesu* case, the ICTR confirmed, however, that acts of rape and other forms of sexual violence can serve as the basis for a genocide conviction, even if the victims ultimately are not killed. It reasoned that "Tutsi women were subjected to sexual violence because they were Tutsi. Sexual violence was a step in the process of destruction of the Tutsi group—destruction of the spirit, of the will to live, and of life itself."[77] It also noted that in patrilineal societies, where a child's identity flows through the father's line, rape can change the demographic makeup of a society. So far, there has been no jurisprudence based solely upon the prevention of births within the group, as with enforced sterilization or forced abortion, or the transfer of children from the group. The revelations in 2020 of the systematic use of forced sterilization against the Uyghur community in China's Xinjiang region provides a conceivable first case. No court has yet asserted jurisdiction over these events to undertake this analysis, though as of this writing lawyers have filed submissions arguing that the Prosecutor should commence an investigation into

---

[75] *Prosecutor v. Al Bashir*, Case No. ICC-02/05-01/09, Second Decision on the Prosecution's Application for a Warrant of Arrest, ¶ 10 (July 12, 2010).

[76] *See Kayishema & Ruzindana, supra,* ¶ 95 (noting that the genocide prohibition covers acts falling short of death).

[77] *Akayesu, supra,* ¶ 732.

crimes against humanity and potentially genocide. To do so, it would have to be shown that part of the alleged crime(s) occurred on the territory of a state party, such as neighboring Tajikistan or Cambodia (which has forcibly deported Uyghur victims back to China), as China has not ratified the Rome Statute. Those arguing for ICC intervention are thus looking to the precedent established by the Myanmar case, where jurisdiction was found because part of the crime of forced deportation—at a minimum—occurred in the territory of Bangladesh, a state party.

By contrast to the genocide definition, the modern definitions of crimes against humanity have always listed some forms of sexual violence as enumerated acts. The Appeals Chamber of the Special Court for Sierra Leone further developed the law by recognizing the crime of forced marriage as a crime against humanity (under the catch-all "other inhumane acts") that was separate and distinct from rape, sexual slavery, or other forms of sexual violence. In so ruling, it overturned the Trial Chamber, which had concluded that forced marriage was fully absorbed into the sexual slavery charges.[78] The ICC is considering a range of forms of gender-based persecution arising out of the Mali situation, which involves crimes committed by Islamist extremist groups. Al Hassan Ag Abdoul Aziz Ag Mohamed Ag Mamoud, the *de facto* head of the Islamic policy, has been charged with enforcing *Shari'a* law through discrimination and violence, including against women.[79]

2. Other Inhumane Acts: An Open-Ended Residuary Clause

The Nuremberg and Tokyo definition of crimes against humanity distinguishes between two broad categories of offenses: inhumane acts ("murder, extermination, enslavement, deportation, and other inhumane acts") and acts of persecution ("on political, racial, or religious grounds").[80] Gradually, this bifurcation has almost entirely collapsed, and modern definitions include persecution in the general list of constitutive offenses. Reflecting humankind's seemingly inexorable ability to devise new ways to brutalize its members, the list of predicate crimes has lengthened over time with the addition in the Rome Statute of new crimes against humanity, such as forms of arbitrary detention or imprisonment, sexual and gender-based violence, disappearances, and apartheid. These additions are clearly meant to reflect past atrocities and the failure of the international community to

---

[78] *Prosecutor v. Brima et al.*, Case No. SSL-2004-16-A, Judgement, ¶¶ 195–196 (Feb. 22, 2008).

[79] *Prosecutor v. Al Hassan*, Document Containing the Charges, Case No. ICC-01/12-01/18 (May 11, 2019).

[80] The Tokyo Charter recognized only political and racial persecutions, probably because religious persecution was less present in the Pacific theater.

adequately condemn them, most notably the crime of apartheid and the use of systematic violence against women to terrorize a civilian population.

Although the enumerated acts differ between the two crimes, can one argue that the same acts could qualify as either genocide or crimes against humanity, depending on the existence of the *chapeau* elements? Certainly one could interpret the phrases "causing serious bodily or mental harm" or "deliberately inflicting" adverse conditions of life under genocide as including all of the more specific acts listed under crimes against humanity. The ICTR, for example, has held that "serious bodily and mental harm" includes acts of physical or mental torture, disfigurement, cruel treatment, rape and other sexual violence, and persecution.[81] The two *ad hoc* tribunals have interpreted "inflicting adverse conditions of life" to include a lack of adequate housing, hygiene, medical care, or subjecting individuals to a subsistence diet, starvation, or excessive physical exercise. Likewise, the expulsion of people from their homes with the requisite intent can also satisfy this element of genocide.[82]

One could also interpret the phrase "other inhumane acts" in the definition of crimes against humanity to encompass most of the enumerated acts under genocide. The ICTY, for example, has interpreted "other humane acts," at times in *dicta,* to include forced displacement, mutilation, beatings, degrading treatment, and forced prostitution.[83] An ICTY Trial Chamber defined "inhumane acts" as "intentional acts or omissions which infringe fundamental human rights causing serious mental or physical suffering or injury of a gravity comparable to that of other crimes covered by Article 5 [the article defining crimes against humanity]."[84] Looking to international human rights standards for guidance, the court identified "inhumane acts" to include the infringement of basic human rights, including "serious forms of cruel or degrading treatment of persons belonging to a particular ethnic, religious, political or racial group, or serious widespread or systematic manifestations of cruel or humiliating or degrading treatment with a discriminatory or persecutory intent."[85] Upholding a conviction for "other inhumane acts," the Appeals Chamber affirmed that the forcible removal of a family and the destruction of the family home constituted inhumane acts that were properly charged alongside the

---

[81] *See, e.g., Prosecutor v. Rutaganda,* Case No. ICTR 96-3, Judgement and Sentence, ¶ 51 (Dec. 6, 1999).

[82] *Musema, supra,* ¶ 157.

[83] *Prosecutor v. Kvočka,* Case No. IT-98-30/1, Judgement, ¶ 208 (Nov. 2, 2001).

[84] *Prosecutor v. Kupreškić et al.,* Case No. IT-95-16, Judgement, ¶ 818 (Oct. 23, 2001).

[85] *Id.* ¶ 566.

crime against humanity of murder based on the killing of a family member.[86] Litigants continue to test the outer contours of this residual clause.

3. Persecution and Extermination: Genocide as Incorporated Within Crimes Against Humanity

International tribunals prove themselves to be quite nimble when interpreting the listed acts under both genocide and crimes against humanity to encompass the same *actus reus*. At the same time, the particular crimes against humanity of persecution and extermination incorporate what appear to be the *chapeau* elements of genocide within crimes against humanity. In other words, it would appear that every act that constitutes genocide would also constitute a crime against humanity under either of these two categories.

Definitions of persecution generally contain a discriminatory intent element, thus approximating the specific intent required under genocide. Article 7 of the ICC Statute, for example, requires proof that the defendant acted "on political, racial, national, ethnic, cultural, religious, gender . . . or other grounds that are universally recognized as impermissible under international law." This latter reference would presumably cover persecutions on grounds of sexual orientation, age, profession, mental disability, health status, and so forth, although the statute leaves the cognizability of these other "suspect classes" open to litigation. The ICTY interpreted the requirement of discriminatory *animus* broadly. For one, it is enough that the perpetrator subjectively believed that the victim was a member of the persecuted group.[87] As discussed above, this is similar to the decisions of tribunals adjudicating genocide claims, which have found that it is the subjective perceptions of the perpetrator, rather than any "objective" identity of the victim groups, that matters. The crime against humanity of persecution, therefore, contains three *mens rea* elements: the mental state necessary for the underlying act, knowledge that the act is committed within the context of a widespread or systematic attack against a civilian population, and a discriminatory intent.

A Trial Chamber of the ICTY set forth a four-part test for determining what constitutes persecution: (1) a gross or blatant denial (2) on discriminatory grounds (3) of a fundamental right found in customary or treaty law (4) reaching the same level of gravity as

---

[86] *Prosecutor v. Kupreškić et al.*, Case No. IT-95-16, Judgement, ¶ 393 (Mar. 7, 2003).

[87] *Prosecutor v. Naletilić & Martinović*, Case No. IT-98-34-T, Judgement, ¶ 636 (Mar. 31, 2003).

other enumerated acts that qualify as crimes against humanity.[88] Applying this test, one Trial Chamber found that denying people the right to employment, freedom of movement, judicial process, and medical care all constituted criminal persecution when committed on invidious grounds.[89] As noted earlier, these types of acts may also be found to constitute "deliberately inflicting adverse conditions of life" under the crime of genocide. In this way, the tribunals have looked to the pantheon of human rights treaties to add content to these open-ended provisions, and to further narrow the gap between the two crimes.

Through adjudicating the concept of "extermination" as an enumerated crime against humanity, the ICTY has identified another category of crimes that closely parallels genocide. Indeed, extermination encompasses the crime of mass killing, which most lay persons equate with genocide. In *Krstić*, the Trial Chamber noted the two crimes' normative overlap and entered only a conviction for genocide on the grounds that extermination was, in essence, a lesser included offense of genocide.[90] Yet, even extermination differs from genocide in that it is a result crime, requiring proof of multiple deaths, rather than a crime of intent. The ICC Elements of Crimes emphasize that it must be shown that the perpetrator killed one or more persons "as part of a mass killing of members of a civilian population." In addition, the ICTY established the following *mens rea* for extermination:

> inten[t] to kill, to inflict grievous bodily harm, or to inflict serious injury, in the reasonable knowledge that such act or omission is likely to cause death, or otherwise [the] inten[t] to participate in the elimination of a number of individuals, in the knowledge that his action is part of a vast murderous enterprise in which a large number of individuals are systematically marked for killing or killed.[91]

The requirement that there be a large number of deaths is a significant difference between extermination as a crime against humanity and genocide (which as noted earlier might, as a theoretical matter, be found with only a handful of deaths or even no deaths at all). Despite this difference, however, there is a significant overlap between extermination and most situations of genocide. Unlike the crime of genocide, the crime of extermination is not limited to groups with a common characteristic. Given the limited

---

88 *Prosecutor v. Krnojelac*, Case No. IT-97-25-T, Judgement, ¶ 434 (Mar. 15, 2002).

89 *Prosecutor v. Stakić*, Case No. IT-97-24-T, Judgement, ¶ 306 (July 31, 2003).

90 *Krstić, supra*, ¶ 685. By contrast, cumulative convictions were entered for genocide and persecution.

91 *Id.* ¶ 229.

number of protected groups within the definition of genocide and the difficulties of proving a defendant's specific intent to destroy the group, the crime against humanity of extermination may over time take on greater prominence in the prosecutor's arsenal as it does much of the work of genocide, and more. As you read through the evolving jurisprudence on persecution and extermination as a crime against humanity, critically assess what is the difference between those crimes and the same acts characterized as genocide. Another way to think about this question is to place yourself in the role of the ICC Prosecutor. What would you consider in determining whether to charge a suspect with persecution or extermination as a crime against humanity, on the one hand, and genocide, on the other?

E. Conclusion: Convergence or Distinction

As noted earlier, there are significant definitional differences between the crimes of genocide and crimes against humanity. First, the prohibition of genocide requires a showing of specific intent, whereas the prohibition against crimes against humanity requires only that the defendant acted with knowledge of a widespread or systematic attack against a civilian population. Second, the prohibition against crimes against humanity requires the existence of a widespread or systematic attack as a circumstantial element, whereas genocide—as a crime of intent—could in theory consist of a single isolated act. Third, crimes against humanity may be committed against any civilian population, whereas genocide is limited to populations with a common race, religion, nationality, or ethnicity. The crime of persecution as a crime against humanity captures attacks against individuals based upon a broad range of characteristics, including political, sex, sexual orientation, and many others.

Despite these exacting doctrinal differences, the emerging jurisprudence tends to downplay them. The *ad hoc* tribunals have interpreted the four protected categories in the prohibition against genocide in an expansive way, incorporating subjective perceptions of difference into the definition of each category. Although the *actus reus* of crimes against humanity contains a more numerous list of acts than does the prohibition against genocide, the list of crimes against humanity includes the crime of extermination, which has been interpreted by the *ad hoc* tribunals to effectively capture all discrimination-based killings and persecutions that are not covered by genocide. Given these similarities between the two crimes, and given the fact that they both describe some of the worst atrocities known to humankind, is it necessary to preserve these two crimes as distinct, or should we rather combine them in a way that ensures that all such atrocities are equally punished and deterred?

Chapter 9

IMMUNITIES, AMNESTIES, DEFENSES, AND EXCUSES

Although opportunities to hold individuals accountable for violations of international crimes have increased tremendously in the last century, potential defendants are not without their own arsenal of defenses. Most of the defenses found in domestic legal systems—such as mistake of law, mistake of fact, incapacity, consent, and self-defense—are also found in the jurisprudence of international criminal law (ICL). We focus here on those defenses that have been most commonly raised in ICL proceedings, or those that raise special issues at the international level. In particular, individuals accused of the commission of international crimes may benefit from the application of immunities, amnesties, and a variety of excuses that predate the development of modern ICL. The first two—immunities and amnesties—have been weakened with the creation of an increasingly robust ICL regime (with the significant exception of combatant immunity, which remains a hallmark of international humanitarian law (IHL)). Most forms of immunity and many amnesty laws are viewed with skepticism by the human rights and international justice advocacy communities, although amnesties are still used frequently by states to facilitate the end of a dictatorship, armed conflict, or atrocities by armed actors. Excuses, a third form of defense, play a similar role at the international level as they do in a domestic system—they lessen, and sometimes negate, liability for an otherwise illegal act.

All of these exceptions to criminal accountability are justified as furthering important social values. Immunities protect the necessary and legitimate functions of government officials by, for example, shielding such officials from politically-motivated or otherwise distracting and disruptive legal claims and charges. Combatant immunity—which provides that privileged combatants cannot be prosecuted for lawful acts of war—is justified to further the regulation of permissible and impermissible warfare and to reflect the fact that combatants act with the approval of the state that deploys them into combat. Amnesties are justified as means to achieve peace and social stability by providing a "carrot" to members of the government or military (and to rebel forces) to lay down their arms and, at times, to participate in transitional mechanisms of accountability and truth-seeking. Excuses (such as self-defense) are justified as furthering fundamental moral values and ensuring that criminal liability only attaches if there is true fault on the part of the defendant.

A. Immunities

The immunities from legal process historically afforded to diplomats, other state officials, and heads of state have all eroded in the last few decades. Defenses that once provided absolute protection to official actors under both domestic and international law now appear to provide little, if any, protection for violations of ICL, especially before international tribunals. The Rome Statute of the International Criminal Court (ICC) with its categorical rejection of most immunities, the transnational prosecutions of Augusto Pinochet (Chile) and Hissène Habré (Chad), the international prosecutions of Charles Taylor (Liberia) and Omar Al Bashir (Sudan), and recent decisions of the International Court of Justice (ICJ) all reflect the demise, or weakening, of official state immunity for certain international crimes. As noted later, exceptions to this general trend are the doctrine of combatant immunity under IHL, although its application to the global "war on terror" remains contested, and head of state immunity, which continues to apply in domestic courts.

1. Functional and Personal Immunities

Under international law, there are two general types of immunity enjoyed by state officials: functional and personal. *Functional immunity* protects an individual from liability for conduct performed on behalf of the state, or "official acts," and is also referred to as immunity *ratione materiae*, or subject matter immunity. Thus, a state official who engages in an ordinary criminal act for his or her own benefit (for example, theft or sexual assault) will not be protected from liability by functional immunity. *Personal immunity*—also referred to as immunity *ratione personae*—attaches to certain state personnel by virtue of the office they occupy, and provides protection from legal process regardless of the nature of the act in question. The protection offered by forms of personal immunity evaporates when the individual no longer holds the official position that granted them immunity. By contrast, officials continue to enjoy functional immunity for their earlier official acts even after leaving office. In all cases, the immunities inure to the benefit of the state; as such, the state can waive the immunity of its officials from foreign criminal jurisdiction.

By treaty and custom, diplomats (who may be dispatched to a foreign country or international organization) enjoy a strong form of personal immunity, codified internationally in the Vienna Convention on Diplomatic Relations (1961). As a result, diplomats and their immediate families are entitled to absolute personal immunity from any civil or criminal process while in a host country and even while transiting through third countries. This immunity applies to any criminal conduct, whether committed before or after they assumed office, regardless of whether the act was committed as part of their official duties and so long as they remain in office. Notwithstanding this seemingly impenetrable barrier to prosecution, diplomats may still be subject to legal process for their activities under certain circumstances.

First, personal immunity may be waived by the diplomat's sending state, as the immunity is a right of the state and not of the individual. If a state waives a diplomat's immunity, the diplomat may be prosecuted while still in office even for acts committed in their official capacity. Second, diplomats may be prosecuted after they no longer hold a diplomatic position for unofficial acts committed while they held their diplomatic posts—in other words, they enjoy functional immunity after they leave office, but not personal immunity. Third, they may be sued civilly for certain real estate, commercial or inheritance-related matters or their separate professional activities. Fourth, a diplomat may be rendered a *persona non grata* and expelled for their bad conduct (called being "PNGed"). Finally, these robust immunities apply only to diplomatic agents; other consular officials enjoy functional immunities but weaker personal immunities.

Personal immunity applies to other government officials, though this expansion beyond diplomats is more a function of customary rather than treaty law. Heads of state, heads of government (e.g., prime ministers), and certain state ministers (primarily ministers of foreign affairs) enjoy such personal immunity. This personal immunity provides powerful protection to these government officials before foreign state courts. Professor Dapo Akande noted in 2004 that he could find no case "in which it was held that a state official possessing immunity *ratione personae* is subject to the criminal jurisdiction of a foreign state when it is alleged that he or she has committed an international crime."[1] Some claim that the one exception to this assertion is the prosecution and conviction of the former President of Panama, Manuel Noriega, by the United States.[2] In that prosecution, however, the U.S. government took the position that Noriega was not in fact the legitimate head of state because he had been replaced by Guillermo Endara in an election that Noriega annulled in order to stay in power. The Noriega precedent, relying as it does on a claim that Noriega was not a *bona fide* head of state, does

1 Dapo Akande, *International Law Immunities and the International Criminal Court*, 98 AM. J. INT'L L. 407, 411 (2004).

2 *See generally U.S. v. Noriega*, 746 F. Supp. 1506 (1990).

not provide a clear exception to Akande's observation, which continues to hold true.[3]

With respect to the personal immunity of certain ministers, in a significant and somewhat controversial opinion the ICJ found that customary international law provides personal immunity to other senior government officials with respect to transnational prosecutions in foreign courts. (The case in question involved an arrest warrant issued in connection with Belgium's attempt to prosecute the sitting Foreign Minister of the Democratic Republic of the Congo for international crimes.) In *obiter dicta*, the ICJ stated that such immunity would not apply in the case of a prosecution before "certain international criminal courts," such as the International Criminal Tribunals for the former Yugoslavia (ICTY) and Rwanda (ICTR) or the ICC.[4] The so-called *Belgian Arrest Warrant* case is significant because it extended personal immunity beyond the category of individuals to whom it traditionally applied, namely heads of state, heads of government, and diplomats. In including foreign ministers within this category of officials (forming what is called the *troika*), the ICJ reasoned that without such immunity, foreign ministers would be hindered in performing a crucial function of their position (that is, international travel and diplomacy). Note that the *troika* does not include Ministers of Defense, who do not possess plenipotentiary powers to represent their home countries abroad in the same way as Foreign Ministers or Secretaries of State.

The ICJ's *dicta* reflects the most significant recent development with respect to official immunities: the erosion of such immunities, most pointedly seen in the weakening of the protections traditionally afforded a sitting head of state under customary international law when such individuals are prosecuted before an international tribunal. Until recently, it was generally accepted that customary international law provided sitting heads of state with absolute immunity while in office from any legal process. This is no longer the case. The first modern indictment against a sitting head of state by an international tribunal was issued in 1999 by the ICTY against the

---

[3] For a more up to date discussion of immunities before international and national courts, *see* Dapo Akande and Sangeeta Shah, *Immunities of State Officials, International Crimes, and Foreign Domestic Courts*, 21 EUROP. J. INT'L L. 815 (2011). In particular see notes 16 and 17 for examples of states recognizing immunity *ratione personae* of heads of state and other officials before their courts.

[4] Arrest Warrant of 11 April 2000 (Democratic Republic of the Congo v. Belgium) (2002) I.C.J. Report 3, ¶¶ 58–61. For a critique of the *Arrest Warrant* decision that argues that the Court did not adequately or clearly address the question of immunities (by not, for example, making a clear distinction between functional and personal immunities, and by confusing the basis for lifting functional immunity for acts that constitute international crimes), *see* Miglin, *supra* at 32–34.

president of Yugoslavia, Slobodan Milošević.[5] Milošević challenged the indictment on a number of grounds, including the absolute immunity traditionally enjoyed by sitting heads of state. The ICTY dismissed Milošević's claims of immunity and upheld the indictment.[6] In Africa, the first international indictment of a sitting head of state was that of Charles Taylor of Liberia in June 2003 by the Special Court for Sierra Leone (SCSL).[7] This was followed by the ICC's indictment of President Al Bashir of Sudan for all three core crimes. Both the President and Deputy President of Kenya were tried before the ICC, though the charges against them concerned actions committed prior to their assuming those offices.

The lack of such immunity before international tribunals is primarily based on subsequent treaties, more specifically the powers accorded to the particular international tribunal by their constitutive instruments (that is, the statutes of the various international criminal tribunals). The instruments establishing the post-World War II criminal tribunals—including the International Military Tribunals at Nuremberg and Tokyo, ICTY, ICTR, SCSL, and ICC—all include provisions asserting jurisdiction over state officials regardless of any conflicting immunity doctrines.[8] Article 27 of the ICC Statute, for example, provides:

> 1. This Statute shall apply equally to all persons without any distinction based on official capacity. In particular, official capacity as a Head of State or Government, a member of a Government or parliament, an elected representative or a government official shall in no case exempt a person from criminal responsibility under this Statute, nor shall it, in and of itself, constitute a ground for reduction of sentence.
>
> 2. Immunities or special procedural rules which may attach to the official capacity of a person, whether under national or international law, shall not bar the

---

5 The Nuremberg Tribunal prosecuted Karl Dönitz, who was made head of state for a short time after Adolf Hitler's suicide.

6 In fact Milošević himself did not raise the issue; it was raised on his behalf by *amici* who were effectively acting as his counsel. *See Prosecutor v. Milošević*, Case No. IT-02-54, Decision on Preliminary Motions (Nov. 8, 2001).

7 *See Prosecutor v. Taylor*, Case No. SCSL-2003-01-I, Decision on Immunity from Jurisdiction (May 31, 2004).The ICTR had previously indicted, tried, and convicted (via a guilty plea) the Rwandan Prime Minister Jean Kambanda, although the indictment was issued after Kambanda was no longer in office. *See Prosecutor v. Kambanda*, Case No. ICTR-97-23-S, Judgment and Sentence (Sept. 4, 1998).

8 *See* ICTY Statute, Art. 7(2); ICTR Statute, Art. 6(2); SCSL Statute, Art. 6(2); and the Nuremberg Charter, Art. 7. The Tokyo Charter had a similar provision (Art. 6), but it noticeably and deliberately does not refer to heads of state, presumably reflecting the earlier decision not to prosecute the Emperor of Japan.

> Court from exercising its jurisdiction over such a person.[9]

When states ratify the Rome Statute, they implicitly agree to abrogate whatever immunities might be enjoyed by their personnel.

Although Article 27 of the Rome Statute purports to prevent the assertion of all immunities before the Court, until recently there remained some debate over whether the nationals of non-party states who come before the Court might still enjoy at least certain prerogatives associated with such immunities. This can arise in connection with Security Council referrals of non-party states to the Court and when the Court asserts jurisdiction over the national of a non-party state who stands accused of committing international crimes on the territory of a state party. Many African states argued, for example, that President Al Bashir of Sudan enjoyed customary international law head-of-state immunity before the Court because Sudan never ratified the Rome Statute. This argument is no longer availing to Al Bashir since a 2019 coup ousted him from power. In any case, various chambers of the ICC consistently rejected Al Bashir's claim of immunity before he was overthrown.

Also at issue are the precise contours of the duties of ICC states parties and non-ICC states alike to cooperate with the Court to effectuate the arrest of indicted government officials hailing from non-ICC states who might otherwise benefit from immunity under domestic or international law—an enforcement jurisdiction question. While Article 27 invalidates all immunities before the Court, it does not necessarily relieve co-equal states of any customary international law or conventional immunities outside of the ICC system that they might be obligated to accord to a non-party state's official, including its head of state or of government. A Security Council referral to the Court, standing alone, does not necessarily cancel out the obligations member states might owe to a government official subject to an arrest warrant. Indeed, the Council in its two referral resolutions has merely "urged" other states to cooperate with the Court in the ICC referral texts and has been silent on the applicability of any enduring immunities. Thus, while it could be argued that the referral resolutions implicitly stripped potential defendants of any immunities they might enjoy before the Court (by operation of Article 27), the Council did not expressly nullify any immunities defendants might enjoy vis-à-vis other U.N. member states. These two open

---

[9] The ICC provision on immunities, Article 27, has two provisions that track the distinction between functional and personal immunity. The functional immunity subsection (Art. 27(1)) replicates that found in the earlier treaties; the personal immunity subsection (Art. 27(2)) is unique to the ICC Statute, leading some commentators to suggest that the earlier immunity provisions may only cover functional, and not personal, immunity. *See* James Miglin, *supra*, at 37–38.

questions arose most pointedly with respect to then-President Al Bashir of Sudan in connection with his travels around the globe in defiance of two ICC arrest warrants issued against him, including one for genocide.

Prior to a recent Appeals Chamber's ruling in the matter of Jordan's noncompliance with the Al Bashir arrest warrants, the Court had not spoken with one voice when it came to the question of states' obligations to arrest Al Bashir in the event that he entered their sovereign territory. Instead, as Al Bashir traveled around the globe, various configurations of judges issued divergent yet complementary opinions on state cooperation, experimenting with a number of theories under customary international law and the U.N. Charter as to why states were obliged to effectuate the arrest warrants against Al Bashir. For example, one Pre-Trial Chamber (PTC) in connection with Malawi's noncompliance cited to the ICJ's *dicta* in the *Belgian Arrest Warrant* case and held that customary international law did not recognize immunities before *international* courts like the ICC.[10] A different PTC in connection with the Democratic Republic of Congo's noncompliance focused on the implicit consequences of a Security Council referral, ruling that the Council's referral resolution "was meant to eliminate any impediment to the proceedings before the Court, including the lifting of immunities."[11] In a case involving South Africa's noncompliance, this same PTC opined that Sudan has the same rights and duties of states parties to the Rome Statute as a result of the referral.[12] A minority opinion also emerged that turned on the fact that Al Bashir has been indicted for genocide, and the Genocide Convention vitiates all personal immunities.[13] Article IV of that treaty states that "[p]ersons committing genocide or any of the other acts enumerated in article III shall be punished, whether they are constitutionally responsible rulers, public officials, or private officials."

---

10 *Prosecutor v. Omar Hassan Ahmad Al Bashir*, Case No. ICC-02/05-01/09-139-Corr, Corrigendum to the Decision Pursuant to Article 87(7) of the Rome Statute on the Failure of the Republic of Malawi to Comply with the Cooperation Requests Issued by the Court with Respect to the Arrest and Surrender of Omar Hassan Ahmad Al Bashir, ¶¶ 33–36 (Dec. 13, 2011), *citing* Arrest Warrant of 11 April 2000 (Dem. Rep. Congo v. Belg.), Judgment, 2002 I.C.J. Rep. 3, 25 (Feb. 14) ("an incumbent or former Minister for Foreign Affairs may be subject to criminal proceedings before certain international criminal courts, where they have jurisdiction").

11 *Prosecutor v. Omar Hassan Ahmad Al Bashir*, Case No. ICC-02/05-01/09-195, Decision on Cooperation of the Democratic Republic of the Congo regarding Omar Al Bashir's Arrest and Surrender to the Court, ¶ 29 (Apr. 9, 2014).

12 *Prosecutor v. Omar Hassan Ahmad Al Bashir*, Case No. ICC-02/05-01/09-302, Decision under Article 87(7) of the Rome Statute on the Non-Compliance by South Africa with the Request by the Court for the Arrest and Surrender of Omar Al Bashir, ¶ 93 (July 6, 2017).

13 *Prosecutor v. Omar Hassan Ahmad Al Bashir*, Case No. ICC-02/05-01/09-302-Anx, Minority Opinion of Judge Marc Perrin de Brichambaut, ¶ 9 (July 6, 2017).

This inconsistent and convoluted jurisprudence led commentators to identify two routes toward accountability for heads of state and other government officials from non-ICC states: the Security Council route and the customary international law route. The former hinged upon a robust articulation of the Council's Chapter VII enforcement powers and of the Court's authority to rely upon the unexpressed implications of Council referral resolutions, particularly when it comes to cooperation obligations placed upon all U.N. member states. This theory was premised on either an implied waiver of any applicable immunities on the part of Sudan (by virtue of its membership in the United Nations and thus acceptance of the Security Council's powers) or the Council's imposition of the terms of the ICC Statute, including its elimination of applicable immunities and its full cooperation duties, on Sudan. The latter turned on customary international law and is based on the view that there is no immunity *ratione personae* for heads of state before international tribunals and that this extends to the horizontal relationship between states when it comes to their cooperation with such judicial bodies.

In a May 2019 opinion, the Appeals Chamber ultimately resolved this debate in favor of a robust interpretation of customary international law. The Chamber agreed that Al Bashir enjoyed no immunity before the ICC, but returned to the Malawi PTC's original line of reasoning, ruling that "there is no Head of State immunity under customary international law vis-à-vis an international court."[14] It noted that every international court to consider the issue has rejected such immunities, thus undermining any claimed customary international law rule. Of note is the Court's identification of a class of "international courts," with an objective legal personality, that exercise a form of jurisdiction that is more than simply the sum of the jurisdictional bases delegated to it by individual states. In this regard, the Court held that the ICC and other international courts, "when adjudicating international crimes, do not act on behalf of particular State or States. Rather, international courts act on behalf of the international community as a whole."[15] This ruling treats the Court's jurisdiction as considerably broader than that of its member states. The immunity question is poised to receive additional high-level attention: the African Union adopted a resolution in 2018 to ask the U.N. General Assembly to seek an advisory opinion from the ICJ on the issue of head of state immunity. It remains to be seen whether the General Assembly will make such a referral (it has not done so as of this writing). If such a

---

14 *Prosecutor v. Omar Hassan Ahmad Al Bashir,* Case No. ICC-02/05-01/09 OA2, Judgment in the Jordan Referral re: Al Bashir Appeal, ¶ 1 (May 6, 2019).

15 *Id.* ¶ 115.

referral is made, the ICJ may take the opportunity to elaborate upon its earlier *dicta*, though it is unclear whether it will agree with the ICC's reasoning on these points or chart a new path.

All of this reveals that such immunities are strongest when invoked within domestic legal systems and weakest before international courts. Although state officials still enjoy the benefit of strong immunity claims (both functional and personal) in national courts, a similar erosion is taking place with respect to functional immunities before national courts, especially where serious violations of ICL are at issue. Indeed, the International Law Commission has been looking at the immunity of state officials from foreign criminal jurisdiction for several years with an eye toward creating Draft Articles on the topic that might serve as the basis for a multilateral treaty. Draft Article 7 indicates that immunity *ratione materiae* applies to acts performed in an official capacity but shall not apply to the commission of crimes under international law:

> 1. Immunity from the exercise of foreign criminal jurisdiction shall not apply in respect of the following crimes under international law: (a) crime of genocide; (b) crimes against humanity; (c) war crimes; (d) crime of apartheid; (e) torture; (f) enforced disappearance.
>
> 2. For the purposes of the present draft article, the crimes under international law mentioned above are to be understood according to their definition in the treaties enumerated in the annex to the present draft articles.[16]

The theory is that although such acts are often committed by individuals in their official capacities—and, in fact, official action is required to trigger international liability for some crimes—as a matter of law, such acts are not considered "official" for purposes of immunity doctrines. As Lord Brown-Wilkinson succinctly stated in the *Pinochet* case before the English House of Lords, "How can it be for international law purposes an official act to do something which international law itself prohibits and criminalises?"[17] By this logic, international crimes have become, *per se*, "unofficial." This is so even

[16] *See* Eighth Report on Immunity of State Officials from Foreign Criminal Jurisdiction, Concepción Escobar Hernández, Special Rapporteur, U.N. Doc. A/CN.4/739 (Feb. 28, 2020).

[17] *R v. Bow Street Metropolitan Stipendiary Magistrate and others ex part Pinochet Ugarte* [1999], 2 All ER 97, 114 (House of Lords). It should be noted, however, that only one of the Lords, Lord Millet, held that immunity is always overridden by ICL; the others who found no immunity based their decision on the provisions of the Convention Against Torture and thus only narrowly found that official immunity would be inapplicable to charges of torture.

though international human rights law requires a showing of some official action or acquiescence for an act to qualify as torture.[18]

As the Draft Articles on immunity from foreign jurisdiction are currently formulated, the ILC has not identified any exceptions to personal immunities before domestic courts for the commission of international crimes. Draft Article 4 on the scope of immunity *ratione personae* states simply that "Heads of State, Heads of Government and Ministers for Foreign Affairs enjoy immunity *ratione personae* only during their term of office." Technically, the project does not involve a consideration of immunities before international tribunals, but the issues are inextricably linked. We suspect that the erosion of official immunity for international crimes that has developed before international tribunals will eventually be replicated before domestic courts. As you read through the materials in your ICL course on immunities, continue to follow efforts to clarify this area of law before the United Nations, the ICJ, the ILC, and state practice.

2. Combatant Immunity

A specialized form of immunity is available under IHL for privileged combatants. Although the Geneva Conventions primarily provide protection to vulnerable individuals (such as civilians, prisoners of war (POWs), the wounded, and the shipwrecked) in international armed conflicts, it also tacitly provides immunity to combatants for acts of violence committed in furtherance of a sovereign military campaign. This immunity applies to privileged combatants for acts of war they commit that are not in violation of IHL. By contrast, no immunity is granted for war crimes—acts that violate IHL and give rise to individual criminal responsibility. Although an attack against a military base or other military facilities might be illegal as a matter of municipal law, an individual combatant acting as part of a national armed force and involved in such an attack within the context of an international armed conflict is immune from such liability so long as he or she meets the requirements of a privileged combatant.

None of the treaties expressly sets forth a definition of "privileged combatant." The Third Geneva Convention at Article 4, however, provides that members of the armed forces of a party to the conflict qualify as POWs in the event of capture or surrender. In addition, members of militias, volunteer corps, and organized resistance movements that "belong" to a party may also qualify as POWs if they satisfy the following four requirements:

---

[18] This is true only when torture is prosecuted as a stand-alone crime, however. Where torture rises to the level of a crime against humanity or constitutes a war crime, no showing of state action is required.

i. the organization must be commanded by a person responsible for his subordinates;

ii. the organization's members must have a fixed distinctive emblem or uniform recognizable at a distance;

iii. the organization's members must carry arms openly; and

iv. the organization's members must conduct their operations in accordance with the laws and customs of war.[19]

That article also identifies other individuals who may also qualify as POWs when they accompany combatants, such as war correspondents and civilian crews. These requirements for POW status have been interpreted to also define who constitutes a privileged combatant entitled to combatant immunity.

Note that the IHL governing non-international armed conflicts does not contain a POW regime or recognize the notion of combatant immunity for fighters who are not deployed by a state. As a result, rebel fighters may always be prosecuted for their acts of violence, even when committed within the context of a non-international armed conflict. In most circumstances, such combatants will be prosecuted under municipal penal law, unless the state has adopted a special penal regime to govern non-international armed conflicts. This is because being an unprivileged combatant *per se* is not unlawful under international law.

The question of combatant immunity has continued to be an issue in the context of the global war against terrorism. The question is: when does an act of violence qualify as a lawful incident of an armed conflict subject to the permissions and prohibitions of IHL, versus when does the act qualify as terrorism and thus trigger international terrorism prohibitions and the municipal law of interested states. The consequences of such a determination are significant. For example, both Afghan armed forces and Al Qaeda operatives were the object of attack in the international armed conflict initiated by the United States against the Taliban regime in Afghanistan in the immediate aftermath of the September 11, 2001, terrorist attacks. The U.S. government took the position that neither members of the Afghan armed forces nor Al Qaeda members qualified as privileged combatants. As a result, the United States argued, they were not entitled to POW status when captured or to combatant immunity for any acts of violence they committed.

---

[19] Geneva Convention Relative to the Treatment of Prisoners of War, Aug. 12, 1949, 6 U.S.T. 3316, 75 U.N.T.S. 135, Art 4(2).

Although we agree with the U.S. government and most international lawyers that Al Qaeda members are not privileged combatants, we think that some members of the armed forces of the Taliban when it was the lawful government of Afghanistan may qualify as such. If so, acts of war committed by Taliban troops should give rise to combatant immunity so long as no war crimes are committed. As unprivileged combatants, Al Qaeda operatives are not entitled to combatant immunity, even for acts of war that would be otherwise lawful under IHL (e.g., attacks on combatants or military objectives). As a result, if they participate in hostilities without the privilege of doing so, they can be prosecuted for acts of terrorism, murder, mayhem, and the like to the extent that there are penal statutes that assert jurisdiction over them. As noted above, however, such conduct does not violate international law *per se*.

The question continues to arise with respect to how determinations of combat immunity are made. The Third Geneva Convention (concerning POWs) states that if there is any doubt with respect to the lawful combatant status of a captured person (and thus whether that person is entitled to POW status), then such person must be treated as a POW until a "competent tribunal" determines his or her status.[20] In response to a challenge by individuals detained at the U.S. naval base in Guantánamo Bay, Cuba, the U.S. Supreme Court held that the United States was obligated to provide some legal process to determine the combatant status of those being detained.[21] As a result, the U.S. government established Combatant Status Review Tribunals, although the focus of these tribunals was to determine whether the individual detainee still qualified as an "enemy combatant," and thus whether he could still be detained, and not whether he was entitled to POW status and all that it entails (including humane treatment and the right to repatriation at the conclusion of hostilities). In 2008, the U.S. Supreme Court found that those being detained by the United States in Guantánamo Bay were entitled to the constitutionally guaranteed right of *habeas corpus*, thus ending the use of the Combatant Status Review Tribunals.[22]

The defense of combatant immunity has been raised in related litigation in U.S. courts. John Walker Lindh, the so-called American Taliban, was prosecuted for his involvement with the Taliban forces in Afghanistan and in particular for remaining with the Taliban after the attacks of September 11, 2001. Lindh raised combatant immunity as a defense, arguing that he was part of an organized military force that was resisting an incursion by then-rebel forces of the Northern Alliance. The federal court in which Lindh's case was

---

[20] *Id.* at Art. 5.

[21] *Rasul v. Bush*, 542 U.S. 466 (2004).

[22] *Boumediene v. Bush*, 553 U.S. 723 (2008).

heard concluded that Lindh had not met his burden of showing that the Taliban met the requirements of privileged combatants under the Geneva Conventions, and thus the defense of lawful combatant immunity was denied.[23]

B. Amnesties

Throughout recorded history, officials have enacted amnesties to prevent the prosecution of state officials for crimes they may have committed while in office and of rebel actors as an inducement to lay down their arms and re-integrate into society. This practice continues today, especially in light of the limitations of functional immunity. Until very recently, state practice has been uncritical of the use of such amnesties. In fact, with a few notable exceptions in Latin America, every state court to consider the question has upheld the legality of a challenged amnesty.[24] In addition to limiting the applicability of traditional immunities to state officials responsible for international crimes, international law is also eroding the strength of amnesties. Indeed, whenever international courts and other similar institutions (such as human rights courts) have confronted domestic amnesties, they have always declared such enactments to be illegal under states' human rights obligations.

1. Amnesties Before the Special Court for Sierra Leone

The first non-domestic criminal tribunal to directly address the legality of an amnesty was the SCSL. In *Prosecutor v. Kallon & Kamara*, the SCSL held that the amnesty provision in the Lomé Peace Accord did not apply to those prosecuted before the Special Court.[25] The Court reasoned that the Lomé Accord was in fact a creature of domestic law, and thus was subordinate to international law. As such, it reasoned, the Accord must give way to the jurisdiction and powers of the Special Court.

The Court took up the issue more directly a short two months later in *Prosecutor v. Gbao,* asserting, first, that "there is a *crystallized* international norm to the effect that a government

---

[23] *U.S. v. Lindh*, 212 F. Supp. 2d 541 (E.D. Va. 2002).

[24] *See, e.g., Azapo v. President of South Africa*, CCT 17/96, 1996 (4) SALR 671 (CC). The recent exceptions concern amnesties passed in Argentina and Chile, which were overturned within their respective countries and are not recognized by other states in the context of transnational criminal prosecutions. Another set of exceptions involve states that have implemented judgments entered against them by the Inter-American Court of Human Rights declaring their amnesties illegal as a matter of international law. For a brief discussion of one of the more recent examples involving an amnesty in Brazil, *see* Alonso Gurmendi, *At Long Last, Brazil's Amnesty Law is Declared Anti-Conventional*, OPINIO JURIS (August 16, 2019).

[25] *See Prosecutor v. Kallon & Kamara*, Case Nos. SCSL 2004-15-AR72(E) & SCSL 2004-16-AR72(E), Decision on Challenge to Jurisdiction: Lomé Accord Amnesty (Mar. 13, 2004).

cannot grant amnesty for serious crimes under international law," and second, that "[u]nder international law, states are under a duty to prosecute crimes whose [sic] prohibition has the status of *jus cogens*."[26] Robert Cryer has correctly noted that both of these statements are controversial, and that the latter—concerning the duty to prosecute—"cries out for greater discussion."[27] Specifically, although there has been a good deal of academic literature concerning a duty to prosecute violations of ICL, it is far from clear whether such a duty exists and what, if anything, are its limits. Treaties prohibiting torture and many acts of terrorism establish a general obligation to either prosecute or extradite a suspect to a state that will prosecute, but it is not clear if such an obligation extends to other crimes as a matter of customary international law, and thus applies regardless of whether a state is a party to a particular treaty. As some of the following discussion with respect to amnesties will suggest, there is a stronger argument that international law requires some form of justice with respect to violations of ICL, but it is less clear that such justice must take the form of traditional retributive-based criminal prosecutions.

2. Amnesties and the ICC Statute

The Rome Statute does not address amnesties expressly.[28] This was a deliberate decision made by the delegates at the Rome Conference, who clearly rejected the arguments of the South African delegation, among others, that some amnesties should be given effect before the ICC. The Rome Statute's silence with respect to amnesties means that we will have to wait for the development of the Court's jurisprudence on this issue before we can say with any certainty which, if any, amnesties may provide protection from prosecution before the ICC. In one of its few decisions regarding the legality and applicability of amnesties, the ICC Appeals Chamber recently declined to follow *dicta* in a Pre-Trial Chamber opinion declaring that

---

[26] *Prosecutor v. Gbao*, Case No. SCSL 2004-15-AR72(E), Decision on preliminary motion on the invalidity of the agreement between the United Nations and the Government of Sierra Leone on the establishment of the Special Court, ¶¶ 9–10 (2004) (emphasis added).

[27] Robert Cryer, *Commentary*, *in* ANNOTATED LEADING CASES OF INTERNATIONAL CRIMINAL TRIBUNALS: THE SPECIAL COURT FOR SIERRA LEONE 2003–2004 60 (André Klip and Göran Sluiter eds., 2006).

[28] Amnesties are one example of a range of mechanisms that provide legal leniency to a perpetrator. An amnesty precludes prosecution and may be blanket and one-sided, or nuanced and conditional. The latter are considered more legitimate than the former and may advance some goals of a justice process, such as truth-telling, reparation, or reconciliation. For a comprehensive assessment of the legitimacy of amnesties, see THE BELFAST GUIDELINES ON AMNESTY AND ACCOUNTABILITY (Transitional Justice Institute, University of Ulster, 2013). Other forms of leniency include pardons issued after a conviction, sentencing ceilings, and alternative forms of punishment, such as house arrest, community service, or specific contributions to reparations, healing, and reconciliation.

an amnesty passed in Libya was incompatible with international law. Instead the Appeals Chamber noted that "international law is still in the developmental stage on the question of acceptability of amnesties."[29] There is no question, however, that the ICC Statute provides ample room for the Court and Prosecutor to defer to a specific amnesty in deciding not to prosecute an individual suspect.

Indeed, there are at least four ways in which an amnesty may be given effect before the ICC. First, the Office of the Prosecutor (OTP) may suspend an investigation "in the interests of justice" (Article 53(c)(2)). Second, the Court may find that an amnesty satisfies the requirements of domestic prosecution under the Statute's complementarity provisions (Article 17). Third, the U.N. Security Council may defer an investigation or prosecution under its Chapter VII powers (Article 16). Fourth, the Court may conclude that the amnesty is the equivalent of a conviction or acquittal that triggers its *ne bis in idem* (double jeopardy) provision (Article 20).

3. Interests of Justice

First, Article 53 of the ICC Statute provides that the Prosecutor may decline to initiate an investigation if it would "serve the interests of justice." Such a decision is, however, reviewable by the Pre-Trial Chamber on its own initiative, and the Chamber may reverse the Prosecutor's decision per Article 53(3)(b).[30] The question then is what would qualify as a basis for declining to initiate an investigation "in the interest of justice." Certainly one could accept as reasonable an interpretation that would allow the prosecutor to reach such a decision if the individual suspect is participating in a justice or reconciliation process other than a traditional criminal prosecution. In other words, one could imagine a prosecutor declining to prosecute (and a Pre-Trial Chamber upholding that decision) if the suspect was subject to alternative accountability mechanisms, whether it be something like the South African amnesty process (which provided some level of accountability) or an alternative dispute resolution mechanism like the *gacaca* process in Rwanda.

---

[29] *Prosecutor v. Saif Al Islam Gaddafi*, Case No. ICC-01/11-01/11-695 OA8, Judgment on the appeal of Mr. Saif Al Islam Gaddafi against the decision of Pre-Trial Chamber I entitled "Decision on the 'Admissibility Challenge by Dr. Saif Al Islam Gadafi [sic] pursuant to Articles 17(1)(c), 19 and 20(3) of the Rome Statute' " of 5 April 2019, ¶ 96 (March 9, 2020).

[30] This is in contrast to a decision by the Prosecutor not to proceed on other grounds (for example, lack of legal or factual basis), which is only reviewable if a state party so moves, or if the Security Council requests a review in a case initiated by its referral. *See* Article 53(3)(a). In these other circumstances, however, the Chamber may only *request* that the Prosecutor reconsider the question, rather than reversing the Prosecutor's decision as can be done in the case of the Prosecutor not proceeding in the interest of justice.

Although such an interpretation is certainly plausible, the ICC has not been operating long enough, and thus has not created enough of a jurisprudential track record, for us to predict with any accuracy whether such an interpretation would be adopted by the Prosecutor and approved by the Court. Central to this determination would be whether the alternative mechanism implemented in the country provides some notion of justice for victims (which might include a truth-telling or reparation scheme). We argue that justice requires some form of individual accountability, although others have posited that achieving "peace" alone (meaning the immediate end of an armed conflict) qualifies as a form of justice. The latter argument may be summarized as follows: The ending of hostilities protects future victims from harm, and this achievement outweighs the lack of retrospective justice with respect to past victims. The ICC Prosecutor appears to have adopted a definition of justice that requires some individual accountability, as a published policy document distinguishes between "justice" and "peace,"[31] and noted that although "interests of justice" incorporates a broader notion of justice than criminal justice, it "should not be conceived of so broadly as to embrace all issues related to peace and security."[32] Human Rights Watch has argued in a very sophisticated policy paper that the phrase "interests of justice" should be interpreted narrowly, and should not be used to decline an investigation or prosecution in the face of a national amnesty, truth commission, or other alternative justice system or process of reconciliation.[33]

A related question is whether the inquiry concerning the interests of justice is focused on the justice of an individual case, or whether it encompasses the more generalized justice policies that a society might enact in a transitional period, as is seen in Colombia. In other words, does the inquiry concerning the interests of justice focus on the specific facts and circumstances of an individual suspect, or is it a more general inquiry concerning a particular society's gestalt approach to justice in the post-conflict or post-repression situation? For example, would (or should) a comprehensive set of responses—involving legal and institutional reforms, promises of non-repetition, lustrations, and a truth-telling process—quality? Carsten Stahn argues that the proper inquiry is on the individual case, and not on the general approach of the state from which that

---

31 *See* Office of the Prosecutor, *Policy Paper on the Interests of Justice* 1–4 (Sept. 2007) (noting the difference between the interests of justice and peace, and that any efforts to secure peace must be undertaken consistent with the legal requirements of the Rome Treaty to hold accountable those most responsible for violations of international criminal law).

32 *Id.* at 8.

33 Human Rights Watch, *The Meaning of "The Interests of Justice" in Article 53 of the Rome Statute* (June 2005).

individual comes.[34] There is a good deal of textual support for this position in the language of the treaty, referring for example to "the crime" and "the victims."

4. Complementarity

Article 17 of the Rome Statute concerning complementarity also provides a possible textual basis for the ICC to defer to a local amnesty. There are two possible avenues for this interpretation: Article 17(1)(a) and Article 17(1)(b). Under Article 17(1)(a), the ICC will defer to a national mechanism if "[t]he case is being investigated or prosecuted by a State which has jurisdiction over it, unless the State is unwilling or unable genuinely to carry out the investigation or prosecution." Under Article 17(1)(b), the ICC will defer to a national mechanism if "[t]he case has been investigated by a State which has jurisdiction over it and the State has decided not to prosecute the person concerned, unless the decision resulted from the unwillingness or inability of the State genuinely to prosecute." The one other provision in this article, subsection (c), only applies if there has been a "trial" by a "court." Even the South African amnesty, which is the most "court-like" amnesty ever adopted, might face difficulty in qualifying as a "trial" before a "court."

In considering the way in which complementarity might lead to the application of a domestic amnesty before the ICC, there are three issues worth highlighting: (1) the interpretation of the term "investigation," (2) the proper focus of an investigation, and (3) the presumptions created by the provisions. The first issue concerns the scope of an investigation. Is a general investigation into the causes, effects, and contours of a history of violations sufficient, or is a more focused and individualized investigation required? As with the idea of taking into account the "interests of justice" under Article 53, it appears clear that "investigation" refers to an individual fact-gathering process focused on the facts of a specific course of criminal conduct or perpetrator—and not the type of general inquiry into the causes and contours of violations that truth commissions routinely conduct.

The second question concerns the *type* of individualized investigation. Some have interpreted the concept of an investigation to mean a criminal investigation that could result in a prosecution and conviction, and then concluded that an amnesty could never satisfy this requirement. A variation of this argument is that the granting of an amnesty after an investigation is *prima facie* evidence of an "unwillingness" to investigate or "to bring the person concerned

---

[34] Carsten Stahn, *Complementarity, Amnesties and Alternative Forms of Justice: Some Interpretative Guidelines for the International Criminal Court*, 3 J. INT'L CRIM. JUST. 695, 717–718 (2005).

to justice," and thus fails under Article 17. Indeed, a definition of investigation anchored in a process of criminal prosecution precludes any form of amnesty (although it might be compatible with a pardon *ex post*). By contrast, a definition of investigation that focuses on gathering and publicizing evidence with respect to the crimes in question but that may not result in a prosecution would describe some amnesties, such as the one adopted by South Africa in 1995. This distinction between criminal investigation and amnesty is misplaced in this context. A conditional amnesty like that adopted in South Africa is consistent with a definition of "criminal investigation," as the investigations undertaken in that amnesty process could have led (and in many cases did lead) to a denial of amnesty and thus the possibility of criminal prosecution. The fact that such prosecutions have not been forthcoming in post-amnesty South Africa is an argument that South Africa's amnesty process might not qualify under this interpretation of "investigation," not that a similar amnesty could never qualify. Support for the position that some amnesties involve an investigation of some sort, and thus might qualify, can be found in statements by certain negotiators at Rome, although such statements are, of course, not authoritative interpretations of the treaty.

The third issue under Article 17 concerns the way in which its presumption operates. Stahn rightly argues that the exceptions to Article 17 should be interpreted narrowly, "since it is drafted in a negative fashion."[35] In other words, the general presumption of the complementarity regime is admissibility unless one or more of the exceptions clearly applies. Stahn thus argues that an amnesty *must* be accompanied by some form of investigation to qualify as a proceeding that would render a case inadmissible. In other words, an amnesty without more would be insufficient, for it would not provide strong evidence of a state's commitment to providing some form of individual justice. All three of these interpretive points underscore the fact that an amnesty could conceivably qualify as an investigation under Article 17, but that such an amnesty must meet a minimum threshold of accountability in order to allow the Court to conclude that a particular case is inadmissible.

5. Security Council Deferral

Article 16 allows the U.N. Security Council to invoke its Chapter VII power to defer an investigation or prosecution for a year at a time. This option may also provide a mechanism for giving *de facto* effect to a domestic amnesty before the ICC. The legal question is whether deferral to an amnesty could ever trigger the Security Council's Chapter VII powers—in other words, could not deferring to an

---

[35] *Id.* at 709.

amnesty be characterized as a threat to, or a breach of, the peace? There are clearly some circumstances in which the question of whether to defer to a domestic amnesty might affect international peace. An amnesty included as part of a peace deal to end a brutal armed conflict could be easily characterized as part of an effort to address a breach of, or threat to, international peace and security. The Security Council might distinguish such a negotiated amnesty from a self-amnesty that applies only to government actors after a conflict has concluded. A negotiated amnesty is more likely to garner the long-term support of the parties to a conflict, and a declaration questioning its validity is more likely to endanger the underlying negotiated settlement. A blanket self-amnesty, on the other hand, is likely to lack legitimacy or acceptance by other parties to a conflict; as such, its non-enforcement before the ICC may be less likely to threaten international peace (either because such peace remains elusive, or because conditioning peace upon the impunity of one side to a conflict is less likely to create a stable or durable peace). Likewise, the differential timing of an amnesty—that is, one enacted in the midst of a conflict or peace process versus one enacted while a repressive regime is in office or during peacetime—might be relevant. Amnesties passed in peacetime, after the end of a conflict, are less likely to affect international peace than amnesties passed in the midst of a conflict as part of a peace process or negotiation.

A Security Council deferral might provide a means of implementing a temporary amnesty—in other words, a provisional suspension from prosecution. Such a temporary amnesty could be conditional on a number of contingencies, including a requirement that the beneficiaries not take up arms again and actively support peace and reconciliation efforts (through revealing information and testifying before a truth commission, or by providing some form of reparation to their victims, whether monetary or through good works). One could thus imagine a state working with the Security Council to craft a period of deferral based on conditions that further peace, justice, and reconciliation. Such a scenario would only arise if the Prosecutor initiated an investigation or prosecution, as discussed earlier. In other words, a deferral on the basis of an amnesty would only come into play if there was a strong difference of opinion between the Prosecutor and a suspect's state and the Security Council.

6. *Ne Bis In Idem*

Article 20 codifies the generally recognized principle of criminal law forbidding double jeopardy, referred to as *ne bis in idem* ("not twice against the same") in ICL. That provision provides that a suspect will not be prosecuted before the ICC if he or she has already been convicted or acquitted by another court, unless the proceedings were: (1) designed to shield the suspect from responsibility for crimes within the jurisdiction of the court, or (2) were not conducted independently or impartially but rather in a manner inconsistent with bringing the person concerned to justice. Saif Gaddafi, for example, argued before the ICC that an amnesty passed by Libya applied to the acts for which the ICC was prosecuting him and thus triggered the Article 20(3) protection against double jeopardy. Without having to address the question of whether an amnesty could trigger the protection against double jeopardy, the Pre-Trial Chamber concluded that the amnesty law in question did not in fact apply to the acts for which Gaddafi was being prosecuted before the ICC.[36] As such, the ICC prosecution was allowed to continue.

For the double jeopardy provision to apply to an amnesty, two interpretive hurdles must be overcome. First, the granting of an amnesty would have to qualify as a conviction or acquittal. Second, such conviction or acquittal would have to be achieved by a court. On the first point, an amnesty cannot be characterized as an acquittal. An individual is acquitted when it is determined that he or she is not responsible for an alleged crime for either factual or legal reasons. An amnesty, by definition, assumes that the individual is guilty, but withholds punishment (and in many respects any criminal process at all). An amnesty that took the form of a pardon might more easily be characterized as equivalent to a conviction if one could establish that the individual was found to be responsible or guilty and subject to some form of punishment. The first element—a determination of guilt or responsibility—is an easier requirement, as most amnesties (and pardons) implicitly, and some explicitly, establish individual responsibility. The second element—the imposition of some form of punishment—is less common with respect to an amnesties. For instance, the East Timorese amnesty did require some form of reparation from its beneficiaries (often in the form of community service), whereas the South African amnesty did not.

On the second point, an amnesty administered by a court may more clearly qualify as a prior adjudication. The question arises when the amnesty is administered by a quasi-judicial body like a truth commission. Some argue that such quasi-judicial bodies could not qualify as a court. We do not think the issue is so clear, and one could argue that a body like the South African Amnesty Committee—consisting solely of judges or attorneys and operating independently of the executive branch—could sufficiently qualify as a court to trigger the attachment of double jeopardy. In any case, this is an area

36 *Prosecutor v. Saif Al Islam Gaddafi*, Case No. ICC-01/11-01/11-662, Decision on the "Admissibility Challenge by Dr. Saif Al Islam Gadafi [sic] pursuant to Articles 17(1)(c), 19 and 20(3) of the Rome Statute" (April 5, 2019).

that lacks firm jurisprudence, so we are left to speculate on when, if ever, the ICC (or other international court for that matter) would defer to a domestic amnesty program.

C. Excuses and Justifications

Most of the defenses available under domestic criminal law are also found in ICL, such as the defenses of mistake, duress, incapacity, self-defense, superior orders, and necessity. The source and elements of many of these defenses within ICL is found in customary international law and general principles of law. Rather than discuss each of these defenses in turn, we focus here on one as an illustrative example—the debate concerning necessity as an excuse for torture.

The prohibition against torture is one of the most codified prohibitions in international human rights law. It can be found in the Universal Declaration of Human Rights, the International Covenant on Civil and Political Rights (ICCPR), all regional human rights treaties, the Geneva Conventions, the Cairo Declaration on Human Rights in Islam, the statutes of all hybrid and *ad hoc* international criminal tribunals, and the Rome Treaty establishing the ICC. In addition, the prohibition against torture has its own dedicated treaty, the Convention Against Torture, which also prohibits acts that fall short of torture but constitute cruel, inhuman, or degrading treatment or punishment. None of these manifestations of the prohibition of torture contains any codified exception. The ICCPR, for example, does not list the prohibition against torture as one of the rights that can be derogated in times of emergency. It is also generally accepted that torture has risen to the level of a *jus cogens* prohibition, binding on all states regardless of treaty commitments or persistent objection.

Despite the universal formal acceptance by states of the absolute prohibition against torture, some individuals, including some government officials in the United States and elsewhere, have argued that there may be circumstances in which torture and other forms of harsh treatment would be morally permissible, and thus should be legally permitted. This debate rose in importance with the launching of the so-called global war on terror in 2001. This debate about justifications for torture has proceeded alongside a second debate about what acts constitute torture. Lawyers within the United States government, for example, argued that "waterboarding," or the controlled drowning of an individual, does not constitute torture. While this interpretation was adopted by the administration of George W. Bush, it was rejected by the administration of Barack Obama, only to be rhetorically revived by the election of Donald J. Trump. By contrast, the Committee Against Torture—the body of experts appointed to interpret the Convention

Against Torture—and other experts have consistently held that waterboarding constitutes torture, full stop.

Those who argue that there are some circumstances in which torture may be permissible most often invoke the defense of necessity to support their position. The necessity defense has arisen in two ways to justify torture. First, the necessity defense has been cited to support the general use of torture in response to threats of terrorism. The argument is that the threat from terrorism is so great, and the consequences of terrorist acts are so immense, that the use of torture on suspected terrorists is justified to prevent a future attack. This defense is more properly characterized as a justification, rather than a legal defense. A legal defense is premised on the idea that the underlying act is in fact wrongful, but that the circumstances remove liability for this otherwise wrongful act. This first use of the necessity defense attempts to provide an *ex ante* justification for torture, in effect arguing quite broadly that the acts that qualify as torture are legal, and thus justified, in all cases involving suspected terrorists.

The two states where this issue has been raised at the highest levels of government are the United States and Israel. The question has not been squarely faced by a court in the United States, but it has been the subject of a Supreme Court decision in Israel.[37] In the Israeli case, the Israeli security forces argued that the necessity defense justified the adoption of an interrogation policy that included techniques that impose severe physical and mental pain and suffering (such as prolonged sleep deprivation and a form of shaking that, in some cases, has resulted in death) given the threat of terrorism. The Israeli Supreme Court rejected this argument, noting that the necessity defense could not be used as "a general authority to establish directives respecting the use of physical means during the course of a[n]. . . interrogation."[38] In other words, the necessity defense cannot be invoked to create a prospective authority for, in this case, an interrogation policy.

Whereas this first use of the necessity defense is forward looking, the second use is backward looking. This would be employed by the individual intelligence agent as an individualized defense in a criminal prosecution or other form of accountability mechanism. The Rome Treaty allows a form of necessity defense before the ICC in Article 31(1)(d), which provides for the exclusion of criminal liability if the act for which the individual was indicted was (1) caused by

---

[37] *Judgment Concerning the Legality of the General Security Service's Interrogation Methods*, 38 I.L.M 1471 (1999).

[38] *Id.* ¶ 36. The Israeli Supreme Court struck down the use of these "enhanced interrogation methods" as unauthorized by Parliament and thus illegal under Israeli law, leaving open the question of whether Parliament could, under Israeli law, expressly authorize acts that would qualify as torture.

duress (2) that resulted from a threat of imminent death or continuing or imminent serious bodily harm (3) against the actor or another person, where (4) the act was reasonable and necessary to avoid the threat, and (5) where the actor did not intend to cause a harm greater than the one sought to be avoided. Note in particular that the impugned act must be in response to an imminent threat, and that there are requirements of both reasonableness and proportionality in his defense.

The paradigmatic example cited to illustrate this use of the necessity defense is the "ticking time bomb" scenario. This fictive narrative contains several elements: A state has in custody an individual who knows the location of a bomb that is set to imminently detonate, the detonation will result in the death of a number of people, the individual will reveal the location of the bomb under torture, and the authorities will be able to defuse it in time to save innocent civilians. The theory is that torturing the suspect to force them to reveal the location of the bomb is justified by the number of lives saved. This scenario of course is dependent on a number of idealized factual premises that will be rarely—if ever—all present in the real world: (1) that the detonation of the bomb is imminent, (2) that the person in custody in fact knows the location of the bomb, (3) that the person will reveal that information if tortured (but not if subjected to other forms of persuasion), (4) that the authorities will be able to defuse the bomb, (5) that neutralization of the bomb is the only way to save lives, and (6) that no other techniques (including the age-old tea and sympathy) will get the individual to talk.

Consider the following, which sets forth the consequentialist justification for the necessity defense:

> Necessity as a justification derives from consequential moral theories, according to which wrongful actions may be morally deemed by the goodness of their consequences. It justifies the sacrifice of legitimate interests to protect other interests of substantially higher value. It does not grant the individual "a license to determine social utility." It is rather limited to emergency cases in which there is an imminent and concrete danger to an interest recognized by the legal system. In the context of this discussion, such an emergency exists in the "ticking bomb" situation, in which a bomb has been set to explode imminently and innocent people are likely to be killed. The only hope for saving their lives is to get information about the location of the bomb in order to defuse it. Should necessity justify the use of force in an

attempt to coerce the person under interrogation to reveal such information?[39]

If necessity is to apply to ticking bomb situations, it will justify the use of interrogational force against the *innocent*. The sacrifice of an innocent person's interests is justified when necessary to save others, when the latter have a higher "value." Taken to extreme, necessity might *prima facie* justify the use of force against a terrorist's child in order to force the terrorist to reveal the information about the location of a bomb he has planted. Even to consequentialists the use of force against the child might seem morally repugnant. No one should torture innocent children—even when done to produce a sizeable gain in aggregate welfare. And no one should be asked to torture innocent children in order to demonstrate their loyalty or patriotism.

Although necessity may not be available in all cases involving the use of torture, might there be some situations when it would be justified under ICL? As you study defenses under ICL, consider when, if at all, a necessity defense might be applicable to a charge of war crimes, crimes against humanity, or genocide.

D. Conclusion

Immunities, amnesties, and excuses all limit the ability to hold individuals accountable for violations of ICL. Immunities are historically well established under international law, although as we have seen they are weakening as institutions for international criminal accountability gain strength and the international community's tolerance for the commission of international crimes wears thin. The recent pronouncement of the ICJ on the issue would limit some immunities to situations involving transnational assertions of jurisdiction by co-equal sovereigns and remove their use before international tribunals. Although ICJ and ICC decisions are not considered precedential or binding on subsequent parties, numerous treaties ratified by the vast majority of states (including the Genocide Convention and the Rome Statute) make clear that such immunities are no longer available to those who commit the most serious international crimes. The recent jurisprudence of the ICC with respect to Al Bashir's claim of head of state immunity supports this position.

Like immunities, the utility of amnesties as a complete defense to a criminal prosecution has also been reduced by a variety of recent developments, including challenges before the Inter-American Court

---

[39] Miriam Gur-Arye, *Can the War Against Terror Justify the Use of Force in Interrogation? Reflections in Light of the Israeli Experience*, *in* TORTURE: A COLLECTION 191 (Sanford Levinson ed., 2004).

of Human Rights. Amnesties are still used by states negotiating the end of a period of violent conflict, but the general consensus is that such amnesties are illegal if they do not allow for some form of individualized accountability. Policymakers are thinking creatively about how to craft diversionary mechanisms that induce warring parties to the negotiating table without foreclosing justice—broadly defined—entirely.

Finally, ICL, like its domestic counterpart, allows a number of defenses, excuses, and justifications to criminal liability. We highlighted one of the more controversial applications of an excuse in the context of torture and terrorism. Whereas in the first two cases—immunities and amnesties—one sees a trend toward increasing accountability by limiting historically used mechanisms, in the case of torture and the necessity defense, one sees a challenge by some states (most notably the United States) to the generally accepted absolute prohibition against torture. The struggle over defining the proper contours of immunities, amnesties, and excuses is a microcosm of the more general struggle between those who push for increased accountability for international crimes and those who resist such incursions on powers historically reserved to states.

Chapter 10

FORMS OF INDIVIDUAL RESPONSIBILITY

> Crimes against international law are committed by men, not by abstract entities, and only by punishing individuals who commit such crimes can the provisions of international law be enforced.

So wrote the Nuremberg Tribunal in its historic judgment. Modern international criminal law (ICL) is premised on individual—as opposed to state or collective—responsibility. Shifting responsibility from the collective to the individual was a doctrinal revolution that has made possible the multitude of international criminal proceedings going forward today. In fact, at the moment, it is far easier to hold individuals responsible for international crimes than states or other collectives. The shift from collective to individual responsibility required the development of *forms* of individual liability. Like domestic law, ICL recognizes different types of responsibility that trigger individual liability. Some—like complicity, conspiracy, co-perpetration, and incitement—trace their origins to domestic law principles that would be familiar to common law and/or civil law lawyers. Other forms of responsibility—such as superior responsibility—are more unique to international law.

Liability may be divided into two broad types: principal and accessory. A defendant can be found liable as a principal if they committed, planned, or ordered a crime. Likewise, a defendant may be found liable as an accessory if they instigated, incited, aided and abetted, or was otherwise complicit in a crime. Many of these forms of liability inevitably involve two or more participants in criminal behavior: the direct perpetrator (who personally commits the crime and is directly liable) and the accessory (who is responsible for making some knowing and substantial contribution to the crime). Domestic criminal law recognizes various forms of complicity liability during the life of a crime, including the roles of accessories before and after the fact. To a certain extent, these forms exist in ICL as well. Domestic penal law systems do not generally recognize criminal liability by omission unless there is some special duty on the part of the defendant to act. This is generally the case in ICL as well.

Because international crimes often involve the participation of multiple individuals over vast expanses of time and space, premising liability on the defendant's relationship, association, or joint action with others has become increasingly important in ICL. In addition, criminal law has long recognized the particular dangers posed by group criminality, where individuals may be influenced and encouraged by their peers and less willing to abandon a criminal enterprise if others are involved. In the United States in particular, prosecutors deploy the doctrine of conspiracy to capture the web of activity associated with organized criminal activity. Internationally, the concept of conspiracy is somewhat disfavored, except with respect to the crime of genocide.[1] Instead, we find a related doctrine of liability in the concept of the joint criminal enterprise, although the two forms present some significant differences.

Forms of liability in ICL find expression in three primary sources of international law: treaty law, customary international law, and general principles of law. Many international treaties, as well as the statutes of the *ad hoc* international tribunals, expressly set forth applicable forms of liability. For example, the Genocide Convention at Article III makes punishable acts of conspiracy, incitement, attempt, and complicity to commit genocide, in addition to the direct commission of genocide. Likewise, the Torture Convention at Article 4(1) obliges states to punish attempts to commit torture and complicity in torture.

Superior responsibility—a doctrine that holds superiors liable for the criminal conduct of their subordinates—was first codified in the 1977 Protocol I to the 1949 Geneva Conventions at Article 86(2), though it was invoked as a mode of liability in the WWII tribunals and well before in historical military justice proceedings. Superior responsibility was later codified in the statutes of the *ad hoc* war crimes tribunals (see Article 7(3) of the Yugoslav Tribunal Statute and Article 6(3) of the Rwanda Tribunal Statute) and the International Criminal Court (see Article 28 of the ICC Statute). The Draft Articles on Prevention and Punishment of Crimes Against Humanity produced by the U.N. International Law Commission in 2019, if converted into a multilateral treaty, would oblige states to "take the necessary measures to ensure that the following acts are offences under its criminal law: (a) committing a crime against

---

[1] The drafters of the Genocide Convention included the crime of conspiracy to commit genocide as a punishable offense because the goal of the Convention was not only to punish perpetrators, but also to prevent acts of genocide. The ICTR Trial Chamber in *Musema,* drawing upon the Convention's *travaux préparatoires* (drafting history) and common law and civil law understandings of conspiracy, defined conspiracy to commit genocide as "an agreement between two or more persons to commit the crime of genocide." *Prosecutor v. Musema,* Case No. ICTR-96-13-A, Judgement & Sentence, ¶ 191 (Jan. 27, 2000). That Trial Chamber held that an accused cannot be convicted of both genocide and conspiracy to commit genocide, as the latter crime merges with the former if genocide is actually committed, *id.* ¶ 198, and that it must be demonstrated that the defendant possessed the specific intent to commit genocide. *Id.* ¶ 192. Musema was ultimately acquitted of conspiracy to commit genocide, because there was insufficient evidence that he conspired with others to commit genocide or reached an agreement to that end. *Id.* ¶ 940.

humanity; (b) attempting to commit such a crime; . . . (c) ordering, soliciting, inducing, aiding, abetting or otherwise assisting in or contributing to the commission or attempted commission of such a crime;" and superior responsibility.[2]

Although these instruments identify applicable forms of responsibility, they provide little in the way of concrete standards for determining when the participation of an individual in the principal crime rises to the level of complicity, conspiracy, or attempt. For this, the modern international criminal tribunals have had to rely on general principles of law, World War II precedent, and other indicia of customary international law to identify more precise elements of proof for establishing the various forms of liability. Furthermore, as is the case in domestic law, the line between these various forms of participation is not a sharp one. As you read the materials in your primary text, consider whether the standards of liability being developed in ICL are consistent with domestic criminal law standards. Where ICL departs from domestic law concepts and standards, ask yourself whether this is attributable to something special about ICL and whether judges are adequately explaining the disparity.

In this chapter, we briefly discuss two forms of responsibility: superior responsibility and complicity (including the concepts of joint criminal enterprise and co-perpetration). As such, we are not offering a complete discussion of the forms of liability used within ICL, nor a thorough discussion of these two specific forms of accessory liability. Instead, we seek to highlight some of the most interesting and controversial challenges facing the development and adjudication of ICL. In particular, these forms of responsibility have the potential to extend liability far beyond the direct perpetrator of international crimes. Consider to what extent these extensions are warranted in light of the collective nature of international crimes and whether ICL, by sanctioning expansive forms of indirect liability, has remained faithful to a foundational principle of the criminal law: individual fault.

A. Superior Responsibility

The doctrine of superior (or command) responsibility originated in international law in the law of armed conflict (international humanitarian law or IHL), although it is often invoked in domestic military justice proceedings. The essence of the doctrine of superior responsibility is that a defendant can be held legally responsible,

---

[2] Draft Articles on Prevention and Punishment of Crimes Against Humanity, with commentaries 2019 art. 6, U.N. Doc. A/74/10, II Y.B. I.L.C. 2019, vol. II. The International Law Commission adopted the Draft Articles at its seventy-first session and submitted them to the General Assembly.

either criminally or civilly, for unlawful acts committed by their subordinates. Superior responsibility attaches if the defendant had actual or constructive knowledge that their subordinates were committing abuses and they did not take necessary and reasonable measures to prevent these abuses or to punish the perpetrators. The theory of liability is thus premised on the commander's failure to exercise powers of command and control over subordinates in the face of a duty to act. The doctrine of superior responsibility in the military context is a direct consequence of the principle of responsible command, which allows military superiors to order their subordinates to engage in acts of violence that—outside of a state of war—would be unlawful. The assumption is that the most effective way to prevent the abuse of this power is to place potential liability on a superior operating within the context of a disciplined military structure. Although originally developed in the military context, the doctrine of superior responsibility applies to both military and civilian superiors, albeit with some distinctions.

1. History of the Doctrine

By way of background, although the concept of superior responsibility can be found in early IHL treaties, it was in the post-World War I period that individual criminal responsibility for command responsibility was first contemplated at the international level. The Commission on the Responsibility of the Authors of the War and on Enforcement of Penalties recommended that the German ex-Kaiser and other leaders be tried for war crimes because they "were cognizant of and could at least have mitigated the barbarities committed during the course of the war. A word from them would have brought about a different method in the action of their subordinates on land, at sea and in the air."[3]

The contemplated trials of responsible World War I leaders, however, never came to fruition. It was not until the post-World War II period that international courts first adjudicated the doctrine of superior responsibility, although neither the Nuremberg Charter nor the Tokyo Charter set forth the elements of the doctrine. With respect to the International Military Tribunal at Nuremberg (IMT), a U.S. proposal to refer to the responsibility for the "omission of a superior officer to prevent war crimes when he knows of, or is on notice as to, their commission or contemplated commission and is in a position to prevent them" was not included in the IMT Charter. Nonetheless, the Nuremberg Tribunal invoked superior responsibility without enunciating the precise elements of the doctrine, no doubt because there was strong evidence of the direct involvement of many accused

[3] See *Report Presented to the Preliminary Peace Conference, in* 1 THE LAW OF WAR: A DOCUMENTARY HISTORY 842, 853–54 (Leon Friedman ed., 1972).

in the design and implementation of the atrocities that were the subject of the Indictment. In contrast, the International Military Tribunal for the Far East (the Tokyo Tribunal) was much more diligent in applying the theory of liability to each defendant pursuant to Count 55 of the Indictment, which read:

> The Defendants . . . being by virtue of their respective offices responsible for securing the observance of the said Conventions and assurances and the Laws and Customs of War in respect of the armed forces in the countries hereinafter named and in respect of many thousands of prisoners of war and civilians then in the power of Japan belonging to the [Allies] deliberately and recklessly disregarded their legal duty to take adequate steps to secure the observance and prevent breaches thereof, and thereby violated the laws of war.

Both military and civilian superiors, including high-level members of the Japanese Cabinet, were convicted by the Tokyo Tribunal solely due to the activities of their subordinates.

In addition to the two International Military Tribunals, a number of prosecutions went forward before military commissions in the Allies' respective zones of occupation. The most famous, and indeed infamous, of the command responsibility trials held in the postwar period concerned General Tomoyuki Yamashita, who was charged with liability under a theory of command responsibility for war crimes committed by Japanese troops in occupied Philippines. General Yamashita's conviction by a U.S. military commission was brought before the U.S. Supreme Court on a petition for the writ of *habeas corpus* to challenge the power of the commission over him. The Supreme Court denied the appeal, finding that the military commission had authority to try General Yamashita and that the Court was without jurisdiction to rule on the substantive issue of the defendant's guilt or innocence. The Court found no issue with the charge asserted, stating that a military commander has "an affirmative duty to take such measures as were within his power and appropriate in the circumstances to protect prisoners of war and the civilian population."[4]

Justices Rutledge and Murphy vigorously dissented from the judgment. In an opinion that has resonance today, Justice Murphy strongly criticized the military commissions that were used to prosecute General Yamashita and the way in which they framed the charge of superior responsibility:

---

[4] *In Re Yamashita,* 327 U.S. 1, 16 (1946).

> [General Yamashita] was rushed to trial under an improper charge, given insufficient time to prepare an adequate defense, deprived of the benefits of some of the most elementary rules of evidence and summarily sentenced to be hanged. In all this needless and unseemly haste there was no serious attempt to charge or to prove that he committed a recognized violation of the laws of war. He was not charged with personally participating in the acts of atrocity or with ordering or condoning their commission. Not even knowledge of these crimes was attributed to him. It was simply alleged that he unlawfully disregarded and failed to discharge his duty as commander to control the operations of the members of his command, permitting them to commit the acts of atrocity. The recorded annals of warfare and the established principles of international law afford not the slightest precedent for such a charge. . . . No one in a position of command in an army, from sergeant to general, can escape those implications. Indeed, the fate of some future President of the United States and his chiefs of staff and military advisers may well have been sealed by this decision. . . . To subject an enemy belligerent to an unfair trial, to charge him with an unrecognized crime, or to vent on him our retributive emotions only antagonizes the enemy nation and hinders the reconciliation necessary to a peaceful world.[5]

General Yamashita was thereafter hanged. The *Yamashita* precedent continues to "cast a long shadow" over subsequent superior responsibility jurisprudence because of lingering concerns about the unfairness of the proceedings against him and whether he was prosecuted under what amounted to a strict liability standard (i.e., a type of liability without fault).[6]

Additional World War II-related prosecutions built on this initial international jurisprudence of individual liability for command responsibility. Most notably, the so-called High Command Case, brought under the authority of Control Council Law No. 10, involved the trial of senior German officers for the execution of civilians and prisoners of war. The tribunal rejected the notion—advanced by the prosecution—that the command responsibility doctrine provided for the *per se* liability of a commander within a chain of command. Rather, the tribunal established the principle that to be held liable, the commander must have had knowledge of abuses by subordinates and must have failed to act in the face of such

[5] *Id.* at 27–28 (Murphy, J., dissenting).

[6] *See* Jenny S. Martinez, *Understanding* Mens Rea *in Command Responsibility: From* Yamashita *to* Blaškić *and Beyond,* 5(3) J. INT'L CRIM. JUSTICE 638 (2007).

knowledge.[7] In the Hostage Case, the tribunal convicted top German officers for war crimes, including the unlawful taking and killing of hostages. The tribunal elaborated on what constitutes negligence with respect to knowledge of the acts of subordinates:

> An army commander will not ordinarily be permitted to deny knowledge of reports received at his headquarters, they being sent there for his special benefit. Neither will he ordinarily be permitted to deny knowledge of happenings within the area of his command while he is present therein. It would strain the credulity of the Tribunal to believe that a high ranking military commander would permit himself to get out of touch with current happenings in the area of his command during wartime.[8]

Courts continue to grapple with the level of information required to put superiors on notice that their subordinates might be committing abuses, which would trigger their duty to inquire and intervene if necessary.

2. Superior Responsibility in Treaty Law

Given these and other precedents, one would have expected the drafters of the Geneva Conventions of 1949—still today the most authoritative sources of IHL—to codify the doctrine of command responsibility. It was only with the drafting of the 1977 Protocols to the Geneva Conventions, however, that a command responsibility standard first entered positive law. Protocol I (which defined international armed conflicts to include those armed conflicts waged for self-determination against colonial domination, alien occupation, and racist regimes) set forth the test for command responsibility in Articles 86 and 87:

> Article 86: Failure to Act
>
> 2. The fact that a breach of the Conventions or of this Protocol was committed by a subordinate does not absolve his superiors from penal or disciplinary responsibility, as the case may be, if they knew, or had information which should have enabled them to conclude in the circumstances at the time, that he was committing or was going to commit such a breach and if they did not take all feasible measures within their power to prevent or repress the breach.

---

[7] The High Command Case, 11 TRIALS OF WAR CRIMINALS BEFORE THE NUREMBERG MILITARY TRIBUNALS UNDER CONTROL COUNCIL LAW NO. 10, 543–544 (1951).

[8] The Hostage Case, 11 *Trials of War Criminals Before the Nuremberg Military Tribunals Under Control Council Law No. 10,* 757, 1260 (1950).

Article 87: Duty of Commanders

1. The High Contracting Parties and the Parties to the conflict shall require military commanders, with respect to members of the armed forces under their command and other persons under their control, to prevent and, where necessary, to suppress and to report to competent authorities breaches of the Conventions and of this Protocol. . . .

3. The High Contracting Parties and Parties to the conflict shall require any commander who is aware that subordinates or other persons under his control are going to commit or have committed a breach of the Conventions or of this Protocol, to initiate such steps as are necessary to prevent such violations of the Conventions or this Protocol, and, where appropriate, to initiate disciplinary or penal action against violators thereof.[9]

Although Protocol I only applies to international armed conflicts, the *ad hoc* tribunals have held that the doctrine of command responsibility exists in non-international armed conflicts as a matter of customary international law, regardless of whether a relevant state party has ratified the 1977 Protocols to the Geneva Conventions.[10]

Subsequent codifications have altered the formulation of the doctrine in subtle but important ways. This doctrinal evolution is most notable with respect to the *mens rea* requirement, resulting in some uncertainty about what level of knowledge is required for a commander to be held liable for the acts of their subordinates. Article 6(3) of the Statute of the Rwanda Tribunal (ICTR), for example, provides:

> The fact that any of the acts [criminalized in] the present Statute was committed by a subordinate does not relieve his or her superior of criminal responsibility if he or she *knew or had reason to know* that the subordinate was about to commit such acts or had done so and the superior failed to take the necessary and reasonable measures to prevent such acts or to punish the perpetrators thereof. (Emphasis added).

---

[9] Protocol Additional to the Geneva Conventions of 12 August 1949, and Relating to the Protection of Victims of International Armed Conflicts (Protocol I), June 8, 1977, 1125 U.N.T.S. 3.

[10] *See Prosecutor v. Hadžihasanović*, Case No. IT-01-47-AR72, Decision on Interlocutory Appeal Challenging Jurisdiction in Relation to Command Responsibility, ¶ 18 (July 16, 2003).

The Security Council in drafting the ICTR Statute thus replaced Protocol I's "had information which should have enabled them to conclude in the circumstances at the time" with the "had reason to know" standard, which sounds more like a traditional negligence test. The ICC Statute includes another, more elaborate, formulation that, for the first time, expressly distinguishes between military and civilian superiors:

> Article 28
>
> Responsibility of commanders and other superiors
>
> In addition to other grounds of criminal responsibility under this Statute for crimes within the jurisdiction of the Court;
>
> (a) A military commander or person effectively acting as a military commander shall be criminally responsible for crimes within the jurisdiction of the Court committed by forces under his or her effective command and control, or effective authority and control as the case may be, as a result of his or her failure to exercise control properly over such forces, where:
>
> (i) That military commander or person either knew or, owing to the circumstances at the time, should have known that the forces were committing or about to commit such crimes; and
>
> (ii) That military commander or person failed to take all necessary and reasonable measures within his or her power to prevent or repress their commission or to submit the matter to the competent authorities for investigation and prosecution.
>
> (b) With respect to superior and subordinate relationships not described in paragraph (a), a superior shall be criminally responsible for crimes within the jurisdiction of the Court committed by subordinates under his or her effective authority and control, as a result of his or her failure to exercise control properly over such subordinates, where:
>
> (i) The superior either knew, or consciously disregarded information which clearly indicated, that the subordinates were committing or about to commit such crimes;
>
> (ii) The crimes concerned activities that were within the effective responsibility and control of the superior; and
>
> (iii) The superior failed to take all necessary and reasonable measures within his or her power to prevent or repress their commission or to submit the

matter to the competent authorities for investigation and prosecution.

The Statute's drafters thus changed the applicable *mens rea* for military and civilian leadership and added a new element (b)(ii) for civilian superiors. As you read cases involving the superior responsibility doctrine, consider the degree to which these alterations affect the prosecution's burden of proof and the defense's ability to mount a defense.

3. Elements of the Contemporary Doctrine

According to most modern formulations as set forth earlier, the doctrine of superior responsibility comprises three primary elements:

1. A relationship of *subordination* exists between the direct perpetrators of the unlawful acts and the superior/defendant.
2. The superior/defendant knew or should have known that their subordinates were committing, had committed, or were about to commit abuses (the *mens rea* element).
3. The superior/defendant failed to take adequate steps to prevent or punish such abuses (the *actus reus* element).

In adjudicating a case against a defendant superior, the finder of fact considers these elements in logical sequence. Thus, the finder of fact's first step is to determine whether the direct perpetrators of the acts that underlie the indictment were subordinates—*de jure* or *de facto*—of the defendant. This prong of the doctrine ensures that any measures undertaken by the defendant to prevent or punish abuses would have reached the individuals accused of directly perpetrating the acts in question. If this prong is satisfied, it must be determined whether the defendant was on notice that their subordinates were committing abuses. It is this knowledge, which may be actual or constructive (i.e., knowledge that can be presumed because it would be acquired through the exercise of due care), that triggers the superior's duty to act. Finally, if the defendant possessed the requisite knowledge, then the finder of fact must determine whether the defendant fulfilled their duty to act in the face of this knowledge. In this regard, the finder of fact must determine whether the defendant did all that was necessary and reasonable under the circumstances to prevent and punish criminal conduct by their subordinates. A defendant is legally responsible for the acts complained of where there is sufficient evidence that they failed to implement appropriate preventative and punitive measures in light of their knowledge that subordinates were committing, or had committed, abuses.

a. Subordination

The requirement of subordination concerns the relationship between a superior and their subordinate and determines the point at which we feel comfortable holding the former accountable for the actions of the latter. If the test is too lax, then we may hold individuals liable for actions over which they effectively had little control (as many argue was the case with Yamashita). If the test is too strict, we risk absolving individuals who had the power to stop ongoing atrocities, and thus send a weak signal of deterrence to current and future leaders.

The International Criminal Tribunal for Yugoslavia (ICTY) found the required relationship of subordination between the defendant and the direct perpetrator(s) if the defendant exercised "effective control" over the individual perpetrator(s).[11] The ICTY required a showing that the defendant had the "material ability to prevent and punish the commission of the offenses" at issue.[12] Under this formulation, a showing of *de jure* (i.e., formal) command over the direct perpetrators within a military hierarchy or formal chain of command is a relevant but not sufficient showing to satisfy this first prong of the doctrine. Thus, even where a commander had the legal authority to control the actions of their subordinates by virtue of their rank or position within a military hierarchy, a finding of liability under the doctrine of command responsibility requires proof that the commander could actually exercise that power. Thus, the Trial Chamber required a showing of *de facto* control in addition to *de jure* command. The theory behind the adoption of this standard is that the "doctrine of command responsibility is ultimately predicated upon the power of the superior to control the acts of his subordinates."[13]

The ICTY developed the effective control standard in the context of allegations that certain defendants' *de jure* positions did not accurately reflect their *de facto* powers to prevent or punish criminal conduct by subordinates. These allegations came from both the prosecution and the defense. For example, in *Delalić,* the prosecution argued that Delalić exercised considerable control and authority within the Čelebići prison camp, even though there was no official instrument or letter of appointment granting him any formal responsibility over the camp. In adopting the effective control

---

[11] *Prosecutor v. Delalić,* Case No. IT-96-21-T, Judgement, ¶ 354 (Nov. 16, 1998).

[12] *Id.* ¶ 378.

[13] *Id.* ¶ 377.

standard, the *Delalić* Trial Chamber noted that such situations are often found in the context of civil wars, in which "previously existing formal structures have broken down and where, during an interim period, the new, possibly improvised, control and command structures may be ambiguous and ill-defined."[14] In other cases, defendants argued that they actually possessed less power than their *de jure* positions would suggest. The ICTY accepted this defense, although it developed a rebuttable presumption that *de facto* control exists where there is *de jure* command. The ICTY thus confirmed that the effective control standard governs the determination of the subordination prong in all superior responsibility situations, including those involving *de jure* commanders whose formal rank or position is uncontested.[15]

Although the *Delalić* tribunal purported to adopt a uniform standard, the doctrine of effective control requires different inquiries and produces different legal strategies with respect to *de facto* and *de jure* command and control. With respect to *de facto* commanders, the effective control standard ensures that individuals lacking formal rank or title, or operating outside of any official or sanctioned chain of command, can still be held liable for abuses committed by individuals under their actual command or control. Conversely, with respect to *de jure* commanders, the effective control standard ensures that they can be held liable for abuses by individuals not formally under their command, but who are nonetheless under their control, such as paramilitary death squad members, civilian defense forces, or even civilians within occupied territory. The effective control standard also ensures that commanders possessing formal command or authority are not held responsible for the criminal conduct of individuals who may be formal subordinates, but who are not under a commander's actual control by virtue of the prevailing circumstances (where, for example, lines of communication or the chain of command have been severed or even, perhaps, where subordinates have gone rogue).

With respect to civilian superiors, the existence of a superior-subordinate relationship may be even more difficult to prove. As noted earlier, the ICC Statute defines subordination in the civilian context in terms of "effective authority and control" rather than "effective command" to reflect the fact that civilian subordinates are not generally considered under the "command" of their superiors. The ICC Prosecutor must also show that the direct perpetrator's actions "concerned activities that were within the effective responsibility and control of the superior." Indeed, political and civilian leaders rarely

---

[14] *Id.* ¶ 610.

[15] *See, e.g., Prosecutor v. Blaškić*, Case No. IT-95-14-T, Judgement, ¶ 302 (Mar. 3, 2000).

possess formal powers of control that match those of military commanders. This does not mean that such individuals cannot exercise high degrees of *de facto* control over their subordinates, but this can be more difficult to prove.[16]

b. Mens Rea

The superior responsibility *mens rea* standard has been formulated in several different ways in the jurisprudence and in treaty law, as discussed above. These permutations span the gamut from those sounding of strict liability to those premised on negligence, recklessness, willful blindness, or even actual knowledge. A more liberal view of the evidence required to show knowledge (for example, an assumption that reports prepared by subordinates were in fact submitted to, and read by, a superior) has the effect of expanding the scope of superior liability. On the other hand, requiring a showing of actual knowledge might be impossible from the perspective of available proof in a wartime situation. Regardless of the standard employed, most tribunals agree that this prong may be satisfied by circumstantial evidence and that knowledge may be inferred. As you read through cases involving superior or command responsibility, pay particular attention to the evidence presented to prove the knowledge requirement, and ask yourself if the tribunal's decision is fair to the accused or creates reasonable expectations and incentives for civilian and military leaders in the future.

The ICC Statute introduced a significant alteration with respect to the knowledge requirement for cases involving a civilian versus a military superior. For a military superior, the knowledge requirement is a form of the familiar "knew or should have known" test; for a civilian superior, the burden on the prosecutor is higher, requiring a showing of actual knowledge or "conscious disregard" of information that "clearly indicated" subordinate wrongdoing. The assumption behind this different standard is that military organizations have more formal and more efficient channels of communication than civilian organizations, and thus it is reasonable to place the more onerous "should have known" test on a military commander. This also imposes a greater incentive on military commanders to seek out information about the actions of their subordinates so as to ensure their adherence to the laws of armed conflict.

---

16 *See Prosecutor v. Akayesu,* Case No. ICTR-96-4, Judgement, ¶ 691 (Sept. 2, 1998) (acquitting defendant mayor on superior responsibility counts for lack of evidence that he controlled *interahamwe* death squads operative in his commune).

c. Actus Reus *(Omission)*

The doctrine of superior responsibility premises liability on an omission: The superior is found liable for failing to act when under a duty to do so. As noted by the ICTY in *Halilović:*

> Command responsibility is responsibility for an omission. The commander is responsible for the failure to perform an act required by international law. This omission is culpable because international law imposes an affirmative duty on superiors to prevent and punish crimes committed by their subordinates.[17]

Under the doctrine of superior responsibility, the defendant superior is thus liable for their own omissions and not vicariously liable for the acts of their subordinates.

This third prong of the command responsibility doctrine is formulated in the disjunctive, providing that a superior is liable when they either fail to prevent abuses *ex ante* or fail to punish them after the fact. That said, the failure to prevent and the failure to punish criminal conduct are related inquiries. A failure to punish infractions may be viewed as a failure to prevent by essentially giving the "green light" to future abuses and contributing to a climate of impunity. Determining what concrete measures the defendant should have taken is intimately connected to the degree of actual power possessed by the superior, so this prong must be established on a case-by-case basis.

Superior responsibility should not be confused with liability for ordering an act, which is a form of direct, not accessorial, liability. The act of ordering usually occurs in the context of a superior-subordinate relationship as well, although proof of *de jure* subordination is not required.[18] A superior prosecuted for ordering a subordinate to commit a crime, however, is held liable for their own affirmative act—the issuing of an unlawful order—not an omission.[19]

---

[17] *Prosecutor v. Halilović,* Case No. IT-01-48-T, Judgement, ¶ 54 (Nov. 16, 2005).

[18] The ICTY and ICTR differed over whether the charge of ordering a crime requires a showing of a superior-subordinate relationship. The ICTR presumed such a relationship in the *Akayesu* case: "Ordering implies a superior-subordinate relationship between the person giving the order and the one executing it. In other words, the person in a position of authority uses it to convince another to commit an offense." *Prosecutor v. Akayesu,* Case No. ICTR-96-4-T, Judgement, ¶ 483 (Sept. 2, 1990). In contrast, the ICTY held that "no formal superior-subordinate relationship is required for a finding of 'ordering' so long as it is demonstrated that the accused possessed the authority to order." *Prosecutor v. Kordić & Čerkez,* Case No. IT-95-14/2, Judgement, ¶ 388 (Feb. 26, 2001).

[19] The doctrine of superior orders works in tandem with direct liability for ordering abuses to ensure that criminal responsibility exists up the chain of command. As formulated by the Nuremberg Charter, the doctrine of superior orders provides that "the fact that a Defendant acted pursuant to order of his Government or of a superior

That said, language within the jurisprudence differs on whether the superior is being prosecuted and punished for the crime ultimately committed by the subordinate (as a form of derivative liability) or for their own dereliction of duty in issuing the order.

This discussion of the elements of superior responsibility confirms that the doctrine is not predicated on a strict liability standard. If the prosecution fails to establish any of the three elements, a defendant should be exonerated. This should occur where there is insufficient evidence that the direct perpetrators were the defendant's subordinates or under the defendant's effective control, or where there is insufficient evidence that the defendant had knowledge, either actual or constructive, of subordinates' abuses. Likewise, acquittal is appropriate where the evidence indicates that the defendant undertook sufficient measures to prevent and punish criminal conduct given their level of command and other relevant circumstances. In any of these situations, a defendant should be exonerated even when the crimes were committed.

This last scenario was in fact the basis of the acquittal of Jean-Pierre Bemba by the ICC Appeals Chamber. The Prosecutor's theory of the case was that Bemba—who was billeted in the Democratic Republic of Congo (DRC)—allowed his subordinates in the Central African Republic to rape and pillage as a form of payment for their services. The Trial Chamber found Bemba guilty as a superior for the criminal acts of his subordinates. In a controversial opinion, the Appeals Chamber reversed, holding that although Bemba did little to prevent or punish the crimes committed by his subordinates, he had not failed, as the Trial Chamber found, to undertake "all necessary and reasonable" measures. As noted by the Appeals Chamber, "the measures taken by a commander cannot be faulted merely because of shortfalls in their execution."[20] Other aspects of the appellate opinion suggested that it is more difficult to hold remote commanders liable for the depredations of their subordinates—a claim that is not borne out by modern forms of warfare and that suggests ways that superiors can avoid liability by simply absenting themselves from the battlespace.

---

shall not free him from responsibility, but may be considered in mitigation of punishment if the Tribunal determines that justice so requires." Charter of the International Military Tribunal of Aug. 8, 1945, art. 8, *annexed to* Agreement for the Prosecution and Punishment of the Major War Criminals of the European Axis, Aug. 8, 1945, 59 Stat. 1544. The ICC Statute at Article 33 provides that superior orders may constitute a full defense where the defendant was under a legal obligation to obey orders, the person did not know that the order was unlawful, and the order was not manifestly unlawful. This provision will be applicable mainly in the war crimes context, as the Article dictates that orders to commit genocide or crimes against humanity are manifestly unlawful as a matter of law.

[20] *Prosecutor v. Jean-Pierre Bemba*, Case No. ICC-01/05-01/08 A, Judgment, ¶ 170 (June 8, 2018).

As important as the doctrine of command responsibility is in ICL, the *ad hoc* tribunals expressed a distinct preference for convicting defendants on the basis of some form of direct liability (ordering offenses, complicity in offenses, and so on) if both direct and superior responsibility had been proven. As the ICTY held in *Blaškić:*

> the Appeals Chamber considers that, in relation to a particular count, it is not appropriate to convict under both Article 7(1) [listing forms of direct responsibility] and Article 7(3) [superior responsibility] of the [ICTY] Statute. Where both [forms of] responsibility are alleged under the same count, and where the legal requirements pertaining to both of these heads of responsibility are met, a Trial Chamber should enter a conviction on the basis of Article 7(1) only, and consider the accused's superior position as an aggravating factor in sentencing.[21]

Given their importance, it is to forms of direct and accomplice responsibility that we now turn. Because of the difficulty of proving effective control and the knowledge element of the doctrine of superior responsibility, prosecutors before the *ad hoc* international criminal tribunals increasingly utilized the theory of the joint criminal enterprise to address crimes committed by multiple individuals, even individuals within a formal chain of command where the doctrine of superior responsibility would also apply. Rather than holding superiors liable for failing to control their subordinates in a vertical fashion, the theory of the joint criminal enterprise allows—under certain circumstances—for the lateral imposition of liability on all members of a group acting with a common purpose when any member commits a criminal act. In the same vein, the ICC Prosecutor has relied on the concept of co-perpetration, as drawn from German penal law, which holds all parties to a criminal course of conduct liable for their individual contributions.

B. Complicity, Joint Criminal Enterprise, and Co-Perpetration

Most international crimes are committed as part of an armed conflict or large-scale atrocities. Such crimes are often the result of concerted action by groups of individuals. Sometimes these groups are formally organized (within a state bureaucracy, military organization, or insurrectionist movement); other times they are less formal or form more spontaneously. How should the law ascribe individual criminal responsibility when various members of a group have contributed to the commission of international crimes in

---

[21] *Prosecutor v. Blaškić,* Case No. IT-95-14, Judgement, ¶ 91 (July 29, 2004).

differing degrees? Which members of such organizations should be held criminally liable when other members are involved in international crimes? When should members of a group be liable for acts that were not part of the goal of a group, but were nonetheless committed in the context of concerted action toward that goal? In addition, how wide should the net be cast? We have so far mentioned the principal actor (i.e., the person who pulls the proverbial trigger) and that person's military or civilian superior. What about colleagues? Support staff? The architect of the concentration camp? The driver who transports civilians to be executed? The person who provides financing to the organization? It is for these scenarios that the doctrine of complicity has been developed.

1. Complicity

The Allied Powers at the end of World War II were confronted directly with the challenge of applying individual accountability for atrocities made possible by organized and cooperating individuals. To respond to this phenomenon, the U.S. negotiators in particular argued for the inclusion of complicity and conspiracy as applicable forms of responsibility.[22] The reference to complicity liability in the Nuremberg charter was, like most of its provisions, general: that "[l]eaders, organizers, instigators and accomplices participating in the formulation or execution of a common plan or conspiracy to commit any of the foregoing crimes [crimes against the peace, war crimes, and crimes against humanity] are responsible for all acts performed by any persons in execution of such plan." The Nuremberg and Tokyo tribunals also recognized a substantive crime of conspiracy to prepare, initiate, and wage aggressive war, although this charge remained controversial given that it was unique to U.S. law.

The World War II-related judgments adopted a liberal view of the *actus reus* of complicity liability, an approach that has been generally followed by the present-day international criminal tribunals. For example, even the provision of moral support conveyed by the mere presence of an individual during the commission of a

[22] The United States also argued for the recognition of the concept of criminal organizations. According to this theory, the Prosecution would seek a declaration from the Nuremberg Tribunal on the illegality of indicted organizations—such as the *Schutzstaffel* (SS), an elite paramilitary unit, and the Gestapo, the secret police. Each member of those organizations would be subject to arrest and prosecution before national courts based solely upon their membership in a convicted organization. The Tribunal's declaratory judgment would be *res judicata* in individual proceedings against organization members. The burden would then shift to the individual defendants to prove either that membership in the organization was involuntary or that he did not know the organization's criminal object and purpose. This doctrine of collective responsibility was adopted but underutilized in the post-WWII period and has not been revived with the rest of the Nuremberg legacy.

crime, without any other specific supportive act, may be sufficient to trigger liability if the presence of the accused provides encouragement to those directly involved in the criminal act.[23] This was the position taken by the ICTR Trial Chamber in *Akayesu,* which found that the presence and verbal encouragement of Akayesu—a local leader of considerable influence—during the rape and mistreatment of civilians was sufficient to impose accessory liability on him for those crimes.[24] The standard adopted by today's tribunals is that an individual who provides knowing assistance that has "a substantial effect" on the commission of the crime may be found liable for aiding and abetting the underlying criminal act. There is general agreement on this formulation of the test for complicity liability; the challenge faced by the tribunals is determining what actions have a "substantial" effect on the outcome of the crime.

The *mens rea* required to hold an accessory liable is also somewhat contested and has attracted considerable academic debate. The first issue is whether the accomplice must have the same *mens rea* as the principal. This question is particularly acute in the case of genocide. In other words, must the prosecution demonstrate that an accessory to genocide had the specific intent to destroy, in whole or in part, a protected group of people? The jurisprudence is now clear that there need not be proof that an accomplice possessed such specific intent to be convicted of complicity in genocide. Some prominent commentators, however, argue that only those accomplices who have genocidal intent should be held liable for genocide.[25] The argument for not requiring specific intent is threefold. First, it is argued that broadening the scope of liability for genocide beyond those with genocidal intent creates greater deterrence and appropriately punishes individuals who knowingly contribute to international crimes. Second, this approach captures the complexity of international crimes by recognizing that they are more difficult to commit without the assistance of others. Third, it creates an additional incentive for potential accomplices to ascertain the nature of the activities they are assisting or supporting since they may still be prosecuted for genocide even if they themselves do not possess genocidal intent. The other side to this argument asserts that broadening the scope of liability runs the risk of diluting the special stigma associated with genocide. By contrast, narrowing the scope of liability by requiring genocidal intent for accomplices as well as

---

[23] See the discussion of related cases during the World War II era involving mere presence in *Prosecutor v. Furundžija*, Case No. IT-95-17/1-T, Judgement, ¶¶ 205–209 (Dec. 10, 1998) (citing to the *Synagogue* and *Pig-cart Parade* cases).

[24] *Akayesu, supra,* ¶ 693.

[25] William Schabas argues that genocidal intent should be required to hold someone liable as an accessory to genocide. *See* WILLIAM A. SCHABAS, GENOCIDE IN INTERNATIONAL LAW 259 (2000).

direct perpetrators preserves the special nature of genocide and is consistent with the distinction ICL makes between crimes against humanity and genocide.

A second, and related, point of contention involves the nature of complicity *mens rea* more generally. Most of the ICL jurisprudence suggests that the prosecutor must demonstrate that the accomplice acted with the "knowledge" that their actions would contribute to the underlying criminal conduct.[26] The ICC Statute, however, has adopted what appears to be more of a "purpose" standard. Specifically, Article 25(3) limits aiding and abetting liability to cases in which the suspect acts "for the purpose of facilitating the commission of such a crime," indicating that more than mere knowledge may be required. This distinction is particularly acute in two circumstances: corporate complicity and the potential liability of states for giving assistance to armed groups. Plaintiffs in Alien Tort Statute (ATS) cases have deployed theories of complicity drawn from international criminal law to sue corporations engaged in joint ventures with repressive states. Corporate defendants regularly argue that the ICC Statute standard should govern this inquiry. Likewise, there are situations in which one nation provides weapons or other *matériel* to another national army, or rebel group, which then commits international crimes. It has been argued that the state providing assistance might be liable under principles of state responsibility if it knows that the assistance provided will be used to commit atrocities. This is the standard adopted by the Arms Trade Treaty, which states at Article 6(3) that:

> A State Party shall not authorize any transfer of conventional arms covered under Article 2(1) or of items covered under Article 3 or Article 4, if it has knowledge at the time of authorization that the arms or items would be used in the commission of genocide, crimes against humanity, grave breaches of the Geneva Conventions of 1949, attacks directed against civilian objects or civilians protected as such, or other war crimes as defined by international agreements to which it is a Party.[27]

These issues continue to be debated.

---

[26] *See, e.g.*, *Prosecutor v. Charles Ghankay Taylor*, Case No. SCSL-03-01-A, Judgment (Sept. 26, 2013).

[27] Arms Trade Treaty, Apr. 2, 2013, 3013 U.N.T.S. The treaty now has attracted over 100 parties.

2. Joint Criminal Enterprise

The concept of joint criminal enterprise (JCE), which in some jurisdictions is referred to as the common purpose doctrine,[28] has been present since the dawn of modern ICL at Nuremberg and Tokyo, but is still the subject of controversy and doctrinal uncertainty. The modern articulation of JCE emerged from an ICTY Appeals Chamber decision. The Chamber identified three categories of JCE liability: The first category is sometimes referred to as basic JCE liability, the second category is systematic JCE liability, and the third category is an extended form of JCE liability.[29] The first category describes an enterprise in which all participants share the same *mens rea* with respect to the criminal activity. The ICTY described the *mens rea* of the first category of JCE as follows: "the accused must both intend the commission of the crime and intend to participate in a common plan aimed at its commission."[30] Thus, an individual who drives soldiers to a village knowing and intending that the civilian villagers will be killed can be found liable under this first category. The second category is illustrated with the prosecution of those involved in the Nazi concentration camps. The *mens rea* for the second category of JCE is intentional participation in an organized system or institution undertaking some criminal purpose. Courts have been particularly quick to imply the intent to further the criminal enterprise in cases involving individuals with authority in the organization.

The third category is the most controversial, and has been the subject of differing, and confusing, doctrinal pronouncements by contemporary ICL tribunals. This extended form of liability attributes to members of an organization responsibility for an act of another member of that organization that was not part of the original common plan, but that was a "natural and foreseeable" consequence of implementing the common plan. The ICTY Appeals Chamber gave the following example of the third category of JCE liability:

> An example of [category three liability] would be a common, shared intention on the part of a group to forcibly remove members of one ethnicity from their town, village or region (to effect "ethnic cleansing") with the consequence that, in

---

[28] The common purpose doctrine is also found in several of the modern terrorism treaties. For example, a person commits an offense under the Terrorist Bombing Convention when they "in any other way contribute[s] to the commission of any offenses by a group of persons acting with a common purpose." Article 2(3), International Convention for the Suppression of Terrorist Bombings, Jan. 12, 1998, G.A. Res. 52/164, U.N. Doc. A/RES/52/, reprinted at 37 I.L.M. 249 (1998). This common purpose liability exists where the person either has the intent to further the general criminal activity or purpose of the group or plays some role with the knowledge of the intention of the group to commit the offence.

[29] *Prosecutor v. Tadić*, Case No. IT-94-1-A, Judgement (July 15, 1999).

[30] *Prosecutor v. Brdjanin*, Case No. IT-99-36-A, Judgement, ¶ 365 (April 3, 2007).

> the course of doing so, one or more of the victims is shot and killed. While murder may not have been explicitly acknowledged to be part of the common design, it was nevertheless foreseeable that the forcible removal of civilians at gunpoint might well result in the deaths of one or more of those civilians. Criminal responsibility may be imputed to all participants within the common enterprise where the risk of death occurring was both a predictable consequence of the execution of the common design and the accused was either reckless or indifferent to that risk.[31]

Does the requirement of foreseeability have any limiting power? Or, in a situation of mass violence or armed conflict, are all international crimes foreseeable? Consider the example presented above. What other international crimes are the natural and foreseeable result of a campaign of ethnic cleansing? Is the commission of rape, torture, or genocide natural and foreseeable under these circumstances?

In a subsequent opinion, the appeals chamber clarified the *mens rea* required for the third category of JCE:

> [T]he accused can only be held responsible for a crime outside the common purpose if, under the circumstances of the case: (i) it was *foreseeable* that such a crime might be perpetrated by one or other members of the group and (ii) the accused *willingly took that risk (dolus eventualis)*. The crime must be shown to have been foreseeable to the accused in particular.[32]

The ICTY has suggested that in the case of the third category of JCE, the prosecutor does not need to prove that there was a specific agreement to further the common purpose between the accused and the person who committed the foreseeable act. In other words, the link between the accused and the person who committed the underlying act may be quite tenuous. The potential expansiveness of the doctrine has led defense counsel to describe the doctrine as "Just Convict Everyone."

JCE and the common purpose doctrine are designed in part to capture the organizational reality of mass atrocities. Although the first two categories of JCE liability will raise difficult issues concerning the type of assistance that triggers liability, it is the third category that has led some ICL experts and human rights advocates to argue for a narrowing of the doctrine to better reflect principles of personal fault. As you read through JCE decisions, ask yourself whether the doctrine has become too expansive by holding

---

[31] *Tadić, supra,* ¶ 204.

[32] *Brdjanin, supra,* ¶ 365 (emphasis in original).

individuals responsible not only for acts they did not commit, but for acts committed outside of the common plan by individuals they may not even know. In the alternative, is such expansive liability appropriate when addressing mass atrocities, particularly if it may increase the reluctance of individuals to join such enterprises?

3. Co-Perpetration

The ICC has not adopted the concept of JCE. Instead, as set out in Article 25(3) of the Rome Statute concerning individual criminal responsibility, a person may be found guilty if they commit "a crime, whether as an individual, jointly with another or through another person, regardless of whether that other person is criminally liable." The ICC in its first judgment, which was against Thomas Lubanga Dyilo for crimes committed in the DRC, identified the following elements of co-perpetration: (1) more than one person (2) agreed to a common plan (3) that includes an "element of criminality" and (4) the accused made an "essential contribution" to that plan.[33] The Trial Chamber articulated the *mens rea* requirement as follows: there must be awareness on the part of the accused of a risk that a consequence (i.e. the criminal activity) will occur in the ordinary course of events. Note that the requirement is not that the consequence "may" occur, but that it "will" occur. This presents a difficult challenge to the Prosecutor who must prove that there was a high level of certainty that the criminal consequences of the "essential contribution" by the accused would occur.

C. Conclusion

As you read through the materials in your ICL course, ask yourself what differences, if any, exist between JCE and co-perpetration as developed by the ICC, and what the differences are between those forms of liability and, for example, superior responsibility. When might one doctrine or another result in a different outcome? You might also take note of the influence that ordinary criminal law concepts have had on this component of ICL given how well developed these doctrines are under domestic law. Whereas the substantive rules developed by the tribunals (e.g., when it comes to the elements of international crimes) is often quite influential in domestic legal systems when they play host to war crimes trials, the influence flows in the opposite direction when it comes to forms of responsibility given the degree to which the international criminal tribunals have adapted these concepts from domestic law for the types of crime bases that come before them.

---

[33] *Prosecutor v. Lubanga*, Case No. ICC-01/04-01/06, Judgment Pursuant to Article 74 of the Statute ¶¶ 976–1018 (Mar. 14, 2012).

Chapter 11

THE ARCHITECTURE OF INTERNATIONAL CRIMINAL LAW

The preceding materials have discussed the range of jurisdictional theories and sources of law that undergird the field of international criminal law (ICL). The norms in question—including prohibitions on genocide, crimes against humanity, war crimes, terrorism, torture, and (to a lesser extent) the crime of aggression—can be litigated in a range of fora: international, regional, and domestic. In addition to giving rise to criminal charges, these norms can also animate civil claims by victims and survivors against responsible individuals, legal entities, and sovereigns.

This chapter considers the global architecture of international justice as a whole and the various options for the enforcement of ICL norms with reference to the matrix of accountability set forth below. This matrix is organized along two axes: the first (x) is premised on the type of tribunal (international, hybrid, regional, or domestic); the second (y) compares the types of justice institutions and legal authorities that are available. The white boxes in the matrix indicate criminal liability options, the pale gray indicate civil liability options. This chapter uses the example of Syria, which has been characterized by massive international crimes and an almost impenetrable impunity, to illustrate the various litigation options available against individual perpetrators as opposed to a sovereign state.

Virtually every international crime that forms part of the international penal code has been committed in and around Syria.[1] The Syrian people have witnessed and been subjected to deliberate, indiscriminate, and disproportionate attacks; the misuse of conventional, unconventional, and improvised weapon systems; industrial-grade custodial abuses in a vast network of formal and informal prisons;[2] unrelenting siege warfare; the denial of humanitarian aid and what appears to be the deliberate use of starvation as a weapon of war; sexual violence, including the sexual enslavement of Yezidi women and girls trafficked from Iraq and the sexual torture of detained men and boys;[3] and the intentional

---

[1] *See* Beth Van Schaack, *Mapping War Crimes in Syria*, 92 INT'L L. STUD. 282 (2016).

[2] *See* Independent International Commission of Inquiry on the Syrian Arab Republic, *Out of Sight, Out of Mind: Deaths in Detention in the Syrian Arab Republic*, U.N. Doc. A/HRC/31/CRP.1 (Feb. 3, 2016).

[3] *See, e.g.*, Special Report of the Office of the Special Representative of the Secretary-General on Sexual Violence in Conflict, *Submission to the Security Council*

destruction of irreplaceable cultural property. Thousands of Syrians are missing, many of them victims of enforced disappearances.[4]

Matrix of Accountability

Respondent/Defendant		Tribunal		
		International	Hybrid/Regional	Domestic
	Individual Perpetrators	International Criminal Court, *ad hoc* tribunals	Special Court for Sierra Leone, Extraordinary African Chambers	Domestic international crimes statutes (e.g., 18 U.S.C. § 2340, German Code of Crimes Against International Law (CCAIL))
	Individual Perpetrators	Ø	Ø	Alien Tort Statute, *partie civile* system
	The Sovereign State	Ø	Ø	Ø
	The Sovereign State	International Court of Justice, human rights treaty bodies (e.g., Committee Against Torture)	African Court of Human & People's Rights, European Court of Human Rights	U.S. Foreign Sovereign Immunities Act or equivalent

Civil Liability (shaded) | Criminal Liability (unshaded)

Even children are not spared.[5] The long-standing taboo against the use of chemical weapons has been repeatedly flouted in ways that

Committee pursuant to resolutions 1267 (1999), 1989 (2011) and 2253 (2015) concerning ISIL (Da'esh), Al Qaida and Associated Individuals, Groups, Undertakings and Entities, U.N. Doc. S/2016/1090 (Dec. 2016).

[4] *See* Independent International Commission of Inquiry on the Syrian Arab Republic, *Without a Trace: Enforced Disappearance in Syria* (Dec. 19, 2013).

[5] *See* Independent International Commission of Inquiry on the Syrian Arab Republic, *"They have Erased the Dreams of my Children": Children's Rights in the Syrian Arab Republic*, U.N. Doc. A/HRC/43/CRP.6 (Jan. 12, 2020).

constitute a double violation of IHL: first, the use of a prohibited weapon, and second, the deliberate targeting of civilians. Finally, the sectarian nature of the violence has raised the specter of genocide against ethno-religious minorities. Indeed, then-U.S. Secretary of State John Kerry announced in 2016 that the Islamic State of Iraq and the Levant (ISIL) was committing genocide against a number of minority groups in Syria and Iraq. Violence in the region has contributed to the biggest exodus of refugees since World War II. Given this enormous crime base, the remainder of this chapter explores the different routes to accountability through the aforementioned matrix and the various advantages presented by, and the challenges encumbering, justice options within each of these cells when it comes to the situation in Syria.

A. International Criminal Courts

1. The International Criminal Court

Starting with the top left corner of the matrix: Early in the conflict, it was clear that events in Syria would easily surpass the International Criminal Court's gravity threshold. As Syria is not a party to the Rome Statute, the ICC would have plenary jurisdiction over international crimes in Syria only in the event that the U.N. Security Council effectuates a referral of the situation to the Court.[6] Even before a concrete referral proposal emerged, many states began to express their support for an ICC referral in their Council interventions. So too did the Commission of Inquiry established by the U.N. Human Rights Council—which on multiple occasions recommended a referral or the establishment of a dedicated *ad hoc* tribunal—and two successive U.N. High Commissioners for Human Rights, South African Navanethem Pillay and Prince Zeid Ra'ad Zeid Al Hussein of Jordan. Likewise, the Working Group on Enforced or Involuntary Disappearances also concluded that the practice of enforced disappearances in Syria constitutes a policy of crimes against humanity and requested the U.N. Security Council to consider an ICC referral.[7] A number of human rights non-governmental organizations echoed this call.

In January 2013, two years after the start of the pro-democracy revolution against Bashar Al Assad's government and the government's brutal response, Switzerland began pushing formally

---

[6] In the event of a political transition, Syria could ratify the Rome Treaty and also accord the Court retroactive jurisdiction through Article 12(3), which allows for an *ad hoc* acceptance of jurisdiction. The Palestinian Authority, Côte d'Ivoire, and Ukraine have all utilized Article 12(3) declarations in this fashion to expand—and control—the temporal jurisdiction of the Court.

[7] *See* Report of the Working Group on Enforced or Involuntary Disappearances, U.N. Doc. A/HRC/27/49, ¶¶ 32, 54, 99 (Aug. 4, 2014).

for an ICC referral by circulating a letter with more than fifty sovereign signatories calling for the Council to refer the matter to the Court. The letter emphasized that although

> accountability is primarily a national responsibility and that the role of international criminal justice is complementary, . . . the Syrian Arab Republic has, so far, not reacted to repeated calls from the international community to ensure accountability through a national procedure that needs to be credible, fair and independent in order to bring all perpetrators of alleged crimes to justice. Without accountability . . . there will be no sustainable peace in Syria.[8]

Absent a referral, the Swiss suggested the Council could "at the very least" announce its intention to refer the situation to the Court unless an accountability process is established "in a timely manner." Russia responded with a statement criticizing the Swiss letter as "ill-timed and counterproductive." The United States did not join the letter, but is not on record opposing the Swiss-led campaign either.

In August 2013, the Syrian government used chemical weapons in Rif Damascus. France initiated a draft resolution that would have condemned the attack; obliged Syria to dismantle its chemical weapons program under international supervision; imposed a chemical, biological, and nuclear weapons embargo; and referred the situation to the ICC. That draft did not move forward, and the international community instead embraced a disarmament plan proposed by Russia. In January 2014, the "Caesar photos" (so named because they were smuggled out of the country by a defector code-named Caesar), which documented the death-by-torture of thousands of detainees in Syrian prisons, came to light. Members of the Security Council viewed the Caesar photos soon after in an informal setting organized by France. The horror depicted in the photos re-galvanized the ICC referral movement. France again grasped the pen. At the time its renewed resolution was being considered, the war in Syria was in its fourth year, and had devolved into a full-scale humanitarian catastrophe. France's initiative earned strong international support from many states and civil society actors. The draft referral resolution boasted sixty-five sovereign co-sponsors by the time it went to a vote—almost a third of the U.N. membership. The United States originally demurred, taking note of the impulse to trigger the ICC and expressing sympathy for the objectives that animated such calls. It urged accountability in vague language, but

---

[8] *See* Letter to H.E. Mr. Mohammad Masood Khan, President of the Security Council for the month of January 2013, from the Permanent Mission of Switzerland to the United Nations (Jan. 14, 2013).

refrained from endorsing any referral proposals or foreclosing any options. The United States had also quietly floated ideas about various alternative frameworks for accountability, such as an *ad hoc* hybrid tribunal or dedicated war crimes chamber that could be established on the periphery of the conflict or in a liberated zone. Eventually, however, it joined the co-sponsors of the French draft.

Once the resolution was put to a vote, it garnered the support of thirteen Council members but also triggered a double veto from Russia and China. As luck would have it, nine of the ten members elected to the Security Council happened to be ICC members as well (all but Rwanda). Russia explained the exercise of its veto (its fourth by that time) by invoking the ghost of Libya, arguing that the draft resolution was a thinly veiled attempt to engage in another armed intervention as had been allowed in an earlier similar resolution involving Libya. Russia also insisted that putting the resolution to a vote threatened to undermine P-5 unity, which was already at a new low. In explaining its veto, China reiterated its long-standing reservations about referring situations to the Court and urged states to recommit to seeking a political solution to the crisis. It also warned of the risk of such a referral undermining the peace process: "to [f]orcibly refer the situation in Syria to the Court in the current environment is not conducive either to building trust among all parties in Syria or to an early resumption of the negotiations in Geneva." Other delegates insisted there was no peace process underway to undermine. Syria was invited to speak and invoked the privilege of complementarity, arguing the government was adequately prosecuting war crimes domestically—a laughable claim.

Although the ICC cannot exercise the full scope of its jurisdiction over events in Syria because of the opposition of Russia and China, there are nonetheless several subsets of crimes related to Syria over which ICC jurisdiction currently exists even without a Security Council referral. First are crimes committed by ICC member state nationals who are operating in Syria. This would include so-called foreign fighters who—motivated by ideology, religion, kinship, or even love—flocked to the region to join the fight. Second are crimes committed on the territory of other ICC member states—both near and far—with a nexus to the Syrian conflict. This might include crimes with an impact on neighboring Jordan, which is an ICC member state, or acts of terrorism committed by members of ISIL in Europe. Third are crimes committed on the territory of other states already before the Court (notably Libya), by individuals also active in Syria, such as ISIL's leadership. Civil society organizations and legal chambers have filed a number of submissions with the Office of the Prosecutor (OTP) advocating that she engage on Syria on the basis of these various jurisdictional angles. So far, however, the

Prosecutor has declined to move forward, indicating (at least for now) that "the jurisdictional basis for opening a preliminary examination into [alleged ISIL crimes] is too narrow at this stage."[9] Finally, given that the Council members have been united in their opposition to ISIL, there is speculation that the Security Council might be persuaded to refer "the situation involving ISIL" to the Court. Such a referral could encompass either the organization itself, untethered from any territorial space, or the transboundary statelet that once encompassed ISIL's self-proclaimed caliphate in Iraq and Syria.

2. *Ad Hoc* and Hybrid Options

It was originally hoped that the establishment of the ICC as a permanent judicial institution with potentially global reach would obviate the need to establish additional *ad hoc* tribunals in connection with particular conflicts. This presumption has proven to be misguided. It is increasingly recognized that the ICC cannot be expected to prosecute all, or even a substantial percentage, of the atrocities ravaging our planet either because of jurisdictional gaps, the unwillingness of the Security Council to refer atrocity situations—such as Syria—to the Court, or basic resource constraints. Indeed, given the duration, scale, complexity, and nature of the Syrian conflict, there is no way that the ICC could take the lead on handling the administration of justice at the international level, even if the principle of complementarity were fully functioning. Although the Court is now operating at peak capacity, its jurisdiction remains incomplete and its resources limited. Furthermore, the Court is plagued by challenges to its legitimacy, erratic state cooperation, and persistent perceptions of inefficacy and inefficiency. Given this confluence of realities, there is an enduring need for the international community to create, enable, and support additional accountability mechanisms. *Ad hoc* tribunals dedicated to particular situation countries thus remain a viable and valuable mechanism for increasing the prospects for justice.

Given the enduring blockages within the Security Council, there are mechanisms available to establish an *ad hoc* tribunal dedicated to Syria without the Security Council or the consent of Syria. These include the establishment of a tribunal through the U.N. General Assembly or an international agreement among supportive and specially-affected states to build an institution akin to the Nuremberg Tribunal. The latter institution could be conceptualized as a membership organization operating on the basis of a pooled repository of states' individual jurisdictional competencies, or it could enjoy an independent international legal personality exercising a

---

[9] ICC, *Statement of the Prosecutor of the International Criminal Court, Fatou Bensouda, on the Alleged Crimes Committed by ISIS* (Apr. 8, 2015).

form of universalist international jurisdiction working on behalf of a subset of the international community. These proposals enjoy some precedent in international law, but run up against legal arguments—which remain controversial—about the propriety of prosecuting potential perpetrators without the nationality state's consent.

Moving across the top row of our matrix, any of these models could be undertaken by the League of Arab States, creating a regional criminal court like the one being contemplated for the African Union. In addition, these institutions could all be hybridized with Syrian elements. Multiple proposals for establishing such a tribunal were floated and were considered, to varying degrees, by members of the international community, both before and after the failed ICC referral effort. None has gathered sufficient traction to date.

B. Domestic Criminal Trials

The top right cell of our matrix is devoted to criminal trials in domestic courts. Ideally, ICL cases should be brought in the domestic courts in the impacted country itself. The proximity to the events in question enjoyed by domestic courts ensures greater societal visibility to maximize the expressive function of the law, to tap into the potential of such proceedings to help instantiate the rule of law, and to prevent impunity and an often-concomitant recurrence of violence. On a practical level, local proceedings also facilitate access to evidence and for a more active engagement with survivors and witnesses. Syrian courts, however, have not emerged as engines of accountability; instead, they are being deployed as tools of oppression against the opposition. Where courts in the affected country are foreclosed, as in Syria, legal processes in the courts of other countries offer an advantageous second-best alternative.

When it comes to events in Syria, European and regional domestic courts have emerged as fertile grounds for justice. A number of domestic trials involving events and actors in Syria are underway, featuring a range of criminal charges and fact patterns. These cases fall into three general buckets. One set of cases involves charges under anti-terrorism legislation or laws criminalizing participation in foreign wars—effectively crimes against the sovereign. These defendants are generally ISIL members and former foreign fighters who have returned to the comforts of Europe. States are highly motivated to prosecute such cases because they perceive these defendants as posing an acute national security threat, both from the perspective of bringing the violence home but also as potential recruiters and radicalizers. A second subset of cases involves individuals who stand accused of committing international crimes *stricto sensu*. These latter prosecutions are enabled by the incorporation of international criminal law—and particularly the prohibitions against war crimes—into domestic penal codes, a global legislative trend occasioned in large part by the ratification of the ICC Statute (even though that treaty technically does not require domestic incorporation of ICC crimes). Finally, although most domestic cases involving Syria feature some combination of these two sets of criminal charges, some states are only able to resort to immigration remedies (e.g., criminal charges for immigration fraud, or the use of deportation measures) for foreign defendants for lack of evidence or other legal impediments—a last-ditch option for accountability.

European courts are playing host to some interesting litigation against corporate actors for their complicity in international crimes being committed in Syria as well. For example, the Swiss cement company Lafarge-Holcim and some of its principals have been questioned, detained, investigated, and/or charged with financing a terrorist enterprise, complicity in war crimes and crimes against humanity, and forced labor (among other charges) in French courts. The suit is based on the company's breach of an E.U. embargo on Syrian oil by Lafarge's cement factory in northern Syria, where ISIL was operating, and the endangerment of its employees. It is alleged that the company paid millions to ISIL in order to further its operations knowing that ISIL was engaged in atrocities. This marks the first time that a parent corporation has been criminally indicted for crimes against humanity, an outcome allowed by French law, although those charges were eventually dismissed. Lawyers representing Yazidi victims of ISIL crimes were granted civil party status in the case.

Facilitating all these cases is the proliferation of special prosecutorial units dedicated to investigating international crimes; global mutual legal assistance arrangements (including Interpol); the formation of multinational "joint investigative teams" focused on the prosecution of transnational crimes; training programs dedicated to investigating international crimes; and Europe-wide institutions such as Europol, the European Arrest Warrant (EAW),[10] and the Eurojust Genocide Network.[11] In addition, domestic prosecutors have

[10] Council Framework Decision on the European Arrest Warrant and the Surrender Procedures Between Member States, 2002/584/JHA [2002] OJ L 190/1. The EAW replaces the process of extradition between E.U. member states and abolishes dual criminality—the extradition requirement that conduct be criminalized in both the requesting and requested state—for many categories of crimes.

[11] Council Decision 2203/335/JHA, Official Journal 118/12, of 8 May 2003 on the Investigation and Prosecution of Genocide, Crimes Against Humanity and War Crimes. Europol and the European Investigation Order Directive also support member states in combating forms of international organized crime and terrorism. A similar network is being established across Africa. *See* Network for Investigations and Prosecution of Genocide, Crimes Against Humanity and War Crimes, *Conclusions of the 16th Meeting of the European Network of Contact Points for Investigation and*

benefited from institutional learning and assistance from non-governmental investigative efforts that jump-start domestic processes and render these cases less daunting. Finally, in reaction to the failed ICC referral, the U.N. General Assembly created the International, Impartial and Independent Mechanism (IIIM) to assist in the investigation and prosecution of persons responsible for the most serious crimes under International Law committed in the Syrian Arab Republic since March 2011.[12] The IIIM has shared information with national authorities to support their prosecutions.

C. Civil Trials

It is usually a state that launches a criminal trial on behalf of a polity whose peace has been breached by criminal behavior. In the process of vindicating social norms, the victims of crime appear as mere witnesses for the prosecution. By contrast, victims are front and center in civil (tort) actions against responsible individuals.[13] As an alternative to initiating criminal suits, some systems enable victims of international crimes to obtain civil redress. This tort liability may be broader than penal liability where, for example, a state has not codified international crimes in its penal code but recognizes private rights of action over violations of international law or the domestic law analogues of international crimes (e.g., assault, battery, false imprisonment, and wrongful death). The second row of the accountability matrix is devoted to such civil actions. It reveals that there are no international, regional, or hybrid fora that allow for civil claims to be advanced against individual perpetrators. As such, these cases must be brought within domestic legal systems under the applicable tort law.

1. Tort Liability in Domestic Courts

Individual civil (tort) liability for violations of ICL is most developed in the United States, although victims of international crimes are increasingly seeking civil reparations in the context of criminal prosecutions in civil law jurisdictions in Europe and elsewhere. In the United States, the over 200-year old Alien Tort Statute (ATS), 28 U.S.C. § 1350, and its more youthful sibling, the Torture Victim Protection Act (TVPA), 28 U.S.C. § 1350 note, allow U.S. federal courts to assert jurisdiction over certain international

---

Prosecution of Genocide, Crimes Against Humanity and War Crimes (May 21–22, 2014).

[12] G.A. Res. 71/248, U.N. Doc. A/RES/71/248.

[13] A tort is an act or omission that results in harm to another but not premised on a contract. Tortious conduct gives rise to a civil claim on the part of the person or entity harmed and legal liability on the part of the person or entity deemed to have caused the harm. The remedy is usually a monetary award to compensate the plaintiff for physical injuries, financial losses, and other provable damages.

torts.[14] In the modern era, the ATS was first successfully invoked in the human rights context in *Filártiga v. Peña-Irala,* in which a federal court found a Paraguayan national liable for acts of torture and summary execution committed in Paraguay against another Paraguayan national, whose sister had serendipitously discovered the defendant living in the United States.[15] Since that pioneering case, dozens of cases have been brought against natural and legal persons (including major multinational corporations) involving allegations of various forms of involvement in ICL violations committed in the United States and abroad. In recent jurisprudence, however, the Supreme Court has significantly limited the reach of the ATS,[16] particularly when it comes to foreign corporations.[17]

To be sure, when serious international crimes are at issue, a monetary judgment will never be commensurate to the harm suffered. Indeed, such judgments perpetuate the fiction that money is equivalent to harm, and that for every pain suffered there is an amount that will adequately compensate the victim. The enforcement of damage awards against human rights abusers has been a challenge in many civil human rights suits in the United States, as defendants rarely have adequate and attachable assets within the forum. Nonetheless, a damage award—even where unenforced—marks a symbolic victory over an oppressor, recognizes concrete damage to individuals, and is symbolic of a plaintiff's loss. Where an award can be enforced, money damages provide economic support to enable rehabilitation and reintegration into society and confer a measure of social standing on plaintiffs.

At the moment, there are no suits under this suite of U.S. statutes involving Syria for lack of personal jurisdiction over any responsible defendants. Syrians simply have not yet traveled to the United States (in part due to severe immigration limitations imposed by the Trump administration) to the same degree as they have to Europe. To the extent that such civil suits are proceeding elsewhere,

---

[14] In 1991, the U.S. Congress passed the TVPA in connection with its ratification of the Convention Against Torture and Other Cruel, Inhuman or Degrading Treatment or Punishment, which obligates state parties to adopt measures to ensure that torturers are held legally accountable for their acts. The TVPA enables suits for torture or extrajudicial killing. The Anti-Terrorism Act (ATA), 18 U.S.C. § 2333, allows for similar civil suits involving acts of "international terrorism" involving U.S. persons. The Trafficking Victim Protection Act, 18 U.S.C. § 1595, is available to U.S. or foreign victims of human trafficking; claims can be asserted against the direct perpetrator or anyone who knowingly benefits financially or otherwise from participation in a trafficking venture.

[15] *Filártiga v. Peña-Irala,* 630 F.2d 876 (2d Cir. 1980).

[16] *Kiobel v. Royal Dutch Petroleum Co.*, 569 U.S. 108 (2013) (limiting the ATS to suits that touch and concern the United States with sufficient force to overcome the presumption against extraterritoriality).

[17] *Jesner v. Arab Bank, PLC,* 138 S.Ct. 1386 (2018).

most are the result of survivors "piggybacking" off criminal charges brought by national prosecutorial authorities. These civil cases in domestic courts exhaust the top half of the accountability matrix involving charges and claims that can be brought against individuals and corporate entities.

2. State Responsibility in International and Domestic Courts

The bottom half of the matrix encompasses cases against sovereign entities. The next row of the matrix is empty, signifying that there is no notion of state criminality under international law. In this regard, the International Criminal Tribunal for the Former Yugoslavia has observed: "Under present international law it is clear that States, by definition, cannot be the subject of criminal sanctions akin to those provided for in national criminal systems."[18] The U.N. International Law Commission (ILC)—a body of experts created by the General Assembly to engage in the codification and progressive development of international law—considered the question of state criminal responsibility in connection with its Draft Articles on State Responsibility. Draft Article 19 recognized a distinction between state responsibility for international delicts (the Roman and Germanic law analogue of torts) and "international crimes," defined as breaches of an international obligation "so essential for the protection of fundamental interests of the international community that its breach is recognized as a crime by that community as a whole."[19]

The most compelling argument for the imposition of criminal liability on the state itself is the need to impose greater condemnation against a state when individuals within its highest echelons of power have devised and implemented a policy to commit international crimes and obstruct justice. Recognizing state criminality might generate heightened stigma and perhaps an amplified deterrence. Nonetheless, a number of countervailing arguments emerged in the debates over the Draft Articles. For one, it was difficult to conceptualize a state's *mens rea,* although notions of corporate criminality exist under domestic law that may provide useful analogs. Secondly, punitive penalties are not traditionally awarded in proceedings against states, even for willful behavior.[20] Ultimately,

---

[18] *Prosecutor v. Blaškić*, Case No. IT-95-14-AR108bis, Judgement on the Request of the Republic of Croatia for Review of the Decision of Trial Chamber II of 18 July 1997, ¶ 25 (Oct. 29, 1997).

[19] International Law Commission, 1996 Draft Articles on State Responsibility, adopted by the Drafting Committee on first reading at the forty-eighth session, U.N. Doc A/51/10, 125, at Art. 19.

[20] MATERIALS ON THE RESPONSIBILITY OF STATES FOR INTERNATIONALLY WRONGFUL ACTS, U.N. Doc. ST/LEG/SER.B/25 (2012), at 261 ("the award of punitive

the concept of state criminality could not overcome the attendant controversy and so was eventually dropped in succeeding versions of the project. Instead, the Draft Articles were revised to attach surplus consequences to serious breaches of peremptory norms of international law, namely that states are not to recognize as lawful a situation created by such a breach or otherwise render assistance to maintain such a state of affairs.[21]

Given this discomfort with the concept of state criminality, state responsibility for ICL violations is limited to civil liability—the final row of our matrix. Starting with international institutions that can adjudicate state responsibility, the International Court of Justice (ICJ), the judicial branch of the United Nations, can hear claims between states that have accepted its jurisdiction. Several ICL treaties grant the ICJ jurisdiction over state parties. For example, Article IX of the Genocide Convention provides that disputes "between the Contracting Parties relating to the interpretation, application or fulfillment of the present Convention, including those relating to the responsibility of a State for genocide or any of the other acts enumerated in article III [conspiracy, incitement, attempt, complicity], shall be submitted to the International Court of Justice." It is rare for states to bring suit against other states before the ICJ absent compelling sovereign interests. Perhaps for this reason, the ICJ has not historically been a forum for states to challenge the human rights practices of other states; this reluctance, however, may be dissipating.

Pursuant to Article IX, for example, Bosnia-Herzegovina sued the Federal Republic of Yugoslavia (Serbia and Montenegro) for committing genocide during the breakup of the former Yugoslavia. The Court determined that Serbia was liable for failing to *prevent* genocide at Srebrenica, where Bosnian Serb troops massacred more than 7,000 Bosnian Muslim boys and men in July 1995, but that Serbia itself was not liable for the *commission* of genocide.[22] Another earlier, yet notable, example is the case of *Nicaragua v. United States*. There, Nicaragua attempted to hold the United States responsible for violations of the laws of war committed by the *Contra* rebel forces, who were receiving considerable U.S. assistance. When the Court ruled in preliminary proceedings that it had jurisdiction over the parties and the dispute, the United States withdrew its

---

damages is not recognized in international law even in relation to serious breaches of obligations arising under peremptory norms.").

[21] INTERNATIONAL LAW COMMISSION, DRAFT ARTICLES ON RESPONSIBILITY OF STATES FOR INTERNATIONALLY WRONGFUL ACTS, WITH COMMENTARIES (2001), at Art. 40–41. *See* Legal Consequences of the Construction of a Wall in the Occupied Palestinian Territory, Advisory Opinion, 2004 I.C.J. 136, ¶ 159 (July 9).

[22] Application of the Convention on the Prevention and Punishment of the Crime of Genocide (Bosn. & Herz. v. Serb. & Mont.), Judgment, 2007 I.C.J. 43 (Feb. 26).

acceptance of ICJ jurisdiction. Nonetheless, the ICJ proceeded against the United States in default and determined that violations by the *Contras* were not attributable to the United States (although the U.S. was liable for its own breaches of international law).[23]

Most recently, the Gambia, on behalf of the Organization of Islamic Cooperation, filed an application with the ICJ against Myanmar alleging that Myanmar's persecution of the Rohingya constitutes genocide, and that Myanmar is in violation of its obligations under the Genocide Convention. In its initial application, the Gambia requested provisional measures—the equivalent of interim injunctive relief—to preserve evidence and protect the Rohingya against further harm while the case is proceeding. In January 2020, the Court issued its decision on the request for provisional measures, ordering Myanmar to "take all measures within its power to prevent the commission of all" genocidal acts against the Rohingya, and to "take effective measures to prevent the destruction and ensure the preservation of evidence related to the allegations of acts" that constitute genocide.[24]

Although these are "civil" suits, where state responsibility for international crimes is at issue, the petitioner state must often meet close to a "beyond a reasonable doubt" standard of proof. In the Bosnia case, the ICJ indicated that

> The Court has long recognized that claims against a State involving charges of exceptional gravity must be proved by evidence that is fully conclusive. The Court requires that it be fully convinced that allegations made in the proceedings, that the crime of genocide or the other acts enumerated in Article III have been committed, have been clearly established. The same standard applies to the proof of attribution for such acts.[25]

This heightened burden on the petitioner state is controversial given the lack of punitive remedies.

Syria has ratified a number of human rights treaties, including the Convention against Torture and other Cruel, Inhuman or Degrading Treatment or Punishment (CAT), to which Syria acceded in 2004.[26] Like many multilateral treaties, the CAT contains a mechanism for resolving disputes between state parties concerning

---

[23] Military and Paramilitary Activities in and against Nicaragua (Nicar. v. USA) Merits, Judgment, 1986 I.C.J. 14 (June 27).

[24] Application of the Convention on the Prevention and Punishment of the Crime of Genocide (The Gambia v. Myanmar), Order No. 178 P 1 (Jan. 23, 2020).

[25] Bos. & Herz. v. Serb. & Mont., *supra*, ¶ 209.

[26] Convention Against Torture and other Cruel, Inhuman or Degrading Treatment or Punishment, Dec. 10, 1984, 1465 U.N.T.S. 85.

the "interpretation or application" of the treaty. Under the system contained within Article 30, the parties concerned must first try to settle their dispute through negotiation and arbitration, if the latter is requested by a state party.[27] This arbitral mechanism has never been activated. If an arbitral tribunal cannot be convened within six months, then state parties have the option of recourse to the ICJ in The Hague.

As a useful precedent for the Syria situation, Belgium initiated proceedings against Senegal under the CAT challenging Senegal's failure to prosecute or extradite former Chadian dictator Hissène Habré, who was enjoying safe haven on Senegalese territory.[28] This was the first opportunity the ICJ had to entertain a dispute under the CAT. In its 2012 judgment, the ICJ ruled that Belgium's claims under the CAT were admissible because all state parties have standing to enforce these obligations *erga omnes partes*. In particular, the Court stated: "The States parties to the Convention have a common interest to ensure, in view of their shared values that acts of torture are prevented and that, if they occur, their authors do not enjoy impunity."[29] In this regard, the Court made a distinction between obligations *erga omnes*, which are owed to the international community as a whole, and obligations *erga omnes partes*, which are owed to a group of state parties to a treaty. It was thus of no moment that no Belgian citizens were harmed under Habré's regime (though one of the complainants had become a Belgian national) or that Belgium lacked any other "special interest" in Senegal's adherence to the treaty.

Given the aforementioned precedent, any state party to the CAT could bring a contentious case against Syria before the ICJ alleging its failure to adhere to its treaty obligations, which include the obligation to desist from torture and to investigate allegations that acts of torture were committed within its territory, including by non-state actors. The complainant state could also seek provisional measures, which—as the Gambia/Myanmar case illustrates—can be achieved relatively expeditiously so long as it can be shown that the measures requested are linked to the claims on the merits and that

---

[27] This precondition is satisfied if negotiations have failed or if they have become futile. Application of the International Convention on the Elimination of All Forms of Racial Discrimination (Geor. v. Russ.), Preliminary Objections, Judgment, 2011 I.C.J. 70, ¶ 159 (April 1) (finding that Georgia had not attempted to negotiate a solution to its dispute with Russia).

[28] Questions Concerning the Obligation to Prosecute or Extradite (Belg. v. Sen.), Judgment, 2012 I.C.J. 422 (July 20). Belgium attempted to advance claims with respect to Senegal's failure to prosecute other international crimes under customary international law, but the Court found that these claims were foreclosed because Belgium had not sufficiently advanced them in its prior diplomatic exchanges; as such, they did not form part of the dispute referred to the Court. *Id.* ¶ 54.

[29] *Id.* ¶¶ 68–69.

there is a real and imminent risk of irreparable harm in the absence of such relief. The challenge is to find a state willing to initiate such a proceeding, either in defense of the anti-torture norm or because they have nationals who have been victimized. As this book is going to press, the Netherlands has just initiated proceedings against Syria before the ICJ under the CAT.

Unless there is another basis to invoke the ICJ's jurisdiction, premising jurisdiction on the CAT would limit the Court to considering Syria's responsibility for acts of torture within its territory. Although torture is a war crime when committed within the context of an armed conflict and is an enumerated crime against humanity, Syria's responsibility for the commission of other war crimes and crimes against humanity would only be tangentially adjudged, if at all. To be sure, a contentious case would not likely result in the participation of the Syrian regime; it would, however, establish the facts, develop the law, order a remedy, contribute "to a change of consciousness," and potentially catalyze new international responses.

The ICJ has jurisdiction only over suits between states. Individuals have no standing to advance claims against responsible states (although the state of which the individual is a national may espouse claims of their citizens). By contrast, various human rights institutions, created either by treaty or as part of the U.N. system, can receive complaints against states by individuals under certain circumstances. These human rights bodies have varying powers of enforcement and thus effectiveness. Europe, the Americas, and Africa boast regional human rights commissions or courts that can accept jurisdiction over individual petitions brought by victims of human rights violations alleging violations of the institutions' constitutive treaties so long as the state has consented to this. In Europe, the European Court of Human Rights (ECHR), based in Strasbourg, France, exercises jurisdiction over states that are party to the European Convention for the Protection of Human Rights and Fundamental Freedoms and its Protocols. The Inter-American system has a Commission based in Washington, D.C., and Court based in San José, Costa Rica (IACHR) that exercise this function with respect to the American Declaration on the Rights and Duties of Man and the American Convention on Human Rights. Africa too has both Commission and Court of Human and People's Rights with jurisdiction over the African Charter on Human and People's Rights and other treaties. There are significantly weaker regional human rights systems in Southeast Asia (but not all of Asia) and the Middle East.

In addition, particular human rights treaties have created a web of enforcement bodies with varying adjudicative powers. Many of these institutions are not courts *per se*, but rather expert bodies that can make recommendations and offer authoritative interpretations of the treaty that brought them into being. The Human Rights Committee (HRC), for example, is a creature of the International Covenant on Civil and Political Rights (ICCPR). It has the power to entertain communications from individuals claiming to be victims of violations of any of the rights set forth in the ICCPR committed by the 116 states that have ratified the Covenant's First Optional Protocol. The Committee then forwards its "views" to the state concerned to promote compliance. Similar quasi-adjudicative bodies hear petitions from victims claiming violations of other multilateral human rights conventions. These institutions assess states' compliance with human rights obligations—those basic rights and freedoms that all states owe individuals within their territories or subject to their jurisdictions. While the enforcement powers of these bodies is low, and while the procedures result in "views" communicated to, instead of binding orders issued against, the responsible state party, some of their decisions have either resulted in the state providing direct relief or have been successfully used by local human rights lawyers and advocates to obtain such relief through further litigation and other advocacy. Many of the human rights norms adjudicated by these bodies, especially those civil rights dealing with the right to life and physical integrity, have analogs in ICL. So, for example, the IACHR found the state of Honduras liable for a practice and policy of disappearances in the seminal case of *Velásquez Rodriguez v. Honduras*.[30] This creative use of international human rights bodies to pursue claims that involve violations of ICL has expanded the institutions before which accountability for international crimes can be pursued and related jurisprudence can be developed.

Besides the ICJ compromissory clause discussed above, the CAT includes several other mechanisms that can be used to enforce violations of its provisions. These include an individual complaint procedure before the Committee Against Torture, an expert body created by the treaty and charged with examining state parties' compliance.[31] The Committee can also conduct independent inquiries into well-founded indications that torture is being systematically practiced in the territory of state parties and entertain

[30] *Velásquez Rodriguez v. Honduras*, Judgment of July 29, 1988, Inter-Am.Ct.H.R. (Ser. C) No. 4 (1988).

[31] Convention against Torture, *supra*, at art. 22 ("A State Party to this Convention may at any time declare under this article that it recognizes the competence of the Committee to receive and consider communications from or on behalf of individuals subject to its jurisdiction who claim to be victims of a violation by a State Party of the provisions of the Convention. No communication shall be received by the Committee if it concerns a State Party which has not made such a declaration.").

communications from a state party that another state party is not fulfilling its treaty obligations. These procedures are unavailing against Syria, however, because Syria has not consented to, or has opted out of, each of these mechanisms. As a result, the CAT Committee can only comment upon reports on treaty compliance submitted by Syria itself and so-called "shadow reports" provided by non-governmental organizations. The Committee's last set of Concluding Observations devoted to Syria (issued following a request for a special report in 2012) reveal the degree to which Syria has utterly and habitually flouted its treaty obligations under the CAT.[32] Not surprisingly, Syria is currently in arrears in responding to the Committee and on its reporting requirements. To date, Syria has generally ignored, rebuffed, or only evasively responded to the overtures and criticism of the U.N. Human Rights Council's various mandate holders (such as the Special Rapporteur on Extrajudicial Killings and the Working Groups on Arbitrary Detention or Enforced Disappearances).

Turning to the final cell in our matrix, domestic tribunals exercise only limited jurisdiction over states for breaches of international law. Historically, states were absolutely immune from suit before the courts of sister sovereigns. By the middle of the twentieth century, however, this immunity began to weaken as the role of the state in international relations diversified and the principle of sovereignty eroded. A new norm of restrictive, or qualified, immunity gradually emerged, which accords immunity for public acts (*acta jure imperii*), but not for acts in which a state is acting in a private or commercial capacity (*acta jure gestionis*). Although some international law instruments address it, foreign sovereign immunity is now largely governed by national law.

For example, the U.S. Congress enacted the Foreign Sovereign Immunities Act (FSIA) in 1976 to "depoliticize" determinations of sovereign immunity and provide courts with concrete standards with which to make immunity determinations.[33] The FSIA was amended in 2008 to withhold sovereign immunity from designated "state sponsors of terrorism" for acts of torture, extrajudicial killing, aircraft sabotage, or hostage taking committed outside the United States where the victim or the claimant is a U.S. national. This amendment has re-politicized the doctrine of sovereign immunity to a degree, as claims can only be brought against a state that the U.S. government has designated as a "state sponsor of terrorism." The

[32] *See* Consideration by the Committee against Torture of the implementation of the Convention in the Syrian Arab Republic in the absence of a special report requested pursuant to article 19, paragraph 1, *in fine*, Concluding observations of the Committee against Torture, U.N. Doc. CAT/C/SYR/CO/1/Add.2 (June 29, 2012).

[33] 28 U.S.C. §§ 1330 *et seq.*

FSIA is unique in that it allows for punitive damages against defendants[34]—a feature that is not without its detractors.

A number of suits have been brought against such state sponsors of terrorism (mainly Libya, Cuba, and Iran) in U.S. federal courts. Most recently, the family of famed war correspondent Marie Colvin won a $300M judgment against the state of Syria for assassinating Colvin while she was covering the war in Syria. As true default judgments are not available against a sovereign under U.S. law, plaintiffs were obliged to establish their claim "by evidence satisfactory to the court" to prevail.[35] In their submissions, the plaintiffs presented a damning array of evidence against the regime, much of it provided by documentation centers that have been collecting information since the start of the conflict. The complaint alleged that the government of Bashar Al Assad used informants and signals intercepts to track Syrian and foreign journalists who were publishing stories that were critical of the regime or exposing the commission of war crimes by state actors. Not surprisingly perhaps, Syria did not formally participate in the litigation; however, it did deny the allegations through its Minister of Information and in the press. Nevertheless, in addition to providing some redress to Colvin's family, this litigation also provided a forum in which the extensive documentation of the Syrian regime's atrocities could be publicized. Although this outcome is welcome, it also reveals a stark asymmetry: while the heirs of a U.S. victim are able to take steps to recover against the Al Assad regime, millions of Syrians are suffering with no access to meaningful justice

D. Conclusion

If we were to take a snapshot of the system of ICL today, here is what we would see. The international community has promulgated a web of human rights and ICL treaties that condemn various forms of violence toward people and property, and during war and peace. Examples include the international "bill of rights" (comprising the Universal Declaration of Human Rights, the ICCPR, and the International Covenant on Economic, Social, and Cultural Rights), the Genocide and Torture Conventions, the four Geneva Conventions, and their collective progeny. At the same time, academics, advocates, and jurists continue to refer to a wide-ranging

---

[34] *See* 28 U.S.C. § 1605A(c)(4) (allowing for punitive damages against state sponsors of terrorism); 28 U.S.C. § 1606 (allowing for punitive damages against agencies or instrumentalities of a state but not the state itself).

[35] 28 U.S.C. § 1608(e). *See Han Kim v. Democratic People's Republic of Korea*, 774 F.3d 1044, 1047–8 (D.C. Cir. 2014) (noting that while "the FSIA leaves it to the court to determine precisely how much and what kinds of evidence the plaintiff must provide" courts should be mindful that Congress enacted the terrorism exception to sovereign immunity with the aim of "prevent[ing] state sponsors of terrorism . . . from escaping liability for their sins.").

body of customary norms that supplement and, in some cases, exceed codified norms. The international community has created a variety of enforcement mechanisms for these norms, some more robust and judicial than others. These include bodies with jurisdiction over individual states—such as the Human Rights Committee—and over individuals, such as the various international criminal courts.

As this chapter reveals, when it comes to the enforcement of ICL, a high degree of jurisdictional concurrence exists between international and domestic institutions and criminal and civil processes. This typology of culpability with its two axes—individual versus state responsibility and tort versus criminal liability—illustrates that liability may exist concurrently at the state and individual level and before domestic and international tribunals. So far, the enforcement of ICL has been so scattered and exceptional that there has been little overlap. The cases against Serbian defendants before the ICTY and against Serbia and Montenegro in the ICJ, and the ICC's work in Bangladesh and the Gambia's suit against Myanmar in the ICJ, present notable exceptions. Given this high level of jurisdictional concurrence, the potential exists for divergent outcomes and the fragmentation of the law. This, in turn, could lead to significant uncertainty about, and distrust of, the international justice system. So far, what we actually see is a high degree of cross-fertilization, which has helped to bolster the customary international law foundation of the field.

Chapter 12

INTERNATIONAL CRIMINAL LAW AND ITS ALTERNATIVES: TRUTH, JUSTICE, RECONCILIATION, AND MEMORY

The fundamental purpose of any system of law is to further desirable social policy outcomes. Most texts in the field of international criminal law (ICL) assume the worthiness of the project to expand individual criminal responsibility for acts that violate international law, regardless of whether the offenders are state agents or private actors. That said, it is worth reflecting for a moment on the articulated justifications for a regime of ICL.[1] The goals of ICL—as advanced over time by its practitioners and supporters—are as varied as they are ambitious: to deter future offenses, mete out just punishment, promote accountability, incapacitate offenders, rehabilitate victims and perpetrators, provide a substitute for vigilante justice, reconcile embattled communities, individualize guilt to avoid collective recriminations, reinforce the rule of law, and heal shattered societies. In this way, ICL embodies some of the goals traditionally associated with domestic criminal law (retribution, deterrence, and rehabilitation).[2] At the same time, it embodies others that transcend those more localized concerns and reflect the expanded interests of the international community. The system of ICL thus aspires to be more than just the extension of the domestic criminal law model onto the international plane.

This chapter reviews some of the articulated purposes of ICL, and weighs them against critiques of the field and alternative models of justice and accountability, both legal and non-legal. The goal is to better contextualize ICL vis-à-vis these alternative responses to armed conflict, mass violence, and repression. As you study the various situations in which states and other members of the international community, acting individually or collectively, have resorted to international criminal justice, consider to what extent the

---

[1] Good discussions of this topic may be found here: Immi Tallgren, *The Sensibility and Sense of International Criminal Law*, 13 EUROP. J. INT'L L. 561 (2002); Robert D. Sloane, *The Expressive Capacity of International Punishment: The Limits of the National Law Analogy and the Potential of International Criminal Law*, 43 STANFORD J. INT'L L. 39 (2007); and MARK A. DRUMBL, ATROCITY, PUNISHMENT, AND INTERNATIONAL LAW (2007).

[2] For a discussion of the traditional justifications of the criminal law, see Miriam J. Aukerman, *Extraordinary Evil, Ordinary Crime: A Framework for Understanding Transitional Justice*, 15 HARV. HUM. RTS. J. 39 (2002).

criminal justice model employed in response to "ordinary" crimes on the domestic level is effective on the international level in response to the "extraordinary" crimes of genocide, war crimes, crimes against humanity, and state aggression. In addition, reflect upon what other policy options were available to these actors and whether these other responses might have achieved more desirable outcomes. Finally, contemplate these issues from the perspective of victims and the local affected communities: Which responses do you think best reflect their interests and priorities? To what extent should the international community seek to incorporate victims' rights and perspectives into the design and implementation of transitional justice mechanisms? What is the best way to accomplish this?

A. The Objectives of International Criminal Law

Although more ambitious motivations have been associated with the project of international criminal justice, the three main justifications for ICL, as articulated by the international community today, are retribution, deterrence, and expressivism. Rehabilitation (of both perpetrators and victims) remains a goal of international human rights law and many domestic systems; however, it is less salient in ICL, at least at the moment. The original *ad hoc* tribunals also envisioned that they would contribute to the reconciliation of warring communities and the establishment of the rule of law. Over time, the tribunals' ability to accomplish this was questioned in light of modern research and their articulated objectives became more modest.

1. Retribution

Theories of retribution are premised on the idea that individuals who disturb the public order must be punished for their actions. This, it is surmised, helps to return society to a prior state of equilibrium. For retributivists, a regime of international criminal justice is justified by the need to avenge acts that disturb international public order. Punishment also serves the purposes of conveying the global society's condemnation of the disruptive conduct. As an alternative to execution or exile, criminal justice creates heightened stigma by ensuring that responsible individuals are publicly condemned as war criminals and génocidaires. Indeed, the imperatives of accountability and anti-impunity are frequent refrains of proponents of international criminal justice.

Punishment can also provide a sense of satisfaction to victims when they see their tormentor reprimanded. A formal system of criminal justice is often justified as a way to avoid cycles of recrimination and other forms of vigilante self-help that may occur where malefactors would otherwise enjoy impunity. The law thus acts as a channel for personal and collective vengeance to prevent the vendetta cycle that may plague fractured societies without effective criminal justice systems.

Retributive impulses and efforts are inherently retrospective—they are focused on meting out just punishment for prior bad acts. The punishment is calibrated to the offender's moral culpability and the harm caused to the body politic. In the context of mass crimes, however, this calculation remains a challenge. Of Hermann Göring, Hitler's designated successor and the highest-ranking defendant at Nuremberg, political theorist Hannah Arendt once wrote: "It may well be essential to hang Göring, but it is totally inadequate. That is, this guilt, in contrast to all criminal guilt, oversteps and shatters any and all legal systems."[3] Similarly, how can those responsible for the deaths of more than 800,000 people in Rwanda be adequately punished?

The international criminal tribunals are often criticized for sentencing individuals accused of heinous crimes too leniently. Dražen Erdemović, for example, was convicted for his involvement in a firing squad that massacred hundreds of Muslim men. Mathematically, he alone was probably responsible for at least 70 of those deaths, yet the International Criminal Tribunal for the former Yugoslavia (ICTY) ultimately sentenced him to five years' imprisonment. The fact that he acted under duress, confessed to his involvement in the crime, expressed genuine remorse, and turned "state's witness" in order to testify in the trials of his superiors, including the late Slobodan Milošević, were all factors in mitigation.[4] The tribunals appear to reserve their harshest sentences (life imprisonment) for the intellectual authors or leaders who order or facilitate international crimes, rather than those members of the rank-and-file who implement such criminal plans. How does one compare the punishment of a person who killed 70 people with that of the leaders who ordered the crime or even for those who created the conditions that led to those killings? These crimes are in many respects incommensurate.

2. Deterrence

As compared with the retributivist approach to criminal justice, theories of deterrence are forward looking in their perspective. Deterrent approaches focus on the prevention of future crimes rather than the punishment of crimes that have already been committed. Deterrence is premised on the interplay between the moral philosophies of utilitarianism (the theory that conduct should be

---

[3] HANNAH ARENDT & KARL JASPERS, CORRESPONDENCE 1928–1969 54 (1992).

[4] *Prosecutor v. Erdemović*, Case No. IT-96-22-T*bis*, Sentencing Judgement (Mar. 5, 1998).

directed toward achieving the greatest happiness for the greatest number of people) and consequentialism (the theory that decisions to act are made on the basis of the expected outcomes or consequences of the action). By this account, the criminal prosecution and punishment of responsible individuals prevents future crimes by triggering two types of deterrence: specific and general. Specific deterrence operates against individuals who have already engaged in undesirable conduct and works through the dual forces of incapacitation and rehabilitation. The goal of specific deterrence is to ensure that the perpetrator not engage in additional wrongful acts. By contrast, general deterrence is directed at society at large. The social condemnation of bad acts, coupled with the visible punishment of the convicted individual, are thought to discourage others from engaging in comparable conduct.

Both theories of deterrence assume a rational actor who will refrain from committing criminal acts after weighing the fear of negative consequences associated with the action (prosecution, punishment, and the concomitant stigma) against the gains to be had by engaging in criminal behavior (which in the ICL realm often include self-enrichment or -aggrandizement, the consolidation of power, the liquidation of an enemy, and sectarian advancement). More idealistically, deterrence assumes that social norms will eventually be internalized, and good conduct habitualized, so that individuals will no longer consider the possibility of engaging in breaches. By this account, a vigorous regime of criminal justice contributes to greater social utility overall. This assumes, of course, that the source of the social norms and any prosecutorial power will be perceived as legitimate and morally credible. Genuine internalization of norms will be resisted where the norms are deemed illegitimate or exogenously imposed or where they are contrary to entrenched attitudes backed by community support.

For utilitarians, a regime of international criminal justice is thus justified as an effort to prevent future violations. Yet testing this hypothesis continues to vex criminologists, as it is virtually impossible to construct a rigorous empirical study to quantify the deterrent effect of prosecutions and sentences in any criminal justice system. Even in the more established domestic context, we are left to theorize how deterrence works with imperfect data and uncertain causal pathways. Nevertheless, some have begun to develop empirical data and studies to track the processes of deterrence in situations in which ICL institutions are operating.[5]

---

[5] *See* Michael Broache, *International Prosecutions and Atrocities in the Democratic Republic of the Congo: A Case Study of the FDLR*, 7 J. MIDDLE EAST & AFRICA 19 (2016); Michael Broache, *Irrelevance, Instigation, and Prevention: The Mixed Effects of International Criminal Court Prosecutions on Atrocities in the*

What we do know is that deterrence requires first and foremost a credible threat of punishment. Indeed, most studies show that ensuring the perception of the *predictability* of punishment (rather than its *severity*) is the most efficacious means of promoting deterrence. If this is true, ICL has a long way to go. Even now, at the height of the ICL renaissance, the existing tribunals are considering only a tiny fraction of the world's international crimes. Although they are high profile, ICL prosecutions may be too episodic, selective, unpredictable, and unsystematic to exert any general deterrent effect. Often, the indicted individuals seem randomly chosen—ill-fated losers in an accountability lottery. And, the ICC's record is mixed at best: more than half of the cases have resulted in acquittals or dismissals.

Even assuming the most robust enforcement, these cases involve extreme conduct that is perhaps less susceptible to processes of deterrence.[6] Until legal censure is more certain, the narratives that explain why seemingly ordinary people do evil things in the context of war or state-sponsored repression—because they are beset by prejudices, intoxicated by power, manipulated by elites, terrified into submission by superior orders or threats, or caught up in a maelstrom of violence—likely still overwhelm any cost-benefit analysis in which individual perpetrators may engage. As a result, we continue to speculate about what, if any, deterrent effect is produced by ICL prosecutions. It is likely that this effect is still small, though perhaps not negligible.

Where deterrence might be at its most effective is at the level of regime elites—those who may deliberately choose to sponsor international crimes to consolidate their power.[7] As international tribunals increasingly focus on prosecuting leaders, rather than low-level followers, political and military elites may face a more daunting cost-benefit analysis that weighs in favor of desistence. As such

---

CNDP/M23 Case, 10 INT'L J. TRANSITIONAL JUST. 388 (2016) (demonstrating that the FDLR and M23 rebel groups were significantly weakened in the Democratic Republic of Congo following arrest warrants by the ICC and national prosecutors in Europe).

[6] For more on deterrence, compare David Wippman, *Atrocities, Deterrence, and the Limits of International Justice*, 23 FORDHAM INT'L L.J. 473, 476, 483 (1999) ("Even if we assume that those committing atrocities engage in rational cost-benefit calculations (weighing the risk of prosecution against the personal and political gain of continued participation in ethnic cleansing and similar acts), most probably view the risk of prosecution as slight. . . . Even if successful, the contribution of such mass prosecutions to deterrence is uncertain at best."), with Payam Akhavan, *Beyond Impunity: Can International Criminal Justice Prevent Future Atrocities?*, 95 AM. J. INT'L L. 7, 12 (2001) ("Where leaders engage in some form of rational cost-benefit calculation, the threat of punishment can increase the costs of a policy that is criminal under international law.").

[7] Kate Cronin-Furman, *Managing Expectations: International Criminal Trials and the Prospects for Deterrence of Mass Atrocity*, 7(3) INT'L J. TRANSITIONAL JUST. 434 (2013).

prosecutions become an expected and anticipated part of international affairs, the possibility of deterrence becomes more credible. This may even be the case for failed prosecutions. Some have speculated that the recent elections in Kenya were relatively peaceful because of the involvement of the ICC after the violence during the 2007 election. The 2007 violence was triggered by allegations that the election had been stolen by the incumbent through manipulation of the voting process. By contrast, similar allegations of voting irregularities were raised in the 2013 and 2017 elections. Instead of resulting in the mass violence that characterized the 2007 elections, the disputes concerning the 2013 and 2017 elections were successfully handled through the domestic court system. While this outcome is attributable to many factors having to do with domestic Kenyan politics, the hard work of peacebuilders and civil society actors, and institutional and political reforms undertaken after the 2007 post-election violence, it is also widely recognized that the possibility that such violence would have triggered additional ICC involvement may have deterred the political elites from fomenting violence after each of those elections.

3. Expressivism

Sociologist Émile Durkheim posits that the criminal law operates as a form of moral communication used to reaffirm societal norms, express condemnation toward a course of conduct, and create and strengthen social identity and solidarity. For Durkheim, the punishment of the individual is of secondary importance; what is paramount is the maintenance of social cohesion.[8] In some ways, even unenforced law may have an "expressive effect" if people comply with a rule despite the fact that there is no risk of punishment. As such, expressivism "strikes an intermediate path between the deontological road of retribution and the consequentialist road of deterrence," and is able to be both retroactive and prospective at once.[9]

Expressivism is prominent in ICL. In the *Erdemović* Sentencing Judgment, for example, the Trial Chamber indicated that "the International Tribunal is a vehicle through which the international community expresses its outrage at the atrocities committed in the former Yugoslavia. Upholding values of international human rights means that whilst protecting the rights of the accused, the International Tribunal must not lose sight of the tragedy of the

---

[8] ÉMILE DURKHEIM, THE DIVISION OF LABOR IN SOCIETY (1893). *See also* Cass Sunstein, *On the Expressive Function of Law*, 144 UNIV. PENN. L. REV. 2051 (1996).

[9] Diane Marie Amann, *Group Mentality, Expressivism, and Genocide*, 2 INT'L CRIM. L. REV. 93, 120 (2002).

victims and the sufferings of their families."[10] Expressivism finds expression in the perennial debate over whether there is a hierarchy of international crimes, with genocide ("the crime of crimes") presumably enjoying pride of place at the pinnacle, followed by crimes against humanity, and then war crimes.[11] Furthermore, the tribunals consider it part of their core functions to articulate a definitive history of collective violence; one consequence of this commitment is that such a narrative, when articulated within the confines of a criminal process constrained by rules of evidence, ends up simplifying complex societal and political dynamics.[12]

Some have argued that prioritizing this account of ICL can overcome some of the limitations of other approaches to criminal justice when applied internationally.[13] Retributivism values punishment for its own, deontological sake, which can feel anachronistic in today's ethical landscape, which values human dignity. Furthermore, it is difficult to imagine what would qualify as a "proportionate" sentence under retributivism for mass atrocities, particularly given human rights constraints around cruel treatment and the general ban on the death penalty under international law. Deterrence relies on the fiction of the rational actor, which often feels implausible in war crimes situations where collective or sectarian violence has become normalized, even valorized. Expressivism seeks to alter behavior through the articulation and internalization of norms about moral and legal wrongdoing to the parties and to society at large. Its transformative potential in ICL, however, has been limited by the fact that international criminal justice trials proceed in venues that are often far from the affected communities, where the impact of the trial is often distant and even distorted by this separation.[14]

4. Rehabilitation

For many years, the rehabilitation of offenders was an express goal of many domestic penal systems. Rehabilitation approaches shift focus from the broader society to the offender, emphasizing efforts to transform an offender from a societal outlier to a productive member of the community. Over time, however, rehabilitation fell out of vogue

---

10 *Erdemović, supra*, ¶ 21.

11 *See Prosecutor v. Blaškić*, Case No. IT-95-14-T, Judgement, ¶¶ 797–804 (Mar 3, 2000) (summarizing jurisprudence).

12 Anette Bringdal Houge, *Narrative Expressivism: A Criminological Approach to the Expressive Function of International Criminal Justice*, 19(3) CRIMINOLOGY & CRIM. JUST. 277 (2019).

13 Tim Meijers & Marlies Glasius, *Trials as Messages of Justice: What Should be Expected of International Criminal Courts?*, 40(4) ETHICS & INT'L AFF. 428 (2016).

14 *See* PHIL CLARK, DISTANT JUSTICE: THE IMPACT OF THE INTERNATIONAL CRIMINAL COURT ON AFRICAN POLITICS (2018).

in many systems (the United States most prominently), and its demise seems to be premised on the unproven conclusion that it is unworkable, unattainable, and unrealistic. Nonetheless, human rights instruments urge states to give priority to rehabilitation in designing and implementing their criminal justice systems. So, for example, Article 10(3) of the International Covenant on Civil and Political Rights urges states to ensure that "[t]he penitentiary system comprise[s] treatment of prisoners the essential aim of which shall be their reformation and rehabilitation."[15] From the perspective of penalties under ICL, the Statute of the International Criminal Court (ICC) at Article 77 does seem to contemplate the possibility of rehabilitation. According to that provision, which mirrors domestic legislation in many continental systems, the default maximum sentence is 30 years, although life imprisonment is contemplated where warranted by the extreme gravity of the crime and the individual circumstances of the convicted person.

For the moment, it is too early to fully evaluate the ability of the international criminal justice regime to prevent recidivism and enable convicted defendants to rejoin society. Defendants convicted by the ICTY have begun to complete their sentences. For example, Erdemović, who served his sentence in Norway, was granted early release and is now in a witness protection program. Many individuals are serving their sentences in national systems that still have faith in the promise of rehabilitation. Most important perhaps, many individuals will be released after the circumstances that led to the violence in which they participated—a brutal war or repressive government—have ended. Where minimum order and a functioning domestic legal system have been restored, and where the moral universe is re-inverted, criminal behavior that had become "normalized" may once again be considered deviant, and ICL defendants may return to their prior, law-abiding lives with little difficulty. Others, of course, will remain unrepentant. They, and their supporters, may forever consider their prosecution and incarceration to be a profound injustice. This reaction of some perpetrators and communities presents a significant challenge to the effectiveness of retributive and rehabilitative approaches to ICL. This may argue, however, for more thoughtful and sophisticated approaches to justice that reach perpetrators and their communities in a more effective way, rather than an argument for abandoning any effort at rehabilitation.

---

[15] International Covenant on Civil and Political Rights, March 23, 1976, 999 U.N.T.S. 171.

5. Peace and Reconciliation

Although many developed legal systems are increasingly turning to mechanisms of "alternative dispute resolution" (conciliation, mediation, and arbitration) in the noncriminal context, social reconciliation is not an express objective of many developed criminal justice systems. By contrast, some domestic systems and customary dispute resolution mechanisms in the developing world do rely on processes and traditions that focus more on the restoration of community balance and less on the punishment of the guilty to enforce societal rules and norms, including ICL prohibitions. Where crimes occur within communities that must continue to live together, as compared with anonymous criminal acts between strangers who will likely never interact with each other again, reconciliation may take center stage as a penological goal.

Since World War II, many of the world's incidents of mass violence have occurred within the borders of a single state, albeit with dramatic spillover effects. This violence has often pitted different groups within society—defined by ethnicity, race, religion, political persuasion, language, class, socioeconomic status, or traditions—against each other and resulted in the destruction of much of the societal infrastructure and social harmony within the body politic. When violence turns inward, entire communities that once inter-married and lived peacefully together can be torn asunder. Under these circumstances, proponents of international criminal justice posit that criminal trials can help societies achieve peace and reconciliation in the wake of mass violence. The U.N. Security Council resolution establishing the ICTY, for example, predicted that the tribunal would "contribute to the restoration and maintenance of peace."[16] Likewise, the Statute for the International Criminal Tribunal for Rwanda (ICTR) promised that the tribunal would "contribute to the process of national reconciliation."[17] The fact that the Security Council can trigger the ICC's jurisdiction by activating Chapter VII of the U.N. Charter in response to threats to the peace reflects this faith in the power of justice to bring about peace.

The presumed connection between justice and reconciliation is premised on a belief that the assignment of individual criminal responsibility will effectively individuate guilt and short-circuit attitudes of collective responsibility. For example, by prosecuting an individual like Duško Tadić, it is hoped that Bosnian Muslims will recognize that responsibility for acts of violence against members of their community is properly associated with the defendant himself and not, in this case, all Bosnian Serbs. Although proponents of

[16] S.C. Res. 808, pmbl., U.N. Doc. S/RES/808 (Feb. 22, 1993).

[17] S.C. Res. 955, pmbl., U.N. Doc. S/RES/955 (Nov. 8, 1994).

international criminal justice have touted reconciliation as a key goal of the system, many remain skeptical that international criminal justice can bring about social repair and reconciliation. Indeed, the results of empirical studies in the states of the former Yugoslavia are mixed. Some suggest that the ICTY has contributed little toward the reconciliation of the various ethnic groups (and, indeed, may have entrenched hostile attitudes, particularly amongst some Serbian communities who reject the conclusion that genocide was committed in Srebrenica by Serbian forces and considered the tribunal to be biased against them), whereas others are more positive about the tribunal's impact.[18] In addition, the outcomes of certain cases remain contentious—thwarting the goal of creating a shared narrative or historical memory—and may have actually fueled tensions. For example, following troubling evidence of witness intimidation and the death of several witnesses, the ICTY acquitted high-level members of the Kosovo Liberation Army accused of attacking Serbian civilians, a verdict that dealt a stunning blow to many Serbian court watchers.[19] It has been opined that the judgment increased bitterness between the Kosovar and Serbian populations of the region and reignited radical Serbian groups. That said, the work of the tribunal did bring a measure of satisfaction to the victims in ways that respected international due process standards. In addition, while it is appropriate to critique how well a tribunal like the ICTY worked to lessen ethnic tensions and foster reconciliation, it is also the case that ethnic conflict and reconciliation are the product of many different factors beyond the control of such a tribunal.

B. The Critiques of International Criminal Justice

While proponents of international criminal justice have advanced these goals and expectations, opponents and skeptics have questioned whether the international community should rely primarily or even exclusively on criminal trials in the face of mass violence at the expense of other preventative and reactive options.[20] These naysayers raise a number of critiques that go to the very heart

---

[18] *See* Laurel E. Fletcher & Harvey M. Weinstein, *Violence and Social Repair: Rethinking the Contribution of Justice to Reconciliation*, 24 HUM. RTS. Q. 573, 606–617 (2002); Marko Milanović, *The Impact of the ICTY on the Former Yugoslavia: An Anticipatory Postmortem*, 110 AM. J. INT'L L. 233, 234 (2016); DIANE ORENTLICHER, SOME KIND OF JUSTICE: THE ICTY'S IMPACT IN BOSNIA & SERBIA (2018); Sanja Kutnjak Ivković & John Hagan, *The Legitimacy of International Courts: Victims' Evaluations of the ICTY and Local Courts in Bosnia and Herzegovina*, 14 EUR. J. CRIMINOLOGY 200, 208 (2017). *See generally* JAMES MEERNIK, INTERNATIONAL TRIBUNALS AND HUMAN SECURITY 110 (2016).

[19] *Prosecutor v. Haradinaj*, Case No. IT-04-84-T, Judgement (Apr. 3, 2008).

[20] *See* CRITICAL APPROACHES TO INTERNATIONAL CRIMINAL LAW: AN INTRODUCTION (Christine Schwöbel ed., 2014).

of the international criminal justice project. This section sets out a few of the arguments that have been made against the international community's focus on international criminal prosecutions in the face of mass violence. The next section considers a range of alternatives.

1. Victors' Justice and Selectivity

An early critique of international criminal justice, with contemporary resonance, is that only those on the wrong side of history are punished. Upon receiving the indictment against him, Hermann Göring apparently scribbled on the margins: "The victor will always be the judge, and the vanquished the accused." His words ring true with respect to the Nuremberg and Tokyo proceedings. The establishment of those tribunals was possible only because Germany and Tokyo had been completely defeated in World War II. As a result, Allied judges considered only crimes committed by Axis defendants.

This one-sidedness led to some uncomfortable hypocrisies, as none of the Allies came to the tribunals with entirely clean hands. The Soviets' were particularly soiled. Indeed, it seemed incongruous to have allowed a Soviet prosecutor and a Soviet judge to participate in the prosecution of German crimes against civilians and prisoners of war in light of the plunder, rape, and mistreatment happening contemporaneously in Soviet-occupied spaces, not to mention the 1940 Katyn Forest Massacre in which Soviet troops secretly executed close to 22,000 Polish military officers and intelligentsia. In a stunningly audacious move, the Soviets attempted to pin this atrocity on the Germans. For its part, the United Kingdom could have been asked to answer for, among other things, the 1945 firebombing of the city of Dresden, an arguably indiscriminate attack that resulted in the deaths of tens of thousands of civilians and the total destruction of the baroque city center—all for little military gain. With respect to the United States, the Nuremberg Tribunal awarded German defendant Karl Dönitz, commander of the German Navy who served briefly as the German head of state after Hitler's suicide, a relatively light sentence in part because the United States had engaged in the same unrestricted submarine warfare with which Dönitz had been charged. (Indeed, U.S. Admiral Chester Nimitz submitted an affidavit in Dönitz's case to this effect.) The legality of the atomic bombings of Hiroshima and Nagasaki look even more suspect today than they did at the time, raising allegations of war crimes and crimes against humanity that were never heard, much less adjudicated. And while the Holocaust was unprecedented, the narrative that it was "exceptional" masks previous mass atrocities, including against indigenous peoples the world over and chattel slavery as practiced in the New World and elsewhere.[21]

One response to this critique of the World War II proceedings is that although the Nuremberg and Tokyo Tribunals meted out victors' justice, it was good justice. These were not sham trials, with predetermined outcomes pursued only for their propaganda value (much to the chagrin of the Soviets in fact). Defendants were accorded due process guarantees, such as the right to counsel and to cross-examine witnesses and evidence, and at least the Nuremberg tribunal demonstrated the true possibility of acquittal. It seems clear that had the Germans and Japanese won the war, no such process would have been provided had tribunals even been convened for Allied personnel. As we noted in Chapter 1 on the history of the field, the British and Soviets originally proposed that there be summary executions rather than trials. All that said, there is still an underappreciated difference between the way the proceedings were undertaken at Nuremberg compared to Tokyo. This observation is underscored by critical race theorists and others who argue persuasively that greater attention was paid to European victims than Asian victims (for one, the charge of crimes against humanity was pursued more vigorously at Nuremberg than at Tokyo, notwithstanding numerous atrocities committed by the Japanese against civilian populations throughout Asia), and that European defendants at Nuremberg were afforded more due process than the Japanese defendants at Tokyo.[22]

The involvement of more, and more diverse, members of the international community in the ICL renaissance in the 1990s, coupled with the existence of a permanent International Criminal Court (ICC), help to dispel some of the concerns arising out of the World War II experiment with international justice. As a result, the critique has shifted to decry the selective prosecution of perpetrators from weaker states and the relative impunity of perpetrators from powerful states. That (as of this writing) only Africans have been indicted by the ICC fuels this political selectivity argument. Likewise, there is no question that international prosecutions have focused more on non-state actors as compared to government officials, lending support, in some cases, to the very state actors who themselves also stand accused of committing international crimes. This is apparent in the asymmetrical indictments generated in the ICC's Ugandan and Côte d'Ivoire investigations. The focus on non-state perpetrators and the failure to indict government officials involved in atrocities enabled those governments to effectively

[21] Gerry Simpson, *Unprecedents*, *in* THE NEW HISTORIES OF INTERNATIONAL CRIMINAL LAW 12, 17 (Immi Talligren & Thomas Skouteris eds., 2019).

[22] *See, e.g.*, THE TOKYO WAR CRIMES TRIAL (C. Hosoya et al. eds., 1986).

outsource the delivery of justice to the Court and sideline their political and military opponents. Pragmatism dictates the need to placate states to ensure their cooperation with, and prevent their defection from, international justice institutions. And yet victims often identify violations by state actors as particularly egregious given the profound violation of the social contract they entail. This one-sidedness may soon change, however, with the Office of the Prosecutor moving forward with investigations in Afghanistan, Georgia, Iraq, Palestine, and Ukraine that implicate the nationals and personnel of more powerful states, including the United States, the United Kingdom, Russia, and Israel.

All that said, the ICC's jurisdiction remains limited. Although most of the world's states have ratified the Rome Statute, the majority of the world's population still lives in powerful and populous non-party states, including the United States, Russia, China, India, Pakistan, Iran, and Indonesia. As such, unless domestic institutions step up to prosecute their own, or are willing to utilize extraordinary bases of jurisdiction to prosecute perpetrators wherever they can be found, international criminal justice is destined to remain episodic and incomplete, perpetuating troubling selectivity critiques.

2. The Myopia of ICL

In the words of Finnish legal theorist Martti Koskenniemi, legal narratives are "mechanisms of blindness and insight."[23] Separate and apart from the selectivity problem discussed above, there is no question that international criminal law focuses on certain forms of violence—"the violence of death by hand [versus] the violence of death by political economy."[24] As a result, ICL has been blind to a myriad of other forms of brutality, such as neglect, discrimination, grand corruption, the destruction of the natural environment, and structural violence that emanates from political, economic, and legal institutions (all the more visible in light of the COVID-19 pandemic).[25] Likewise, ICL can only partially respond to corporate depredations—in the extractive industries and elsewhere—foreign policies that keep the Global South in a state of relative poverty, or business practices that subject workers of the world to acute economic exploitation. Profound societal transformation is required to adequately redress these forms of harm, and yet international criminal law is devoid of an agenda for such reform. Instead, efforts

---

[23] Martti Koskenniemi, *Histories of International Law: Dealing with Eurocentrism*, 19 RECHTSGESCHICHTE 152, 176 (2019).

[24] Gerry Simpson, *Human Rights with a Vengeance: One Hundred Years of Retributive Humanitarianism*, the Annual Kirby Lecture on International Law, 2015, ANU College of Law, available at https://www.youtube.com/watch?v=bxzJK0nlNrY.

[25] For a recent discussion of the importance of acknowledging and addressing structural violence, *see* JUDITH BUTLER, THE FORCE OF NON-VIOLENCE (2020).

are made to enact more modest reforms, such as the expansion of responsibility for crimes against humanity to corporate entities included in the ILC Draft Articles on crimes against humanity, and the inclusion of multinational corporate violence and environmental crimes as part of the proposed African regional criminal court. We elaborate on some of these critiques below in our discussion of the neoliberal appraisal of international criminal law.

A similar critique of ICL exists in the human rights world, where it is argued that the demand for individual criminal accountability has shaped, and limited, the aspirations of the human rights movement. ICL valorizes the criminal law, which has historically been seen as a tool for domestic oppression given tendencies towards prosecutorial over-reach, over-investment in the carceral state, due process violations, racial injustice, impunity for sexual and gender-based violence, the abandonment of a commitment to rehabilitation, and the prevalence of the death penalty and other excessively punitive practices. In fact, human rights advocates historically have viewed the state and its coercive power as one of the major, if not primary, violators of the rights they seek to protect. There are also "disabling effects" to this turn to the criminal law wherein ICL advocates "reinforce an individualized and decontextualized understanding of the harms they aim to address, even while relying on the state and on forms of criminalization of which they have been long critical."[26] Human rights courts themselves have contributed to this shift by demanding prosecutions of human rights crimes—human rights with a vengeance.[27]

This shift in human rights discourse towards a more punitive model of enforcement was also present in feminist debates, particularly in discussions about addressing sexual violence and trafficking.[28] This turn to "carceral feminism"[29] has been decried as a move to align with state criminal justice systems that have systematically downplayed violence against women, at times protected the perpetrators of such violence, and themselves

---

[26] Karen Engle, *Anti-Impunity and the Turn to Criminal Law in Human Rights*, 100 CORNELL L. REV. 1069, 1071 (2015).

[27] Simpson, *supra*. *See* Alexandra Huneeus, *International Criminal Law by Other Means: The Quasi-Criminal Jurisdiction of the Human Rights Courts*, 197 AM. J. INT'L L. 1 (2013).

[28] *See generally* LOUISE CHAPPELL, THE POLITICS OF GENDER JUSTICE AT THE INTERNATIONAL CRIMINAL COURT: LEGACIES AND LEGITIMACY (2015), which was the subject of a mini-symposium at *EJIL: Talk!*, the blog of the EUROPEAN JOURNAL OF INTERNATIONAL LAW, starting on December 19, 2016 (https://www.ejiltalk.org/book-discussion-introducing-louise-chappells-the-politics-of-gender-justice-at-the-international-criminal-court-legacies-and-legitimacy/).

[29] Elizabeth Bernstein, *Militarized Humanitarianism Meets Carceral Feminism: The Politics of Sex, Rights, and Freedom in Contemporary Antitrafficking Campaigns*, 36 SIGNS: J. WOMEN CULTURE & SOC'Y 47 (2010).

perpetrated such violence in custodial settings and out in the world. Echoing debates within other critical schools of thought, some feminists argue that, though imperfect, international criminal justice institutions should be reformed rather than rejected, while others argue that international criminal justice is at best irrelevant to dismantling sexism and patriarchy, and at worse supports and perpetuates such oppression.

In addition, a tradition of liberalism—in the sense of an ethos of liberal individualism, agency, and autonomy, and a belief in the centrality of the atomistic rational actor—has conditioned many of us to overlook potent forms of human interdependence and collective action. This singular focus also obscures communal forms of violence, the role of sociological conformity in emboldening participation in group-based harm, the power of willing bystanders to encourage brutality, and the harm that may be experienced by entire communities who perceive themselves as more than the sum of their members.[30] Furthermore, as currently constituted, our system of individual criminal responsibility cannot adequately redress the role that states, bureaucratic institutions, corporations, and other legal entities play in perpetuating, enabling, and fomenting mass violence.[31] The fixation on individuating guilt also decontextualizes violence; this ahistoricism can, in turn, distort any genuine search for a definitive or shared truth.[32] Given these limitations, the justice meted out by international criminal tribunals is inherently underinclusive, and the international community continues to grapple with ways to adequately redress collective violence without descending into illiberal forms of collective guilt (e.g., guilt by association or collective punishments).

3. Prevention in Lieu of Justice

Deterrence through criminal prosecutions is not, of course, the only way to prevent crime. Many would prefer to see the international community invest in more robust prophylactic measures and strategies *ex ante* to obviate prosecutorial responses *ex post*. In fact, compelling critiques of international criminal justice situate international prosecutions as a second-best option that allowed the international community to assuage its guilt for failing to prevent yesterday the very atrocities that are today the subject of

---

[30] Mark Drumbl, *Collective Responsibility and Post-Conflict Justice*, *in* ACCOUNTABILITY FOR COLLECTIVE WRONGDOING 23 (Tracy Isaacs & Richard Vernon eds., 2011).

[31] Note that the African Union's proposal to create a criminal chamber within the African Court of Human and People's Rights would result in the first international tribunal with jurisdiction over corporate entities.

[32] Martti Koskenniemi, *Between Impunity and Show Trials*, 6 MAX PLANCK Y.B. U.N. L. 1, 13 (2002).

criminal prosecution. The ICTY—established in the midst of the ongoing conflict in the former Yugoslavia—was roundly criticized by many as a feeble substitute for a more robust military response to atrocities. Likewise, the ICTR—established after the international community stood by while genocide engulfed Rwanda—was condemned as too little, too late. Worse still, Cambodian survivors of the Khmer Rouge waited decades for justice; even after Vietnam ousted the Khmer Rouge in 1979, the latter's leadership-in-exile was entitled to keep its U.N. seat as a function of enduring U.S. animosity towards Vietnam stemming from its misguided war. Under these circumstances, justice emerges as a consolation prize to communities torn asunder by violence.

A genuine commitment to up-stream prevention requires the provision of international aid and development in times of peace, the creation of measures to address structural violence and avert the escalation of brutality, and programs to establish the fair and effective rule of law around the world. It also requires an honest assessment of the way in which exploitative and extractive economic relationships emanating from the proverbial Global North, and the corrosive global market for arms and armaments, perpetuates conflict and repression in the proverbial Global South.

A prevention mandate also forces a consideration of the historic, and contested, doctrine of humanitarian intervention. Humanitarian intervention involves the armed intervention into a state by another state or a collective of states for the promotion or protection of basic human rights where the territorial state is perpetuating abuses or is unable, or unwilling, to provide the necessary protection to its inhabitants. Under the leadership of Kofi Annan, the United Nations recognized the obligation of states to intervene in extreme cases of mass atrocity under certain circumstances within the U.N. framework. This Responsibility-to-Protect (R2P) initiative recognizes:

> The international community, through the United Nations, . . . has the responsibility to use appropriate diplomatic, humanitarian and other peaceful means . . . to help protect populations from genocide, war crimes, ethnic cleansing and crimes against humanity. In this context, we are prepared to take collective action, in a timely and decisive manner, through the Security Council, in accordance with the Charter, including Chapter VII, on a case-by-case basis and in cooperation with relevant regional organizations as appropriate, should peaceful means be inadequate and national authorities manifestly fail to protect their

> populations from genocide, war crimes, ethnic cleansing and crimes against humanity.[33]

Under this framework, kinetic action must involve the Security Council and be a last resort measure. Pillars 1 and 2 of R2P provide that each individual state has the responsibility to protect its populations from international crimes and that the international community should help vulnerable or at-risk states carry out this responsibility. Pillar 3 indicates that if a state is failing to protect its populations, the international community must be prepared to take appropriate collective action, in a timely and decisive manner and in accordance with the U.N. Charter. So far, implementation of this initiative has been halting, particularly Pillars 2 and 3, as illustrated by the continued failure to intervene to prevent atrocities in, among other places, Syria, Myanmar, Palestine, Yemen, and North Korea.

4. The High Costs of Criminal Justice

The international community has expended significant time, energy, intellectual effort, and funds to build and maintain these judicial institutions—resources that could have been deployed for other initiatives, including preventative action and economic development. Critics of ICL will point to the fact that the ICTY consumed $3B to convict around 100 individuals. To be sure, the tribunal made many other valuable contributions as well, including the issuance of a vast ICL jurisprudence; nonetheless, the cost per defendant is staggering. The ICC, with a budget of approximately $120M/year, has achieved only a handful of convictions during its close to two decades of operation (with one by guilty plea and several for obstruction of justice rather than for the underlying international crimes); other cases have stalled for lack of state cooperation, ended in acquittals, or been dismissed for lack of evidence, at times in the face of rampant witness intimidation. As this book goes to press, the working methods of the ICC are finally under review by the ICC's Assembly of State Parties and outside experts; it remains to be seen if the Court can be transformed into the more efficient and effective institution that was envisioned in Rome in 1998.

The costs of international criminal justice are dramatically lower than the costs of regional human rights institutions (although the latter are woefully underfunded). Arguments have been made that the international community should invest more in human rights institutions with the power to adjudicate state responsibility, make concrete recommendations for reform, and order reparations

---

[33] World Summit Outcome Document, ¶ 139, U.N. Doc. A/60/L.1 (Sept. 15, 2005).

for victims.[34] Similar arguments are made to shift resources to rule of law programs and to local peace-building efforts that will better equip national jurisdictions to prevent the eruption of such violence and ensure accountability and reparations when such atrocities are committed. Such initiatives, however, have not captured the international community's imagination in the way that ICL has, perhaps because of the difficulty of measuring the effectiveness of preventative measures as compared to tangible reactions to events in the past.

5. The Judicialization of Peace

A tension often exists between efforts to seek justice and efforts to achieve peace in conflict situations.[35] In particular, tribunals that operate while abuses are ongoing may complicate efforts to negotiate with potential, or even indicted, war criminals, who may demand amnesty from prosecution in exchange for laying down their arms. This argument against ICL posits that those fixated on the quest for justice pay insufficient attention to political realities and that the international community should not support any measures that delay peace and thereby increase the number of victims. According to one commentator, who wrote anonymously about the implications of simultaneously pursuing peace and justice in the former Yugoslavia,

> Targeting violators of human rights and bringing them to justice is essential. Accusation, however, comes more easily than making peace. The quest for justice for yesterday's victims of atrocities should not be pursued in such a manner that it makes today's living the dead of tomorrow. That, for the human rights community, is one of the lessons from the former Yugoslavia. Thousands of people are dead who should have been alive—because moralists were in quest of the perfect peace. Unfortunately, a perfect peace can rarely be attained in the aftermath of a bloody conflict.[36]

While the Dayton Peace Accords were being negotiated, two men who had the real capability of improving conditions on the ground—Radovan Karadžić (the self-proclaimed president of the Serb enclave

---

[34] James L. Cavallaro & Jamie O'Connell, *When Prosecution is Not Enough: How the International Criminal Court Can Prevent Atrocity and Advance Accountability by Emulating Regional Human Rights Institutions*, 45 YALE J. INT'L L. 1 (2019).

[35] Courtney Hillebrecht et al., *The Judicialization of Peace*, 59(2) HARV. INT'L L. J. 279 (Summer 2018).

[36] Anonymous, *Human Rights in Peace Negotiations*, 18 HUM. RTS. Q. 249 (1996). (It has been speculated that this article was written by Bertrand Ramcharan, former acting High Commissioner for Human Rights and once an assistant to Thorvald Stoltenberg, Special Representative of the U.N. Secretary-General for the former Yugoslavia). For a response, *see* Felice D. Gaer, *U.N.-Anonymous: Reflections on Human Rights in Peace Negotiations*, 19 HUM. RTS. Q. 1 (1997).

in Bosnia) and Ratko Mladić (the chief of staff of the Bosnian Serb Army)—had both been indicted by the ICTY. (Slobodan Milošević had not yet been formally indicted, although it was later revealed that he had been under investigation). The two were excluded from the peace negotiations and were presumably less inclined to go along with the results because they faced trial once peace was achieved. The negotiations resulted in the Dayton Peace Accords even with the two indictees sidelined, though atrocities continued, raising the question of whether the outcome would have been different if Karadžić and Mladić had been integrated into the negotiations.

Victims, human rights advocates, and others responded to efforts to prioritize the end of conflict by subordinating, or even foregoing, legal accountability with the rallying cry "no peace without justice." As a response to the charge that the pursuit of justice can prolong conflict, human rights activists point the finger at the international community for lacking the resolve to follow through on threats to intervene and thus emboldening war criminals to keep fighting. They also argue that any peace without justice is not a viable or durable peace, because the presence of war criminals enjoying impunity prevents the peaceable stabilization of societies, a claim that is borne out in the academic literature.

The architects of the ICC had these concerns in mind and included mechanisms to balance the pursuit of peace and justice in the Court's design. Article 16 of the ICC Statute allows the U.N. Security Council, acting within its Chapter VII mandate to respond to threats to and breaches of the peace, to defer an ICC investigation or prosecution for a renewable period of twelve months. Although Sudan and Kenya both tried to invoke Article 16 under dubious circumstances, so far this power has remained dormant. Concerns about peace versus justice remain salient even with the Article 16 safety valve. For example, when it comes to the Lord's Resistance Army in Uganda, there is speculation that Joseph Kony rejected the peace deal brokered in Juba, now the capital of South Sudan, in 2008 because it did not sufficiently protect him from the ICC.[37] That said, it is not clear that he would have adhered to the deal in any case, and his followers continue to defect notwithstanding a threat of prosecution.

While proponents who emphasize peace over justice and those who prioritize justice over peace make compelling arguments, the debate of which they are a part is too often reduced to a false binary choice. Real world efforts to end atrocities and provide accountability for those responsible underscore the misleading oversimplification

---

[37] LINE ENGBO GISSEL, THE INTERNATIONAL CRIMINAL COURT AND PEACE PROCESSES IN AFRICA: JUDICIALIZING PEACE 61 (2018).

presented by this debate. Experience teaches that ending conflict at all costs—with no accountability, reparations, healing, truth-telling, or other elements of justice, broadly defined—creates a short-lived peace. At the same time, pursuing accountability through robust criminal prosecutions with no attention to addressing the root causes of the conflict and without incentives for perpetrators to forego violence as a viable option, risks creating more conflict and more victims. Innovative experiments in artfully combining the demands of peace and justice, inspired by the lessons of transitional justice, suggests the value of rejecting the often-presented binary choice between peace and justice and exploring the creative space that allows for the furtherance of both. There is still much work to be done in fine-tuning these approaches, but current efforts underway in Colombia, among other places, suggest that there is much to be gained through a more nuanced and sophisticated layering and sequencing of interventions.

6. Neo-Colonialism/Neo-Imperialism

The outsized role of the Global North in creating the system of international justice, and the fact that many institutions are focused on violations in the Global South, have given rise to concerns that ICL is essentially a neo-colonial or neo-imperial enterprise. This critique provides a counter-narrative to the dominant positive and progressive story of Nuremberg and Tokyo by correctly noting that while the United States and its allies prosecuted the Germans for their brand of racial supremacy, those same states had fostered, and continued to practice, racial supremacy at home and abroad through, *inter alia*, colonialism, slavery, and variations on apartheid. Drawing upon domestic alternative approaches to law such as critical legal studies, critical race theory, and feminism, these critiques highlight crimes and other injustices that are ignored or under-represented by the dominant international criminal justice system. These voices also underscore the importance of acknowledging the privileges, preferences, and immunities enjoyed by the Global North and embedded in the dominant international criminal justice institutions, and international law and politics more generally. A prominent school of thought advancing these critiques is organized under the banner of Third World Approaches to International Law (TWAIL).[38]

With respect to the structural preferences, and even violence, embedded in the current international criminal justice system, critics point to the power given to the U.N. Security Council to refer even

[38] For a good introduction to TWAIL and its critique of international criminal law, *see Symposium on TWAIL Perspectives on ICL, IHL, and Intervention*, 109 AJIL UNBOUND 252 (2015).

non-state parties to the ICC, and its ability to halt ICC proceedings for renewable one-year periods. This critique of structural injustice is underscored by the fact that three of the five permanent members of the Security Council have refused to join the Court, and, in the case of the United States, laid the groundwork to sanction the Court for its efforts to investigate alleged crimes committed by U.S. personnel in Afghanistan. In addition, in the two situations in which it imposed jurisdiction on non-party states (the Sudan and Libya), the Security Council expressly excluded from the jurisdiction of the Court any acts committed by other non-party states within the territory of the two referred countries. This was a clause demanded by, among others, the United States to protect it and its allies from any claims of violations of the laws of armed conflict, in particular in Libya where NATO undertook an air campaign that resulted in a number of civilian casualties.

More broadly, these critiques view international criminal law as part of a broader project of political economy that supports, and even imposes, globalization and neo-liberalism on the Global South. Some of these critiques echo those set out under the "Myopia of ICL" heading above, arguing that focusing on individual accountability decontextualizes the structural and institutional forces (arising out of, for example, the pernicious vestiges of colonization and economic exploitation) that create the environment for such crimes. This has led some critics to conclude that "the international criminal law project . . . has reproduced colonial legacies more than it has challenged them."[39] As a prescriptive matter, these same critics argue

> If international criminal law is to take seriously its claim to be part of a project of global justice, it must at some point begin to tackle the economic contexts of war, exploitation and scarcity: 'to reconsider the boundaries of criminalization' and question, for example, 'the legality of sanctions regimes, the role of structural adjustment and austerity programs imposed by international financial institutions, the competition between China and Western states for access to resources in third states, or the propriety of reparations for slavery and colonialism.'[40]

While we agree that these and other systems of oppression need to be addressed, it is not clear that international criminal law, or criminal law generally, is best-suited to remedy all of them. As you

---

[39] John Reynolds & Sujith Xavier, *"The Dark Corners of the World:" TWAIL and International Criminal Justice,* 14 J. INT'L CRIM. J. 959, 975 (2016).

[40] *Id.* at 980 (quoting from A. Kiyani, *International Crime and the Politics of Criminal Theory: Voices and Conduct of Exclusion,* 47 NYU J. INT'L L. & POL. 129, 200 (2015)).

engage with the theory and practice of international criminal law, ask yourself how you would modify the current institutions to address some of these injustices, and how you would invoke other bodies of law, or even non-law solutions, instead. As one example, the Malabo Protocol[41] establishing an African regional criminal court provides a vision of a criminal court that is empowered to take on crimes of particular concern to Africa and the Global South (including the use of mercenaries, multinational corporate violence, environmental crimes, and corruption), and thus may provide a template for using a more traditional criminal justice model to address some of these larger structural injustices, though it appears the new Protocol will not be activated any time soon.

C. Alternatives to International Criminal Justice

There is no question that ICL favors retributive justice over other forms of justice, including restorative justice, that focus on repairing harm and not just meting out punishment. In situations in which ICL is applicable—during or following armed conflict, repression, and mass violence—there are a multitude of other ways a state or the international community can respond. This dilemma marks the field of transitional justice. A full discussion of transitional justice is beyond the scope of this text; however, it may be useful at this point to consider what other alternatives to criminal prosecutions are available to address the commission of international crimes. As you review these various options, consider what commends them and what problems they may present.

1. Do Nothing

One option is, of course, to do nothing at all. Where the past is controversial and painful, societies may prefer to draw a thick line and essentially start over rather than grapple with what happened and who was responsible. This is essentially what happened in fascist Spain after World War II. Francisco Franco, *el generalissimo,* remained in power until his death in 1975. He rose to power in 1936, in the midst of the Spanish civil war. During World War II, he was supportive of the Axis side, but managed to largely stay out of the war; he declared total neutrality by 1943 when the tide was turning against Germany. Throughout his reign, his focus was more internal, overseeing a repressive apparatus that some historians say is responsible for up to 80,000 executions. Because he was not involved in acts of international aggression, the Allies largely left him alone

[41] African Union, *Protocol on Amendments to the Protocol on the Statute of the African Court of Justice and Human Rights,* Annex (Statute of the African Court of Justice and Human and People's Rights) (adopted June 27, 2014).

after World War II, although Spain was for a time quite marginalized in Europe.

The Spanish example, however, suggests that the ability to move forward without addressing a violative past is limited. In the last two decades, Spaniards demanding an accounting for the crimes of the Franco era have succeeded in redirecting attention to this period of Spanish history. For example, legislation was passed calling for the exhumation of mass graves to determine the fate of the disappeared and the removal of the few remaining monuments to Franco. In 2007, the most senior bishop of the Catholic Church formally apologized for the Church's support of Franco. Efforts to open cases in Spain, however, have been unsuccessful. In a poetic exception to the prevailing norm of courts in the Global North reaching out to adjudicate international crimes in the Global South, Argentina has initiated an investigation into Franco-era crimes under its international crimes legislation.

2. Amnesty

National governments often resort to amnesty laws in the face of prior abuses by government officials. The most problematic form of amnesty—often passed by officials to protect themselves and their allies—completely prevents the investigation and punishment of individuals who committed abuses. These blanket self-amnesty laws, which also obviate civil claims, are often defended as a necessary evil to encourage members of a repressive regime to relinquish power by eliminating the possibility of prosecutions. Early amnesty laws passed in Latin America and elsewhere generally took this form of self-amnesty and prevented any form of reckoning with prior crimes. Such blanket amnesties frustrate victims and their communities by denying any form of civil or criminal redress for violations perpetrated by the amnesty's beneficiaries. Partly in response to this criticism of such amnesties, South Africa revolutionized the use of a conditional, or individualized, amnesty in connection with opportunities for victims and perpetrators to give testimony about what they experienced under apartheid. The amnesty law administrated by that country's Truth and Reconciliation Commission (TRC) protected individuals from prosecution and civil liability in exchange for their cooperation in establishing the full truth about the past. While no other society has adopted a similar amnesty process, the use of an amnesty or other form of legal leniency to entice truth revelation, further reconciliation, and social repair has been adopted in other contexts, the most recent and innovative being the "Special Jurisdiction for Peace" developed in Colombia.

Human rights organizations generally oppose the use of amnesties in any circumstances, arguing that they further impunity and undercut domestic and international efforts to deter future gross violations of human rights. Most domestic courts that have reviewed their own amnesties have upheld their legality, although some states in Latin America have begun to deviate from this norm by reversing amnesties that were passed in the 1970s and 1980s. By contrast, international tribunals that have evaluated the legality of amnesties have found many of them to violate fundamental principles of justice, including the right of victims to judicial protection. For example, the Inter-American Court of Human Rights has ruled that the "self-amnesty" promulgated by General Augusto Pinochet is incompatible with the American Convention on Human Rights.[42] It is generally agreed that blanket self-amnesties, such as that adopted in Chile, are illegal under international law. In one of its only decisions addressing an amnesty, the ICC's Pre-Trial Chamber in the *Gaddafi* prosecution opined that an unconditional amnesty that Gaddafi raised in defense of his prosecution was incompatible with international law.[43] Conditional amnesties, like that adopted in South Africa, raise the question of whether a quasi-legal process that includes a truth-telling or reparative component, but results in legal protection, rather than punishment, provides a minimum level of justice that satisfies international law. No international tribunal has evaluated the legality of such an amnesty, although the ICC may be faced with the question in Uganda, which adopted a weaker form of conditional amnesty than that adopted in South Africa. Recent opinions by both the Inter-American and European human rights systems leave open the possibility that such amnesties may be compatible with international law.[44]

[42] *Almonacid-Arellano et al. v. Chile*, Inter-Am. Ct. H. R. (ser. C) No 154, ¶ 114 (Sept. 26, 2006).

[43] *Prosecutor v. Gaddafi*, Case No. ICC-01/11-01/11-662, Decision on the "Admissibility Challenge by Dr. Saif Al Islam Gaddafi pursuant to Articles 17(1)(c), 19 and 20(3) of the Rome Statute" (April 5, 2019). On appeal, the Appeals Chamber found that this part of the Pre-Trial Chamber's opinion was *dicta*, and thus did not address whether it adequately reflects international law. *Prosecutor v. Gaddafi*, Case No. ICC-01/11-01/11-695, Judgment on the Appeal of Mr. Saif Al Islam Gaddafi against the decision of Pre-Trial Chamber I entitled "Decision on the 'Admissibility Challenge by Dr. Saif Al Islam Gaddafi pursuant to Articles 17(1)(c), 19 and 20(3) of the Rome Statute' " of 5 April 2019, ¶ 96 (Mar. 9, 2020).

[44] *See Case of the Massacres of El Mozote and Nearby Places v. El Salvador*, Separate Opinion of Judge Diego García Sayán, Inter-Am. Ct. H. R. (Ser. C) No 252 (Oct. 25, 2012) (suggesting that amnesties enacted after a civil war should be examined with respect to how well they balance victims' rights to truth, justice, reparations and guarantees of non-repetition with the right to peace); *Marguš v. Croatia*, Judgment, App. No. 4455/10, 2014 Eur. Ct. H.R., 53 I.L.M. 751, ¶ 139 (2014) (leaving open the possibility that amnesties promulgated as part of a reconciliation process or combined with compensation to victims might be compatible with international human rights law).

3. Truth and Investigatory Commissions

The phenomenon of the truth commission emerged initially as a response to mass violence in countries (mostly in Latin America) where prosecutions were precluded by the operation of an amnesty law, the lack of political will, a still-entrenched military, or other obstacles. Under these circumstances, truth commissions have often represented a compromise between "former abusers and their victims, who settle for the limited satisfaction of truth, rather than receive actual redress through punishment."[45] Truth commissions are often presided over by respected public figures (foreign and/or domestic) rather than trained lawyers or judges. They typically provide a space for victims, perpetrators, and experts to testify and tell their stories, thus creating a narrative history of past violations. They often provide an opportunity for deep analysis of the structural and institutional causes of violations which may elude more traditional adversarial processes. Based upon these testimonies and its own investigations and research, the commission issues a final report that includes their findings and recommendations.

Truth commissions further justice by establishing a historical record of abuses, providing a forum for victims (and at times perpetrators) to bear witness, investigating the fate of the disappeared, creating an environment more ripe for reconciliation and forgiveness than an adversarial trial, issuing or recommending reparations, and proposing institutional reforms to prevent the repeat of past violence. Some truth commissions, such as the commission established in El Salvador, identify individual perpetrators by naming names; others are content to present the causes, patterns, and consequences of violence. By generating a "definitive" history of abuses, truth commissions can undercut revisionist accounts that might develop about a country's past history of violence. While truth commissions do not claim to produce the ultimate truth of the past, they can reduce the number of lies that may legitimately circulate as part of the public discourse, as Michael Ignatieff famously observed.[46]

Truth commissions have the advantage over criminal trials of focusing on the victims and their experiences rather than on the defendants. Where they "name names," truth commissions can also achieve some measure of stigma and accountability, although the *ex parte* designation of individuals as responsible for human rights violations with limited opportunities to be heard raises due process concerns. Truth commissions can also award compensation to

---

[45] Ivan Simonovic, *Attitudes and Types of Reaction Toward Past War Crimes and Human Rights Abuses*, 29 YALE J. INT'L L. 343, 346 (2004).

[46] Michael Ignatieff, *Articles of Faith*, INDEX ON CENSORSHIP, Issue 5 (1996).

victims, assuming there is a fund from which to draw. Finally, where truth commissions invite the participation of both victims and perpetrators, they can encourage acts of contrition and forgiveness that may lay the groundwork for a more community-wide reconciliation.[47] While truth commissions can, and often do, further many of these important goals, their track record has been mixed, particularly in the area of recommendations and reparations, which have rarely been implemented. Critics point to the failure of the South African TRC to tackle in a meaningful way the crime of apartheid itself, as distinct from the crimes committed in the name of apartheid (such as summary executions and torture), as contributing to the continued racial, class, and other divisions that persist in South African society today.

4. Lustration

Potentially guilty individuals can also be barred from political office or other positions of influence. The term *lustration* derives from the Latin for "purification." Following World War II, the Allies launched a de-Nazification program in Germany and its former spheres of influence. After the fall of communism, similar efforts were launched in Eastern Europe to address the systemic bureaucratic repression that characterized life within the former Soviet client states. As a result of these efforts, thousands of individuals were disqualified from public life and even from some private enterprises and industries. In May 2003, the Coalition Provisional Authority in Iraq began lustrating members of the Ba'ath Party—a party considered to be synonymous with the Saddam Hussein regime. Under this policy, all senior members of the party were banned from public life (including employment as doctors at hospitals, as university professors, and other ostensibly nonpolitical posts); some more junior people could appeal their exclusion. As seen in Iraq, lustration can contribute to destabilization by leaving important posts empty or filled by untrained or inexpert individuals and by removing incentives for individuals to contribute to the rebuilding of society.[48]

D. Conclusion

This chapter has explored the question of what a regime of international criminal justice can reasonably be expected to

---

[47] For more on truth commissions, *see* PRISCILLA B. HAYNER, UNSPEAKABLE TRUTHS: TRANSITIONAL JUSTICE AND THE CHALLENGE OF TRUTH COMMISSIONS (2nd ed. 2010); MARK FREEMAN, TRUTH COMMISSIONS AND PROCEDURAL FAIRNESS (2006); CHARLES VILLA-VICENCIO & WILHELM VERWOERD, LOOKING BACK REACHING FORWARD: REFLECTIONS ON THE TRUTH AND RECONCILIATION COMMISSION OF SOUTH AFRICA (2000).

[48] For a recent critique of lustration in Iraq, *see* Peter Shirlow, *Lustration in Iraq: Regime Change as Exclusion and Control*, CAPITAL AND CLASS (June 5, 2020).

accomplish. Where judicial mechanisms fall short, or are unavailable, societies and the international community must consider alternative mechanisms to address the misdeeds of the past. Indeed, many of the measures discussed here can be adopted alongside criminal prosecutions before domestic or international tribunals as part of a comprehensive response to situations of societal breakdown, ethnic conflict, and mass violence. For example, in Sierra Leone, the Special Court operated simultaneously with a Truth and Reconciliation Commission as an element of the Lomé Peace Accord "to address impunity, break the cycle of violence, provide a forum for both the victims and the perpetrators of human rights violations to tell their story, [and] get a clear picture of the past in order to facilitate genuine healing and reconciliation."[49] Depending on the circumstances, these various mechanisms may complement or complicate each other. Although conflicts developed between the two Sierra Leonean institutions, there is a growing consensus that pursuing such a two-track process may more adequately address the demands of victims, international justice, peace, and reconciliation than any one approach on its own. Modern research in this area confirms that there is no one-size-fits-all model. Efforts at transitional justice must be bespoke and holistic, reflecting the priorities and constraints of different segments of societies and responding to different goals and objectives.

---

[49] Peace Agreement Between the Government of Sierra Leone and the Revolutionary United Front, Art. VI(2) (1999).

TABLE OF CASES

INDEX

References are to Pages.
We have italicized those page numbers that indicate an important treatment of the topic.